D0932081

The Roving Eye

A Reporter's Love Affair with
Paris, Politics & Sport

by Richard Evans

Clink
Street

London | New York

Published by Clink Street Publishing 2017

Copyright © 2017

First edition.

ISBNs:
978-1-911525-47-9 paperback
978-1-911525-48-6 ebook

Photographers' credits: Linda Gunter 1; Richard Evans 2, 4, 5, 13, 15, 17, 18, 19, 20, 21, 23, 27, 28, 30, 31, 33, 37; Le Roye Productions 6; Pictorial Parade 8; Roxanne Francois 12; Jon Swain 22; Bob Strauss 32; Lynn Evans 26, 36; Frank de Jongh 35; Mark M. Mayers 25.

For Ashley
So that he knows what his father has been up to

CONTENTS

INTRODUCTION

This is the story of a long, varied and, I hope, interesting life. It is the story of a reporter's life – a reporter who turned himself into a writer and broadcaster, skills that overlap and intertwine.

It is the story, inevitably, about aspects of our world which are of particular interest to me. Journalism, broadcasting, sport, politics, travel and people. And it is the people that make the whole thing worthwhile. Without people, as Nelson Mandela must have contemplated on occasion during his 27-year incarceration, what is there?

I have been uncommonly lucky in knowing both private and public people and, if this story concentrates more on the latter, it is because many of them have shaped our world, using their exceptional gifts to add colour and mood, excitement and controversy, all embellished with the headlines that my profession enjoys so much.

I am not one of those people who scorn the idea of having heroes. Most of us need someone to inspire and guide us; to quicken the heartbeat and bring us joy.

In journalism, no one inspired me more than James Cameron, not the film maker but a sardonic Scot whose view of life was forever tainted by having witnessed, from a dubiously safe distance, the atomic bomb tests over the island of Bikini in Micronesia. Cameron wrote of it at the time: 'This enterprise was a pantomime of such hilarious tragedy, compounded of every factor from the banal to the appalling, that it remains in my mind as a kind of slapstick nightmare.'

As we shall see, from his description of a visit to the Gabon to meet Dr Albert Schweitzer, Cameron possessed a talent that enabled him to write from the heart and leave his readers in no doubt as to where he stood. Needless to say, I admire that.

It unleashes a whole discussion about the divisions between reporting and commentating – in Britain the two are allowed to merge far more than they are in the United States – and Cameron did not shy away from it.

1

Writing in 1967, Cameron, in the last chapter of his captivating auto-biography, *Point of Departure*, said this: 'Today, we journalists spend our time splashing in the shallows, reaching on occasions the rare heights of the applauded mediocre. It looks, perhaps, easier than it is.

'To the individual in this machine (of journalism) it brings its own dilemma: the agonising narrow line between sincerity and technique, between the imperative and the glib – so fine and delicate a boundary that one frequently misses it altogether, especially with a tight deadline, a ringing phone, a thirst and an unquiet mind.'

Not many in my profession would disagree with that.

As I write, a man who likes only journalists who write nice things about him has gained entrance to White House. It is too early to know where that will lead but I fervently hope it will ensure journalists are made ever more aware of the very serious duty to tell the truth.

On a more personal level, I owe my whole career to Reg Hayter, who took an extraordinary punt on a seventeen-year-old when he had just set up his freelance agency in Fleet Street with Ron Roberts and Freddie Garside and offered me a job. Whatever skills I have as a reporter were learned while grappling with the assignments Reg gave me. There are many others who can say the same thing. Hayter's became the best school an aspiring sports writer could ever attend.

Even before I started wearing long trousers, I became captivated by a genius in white flannels, a cricketer called Denis Compton, a batsman of such carefree abandon that he left thousands of runs unscored, giving his wicket away because he may have picked up the wrong bat in the dressing room (he often mislaid his own) or was wondering if his nag had won the 3.30 at Epsom.

Before his cartilage blew up, Denis played on the left wing for Arsenal with his brother Les. Like thousands of others, my day was made or ruined by a Compton century or a Compton duck. It is the same, even now, depend-ing on whether Arsenal win or lose. Those who captivate you in childhood have you forever.

In politics Winston Churchill was my hero. I grew up in England during World War Two. Do I need to explain? Much later, when I came to cover politics for the London Evening News and BBC Radio in America, I found Robert F Kennedy to be the most special of people; a haunted, evolving human being who became a unique politician. It is almost unbearable to think how much better a place the entire world would have been had he become President instead of Richard Nixon.

There have many other people I have admired from near or far and I will remain indebted to those who have offered their friendship. Many will appear in this story. Inevitably some will not and to them I apologise. Omissions are purely the result of how narratives unfold, as anyone who has tried to write a book will understand.

It has been a life carried out on the hoof; in hotels and airports and 747s, leading to an ever-changing vista of what this amazing world has to offer. I have had homes in Paris, London, Stockholm, New York, Mijas, El Castillo de Castellar and now, under the blazing Florida sun, in Delray Beach. I should have spent more time in each but then, what would I have missed? Curiosity and the need to earn another dollar always drove me on and there is little that I regret.

Somehow in the middle of it all – or, to be precise, at the beginning and towards the end – I managed to persuade two remarkable women to marry me. Glenys has remained a lifelong friend and I think Lynn will, too. And, of course, I cannot find adequate words to thank Lynn for producing Ashley, a son to cherish.

I also want to thank those friends who not only put up with my stories, but encouraged me to write them down. That is what I have tried to do here. During the process, Chris Bowers, a great friend and partner of mine at the Tennis Radio Network, volunteered to read the manuscript and offer suggestions. As a biographer himself, Chris has a shrewd eye for detail and nuance and I have taken heed of many of his observations. My thanks, too, to Gayle Hunnicutt, Heather Mitchell and Robert Sackville West who were kind enough to read early chapters and offer the kind of encouragement one needs on those darker days when one thinks 'What the hell am I doing?'

They seemed to enjoy what they read. I hope you do, too.

Chapter 1
PARIS: THE BEGINNING

Parisian air was the first air I breathed; her trees the first trees I saw. The chestnuts, a shiny mahogany as they split from their green casings, fell at the foot of my pram as my mother wheeled me down the quayside by the Seine, which flowed less than a hundred yards from the room where I was born.

I left before I could talk, returned before I could write and went off to be educated elsewhere. But, of course, you never leave Paris. Hemingway uttered many truisms but, for me, none more accurate than his remark to a friend in 1950: "If you are lucky enough to have lived in Paris as a young man, then wherever you go for the rest of your life, it stays with you, for Paris is a moveable feast."

Feasts were difficult to put on the table in France in December 1945. Since the day of my birth on 10th February 1939, the Second World War had dimmed the lights, swept the gaiety from the boulevards and turned the world's most glamorous city into a place of fear and suspicion as it struggled under the Nazi jackboot.

So allow me to re-trace some steps to the beginning. I had been born at home in my father's dressing room, on the 3rd floor of a typical Parisian apartment at 6, Rue Francoise 1er. The flat ran the length of the building and from the balcony you could see the Seine and the glittering Pont Alexandre 111. The Champs Elysees was a few steps away but to get to his office in the Avenue de l'Opera every morning my father had Rene, the chauffeur, to whisk him across the Place de la Concorde in our splendid Renault tourer. Lassere, still one of the city's finest restaurants, was just around the corner. My silver spoon was waiting for me in our dining room.

Inevitably, I have often wondered how I would have grown up had the Maginot Line held and the war been kept at a distance. Spoilt brat would have been the obvious outcome. We would certainly have continued to live in considerable luxury, presuming the Paris office of Price Waterhouse had continued to function.

My father, C.H. (Harry) Evans was a founding partner of the European firm, in 1921, I think it was. For a lad born in the previous century in Beverly and educated in Whitby, he had risen fast in his chosen occupation of accountancy and, by an extraordinary quirk of fate, had avoided the worst horrors of the First World War. This came about because he was given the singular task of saving the margarine in Holland. No, really. In 1914, Britain imported most of its margarine from Holland but some of the ingredients were made in Germany. The British government decreed that the margarine could still be imported as long as no part of it was manufactured in Germany. So some Minister or other selected Price Waterhouse as the firm that would be responsible for overseeing this operation, which was of considerable importance because butter would be scarce to non-existent once war time rations took hold.

By chance, my father had already been to Holland on one of his first foreign trips for the firm and had picked up a little Dutch. "So give the job to the young man from Yorkshire," someone must have said at the PW headquarters in London. "Tell him to make sure the margarine is pure Dutch."

There was just one problem. The young Yorkshireman had just been called up to join the London Rifles in the City. My father had barely got his boots on before a phone call from Whitehall had him back in mufti and on a cross-channel steamer to Rotterdam. And there he stayed for the duration. He never told me much about his exploits, not even how he made scores of dangerous cross-channel journeys, once ending up in a lifeboat just outside Tilbury after the ship had been torpedoed.

But he obviously got the job done because Britain had a regular flow of margarine throughout the war. Soon after the hostilities ended, my Dad got himself transferred to the newly opened Paris office and was offered a partnership in the European firm.

Around that time, he married an American, had two children, Patricia and Tony, who would become my half-sister and half-brother, and lived in the Villa Montmorency, a complex of town houses near the Porte d'Auteuil. Stade Roland Garros, which I would be visiting so often in later years, was in the process of being built little more than a mile away.

The marriage didn't last and by 1935, Daddy had met my mother, a blonde-haired beauty who was also a divorcee. They were married the following year, lived briefly in Neuilly, and then bought the splendid apartment on the Rue Francois 1er.

By the time my first birthday came around, war had been declared and things were getting sufficiently uncertain for my mother, a nanny and me to be packed off to a rented house in Niort, a town in northwest France not far from where my mother's daughter Margot, then twelve, was at school. Apparently, we stayed there for several months while my father continued to work in Paris but, by June 1940, it became obvious that the game was up. "Pack," said my father when he called. "I'm closing the flat and we're taking a boat out of Bordeaux."

And so we joined the pathetic ragtag army of refugees streaming south as Hitler's forces burst through the paper-thin Maginot Line, skirted whatever other resistance remained and descended on Paris. Margot, who had been rescued from school by Alma Dax, the wife of our family doctor in Paris, remembers low-flying aircraft and the sound of distant bombing. My father had booked us into the Grand Hotel in Bordeaux but we never made it to our rooms. Right in the middle of lunch, the manager ordered us out. "The Government is arriving!" he announced in a panicky voice. "They are taking over the hotel!"

They were indeed. Realising Paris was no longer safe, Ministers, their secretaries and their entourages, probably including a mistress or two, were arriving in droves. In an instant, we found ourselves sitting on our luggage in the big square outside. And it was stinking hot.

So there we were, the well-heeled family of a Price Waterhouse partner, with a future that could best be described as uncertain. According to rumours – and there were plenty of those – the Germans were nine miles away.

With no time to lose, my father checked on the ship reservations he had made and discovered that our boat was not only going to be one of the last to leave but was, in all its glory, a coal boat that had been sunk in the Spanish civil war, dredged up and put back into the service. Normally it had a crew of 30. Now it was going to be filled with 300 refugees.

My father decided the best thing to do was to get my mother and me down to the boat. After a quick look at what was on offer, it was clear that water was going to be in short supply, especially as it was turning out to be one of the hottest French summers on record. So Daddy drove back to the square to pick up Margot; pay off the nanny who was, of course, in tears; and go off in search of Evian.

Meanwhile, back at the ship, the captain was calling my mother up onto the bridge. Evidently, I was left screaming in a sailor's arms at the foot of the steel ladder as Mummy, who was never good with stairs at the best of times, struggled to the top.

"I am afraid I have some bad news," the captain said. "I have orders to sail immediately."

"But you can't do that!" replied my horrified Mum. "You said two hours and my husband has all our passports and our money!"

Taking pity on her, the captain offered his cabin as I was the only infant on board. But that was scant consolation to a woman faced with the prospect of arriving in England with nothing except what she stood up in and a babe in arms. Not to mention the thought of a husband and daughter left to face certain incarceration in a prison camp. She never discovered what happened next and never knew whether it was an act of God or a captain disobeying orders. But the story was that the anchor got stuck.

Half an hour later, the Renault hove into view and, with passengers yelling encouragement from the ship, Daddy and Margot grabbed the cushions from the back seat and ferried the water bottles up the gangway. With what must have been a very regretful backward glance at the beautiful Renault – soon to be driven, no doubt, by the chauffeur of some Nazi General – we set sail.

It would probably have been quicker if we had, indeed, had sails. The old boat chugged along, somehow avoided some bombs that were dropped in our vicinity at the mouth of the Gironde, and took no less than four days and three nights to get to Falmouth. Other ships had sailed with us but they soon steamed off into the distance, leaving us as the very last refugee ship to make it out of Bordeaux. From the description in his autobiography, *Anyone Here Been Raped and Speaks English?*, Ed Behr, the celebrated Newsweek correspondent, might well have been on our boat. If so he, too, would have arrived in Falmouth covered in soot because no one had cleaned out the hold and soon coal dust was flying everywhere, impregnating every pore and making everyone, including my very blonde mother, look as if they had just arrived from Africa.

I think a little place called Pra Sands was our first stop and it seems to have provided me with my first memory. My mother and I were walking down a Cornish lane when I saw a black horse. Then somehow it disappeared and I remember saying, "Mummy, mummy where did the horse go?" I never found out.

After a while in the West Country, we gravitated towards London and found a spacious house in Knapp Hill near Woking. My father, too old now to be called up, was given a job at the Ministry of Supply which was under the direction of Lord Beaverbrook, who, on orders from the new Prime Minister, Winston Churchill, was busy getting Spitfires built. Sometimes Daddy would commute back to Woking but, more often during the week, he would stay in town, taking turns to do look out duty on the roofs of Westminster, tin hat firmly on his head.

My mother used to go up to London as well and help serve tea to the troops on Waterloo station. Once, she took Margot and stayed the night at a hotel. The Blitz had started but that didn't seem to deter anyone very much. "There was an amazing spirit of defiance," I remember her telling me. "One night some friends and I had a few too many cocktails and ended up on the balcony of the hotel as the searchlights lit up the sky and the bombardment started, as it did every night, and we just laughed at Hitler. We didn't seem to care. If he'd seen us it would have confirmed his opinion that the English were crazy. It was what got us through the whole thing. Have another pink gin and to hell with it."

Or have a 'nice cuppa tea'. It was the great phrase of the war years. "The 'ouse next door just got hit, love."

"Yes dear, just have a nice cuppa tea."

But, of course, the humour couldn't cover up the carnage as the German bombs rained down night after night, not just on London, but Liverpool, Plymouth, Coventry where the trucks and tanks were being built as well as other industrial centres. Swathes of England were laid to waste and the nation clung to the radio to hear Churchill's bulldog tones.

"We shall never surrender."

It is impossible to overestimate the effect that man had on a nation's morale. The jutted jaw, the cigar, the Homburg hat – clichés now, but very real as the bombs fell and the news went from bad to worse.

It wasn't getting any better in Surrey. We had moved to a new house near Guildford which happened to be the marker for the Luftwaffe as the bombers turned to head into London. The town bristled with ack-ack guns and if the German pilots thought it was all a bit too much, they just dumped their bombs right there and went home. For fourteen consecutive nights, I remember being lifted into my mother's arms from a dead sleep and taken down to sit it out under the stairs. A tree was uprooted by a direct hit in the garden next door but, physically, we survived. Not so my mother's nerves. Calm during the bombardment, she tended to collapse with fatigue and anxiety the next day and, finally, she decided we had had enough.

Margot's boarding school had been moved, lock, stock and barrel from an exposed position at Cooden Beach, near Eastbourne on the south coast, to the depths of Shropshire. We found a little barn of a house not too far away in a tiny village called Leintwardine where there was a pub called the Red Lion, a butcher, and not much else. The butcher, a Mr Griffiths, was our defence against the Germans. He had a shotgun. He was the Home Guard. All 5' 10" of him. The war? Yes, everyone knew about the war but it hadn't really penetrated deepest Shropshire and so we settled down to a calmer life and I made my first real friend, the butcher's son. He was called Eric and we used to chase cows in the fields behind our cottage and do all the naughty things five-year-olds will do when left to run free.

For my mother, with a husband hundreds of miles away in bomb-stricken London, no help and no idea how to gut a trout, it must have seemed a very long way from the Rue Francois 1er. But, unlike so many, we were safe and we survived.

The next move, as a staging post to return to Paris, took us to Bournemouth and the Dover House Hotel on Dover Road. If the film of Terence Rattigan's play *Separate Tables*, which had starred Burt Lancaster and Deborah Kerr, was not filmed there it could have been. It typified Bournemouth down to the last pine needle in the garden.

I remember Margot taking me down to the town square to join in the throngs rejoicing in VE Day, which signaled the end of the war in Europe, but, shortly before, I had received a brief visit from the only grandparent I ever met – my father's mother. I am afraid my only memory is of a slightly formidable old lady dressed in a long black coat with a squat black hat covering wisps of grey hair. Sad.

My father had already left for France, virtually tailgating the French and American forces into Paris. He arrived back only a week or two after General de Gaulle had marched up the Champs Elysee at the head of his troops, defying the last remaining German snipers to shoot at him. If they tried, they missed of course, as did everyone who tried to kill this immense figure. As my father turned the key in the lock of the Price Waterhouse office on the Avenue de l'Opera he could hardly have imagined that it would fall to his son to be the first voice heard on the BBC announcing the death of de Gaulle nearly 30 years later. Le Grand Charles had outwitted all his enemies, dying of a heart attack in his own living room.

When Mummy, Margot and I returned later in 1945, we constituted the first British family to take up residence in the city after the war. For the first few months we lived primarily off Red Cross parcels that had been prepared for the prisoner of war camps and were no longer needed. I can still remember sticking a finger into the glutinous and wonderfully creamy condensed milk. Occasionally my father's contacts would produce something from the thriving black market – a chicken, a piece of tough meat or, at Christmas, a turkey.

We were luckier than some foreign residents who found their homes virtually destroyed. Ours had been occupied by three young German officers who, apart from drinking my father's extensive wine cellar dry and throwing some dregs onto the carpet, had not done any lasting damage. It was pot luck as to who you got as uninvited guests. One friend of ours returned to find a note on the burnished dining room table. It was from the German Admiral who had occupied their apartment, thanking them for their hospitality and apologising for two pieces of broken crockery from the carefully detailed inventory. The note said that he would be happy to return their hospitality should they visit Berlin. So there were some gentlemen fighting on the other side.

But it was difficult to forgive and forget. I shall always remember the look of disgust on my mother's face when she dropped a knitting needle down the side of the sofa one afternoon. In pulling it out she came up with a photo of three German officers. The French family living upstairs confirmed it was the trio who had been sleeping in our beds.

Christmas provided momentary relief from the horrors of the past and, on a purely personal level, an extraordinary piece of luck. As far as we could make out from our fairly wide circle of new friends, I was the only British or American child in the capital. Almost everyone we knew was in the military and it was much too early to think of bringing families over to join them. So … guess who got the presents?

We must have invited nearly a hundred people for drinks on Christmas Day and, of course, nearly all brought something for the 'young man'. The prize present was a huge toy fortress, complete with turrets and passageways, soldiers, armoured cars and tanks. The vivid memory of playing on the floor amidst a forest of uniformed legs as the guests moved around me remains to this day. There were the blue legs of the RAF officers; khaki of various shades; the occasional dark Royal Navy blue; and then, of course, the light tan of US Army colonels and captains. They were the ones that impressed me most because of the smart contrast between what the Americans somewhat strangely called their pants and the chocolate coloured tunics.

In return for all this attention, I had a bizarre job. The lift in our apartment building was one of those open topped contraptions which would not move until the swinging, wrought iron gates had been properly closed. A load of more than three people caused it to slow down alarmingly and by the time it reached the third floor it would often need some assistance. This I was able to provide by leaning over from the staircase and physically pulling it up the last few inches.

"Hey! Swell, kid! Great job!" I got a lot of praise from crew-cut Americans with ribbons all over their chests.

And, out on the street, the GIs were no less generous. The young men from Alabama and Ohio used to sit on the balustrades of the Metro stations on the Champs Elysees, their caps in their epaulets, legs swinging free as they watched the young ladies of Paris parade before them. And for a child it was always, "Hey! Have some gum, chum!"

There was, of course, a lot going on in Paris that a six-year-old didn't understand. While I was taken for walks and offered the treat of a very watery ice cream at Pam-Pam's on the Champs Elysees – or occasionally at the Marigold, a café which existed until very recently – some nasty recriminations were taking place as the French turned on collaborators, of whom there were more than anyone wanted to admit. And they were not only little businessmen who had been out for a quick buck or women who had slept with German officers. The great Maurice Chevalier, who was deemed to have performed too willingly for the Nazis, was banished to small theatres off the boulevards and had to work his way back into favour. It took a while.

More amusingly, Maxim's, the iconic restaurant situated between the Madelaine and the Place de la Concorde, was heavily penalised for having made a fortune off the gluttony of the Nazi High Command. Not wishing to deprive Parisians of such haute cuisine – heaven forbid – the new Government came up with the perfect penalty. Maxim's would feed all Allied officers for the next two years at cost. Inspectors would visit regularly to ensure that culinary standards were maintained and that the profit would be zero.

So slowly Paris regained some vague semblance of its former self and, from what my parents told me after a night 'up the hill', as they called it, the Montmartre haunts of Le Lapin Agile or La Cremaillere were soon alive with the sound of the accordion and the haunting songs of Edith Piaf. She was brave to 'Regret Rien' because there was so much to regret. Even so, some had managed to live passable lives during the occupation and my Godmother, Joyce Bayol, was one of them.

Although English, her marriage to a Frenchman had enabled her to remain in Paris for the duration. With their two sons, the couple lived at 102 Avenue des Ternes, which, much later, would fall into the shadow of the monstrous Concorde Lafayette Hotel. Joyce told me some harrowing stories of the occupation. One of Britain's best secret agents, code named The White Rabbit – an incredibly brave man whose real name was Wing Commander Tommy Yeo Thomas – hid out for several months on the second floor right above their flat. He used to come down and play with the boys, Jerry and Max, who both loved jazz music. But, after twice returning to England following invaluable work with the Resistance, he was betrayed on his third visit in 1944 and arrested at the Passy Metro station. The Gestapo tortured him for four months but he never revealed a thing. Eventually, he was sent to Buchenvald and other camps. After several attempts, he escaped and, after testifying against Nazi Guards in trials held at Dachau in 1947, he returned to his pre-war job as an executive at Molyneux, the Paris fashion house. Joyce thought him to be the bravest man she had ever met and she was not alone.

Others were less fortunate. Joyce knew a young couple who had been round at their place for dinner and, foolishly, had decided to risk breaking the 9.00 pm curfew. They were arrested while walking home and sat in the local police station waiting for the customary fine. But a German soldier had been shot by the Resistance that night. So, caught in the trap of time and circumstance, they were included in a group of a dozen Parisians who, next morning, were taken out and shot.

The manner in which the French Police enforced this barbarous justice on behalf of their German masters was a sore that took a very long time to heal.

After nearly a year of Red Cross rations, my father sent us off on holiday to Switzerland. On the sleeper to Geneva I had my first banana. I had never seen one before. Nor I had skied and that, partly, was the purpose of the trip. We were heading for Villars, a resort above Lake Geneva, and all seemed new and exciting until, as Margot and I got ready for dinner, an earthquake hit. I vividly remember sitting on the bed watching the tallboy sway towards us before settling back against the wall.

The next day I was dressed up in all the right gear with big boots and children's skis and taken out into the glistening snow, which looked remarkably unruffled by the earthquake.

"I don't want to ski, I don't feel well," I moaned and my mother told me not to be silly, thinking it was just a reaction to the night before. But it wasn't. I had scarlet fever and soon developed a temperature of 104. So it was down the winding mountainous road, in a swaying car smelling of petrol and leather, and six weeks in a sanatorium in Montreux. End of holiday.

At least Margot had a good time. She and my mother stayed in considerable comfort at the Metropole Hotel where, every three days, a new batch of young American officers arrived on leave. As one of the few young ladies around who could speak English, she was not short of dates and spent most of her days escorting a stream of young men with crew cuts on trips to Lord Byron's castle, which stood a little further down the lake.

On returning home to Paris, my father got some surprising news. The Stockholm office was not doing well and the PW partners decided that he should be transferred to Sweden to take care of the problems. So it was that, on Christmas Eve 1946, we found ourselves spending our last nights in Paris at the Hotel Regina, right next to the Louvre. Joan of Arc, now all golden on her horse but less lovely then, sits outside in the little square. We were to take the train to Stockholm on Boxing Day. I still had one eye open as Mummy and Margot tip-toed into our room to leave Santa's presents and I just got an inkling that maybe Father Christmas wasn't quite who they said he was.

The growing up continued as the wagon-lits carried us, for four days and four nights, across the wreckage of Europe. Bombed out buildings flitted by as we picked up speed through Belgium and on into Germany. But the image which remains is that which greeted us at the main station in Hamburg. The platform is raised above street level and we found ourselves looking down on a scene of total devastation, alleviated only by two or three stalls selling fruit and vegetables to huddled figures clad in little more than rags or old pieces of uniform.

The ferry from Copenhagen carried us across the Oresund Straits to a different world.

There was – and, indeed, still may be – a sweet shop at the Stureplan in Stockholm. On one of our first walks around the city I stopped and gaped. There were chocolates and Smarties in the window. I had never seen a box of chocolates and nothing as colourful as Smarties. Sweden had worn the war years well, wrapped in its neutrality.

The Grand Hotel, an establishment that really was grand in every sense, turned into our home for the first three months as my parents searched for a flat. The year of 1947 turned out to be a freezing winter, even by Swedish standards, and although the snow along the Stromgatan just outside the hotel was deep and inviting, it was not long before I caught a bad chill and was confined to barracks. So I had the corridors and nook and crannies of the Grand Hotel to play in and, from what I remember, had a pretty good time.

We eventually found a lovely apartment at 101 Karlavegan but life turned out to be a little more difficult. The war had damaged my parents' relationship, not least because of an affair my father had been having with his secretary in London, and it was not long before my mother went back to England.

So, with the aid of a Scottish governess, I lived in Stockholm with my father and Margot and became a movie addict. Apart from enjoying my toboggan in the local park, I knew nothing of sport and my motivation each day was to find a movie that was marked 'Barntil' instead of 'Barnforboten'.

The problem was that the censors thought *Robin Hood* unsuitable for children because Errol Flynn kissed Olivia de Havilland yet considered *Great Expectations*, with its truly terrifying scene of John Mills as Pip being confronted by Finlay Currie, the convict, in the graveyard, quite all right. I didn't sleep for a week.

But Westerns seemed to be OK and I remember insisting that Mummy took me to see Randolph Scott in *Western Union* for a second time at the Rialto or Rio or Rigoletto – the cinemas in Stockholm all had those sort of names. These and some musicals like *Blue Skies* with Bing Crosby became my window on the world, opening up new vistas for a child who was trying to grasp just what life had to offer.

Chapter 2
SCHOOL

None of it prepared me for the jolt of reality which confronted me when I was sent to prep school at Cooden Beach in Sussex. The school was called Seafield and was run by two brothers: Granville Coghlan, a former Cambridge rugby blue, and his younger brother Pat. They were a spartan pair who insisted on cold showers in the morning, winter and summer, and a heavy regimen of sport. Pat, who wore dark prescription glasses because he had fallen back onto his head as a child and damaged his eyesight, almost always wore a pair of blue shorts and knee length socks under his black gown as he strode about the school from class to class.

If I have made them sound somewhat frightening, that would be unfair. It would have been difficult to find a more conscientious, intelligent and caring pair of headmasters than Granville and Pat.

The teaching staff were a memorable bunch, too. There was genial Major Bennett with his military moustache; Captain Wheeler, gaunt and faintly yellow from the malaria he had caught in the jungles of Malaya; and Mr Kempson with his shock of white hair that stood straight up and a nose that, alarmingly, bent sideways when he blew it. The nose was boneless.

The problem for me – one of many, actually – was that I was frequently speechless. I had a stammer. Maybe it was the trauma of leaving France or the nights under the stairs in Guildford, but, for whatever reason, I had developed quite a bad speech impediment. Answering questions in class was often agony and I was only too happy when my mother told me that she had found a speech therapist – a Miss Scott – who was willing to come round twice a week and help me.

My mother said she never charged a penny which was amazing because, God knows, I owe my radio career to her. I remember Miss Scott as quite a young-looking woman despite her grey hair and she had a warm, comforting smile. First of all, she made me lie flat on my back and told me to concentrate on my feet. "Feel your feet on the floor," she instructed. "Feel them get heavier and heavier. Now your calves …"

So she went on with her method of total relaxation. When I felt like a lifeless lump she made me read to her, still lying on the floor. I think she came to see me through an entire winter term and a few weeks into the next one. And my stammer disappeared. Thank you, thank you, thank you, Miss Scott.

By then I was beginning to get over the shock of being thrown into this alien world, but I still pined for the rare weekends when Mummy would come down to take me out for a trip to Eastbourne or tea at the Cooden Beach Hotel. One weekend I got Lord Tennyson, the former England cricket captain and grandson of the poet, to sign my autograph book. It must have been the year before he died just down the coast at Bexhill-on-Sea in 1951.

Sport was fast becoming part of my life but I had needed a crash course in the subject. When I first arrived, I remember listening to the boys chatting about who was playing centre forward or who should have been chosen for left back. I had absolutely no idea what a left back was. And I was nine.

My saviour was a boy, as chance would have it, called Nick Evans. No relation, of course. But as he was Evans 1, I became Evans 2 and he sort of took me under his wing. Or, to be more accurate, he taught me everything I needed to know about sport. Nick was a natural at ball games and went quickly into the First Eleven at everything – as he did when he went on to Lancing College. Having started so late I was not First Eleven material, but soon took a liking to cricket and football; somewhat less so to rugby because, being quite tall, I was put in the second row of the scrum. Being shoved up the arse while your nose was in someone else's was not my idea of fun and it was only much later, when I joined Richmond and played centre or on the wing, that I really enjoyed the game.

I also picked up a tennis racket for the first time although I had already seen the game played when, one May day in 1946, Margot had taken me to Roland Garros. I only have haziest memories of people in long whites, running around hitting balls on what is still Court No 2.

Tennis at Seafield was a Sunday sport, the serious stuff like rugby and cricket being played on Wednesday and Saturday afternoons. The rackets we used were those old Slazengers with laminated white frames and they seemed faintly glamorous. Pat Coghlan, still in his blue shorts, used to play with us energetically. The idea that, one day, I might get on the same court with Frank Sedgman or Ken Rosewall, names I was beginning to recognise from the sports pages of the Daily Express, never entered my mind. Sedgman, all dressed up in a white tuxedo for the 1952 Wimbledon Ball was, in fact, the first tennis player ever to catch my eye when his photo appeared on the front page of the Sunday Express.

Nick lived with his mother at Broadstairs in Kent, and during a couple of holidays I went down to stay with him. Apart from stinging my hands from his penalties when we messed around on the local recreation ground, we went to watch Kent play county cricket at Canterbury and he introduced me to my first real sports star, Colin Cowdrey, captain of Kent and later England.

Given how late I had been introduced to sport, I rather envied Colin because his father, who I met briefly some years later at a Test match at the Oval, had had the nerve to give his son the initials M.C.C. Michael Colin Cowdrey. He had done so quite deliberately so what were the odds on Colin, who was always slightly overweight and not an obvious athlete (until you saw him take dazzling catches at slip), turning into an England cricketer or, more amazingly still, being voted President of the Marylebone Cricket Club, which owns Lords and writes the rules of the game? Long odds, I would have thought.

In the class room, it was quickly becoming apparent that English, History and Geography were my best subjects and that Maths wasn't. It was my general inability to decide whether x equalled y or vice versa that ruled me out of Charterhouse, the public school that my Carthusian godfather, Sir Anthony Hawke, was keen for me to attend. Tony Hawke was Common Serjeant at the time (a typically understated British name for something terribly import in the judiciary) but even his influence could not persuade Charterhouse to accept a dunce at Maths.

So my father came up with Canford, a new school by English standards as it was only founded in 1923. I was never quite sure why Canford was chosen for my further education but, in September 1952, I found myself being admitted to this fine establishment which encompasses Lord Wimborne's sprawling estate on the edge of the Dorset town of the same name. It is a beautiful place with playing fields stretching as far as the eye can see from the top of the tower, which forms part of the magnificent 19th century grey stone mansion. Canford enjoys many unique features such as John O'Gaunt's Kitchen, a Norman church and a splendid Real Tennis court but, to be honest, these assets were not sufficient to make my first year being anything but thoroughly miserable.

I was homesick and even missed Seafield which had become an enjoyable experience during my last two years. But I was being put through the essence of the British private education system. The building up and the knocking down. "Riding high in April, shot down in May ... back on top in June" – Frank Sinatra offered a speeded-up synopsis of how it works. You can be strutting about as a terribly important prefect or cricket captain at your prep school in June and, come September, be regarded as little more than dirt when assigned to some disdainfully superior eighteen-year-old as his 'fag' at the bottom of a ladder you have to climb all over again.

There were various names for being a 'fag' at public schools – Canford used a different term which I have forgotten – but it basically meant that you were at someone's beck and call day and night. Shining his shoes, making his bed, fetching him a cup of tea – basically you were reduced to being a low-grade servant and if he didn't think you were doing your job it was within the prefect's remit to find some obscure rule you had unwittingly broken and give you six of the best with a nasty looking cane.

Such practices are, I believe, no longer and Canford had certainly changed when I took my son Ashley and his mother back for a quick tour a few years ago. For a start there were girls! In my day the House Matrons were the only young women we saw during term time and, unhappily, my house – Wimborne – did not have a Matron as accommodating as the young lady at School House who, it transpired, enjoyed introducing the delights of erotic entertainment to a select group of prefects in her room late at night! Needless to say, Matron was sent packing and the Head Boy, who had been one of her chosen amours, was promptly demoted.

I would not have enjoyed facing the headmaster after that little escapade. John Hardie was a stunningly good-looking man with deep dark eyes and the upright bearing of a Guards officer who put most of the boys' mothers under his spell with a single glance as he swept into his study with his black gown billowing. He was a Welsh hockey international and fine academic who, rather surprisingly, I thought, ended up at Loughborough College, an institution that specialises in sport.

Apart from the girl students who are housed in their own specially built complex behind the gymnasium, the other major change I noticed on my return was the absence of dormitories. Every single boy now has his own room from day one. Talk about luxury. To say the dormitories I endured were spartan would be an understatement. Any attempt at heating was made redundant by the fact that our Head of House, a lean faced, wiry cross country runner called Bulleid, insisted on keeping the fire escape door open at night through the dead of winter. And my bed was next to that door. Frequently, my face flannel was literally frozen stiff in the morning. Not that I got to use it immediately, because an early morning run was the first item on the day's agenda. Up to the Bournemouth Road and back. A nice little couple of miles. In retrospect, I am not sure how I survived.

But, eventually, I made friends – Hood, Reed and Rowe were three names that linger although I never saw them again after leaving – and made a bit of a mark with my riding. By my third year I was made captain of the Canford School Riding team and was therefore a focus of some envy as we were the only sports team to compete against girls! We had day trips for cross country matches at nearby girls' schools, but even so fraternisation was kept to a minimum.

The dressage bored me but I loved the show jumping. I rode a grey who seemed to accept that I was trying to do my best and there is nothing more exhilarating than clearing a jump when you and your horse are in perfect harmony. It was not, of course, always the case and I was thankful on occasion that English rain usually made for a soft landing.

By then the early miseries had subsided somewhat and I had begun to enjoy life in a setting of such beauty. Weekends spent in Bournemouth when my mother came down to rescue me for a couple of days remained highlights of my existence, but no one could suggest that Canford lacked a choice of pastimes for anyone energetic enough to grab the opportunities on offer.

Cricket was played in the shadow of the main house in the summer with tennis an alternative (which, ironically, I did not take up) while the winter term was reserved for rugby – cheering on big First Fifteen battles against local rivals like Sherborne or Bryanston – and then, during the Easter term, hockey took over. Somebody suggested I should play for my house in goal and I spent a few happy afternoons kicking everything in sight, but it was never really my sport.

Nor was boxing but I represented my house in that, too, for some absurd reason, and discovered being hit on the nose by someone bigger and faster than you to be a most unpleasant experience.

I enjoyed nothing more than the evenings when films were shown on the big screen in the gymnasium. I particularly remember seeing the crime thriller *The Blue Lamp* in which Dirk Bogarde played an East End boy with a Cockney accent. So unaware was I of acting skills that I was amazed to hear him using his proper cut glass vowels while rising to fame in all those 'Doctor' comedies a few years later.

It was fortuitous that *Julius Caesar* was our prescribed Shakespeare play in my final year, because that magnificent film production starring Marlon Brando as Anthony, John Gielgud as Cassius and James Mason as Brutus had just came out, so an entertaining evening became educational, too, and brought Shakespeare vividly to life for a young student.

Generally nothing changed as far as my academic studies were concerned. Mr Willis, my bespectacled Maths master, used to peer at me in despair at the back of his class and was probably surprised to hear better things being said about me in the Common Room from his colleagues, Mr Vaughan and Mr Rathbone. Mr Vaughan, my English master, was a slight figure with a nasal voice and ready sense of humour who quickly spotted a certain talent when it came to marking my essays. He became a great source of inspiration and encouragement as I began to lean more and more to a career with the pen.

Mr Rathbone, who we inevitably called Basil because of a well-known actor of that period, was a large, untidy man, slow of movement but sharp of mind who spoke in deliberate, strangulated tones. He umpired our house cricket matches and was kind enough to compliment me on my cover drive. Funny how tiny, irrelevant incidents stick in the memory. Of more import was the fact that 'Basil' evidently had his ear close to the ground when it came to exam time and guided us to subjects that might, just possibly, be on the question sheet.

There was much mention of Bismarck – hint, hint – so I spent two nights with very little sleep swatting up on the life of the great German. Utilising a nascent journalistic ability, I wrote reams on the subject and it seemed to do the trick. The note from 'Basil' a while later read – and I can confidently quote from memory – "I must congratulate you not merely on passing in History but the manner of your passing. Your score of 94% is the highest yet recorded in the school's history."

So, evidently, I could do something. I could write.

In between times, we would laze around, using up our pocket money by stuffing ourselves with Cadbury's chocolate and other delicacies in the school tuck shop. We used to sit, obliviously, under a strange looking object that we idly presumed was some pre-historic slab of art. We were right. But no one said anything.

"Excuse me, sir, have you had that thing looked at?" It never happened.

Until a real art expert, John Russell from Columbia University, passed by on a visit to the school one day in 1992 and did a double take. After having it properly looked at, Canford School found itself a great deal richer. Richer, in fact, to the tune of £7.7 million. The 'find' which had been so visible to all and sundry for so long turned out to have adorned a wall alongside the throne of King Assurnasirpal 11 of Assyria, who ruled from 883 to 859 BC. If that's not pre-historic, it's close.

It had been brought to England from Nimrud in northern Mesopotamia (now Iraq) by Sir Henry Layard. But the original was thought to have been lost in a river accident and everyone had assumed in the years preceding the foundation of the school that the object hanging on the wall of what was known as the Grubber was a plastic replica. Not so.

The seven-million-plus pounds was the highest sum ever paid for a piece of antiquity at the time and it enabled the school to build a splendid new gymnasium and sports facility. Generations of Canfordians have been kicking themselves ever since. Even the tiniest slice of £7.7 million would have been nice. "Excuse me, sir …"

By 1956 my father and I had a decision to make. Canford was expensive and Daddy was not getting any richer on a Price Waterhouse pension that showed a shocking disregard for inflation. Should I stay on through my eighteenth year and try for some A levels so that I could go on to university? Or should I march out into the great big world and see what I could achieve?

I think Daddy was relieved when I said that I was prepared to give it a go in journalism and he busied himself writing letters to such local publications as the South Croydon Advertiser and the Richmond & Twickenham Times. At least most of them replied. But none were interested in offering a seventeen-year-old a job. So I took a different tack and went to a man who I thought might just possibly have an idea or two.

Chapter 3
A CAREER BEGINS

By the time, I left school, my mother and I were living in a block of flats called Southfields at the top of Putney Hill next to The Telegraph pub which turned out to be the first drinking establishment I ever entered.

My love of cricket led me to getting the occasional game for a Roehampton team which played on a nearby field and, as my game needed considerable improvement, we found enough money for me to attend an indoor school on Chiswick High Road which was run by someone called Joe Gaby.

Joe had another job. He and his brother were the doormen at the Lords Pavilion. Rather more amenable and welcoming than some of their successors, Joe seemed like a good person to ask about contacts in sporting journalism so, the next time I went to watch Middlesex play, I went up to him to say hello. He knew me, of course, as one of the pupils at his school.

"I want to write about sport, Joe," I said. "Do you happen to know anyone who might have an opening?"

"Funny you should mention it," he replied with a sentence that changed my life. "There's this new freelance agency in Fleet Street that three fellows from the Press Association have set up. Reg Hayter is the chap's name and his partner Ron Roberts – you know, R.A. Roberts who writes in the Daily Telegraph? – will be here tomorrow. Come along and I'll introduce you."

I was back before play started the next day and, sure enough, Joe presented me to Ron Roberts, who was not a man with time for small talk. He usually had two books and half a dozen articles to write at any given moment and, after taking one good look at me, he came straight to the point.

"We are actually looking for someone who can write and make the tea," he smiled. "Reg and I will be in the office next week. Come round and see us. Here's the address."

So it was that I found myself searching for an office in Bridewell Place, round the corner from the Albion pub just off Fleet Street. Full of apprehension, I checked the number on the door and, on walking up a flight of stairs, I found myself confronted by a burly individual with an enquiring eye.

"C-c-come in!" Reg Hayter exclaimed. "I hear you want to w-w-write for us!"

Oh, God, he stammers like I used to, was the first thought that flashed through my mind but, after saying hello to Ron who was typing furiously on a little portable typewriter and Albert Sewell, a small, serious looking fellow who was working in the adjacent office, I was told to sit down and tell Reg a bit about myself.

After a while an older man arrived. White haired and avuncular with a warm smile, he turned out to be the third partner, Freddie Garside – Sewell being the first man they had hired when Hayters Sports Services was born just a few months before.

If I remember correctly, I had given Roberts a report I had written as a trial run for myself on a football match I had gone to at Craven Cottage the previous year. Fulham were not my team but they were nearest big club to where I lived and I had wanted to prove to my father that his warning of 'You can't earn a living watching football matches' was not necessarily true.

So Reg Hayter had some proof that I could string a sentence together but that did not dilute the surprise when he said, "Saracens are playing Wasps at Southgate tomorrow. We'll get you a press pass. The T-T-Times want 300 words. Bring your story back here on Sunday, we'll t-t-take a look at it and if it's OK, we'll send it across the road."

'Across the road' meant Printing House Square, home to the world's most famous publication since the previous century. I was going to write for The Times? Really?

I left Bridewell Place in a bit of a daze. If I didn't have a job, I certainly had an assignment and no one needed to tell me how important it was not to screw it up. Forty-eight hours later, I handed over my hand-written 300 words which was typed up in the office and duly dispatched, untouched. To my amazement, the rugby report appeared, as written, in The Times that Monday.

"We can offer you five p-p-pounds a week," Reg said. "But I'll expect you to work for it. We're here seven days a week. You will be, too."

I'd have slept there if they'd asked me to. If five pounds a week was barely a living wage in September 1956, it didn't seem to matter much to me. I was just delighted to be able to contribute to the housekeeping money and overwhelmed with joy at the thought of having a job that would immerse me totally in the world of sport.

And so it began. The District Line from Putney Bridge to Blackfriars every morning; all day in the office phoning over scores to newspapers or writing short feature articles for magazines; and then, most evenings, off to Brentford, Millwall or West Ham for a football match of some sort. I would learn how to knock together three or maybe even four different reports of 150 to 400 words for papers ranging from the august Daily Telegraph to the Scunthorpe Echo or some such. Home at midnight and off again the next day, yes, including Sundays. I was in heaven.

I was also getting the best journalistic education you could imagine. I have never been certain what those journalism schools teach – I am sure they are worthy and useful institutions – but, for me, learning to be a reporter is not something you can do in a class room. Out in the field, on a deadline, an editor yelling at you – that is how you discover if you can do the job. And it is how you improve. I know many Hayters men will agree when I say that Reg's little organisation was providing as good a journalistic education as you could find anywhere in the world.

It was a bit of a miracle that it existed at all. With Freddie Garside and Ron Roberts in tow, Hayter had sold the idea of a freelance agency providing a reporting service on sport to the twenty or so daily and Sunday Fleet Street (national) newspapers which existed at the time. Reg had cultivated relationships with the top sports editors during his years at the Press Association and now he made it pay off – simply by persuasion which, for a man with a bad stammer, was quite an achievement.

Somehow Reg managed to convince them that his reporters could provide, on deadline, a report on a cricket, football or rugby match which would be especially tailored to their own style, thus saving them the cost of sending their own man. So that's what we did. The report for the Daily Mirror needed a wham, bam personality driven intro while the Times wanted a more carefully written appraisal of the match as a whole. And if Crystal Palace were playing Northampton Town, the Northampton Chronicle required a report heavily angled to what their team and their players had done.

At a Saturday afternoon match, with its traditional 3.00 pm kick off, you had a bit of time. Not so for a 7.30 pm start under the lights. At most London football grounds you at least had a telephone within reach, sometimes even on your desk in the press box, but the deadlines were ridiculous. The match would finish at around 9.15 and by ten everyone was screaming for copy. By then you were supposed to have not only written three separate reports but also dictated them to copy-takers of varying competence. Oh, the joy of having a copytaker who knew how to type Johnny Haynes or Tommy Lawton without needing to spell it out!

There was a night at Millwall's old ground, so aptly called Cold Blow Lane, when the lights went out just as I was half way through dictating copy. So, for the first time in my career but not the last, I had to ad-lib what I had scrawled in my note book. It probably read OK, just, but could never have matched the prose of the incomparable Geoffrey Green of the Times who sat next to me one night in a darkened White Hart Lane and ad-libbed 500 of the most beautifully constructed words you have ever heard on the Tottenham Hotspur match we had just seen.

The match came alive again before my eyes and when he had finished Geoffrey, looking marginally satisfied, turned to me and said, "Well my old Commander, time for a quick one?"

Everyone was a Commander to Green, a sartorial figure with half-moon glasses and flowing grey hair whose ability as a wordsmith was only matched by a willingness to drink any of his colleagues under the table and emerge next morning apparently none the worse for wear.

The same could be said for someone else I met on one of those cold nights at football matches – an encounter that made Cold Blow Lane a much warmer place in my heart. One afternoon at a Millwall game, I found myself sitting next to my idol, the one and only Denis Compton. A lingering cartilage problem in his left knee had eventually forced this genius of a batsman to retire from cricket a couple of years earlier and he had taken a part time job writing on cricket and football for the Sunday Express. I don't use the word genius lightly. With a willow in his hand, Compton batted like no one before or since. He late cut fast bowlers; swept off-spinners to the square leg boundary from balls pitching outside off-stump; and charged down the wicket on a whim to drive the ball over bowlers' heads. He retired before one day cricket was born but what an impact he would have made.

I could, of course, write a biography right here about Denis, the Brylcreem poster boy with the slicked back dark hair and charming smile who had whizzed down the left wing for Arsenal (and England in war time Internationals) in between scoring centuries for England and Middlesex. Like Len Hutton, Bill Edrich, Alec Bedser and other great sportsmen of his era, a five-year chunk of playing time was taken out of his career by World War Two but even then he scored seventeen Test hundreds and in that scorching summer on 1947 compiled over 3,000 first class runs, bringing people to Lords in their thousands as he and Bill Edrich, the 'Middlesex Twins', injected some cheer and light to those days of rationing and gloom in post-war London.

Decades later, a photographer friend of mine, Nik Wheeler, took me to visit his sister and brother-in-law, John Bardner, at their lovely house in Highgate in north London. John was my age and we soon started talking about sport. I complimented him on his garden and he said, "Yes, but you know the best thing about this house? It is perfectly situated. It is one hour's walk to Lord's and one hour's walk to Highbury!"

He then confirmed what I had already suspected. "Yes, of course I support Middlesex and Arsenal and, of course, it's all about Denis Compton. There are a whole generation of us." There are indeed.

So, slowly, I was gaining confidence in my ability to produce what Hayters required even though the hours were long and the days intense. However, one morning, something happened that might interest speech therapists. When I picked up the phone to call over some rugby results to the Daily Telegraph, I found myself stammering again. "Oh, shit!" was my immediate reaction. Where had that come from? The source of the problem presumably lay in the fact that I was expending a great deal of nervous energy in a new job and that, for long periods of the day, I listened to a man who stammered. Which of those two factors played the bigger part I have no idea but the combination was obviously lethal to smooth speech.

Every speech impediment seems to be slightly different. Reg Hayter had most trouble with hard consonants. I had trouble with vowels like 'e' and 'a' so had trouble saying my own name. The next few days were hell as I tried to read out names like Epsom and Abertillery but, for reasons unknown, the problem disappeared after a week and I have never been afflicted since.

The work rate, however, did not decrease and by the first week of December I plucked up enough courage to ask Reg if I could have a day off.

"D-d-d-day off!" he spluttered. "What do you want a d-d-day off for?"

"Maybe for a chance to do some Christmas shopping?" I replied plaintively.

Underneath the bluster, Reg was not an unreasonable man so I got my day off. But that didn't mean I wasn't working on Christmas Day. Oh, no! In those days there was a full league programme of football matches at 11.00 am on Christmas morning and so Leyton Orient down the Mile End Road it was for this Hayters man. In those days, matches on Christmas morning were deemed perfectly logical. The men were supposed to be useless in the kitchen, so pack 'em off to watch their football while the wives prepare the Christmas dinner. As Marvin Hamlish wrote many years later, "It all seemed so simple then …"

Sometime early in 1957, the partners decided Hayters Sports Services needed more space so we moved across Fleet Street to Shoe Lane and offices next to the Evening Standard. Apart from Albert Sewell, so immaculate with his facts and figures – especially those concerning his beloved Chelsea for whom he worked towards the end of his career – Hayters had hired a smart young man from the West Country called Roger Malone, who went on to write for the Daily Express through a long career, and after me came John Thicknesse, a large, jovial man who became a longstanding cricket correspondent for the Evening Standard. Soon after Christopher Ford arrived and he, too, blossomed under Reg's tutelage. Christopher leant to the left politically and enjoyed a deep love of classical music so The Guardian was his natural habitat and he wrote elegantly for them for many years.

The number of sports writers who followed, 'graduating' from the Hayters 'academy' to achieve great things in Fleet Street are too numerous to mention in their entirety … Peter Smith, Barry Newcombe, John Etheridge, Glenn Moore, Martin Samuel, not forgetting Reg's own son, Peter Hayter … the list goes on. But the reason for our success was not hard to fathom. If you could produce three well written reports under difficult conditions and absurd deadlines on time, graduating to a newspaper that required only one was, as Reg would have said, "A d-d-doddle."

Hayter himself was always available for advice, as was Garside and Roberts whenever he was around, but one must not forget the diligent editing of Ron Surplice, who arrived soon after we moved to Shoe Lane. Ron was a straight-backed, sharp-featured man with a good sense of humour but a sergeant-major's attitude to discipline and detail. He wanted the apostrophe in the right place and kept us on our toes.

Chapter 4
THE IRON CURTAIN

In April 1957, two months after I had turned eighteen, Reg called me into his office one morning and told me that Hayters had received three orders to cover the England Under 23 football tour to Bulgaria, Romania and Czechoslovakia and, to my utter astonishment, asked me if I wanted to go.

"It won't be easy and I am p-probably t-taking a chance sending someone of your age and experience," he said. "But I think you're up to it. Just remember you will be carrying the reputation of the company with you so don't mess up!"

To say that Hayter was taking a gamble was putting it mildly. I suppose, during the preceding six months, I had shown him that I could do the job but catching the Piccadilly Line to Arsenal was pretty straightforward compared to getting oneself from Sofia to Bucharest. Travelling around Europe was not, of course, new to me but this trip would be behind the Iron Curtain at the height of the Cold War. Daunting? A little … but I was thrilled and couldn't wait for the adventure to start.

The orders had come in from the Daily Telegraph, the Daily Mail and the News Chronicle. The Telegraph would require its own report but Reg, correctly visualising the problems that might arise from having to phone copy through from these countries, had done a deal with the Mail and News Chronicle. On alternate days, I would file to one paper and then the other. The day I filed for the Mail, they would run the copy over to the News Chronicle, a few yards down Bouverie Street, and their subs would re-write it. This way I only had to write two stories.

That, however, was still double the work load of the three experienced football writers who would be my competition on the trip. Bob Pennington, chief football writer of the Daily Express, Frank McGhee of the Daily Mirror and Peter Lorenzo of the Daily Herald were, thankfully, a pleasant trio to travel with and never tried to cut me out of any snippets of information they picked up along the way.

The England team was managed by Walter Winterbottom, the long serving manager of the full England side and he had the future Tottenham Hotspur manager, Bill Nicholson, as his trainer. Although they were all young and largely untested at the time, the team itself was full of players who would go on to make a name for themselves in England colours starting with the captain, Ronnie Clayton and his Blackburn Rovers colleague Bryan Douglas. Then there was the Manchester United pair of Duncan Edwards and David Pegg; Fulham's brilliant inside forward Johnny Haynes; a centre forward from Middlesbrough called Brian Clough who would later lead Nottingham Forest to European Cup titles and make a great deal of noise doing it; Arsenal's clever Jimmy Bloomfield; Blackpool's elegant full back Jimmy Armfield who went on to enjoy a fine BBC radio career on retirement; Tottenham defender Maurice Norman and the big, blond West Brom centre forward (they weren't called strikers on those days) Derek Kevan. One of the goalkeepers was Alan Hodgkinson of Sheffield United who, despite being first choice for the full England team at the time, could not dislodge the other keeper, Bolton's Eddie Hopkinson, when he arrived for the last two matches of the tour.

So off we flew one fine morning in May 1957 on BEA (which, with BOAC, later became British Airways) to destinations that seemed far away and quite mysterious. They became more so when the door of the plane opened on the tarmac of Sofia Airport and the greeting party of Bulgarian FA officials boarded. I smelled garlic from that moment on until we left four days later. The entire city reeked of it. Every hotel lobby, every restaurant, every taxi gave off this aroma of garlic and when I put my head on the pillow that evening, the pillow seemed impregnated with it, too. It took years before I could enjoy garlic in my food.

There was one good hotel in town and we weren't in it. A Communist delegation from Moscow had turned up and although the players were allowed to keep their rooms, we journalists were downgraded to a place which, from memory, was aptly called the Hotel Moskva. At least we were able to go and have a drink at the players' hotel and I made the mistake of accepting a second Mastika from an all too hospitable Bulgarian. When I stood up the room went round, something that had never happened to me before or since. Mastika is the Bulgarian version of raki in Turkey or ouzo in Greece and is aniseed based. It clouds when you add water and your head is in the clouds afterwards.

The real fun began when, having watched the England team train that afternoon, we returned to our basic quarters at the Hotel Moskva to write our stories and, just as importantly, book our phone calls to London. We asked the receptionist how long it would take. The answer was a shrug. "One, maybe two hours," was about as much as we could get out of him. Two hours passed. A short while later, the phone rang in Lorenzo's room. It felt as if he had won the jackpot. Not only had Peter's call come through first but the Daily Herald was renowned for having the best copytaker in Fleet Street so he was all done and dusted and grinning broadly when he came in to my room to check on my progress. Minimal. The danger was that the Telegraph and the Mail would call at the same time and I would have to reject one of them. The Telegraph came through first and I dictated the longer of the two stories I needed to write.

By then Pennington was on to the Express. He was a burly man with a lopsided grin and a stentorian voice which he now proceeded to use to full effect. "No, ARMFIELD!" he bellowed. "A for apple, R for roger, M for Mary …" The thin walls shook and Eastern European ladies of a certain age began emerging from their rooms in their nightgowns with their hair in curlers. There was a lot of 'shushing' and angry looks but nothing was going to stop Bob. "F for …" He probably wanted to say something else but kept it to 'Freddy'.

Somehow we all got through the ordeal, which was five times as exhausting and nerve-racking as writing the stuff and, of course, it was repeated each night in some form or other throughout the tour. Primitive was the best way to describe trans-European phone services in the 1950s. Email? Hah! It was literally unimaginable.

What should have been imaginable, however, was a fax. Because the technology was available and had been ever since the invention of the telephone some 70 years before. And newspapers had been using it for decades. How do you think pictures were wired? By telegraphing a collection of dots on a piece of paper. Which is what the fax does. But for some weird reason, no one thought of sending the printed word by the same method until the 1970s, and even by 1980 a lot of top class hotels in Europe still didn't have a fax machine.

Along with Haynes, Edwards and a couple of other players who had been on full England duty, Ronnie Clayton was not with us for the first match so Birmingham's Trevor Smith captained the team. But it was not an auspicious start. Bulgaria's Under 23 side won 2-1 and Sunderland's Stan Anderson got himself sent off for kicking Doicho Batchev as he went to pick up the ball for a throw in. Not clever.

Clough scored England's goal and Hopkinson's fine shot-stopping prevented a heavier defeat. Winterbottom looked unhappy and Nicholson's creased features, which never changed too much, were set in stone. On to Bucharest.

Pennington, McGhee, Lorenzo and myself had booked ourselves into a four bed sleeper compartment on the Sofia-Bucharest Express. It turned out to be stuff of which novels are made. For a start Pennington and McGhee, honouring the great traditions of Fleet Street, brought along a bottle of Scotch. That, fatally, was augmented soon after we pulled out of the station by a bottle of brandy which was acquired from a dilapidated looking wagon-lit attendant in exchange for two packets of Senior Service cigarettes. Whisky and brandy – bad mix. Especially when Bob and Frank proceeded to guzzle both before we had even got out of Bulgaria. Peter and I had had a sip each but our two colleagues had taken care of the rest.

So by the time we reached the border, they were both out cold. Pennington's snores almost drowned out the noise of the engine while little McGhee was all snuggled up like a baby. All that was fine until the Romanian solider opened the compartment door with his machine gun slung over his shoulder and demanded our passports. Frantically Peter and I tried to bring the pair back to life. Bob was on the lower bunk and I literally dragged him off it, so that his heavy frame thumped onto the floor from two feet up. Not a flicker. Not a twitch of an eye lid. If his chest hadn't been heaving I would have thought he was dead. McGhee might never have been born and Peter certainly couldn't get him out of the womb of his slumber. So we scrabbled around in their coat pockets and handed over their passports to the unsmiling soldier, hoping to God all the visas were in order. After what seemed like an age, he grunted and handed them back.

Under the circumstances, it was a good thing that the journey took several more hours and by the time we pulled in to Bucharest Station Pennington and McGhee were rousable, although barely able to stand without assistance. Somehow we hauled them down the platform and into a taxi.

"Athenee Palace!" we told the driver and were duly taken to one of Eastern Europe's great old hotels which, at the time, was reputed to have one of the longest bars in the world. It was certainly needed as the Athenee Palace had a well-earned reputation for being the meeting place for every spy of every stripe operating behind the Iron Curtain. If Graham Greene never visited the place, he should have. Books would have flowed.

We were warned that rooms were probably bugged but no one said anything about the General Manager being an undercover Colonel with the Romanian Counter-espionage Directorate or the fact that every chamber maid, porter, and waitress reported to him – not to mention the slinky, sexy floozies who hung around the bar.

However, as far as comfort was concerned, the Athenee Palace was a big step up from the Hotel Moskva and, once Bob and Frank had stuck their heads under the cold tap, we headed off for the amazing August 23 Stadium which could hold 100,000 spectators – just a third, we were told, of the number of fans clamouring for tickets. I reported this under the by-line of Hadley Stevens which was the name the Daily Mail was using for my reports. The pitch looked perfect as the England players had a light work out and I quoted Bill Nicholson as saying, "There can be no excuses now."

Looking back at my reports, yellowing now with age in my cuttings book, I see that it was almost the only time I used a quote during the entire tour. That would be unthinkable in this quote-crazy age of endless press conferences but it was just the style of the time. We had plenty of informal access to the players but virtually nothing they said found its way into print. The sports editors just weren't interested. There has been no more profound change in sports reporting than that.

The following day something quite incredible happened. I got conscripted. To play. Yes, with that lot. Winterbottom wanted a fully-fledged eleven-a-side practice match and he had eighteen players. Adding Billy Nick and himself made twenty. That was it as far as staff was concerned – another sign of the times. So Nicholson's eyes strayed to the quartet of British reporters standing innocently on the touchline. Oh, dear God, I thought to myself, there can only be two options. Even without hangovers, Pennington and McGhee were overweight, unathletic and in their late thirties. That left Lorenzo and you know who. Peter was thrilled. He was a good footballer and had played for Leyton Orient reserves. Then there was me: eighteen, which was good, but fit? Not so good. Quite apart from not having played football, as opposed to rugby and field hockey, since prep school, the only thing I had run after since joining Hayters nine months before was a bus.

I tried to point this out to Winterbottom but he just said, "Don't worry, son, you'll be fine." But I wasn't. I was terrible. I managed to survive the half hour of rigorous exercises the squad was put through before the game, but once the whistle went I had no idea what was happening. Once, when it occurred to me that a tackle might be in order, I found myself facing Johnny Haynes of all people and literally in a blink of an eye, he was gone, vanished, playing on some other planet. I had never seen anyone move so fast. By today's standards I suppose it was slow but it left me gasping and, inevitably, late when I did try to tackle and put out a foot. I caught David Pegg and send him sprawling. "Don't kick him, for God's sake," Billy Nick growled at me. "We want him for Saturday!"

Meanwhile Lorenzo was having what, I am sure, remained one of the most joyous days of his life. Haynes and other midfielders kept feeding him delicious passes out on the right wing and he kept cutting in and banging the ball past poor Alan Hodgkinson. Seven times. His paper ran with the story the next day and led the back page with the headline 'Herald man puts seven past England goalkeeper!'

Peter was a lovely guy, of Italian parentage as his name suggests but English to his fingertips, and he went to enjoy a successful career in radio, eventually rising to Head of BBC Radio Sport. His son Matt followed him into the medium and was well known on TV as a sports presenter in the nineties.

We were all thrilled for Peter and his goal scoring spree and, of course, he dined out on it for years afterwards. I said as little as possible about my performance and tried to forget it, which was difficult as I could hardly get out of bed the next morning. Every previously unused muscle in my body was screaming and I was still feeling the effects when match day arrived 48 hours later.

With Clayton, Haynes, Edwards and Pegg coming into the side, England put in a much better performance than we had seen from them in Sofia despite the fact that they had to wait until two minutes from time for Haynes, lashing in an Edwards free kick, earned them a 1-0 victory. The team did well to keep their composure in front of 100,000 screaming Romanians, which was easily the biggest crowd any of them had encountered, but the locals were not unfair and generously applauded Haynes for his brilliance throughout the match. In my piece for the Telegraph, I likened the Fulham star to Wilf Mannion and Raich Carter, two of England's most skilful post-war inside forwards and Johnny went on to justify the comparison during an illustrious career.

As far as I can remember we flew to the picturesque city of Bratislava for the final match of the tour against Czechoslovakia's youngsters and, as fate and timing would have it, I could have had a major impact on the selection of the team. We were staying in the same hotel as the players and, on the eve of the match, I returned from dinner and was fumbling around trying to find my hotel key when the door directly opposite mine opened. To my obvious surprise a somewhat disheveled but quite attractive young lady was ushered into the corridor by two large and even more unkempt members of the England team – both of whom were on the team sheet to play the next day.

I sort of stopped and gaped and seeing me, the players slammed the door, leaving their lady friend to find her way downstairs, hopefully by way of the ladies' room so that she could tidy herself up before being seen by her father, who just happened to be a very senior member of the Czech FA. To make matters worse he was, at that very moment, enjoying a late night cognac with his England counterpart, Sir Stanley Rous!

As the door slammed upstairs, I caught sight of a figure further down the corridor. It was Bill Nicholson, who had evidently seen everything I had seen albeit from a greater distance. Every word counted with Billy Nick and he didn't use many. "Write that and they'll never play for England again," he said. It was one of those quotes you don't need to write down and which stay with you the rest of your life.

There was no arguing with Nicholson's warning. I held the careers of two England footballers in in the palm of my hand. It wasn't just that the pair had been enjoying the company of a girl in their room at midnight on the eve of the match. The story was, naturally, made all the juicier by the fact that one could have called her a member of the opposition. Can you imagine what the News of the World would have done with it? If Arsenal's Jack Wilshere smoking a cigarette at a party in Las Vegas warranted two pages of guff in the Daily Mail today … well, the times were different. The red top tabloids were still in incubation in the gutters of British journalism and although the newspapers of the day loved a scurrilous story, reporters were not under the same pressure to produce one.

So I retired to my room to think about it. I was nine months into a journalistic career and I suppose I could have made a major name for myself. But I just couldn't bring myself to ruin someone else's career in the process. I have no idea what my three colleagues would have done or advised if I had gone to them with the story. But I didn't so the decision was left to me and my conscience. I never told a soul.

Of course it was pure supposition as to what actually went on in the players' room and it may well have been little more than a kiss and a cuddle. But they had put themselves in a ridiculous position and I am sure Nicholson – probably without telling Winterbottom – let them know just how ridiculous the next day.

They both played; England won 2-0 courtesy of two power-driven goals from Duncan Edwards and a fascinating tour came to an end. But not before one more incident occurred that provided another kind of test for a young and pretty green reporter travelling abroad. On the last night, I was having a drink the bar when a young man came up to me, carrying quite a large package the size of a coffee table book.

He excused himself for butting in but said he knew that I would be flying back to England the next day and maybe I could do him a great favour. "I have relatives in England," he said. "In Essex; the address is written here. Would it be possible for you to post the book to them when you get to London? It is just a picture book of my country and I would so like them to have it."

He took the book out of the wrapping paper and it was, indeed, one of those official tourist publications, airbrushed to show only the beautiful aspects of life in Czechoslovakia. He was only a little older than myself and eagerly persuasive. I won't say that I accepted in a state of blissful ignorance but, in the minute or two I had to think about it, I couldn't see a proper reason for saying 'no'. It was, after all, only a book and, on the face of it, hardly a subversive one.

I wish I could weave some wonderful tale of espionage into this story and, who knows, there might have been one. It is not entirely beyond the realms of possibility that there was an elaborate code woven into the words of that book which would be deciphered by some Czech resistance movement in a semi-detached in Basildon – for that, I seem to remember, was the book's destination. It would have been very Le Carré.

I never found out. I dutifully mailed the book at the Putney Post Office and hoped that I was doing nothing more than fulfilling a favour for someone living in an unfree society. Even if I had known him for all of four minutes.

Of more consequence to me at the time was the reception I got back at the office in Shoe Lane. Pats on the back and a, "J-jolly good show," from

Reg and even, I believe, a couple of days off. But I was soon to find myself at Lords watching Middlesex and so it continued through the summer. I took no more than a passing interest in the fact that Lew Hoad destroyed Ashley Cooper in straight sets in the Wimbledon final or that Althea Gibson made history by winning the women's title over Darlene Hard, thus becoming the first black person to lay their hands on a Wimbledon trophy. Tennis was not my beat and if anyone had told me Lew would become a close personal friend and that, three years later, I would be escorting Althea to the Wimbledon Ball, I would have queried their senses.

And so the summer waned as did the career of Denis Compton. I had watched him occasionally during the season but, regretfully, missed the dashing 143 with which he signed off against Worcestershire in his final appearance at Lords. He had played his last Test for England the previous summer despite having the knee cap on his left leg removed. It was an old problem. He was bothered by the injury when he played on Arsenal's left wing in the 1950 FA Cup Final against Liverpool. His first half display was poor but, after the former Arsenal star Alex James had poured a hefty dram of Scotch down his throat in the dressing room, Denis returned to the Wembley pitch to help Arsenal win the Cup with an energised display that showed just what kind of footballer he could have been.

In the mid-fifties, cricket was inestimably the poorer for his retirement. His batting, which brought him 123 first class hundreds of which seventeen were made for England, was of a type that almost defies description. He teased bowlers, thrilled spectators and amused himself. Compton was, as the Daily Telegraph obituary said when he died in 1997 at the age of 78, 'the cavalier of cricket'. We have never seen his like again.

And so by September it was back to the enjoyable grindstone for Hayters, watching Queen's Park Rangers beat Coventry City 3-0 for the Sunday Pictorial on a Saturday afternoon or off to Vicarage Road for a midweek game. My cuttings book reminds me that I did a piece for the Daily Herald and was presumptuous enough to suggest that Watford's George Catleugh, who smacked home the 35-yard winner against Torquay United, was the only player on the pitch to deserve his £20 a week wages. That was the salary cap in those days – twenty quid a week and not a penny more. It took that fine shop steward and Fulham right half Jimmy Hill to stick his long jaw into football's finances before the Professional Footballers Association (of which Hill had become chairman in 1956) was able to force the reactionary

Football League to scrap the wage restriction. But it took Hill until January 1961 to get it done and, not soon after, Johnny Haynes became the first £100 a week footballer. But even Jimmy, who went on to become a popular, controversial and top quality broadcaster, could never have envisaged the 52-year leap from £20 to the £200,000 a week that a few stars like Wayne Rooney and Diego Costa earn today. Are they worth it? One could probably say that they are as overpaid as their predecessors were underpaid.

Meanwhile I was dashing about having the time of my life on a fiver and was grateful for it. (Actually I think I got a one pound a week raise after that England Under 23 tour.) No matter, it was off to Colchester or Brentford or Wycombe Wanderers for football or, for rugby union, the Richmond Athletic Ground – home of Richmond and London Scottish – Teddington where St Mary's Hospital played, or Old Deer Park where London Welsh and Rosslyn Park shared the ground at that time.

Occasionally I would be given a plum assignment for The Guardian – or Manchester Guardian as it was in those days – and, early that season, I was at White Hart Lane to see Tottenham Hotspur, inspired by that magical Irishman Danny Blanchflower and little Tommy Harmer, beat Burnley 3-1. A year into the job, I was feeling like a reasonably experienced eighteen-year-old!

But I knew there would be a significant interruption of my journalistic journey. I was going to be called up for National Service. As it turned out I was the last lot in – they took one look at me and pulled the plug! Silly joke and, anyway, it was going to be all too real come June of 1958 when I would be told to report to barracks.

In the meantime, all went smoothly in Britain's sporting world except for one total tragedy. On the 6th of February, I remember being in the Hayters office when news that the chartered aircraft carrying Manchester United home from a Europe Cup match had crashed on the snow-splattered runway at Munich. The scene is etched in my mind. Christopher Ford was at his desk in front of me; Albert Sewell over to my left; Reg and Freddie Garside were in their offices and Ron Surplice was marching around giving orders. All work stopped. There had been casualties – no, worse than that, fatalities.

As we sat glued to the radio; ripping the next dispatch off the Reuters and PA wires, the names started to come in – Tommy Taylor, Roger Byrne, David Pegg, my little 'opponent' in Bucharest. Oh my God! This was too awful to comprehend. If we were white with shock, heaven knows what it must have been like for people in Manchester. Apart from the individual human trag-edy it was their team that had been ripped apart.

Eventually everyone had to face the stark truth. Of the 43 people aboard that flight, 23 had died. Mark Jones, Eddie Colman, Liam Whelan and Geoff Bent were other players to be killed outright while Duncan Edwards, emerging as one of England's greatest players – so tall, so talented, so seem-ingly indestructible with a golden future ahead of him – fought for his life for fifteen days in a Munich hospital before succumbing to his injuries. Big Dunc dead? How could that be?

Bert Whalley, United's long serving coach, also died, as did the co-pilot and a steward. But, apart from the team, it was our profession that was hard-est hit. Eight journalists died – Frank Taylor being the only survivor from the press corps. Henry Rose, a super star of a reporter for the Daily Express in Manchester; the Guardian's Don Davies; George Follows, whose match reports I always admired; Eric Thompson, Tom Jackson, Archie Ladbroke, Alf Clarke as well as Frank Swift, a Manchester City legend who had taken up writing for the News of the World – they all perished.

Fate of course played its part. Don Davies, who had been capped by the England Amateur football team of 1914 and had played cricket for Lancashire, wrote under the pseudonym of 'An Old International' and had a large follow-ing. As a fighter pilot he had been shot down over Douai in World War One and spent years in a prisoner-of-war camp, arriving home weighing less than six stone. But he recovered his health and it was only a minor ailment that put his trip with Manchester United to Belgrade in jeopardy. The Guardian, feeling he would not be well enough to travel, assigned John Arlott, the famous BBC cricket commentator who also wrote for the paper, to take his place. At the last minute Davies said he was well enough to go and so re-claimed the assignment. At 65, he was the oldest person to die at Munich.

The grief was immeasurable and we all clung to stories of the survivors; of goalkeeper Harry Gregg, who had only joined the club two weeks before, turning hero as he ploughed back into the burning wreckage to rescue a woman and her baby daughter; of manager Matt Busby fighting through his awful injuries and eventually recovering to re-build his team around the inspirational Bobby Charlton – a team that would become known as The Busby Babes. Dennis Violett was another who was able to continue an already noteworthy career, but Jackie Blanchflower and Johnny Berry were too badly hurt to ever play again.

If Gregg became a hero it was a deserving accolade. Although wounded in the head, he refused orders to run away from the aircraft and went back in, first to grab a 22-month-old baby, and then returned to search for her mother who was the wife of a London-based Yugoslav diplomat and was hitching a ride back with the team. She was Vera Lukic and she was five months pregnant with her son. Miraculously her unborn child survived the severe injuries suffered by his mother whom Gregg literally had to kick out of the plane to get her free of the wreckage.

Any plane crash is a horror story but, of course, this one resonated to a far greater extent with the public because of the youth and fame of so many of the victims. The psychological wounds felt by multitudes of people were eventually assuaged, in part, by the remarkable achievements of the team Matt Busby re-built and the wonderful spirit of those 'Babes' as they strove to do justice to the memory of their fallen colleagues.

With Busby in hospital for two months and unable to take over the reins from his deputy Jimmy Murphy until the following season, United were unable to maintain their League One title challenge – despite beating Sheffield Wednesday 3-0 in their first match after the crash – and slipped to ninth in the table but they did manage to reach the Cup Final, losing 2-0 to Bolton Wanderers.

It took ten years before Manchester United could complete what they had set out to do in 1958 and by then those two icons, George Best and Denis Law, were bamboozling opposing teams with their magic. When they helped the team win the European Cup against Benfica, only Bobby Charlton and Bill Foulkes remained from those who had survived Munich.

Spring saw me return to the cricket grounds I loved but, after a few short weeks, the happy sound of leather on willow would be replaced by the bark of a foul-mouthed sergeant major in a desperate place called Warley Barracks at Brentwood in Essex. The contrast was stark.

Chapter 5
THE ARMY

It was Harold Macmillan's government that decided to start phasing out National Service in 1957. Conscription had started, of course, with the advent of World War Two and, at the end of hostilities in 1945, it was decreed that all men between 18 and 51 would have to serve Her Majesty in one of the three main services for a period of eighteen months. When the Korean War broke out in 1950 that was increased to two years and many conscripted servicemen found themselves fighting – and dying – on the Korean Peninsula, as, indeed, some had in Malaya, Cyprus and Suez.

The cut off birthday was 1st October 1939, so having been born in February that year, I was well inside the date. I thought about the RAF but, unlike my half-brother Tony, who ended the war as an RAF fighter pilot, I had no real urge to fly and I certainly didn't fancy being sea-sick all over the North Sea with the Royal Navy. So the Army it was and I was duly told to report to a military depot just down the road from Primrose Hill in north London. After all the paper signing, I was informed I would be joining the East Anglia Regiment which, not too many years before, had been formed by merging the Essex and Suffolks.

I would have preferred the Middlesex Regiment for obvious reasons but in the Army you don't argue. Sorry, make that 'cannot' argue. It took a while for some of my less well trained colleagues to understand that basic fact of army life and, as a result, they spent varying amounts of time in 'jankers' or a very small cell at Warley Barracks in Brentwood, Essex. God knows what that was like because Warley Barracks itself was the next best thing to a prison. The place had been condemned as unfit for human habitation at the start of the Great War in 1914 and here it still was, a dirty looking heap of masonry which would be my home for the next three months.

Looking around the dormitory as we collected our kit, the makeup of the bunch of young men I was destined to live amongst did not come as much of a surprise. Ninety percent were cockney kids from somewhere down the Mile End Road -- Barkingside, Romford, Hornchurch or Leytonstone where, decades later a baby called David Beckham would be born.

One needs to understand the part that vowels play in the pronunciation of the English language in British society to fully comprehend why Brian Henderson, a Scot, and I stood out somewhat starkly from the rest as soon as we opened our mouths. Any non-Brit who has seen My Fair Lady will have some understanding of what I mean. We were the only two in our company of about 30 who had been privately educated. In other words, we were Public School boys. Brian, being Scottish, had an upper-class burr in his speech that made it sound very different from mine but nonetheless we were set apart.

Henderson, with his flaming red hair, ready smile and the kind of bulk that enabled him to go on to win numerous caps for Scotland's rugby union team as a hard tackling centre three-quarter, was not going to be messed with and, anyway, his bonhomie made him instantly likeable. I had to be careful, however. It was going to be all too easy for the Cockney lads to dismiss me as a snooty, upper class git who needed taking down a peg or two.

I think the overriding factor which prevented that from happening was that they were scared shitless. Not of me. But of the sergeant-major, the sergeant and all the nasty little corporals who did their bidding. They were scared of the whole set up because, poor kids, this was going to be the first night they had spent away from Mummy in their entire lives.

There were muffled sobs when the lights went out and no wonder. They had nothing to prepare them for this. For Brian and myself it was, "Here we go again!" We had been yelled at by prefects and occasionally by masters at prep school when we were eight or nine and again by bigger prefects when we went to our public schools at thirteen. It brought home one of the great advantages of a private education in Britain and, to a lesser extent, I imagine, in the United States. It prepares you for life. Once you have been bounced up and down through two schools, very little is going to surprise you, especially if they have been boarding schools.

So, opening an eye the next morning I took a look at the Corporal banging his stick on the metal bar at the bottom of our beds yelling, "Get out of bed you lazy fuckers," and I thought, Oh, he's wearing a uniform this time. It was such old hat.

Naturally, Brian and I didn't say too much about this. Rubbing in our nonchalance would have been very bad tactics. The thing to do was to be as nice as possible and talk about football. It helped that I had been to Leyton

Orient. Slowly, once they realised I wasn't laughing at them, we started to make tentative social contact and shared a few jokes.

After a few days, one guy came up to me a trifle shyly and said, "I could help you get a real good shine on your boots if you could help me ... help me ..."

"Help you do what?" I replied quietly.

He fidgeted a bit and then said, "Well, like you being educated an' all ... I thought perhaps you could help me write a letter to my girlfriend."

Supply and demand. And so it was that I became the romantic scribe, inserting all manner of sweet nothings and delicate turns of phrase into the missives mailed off to loved ones from Bert or Joe or Bill and, in return, my shoes and even the state of my bed passed muster at every inspection. Which was very useful because they might well not have done otherwise.

In a very minor way, I got a whiff of what had enabled their parents to survive the Blitz during the war. There's nothing downbeat about a true Cockney. You get it from their speech. "How yer doing, mate? Everything aawlright then?" Practically every sentence ends with an upturned inflection, inviting a positive response. And their humour overrides everything. They are also very loyal. Once you have been accepted, they'll do anything for you. I didn't test that theory too far but, once when I lost a buckle on my belt, knowing that I would never pass the sergeant's inspection without it, one of my mates said, "Don't worry. I'll see what I can do." The big wink was followed about an hour later with a replica buckle appearing out of nowhere. No questions asked.

I made two decisions at Warley, one of which was quite brilliant, although I say it myself, and the other which was damn stupid. Let's take the latter first. When asked which sports I had played at school, I included boxing. Bad move. Within a couple of weeks, I found myself in the ring facing a little thug from Barking who was three inches shorter than me but twice as broad and about three times as strong. He hit me so hard on the nose that it broke and the fight was stopped with blood everywhere. I had broken something else, too – a rule in the Army which says 'Never Volunteer'. Owning up to a very brief and unsuccessful career in the ring for Wimborne House was not quite volunteering but it amounted to the same thing and it proved painful. Idiot.

But I used a bit of cunning to fight back when the injury threatened to keep me at Warley Barracks for an extra six weeks. The doctor had taken a look at the nose and decided that I needed to go into Millbank Hospital in London to be kept under observation for a few days in case I caught a cold which, apparently, would cause the bridge of the nose to collapse. Then, I suppose, I would have ended up like Mr Kempson, my Latin teacher at Seafield, with a nose that flapped in the breeze.

The problem was that I had been accepted for Officer's Training School in Aldershot which, quite apart from anything else, would get me away from dreaded Warley Barracks. Intakes only occurred every six weeks and, if I was in hospital at the time, I would miss the next one. I knew how long it took for names to work through the pipeline and, as my case was not life threatening, I would not be far up the list. If I didn't get to Millbank inside two weeks I would face another six at Brentwood.

So, I decided the play the upper class accent card. I had got to know the Medical Officer's orderly during my visits to his office and I had a quiet word.

"When the captain goes off to lunch, do you think you could look the other way while I use his phone?" I asked my pal. Being a good lad, he agreed. So I nipped in to the MO's office one lunchtime, picked up the phone and asked for Millbank Hospital.

"Hello, it's the MO's office at Warley here," I said, accentuating the authority that came with my officer-like voice. "Need a favour, old chap. You've got a Private Evans on your list, due to come in for observation. Bump him up to the top for me, would you? Need him back here sharpish."

Worked like a charm. I was at Millbank the following day for a few tests and precious little else. I ascertained that I could get six hours leave on the Saturday to do pretty much as I pleased so I phoned up Reg Hayter and asked if there was any work on the go.

"Actually, there is," Reg replied. "C-convenient for you. Just across the river at the Oval. Alan Ross c-can't make it down on Saturday and we need someone to write a piece under his by-line for The Scotsman. Read his stuff so you get a feel of his style."

I had been reading Alan Ross for years, as had most people interested in fine cricket writing. It was quite a daunting assignment but it was certainly better than sitting on my bed at Millbank so off I went to cover England's Test Match against New Zealand. As luck would have it, a saturated outfield prevented any play on that Saturday but I filed anyway, picking up on the state of the match from Friday's play. The Scotsman should not, of course, have carried the Alan Ross by-line on the piece but such niceties were overlooked in those days and I apologise, half a century too late, for those readers I fooled – if, indeed, I did. One or two of Alan's more discerning fans might have thought, "Mmm … not quite on form today."

At any rate, it provided a nice little interlude from army life quite apart from the ten and sixpence Reg paid me for the job and I returned to Warley in a good mood, knowing the stay would be brief.

Being accepted for a commission in the British Army as a national serviceman was not automatic. One needed to travel down to Warminster in Wiltshire to be interviewed and undergo a few basic tests. There were eight of us who turned up one weekend at the beginning of August – this was before the Millbank interlude, of course – and a quick look around the waiting room suggested that a few might have a problem passing muster. One who stood out was a chap called Keith Turner who would become a life-long friend.

One of the dubious things about the interview with a faintly bored looking major was the fact that he asked you to comment on your fellow applicants. I mentioned a couple of guys about whom I found something nice to say but admitted, "Keith Turner is the one with obvious officer potential." Apparently, Keith had something nice to say about me, too, thank goodness, and in the end we were the only two from our group to be accepted as Officer Cadets, with orders to report to Mons Barracks at Aldershot. Keith and I celebrated by going into town and seeing *Three Coins in the Fountain* with Louis Jourdan and Dorothy MacGuire. I had not been to Rome at that stage of my life and the romantic scenes of the Eternal City in that movie only made me more determined to put that right as soon as possible.

It was a strange fact that I travelled less during my two years in the army than I had done at any time of my life. I had put my name down for the Jamaica Regiment – yes, I was dreaming about tropical isles already – but I don't think I ever got close and I had to wait several years before that magical island began to play a significant part in my life.

So I left Warley with its contrasting personalities ranging from our company commander, a terribly precious young man who had been Sword of Honour at Sandhurst called Lt Sincock, and nasty little sergeant who rendered the word 'fucking' redundant through serious overuse, and hoped that Mons would offer something better.

It did in a way. Certainly the level of non-commissioned officers in charge of us went up a notch and I became quite fond of the Welsh Guards' Sergeant-Major who told us exactly where we stood at the first parade.

"Now listen carefully, gentlemen," he said in his best parade ground voice. "You may be Officer Cadets but don't get any funny ideas. Here at Mons I call you 'Sir' and you call me 'Sir' and the difference is YOU MEAN IT!"

And so it went. "You are the biggest load of lazy fuckers it has ever been my misfortune to come across – Sir!" That sort of reprimand could take place anywhere but it was certainly applicable when we were dragged off to Sennybridge in Wales for a week in the Brecon Beacons in November. As any Welshman will tell you, the mountainous terrain behind Cardiff is not particularly hospitable in high summer but, with winter winds picking up and snow on the ground, trying to stay warm became a primary occupation. Just two weeks before we arrived, two soldiers had died of exposure after losing their way so we paid special attention to the map we were handed as our commanding officer, a gung-ho fellow who wore his Parachute regiment wings and red cap with pride, told us we were to set off in groups of four to find a place called Llanddewi-Brefi. It's not just because I have Welsh ancestry that I found it easy to remember the name. It became embedded in my brain.

So we set off and after several hours trekking up and down mountainsides we found a couple of Welsh farmers with their carts on the side of a road we came across. We asked for the best way to Llanddewi-Brefi. I'll never forget their reply as they looked at each other and chuckled. "Oh, boy-o," one said. "They're going across the ROOF of Wales."

Our hearts sank and it was at this point that I became even more grateful that Brian Henderson was a member of our quartet. We were not just carrying rifles – the good old Enfield that had been used in the trenches of the First World War – but also a full kit bag. This was a big enough load on tarmac but the Roof of Wales, as our farmer had so aptly called it, wasn't paved and we soon found ourselves sloshing through terrain that is the very worst to traverse – the kind of marshy bog that gives you a solid footing after one stride and a slushy mess on the next as your ankle sinks into a mixture mud and melting snow. It was totally exhausting.

Inevitably Henderson strode on ahead of the three of us, handling the conditions with his rugby player's thighs, and eventually had the decency to look back at us pityingly. By that stage we were, indeed, a pitiful trio and it was obvious that we could use some help. So the mighty Scot volunteered to take one of our kit bags in turn for about twenty minutes each – rifle slung across his back; his own kitbag on one shoulder and one of ours on the other.

I've been very respectful of Scots ever since. Proceeding thus for a total of some 45 miles to the northwest, we finally made it to the little village of Llanddewi-Brefi and virtually passed out. I have no recollection of the night we spent there or the journey back to Aldershot. I returned to south Wales on many occasions to cover rugby matches but stayed well clear of the bloody Brecon Beacons.

Life at Mons continued in a military sort of way with a bit of parade ground bashing and endless lectures on what to do with your platoon when confronted by an enemy behind a hedge. All the maps and drawings were of nice rolling countryside with little hedgerows and dips and valleys and had absolutely nothing to do with what one might have encountered in a Malayan jungle – or up a mountain in the Brecon Beacons for that matter.

We were taught to clean and fire a Bren gun and, something I found harder at the first attempt, how to handle a large army revolver. Having been a reasonable marksman with a rifle in the Cadet Corps at Canford, I thought hitting a life-size target of a human figure at 30 paces would be easy. But the thing jerked viciously in my hand and the bullet flew over the target's head. So Randolph Scott must have had a very strong wrist as he blazed away bringing down all those baddies with his Colt .45 in the Westerns I had grown up with. Sad how reality kicks in.

Far from reality, I yearned for a bit of escapism as the weeks rolled by and I found an hour of it every Monday night as I parked myself in front of the only TV set in the Cadet Officers' mess and soaked up *The Perry Como Show* with the Janeiro Dancers. Relaxation was Perry's speciality and sometimes I wondered if he would get through one of his love songs without nodding off. But I loved his voice and the dancers were magic and I was able to forget the army for a blissful hour.

It was good having Keith around and we made friends with a few other guys one of whom, Ian Todd, went on to have a good career writing cricket and rugby for The Sun. There was also a jolly fellow called Peter Burge who had a passion for vintage cars and, one Friday afternoon, he offered to drive me up to London in his 1925 Bentley. It was a magnificent looking machine but it had one drawback for journeying in December. It was open on all sides and the seats were elevated above the windscreen. It was like being back in the Brecon Beacons and, while grateful for the ride, I was lucky not to arrive with frostbite.

Towards the end of our three months at Mons, we were all anxiously waiting to see to which regiment or corps we would be posted. Keith had done his basic training with the Green Jackets, a singular regiment with a great tradition which quick-marched its troops everywhere, and was duly posted back to them. I had no idea where I was going and was somewhat disappointed to see the 'General List' attached to my name when the orders were posted.

In fact the Army had been quite logical for once and was attempting to put a round peg into a round hole, having noted my eighteen months as a journalist. I was to go to HQ Eastern Command at Hounslow, Middlesex as deputy Public Relations Officer. So much for Jamaica or even Cyprus where there was still a bit of excitement going on. My Army career would see me posted nowhere more glamorous than Brentwood, Aldershot and Hounslow. Join the Army and see your back yard.

Anyone who has taken the Piccadilly Line to Heathrow will have passed through Hounslow West and the army barracks was just a short walk away, hidden behind the Bath Road. It wasn't exotic but, as it turned out, extremely convenient. As soon as I received my commission and became a 2nd Lieutenant, life became a great deal more comfortable. I was an officer in the British Army! The perks that came with the job included my own comfortable room in the main building at HQ and a batman who I really didn't know what to do with. The poor fellow was supposed to iron my shirts, shine my shoes and bring me my cup of tea in the morning before I descended to the Officers' Mess for breakfast. Being waited on hand and foot was not something I was used to – having left Canford before I became a school prefect – and I found it faintly embarrassing. Anyway we came to a sort of understanding that he wouldn't fawn too much and let matters run their course.

Our Commander-in-Chief was a splendid man called General Sir James Cassels who had survived Normandy, Malaya and Korea in one piece, commanding various battalions and would go on, a few years later, to be appointed Chief of the General Staff, which meant he was Britain's top soldier. He was a man of great charm and civility and I felt honoured to share the long table at dinner with him. As junior officer, it was my task to start passing the port at the end of the meal and to know which way to pass it. To the left is the correct direction.

Our mess, being made up of a hotchpotch of officers from all branches of the army, was a good deal more relaxed than some I was to visit in the coming months, especially the Guards regiments where the Grenadier, Coldstream,

Welsh, Scots and Irish Guards would adhere to rules and traditions born centuries before. These were the fellows who commanded those poor souls who have to stand outside Buckingham Palace in their bearskins, unflinching in the face of having their photo taken a million times a day. It is very easy to underestimate the Guards soldier, who seems so ceremonial, and his officers who loll about their Mess sipping gin and swapping yarns in a languid, terribly upper-class manner. Put them on the battlefield and all that changes as Nazis, North Koreans and Chinese have discovered to their cost. It was, however, fascinating to visit Wellington Barracks near Whitehall and observe the etiquette required to gain entry; the proffering of one's card and then the acceptance of the promptly offered gin and tonic, even at 10.30 am.

My job, basically, was to advise General Cassels and his staff of how to handle the press while finding interesting things to feed through to Fleet Street newspapers so that the Army would be seen to be doing something useful while at home. My boss was, in fact, a civilian PR expert under contract to the Army. Don Leslie was a busy, bustling and very bald chain-smoker who happily possessed a sharp Scottish sense of humour and we got on well.

After a couple of weeks it became evident that I spent a fair amount of time if not telling, then certainly advising, Lt-Colonels and Brigadiers what to do. "Sonny boy," Don chuckled, "that is not the way the Army likes to do things. Can't have a Second Louie telling the brass how to behave! We'll have to get you some more pips."

As it was, my solitary pip was not often visible because, on a normal day, we worked in mufti. But Don knew something had to be done about it and put in a request for me to be promoted to Acting Captain. Inevitably, even though the request was approved, it got stuck in the pipe line and nothing happened. So I decided to give them a nudge and turned up at the Friday staff meeting in uniform – something I didn't need to do. I'm not sure there was even another Captain there, just a roomful of Majors and up, all the way to the General himself.

It was all too much for the fussy Major who thought of himself as Don Leslie's boss – it was not reciprocal – and he phoned up immediately after the meeting. "Tell that 2nd Lieutenant of yours to go to the Quartermaster and get his extra pips. Can't have that happening again. Won't do, won't do at all!"

It did very nicely for me because, apart from the added prestige, the higher rank meant higher pay which was very useful indeed. And I must confess I played on it a bit. When making a reservation for dinner at a West End restaurant I always emphasised the 'Captain' Evans bit and, in those days, it still carried a little weight, although I'm not sure it would now.

The pips went up at the end of February 1959 which meant I had only missed being a teenage Captain by a couple of weeks and that might well have been a first in the British Army. I felt a bit of a fraud because there is a considerable difference between being an Acting Captain and a fully-fledged one -- the latter rank, after all, might well have had to have been earned in places far more demanding and dangerous than Hounslow. But, of course, the three pips on the shoulder revealed nothing of that.

The moment when I felt most awkward arrived when I had to return to Warley Barracks for some function or other and found myself sitting down at the same table as Lt Sincock, the Sword of Honour fellow from Sandhurst who was a professional soldier to his fingertips. What he thought of this National Service upstart who had been a private under his command six months before and now outranked him, I cannot imagine. At least he had the decency not to mention it.

My duties took me all over East Anglia and I found myself handling the press at Royal occasions as Princess Margaret visited the Cathedral at Ely or the amazing Queen Mother inspected the troops in Norwich. She was not young, even then, but she never faltered in the heat, chatting to crowds and being out on the parade ground for long periods of time. She worked very hard for the Royal Family and kept at it throughout her nineties before she died at the age of 101 in March 2002. A remarkable woman.

I had two assignments which took me to the Chelsea Hospital, home of all those old-age pensioners who one sees around London to this day in their scarlet tunics and blue caps. On the first occasion I was acting as temporary ADC to Field Marshall Sir Gerald Templar at his daughter's wedding and, secondly, for the visit of President Charles de Gaulle.

The man of whom Winston Churchill had said during the World War Two, "The greatest cross I have to bear is the Cross of Lorraine," had vowed never to return to Britain, where he had spent much of the war, until he was President of France. Given the state of French politics, it had taken him a while. Various left wing governments had failed to bring the country back to full prosperity and showed no signs of being able to handle the growing crisis in Algeria, so the country turned to its war time leader and de Gaulle was duly elected. Only then did he feel able to accept an invitation from the Queen to return to the country that had sheltered him during his own nation's darkest hour.

He was accompanied to the Chelsea Hospital by Prince Philip who is hardly an unimposing figure. But he was dwarfed by the French President. I was standing a few yards away while they inspected the old war veterans and I was struck by the haughty grandeur and sheer ugliness of de Gaulle with his huge nose sticking out from under his peaked cap. He was a giant of a man and he loved France probably more than France loved him. Certainly the French people were unable to live up to the grand vision Le Grand Charles had for them.

But, quite often, I had more serious duties to perform. Luftwaffe bombs were still being dug up all over London as re-building increased apace and there was an incredibly brave Major Hardy who was London's leading bomb disposal expert. The soldiers from the Royal Corps of Engineers were heroes, too, as they fiddled around with fuses and detonators that could blow up in their faces any moment. It was my job to keep the reporters at a safe distance while Major Hardy went to work, frequently around Wapping and other parts of the East End by the Port of London that had been blasted to high heaven night after night during the blitz. The good major was so expert at his job that, as far as I know, nothing went off unexpectedly and everyone survived.

So my life at Hounslow was varied and often interesting but, I have to admit, nothing pleased me more than the 5.30 sign off on most Friday evenings and the quick dash home to spend the weekend doing what I loved best – reporting on football matches! There was nothing to stop me working for Hayters at the weekend so I spent many a Saturday back at my old stomping grounds – Highbury, White Hart Lane, Griffin Park and Craven Cottage. There was also rugby to report which was always more challenging as the press facilities at places like Motspur Park and Imber Court, where the Met Police played, were non-existent. It was touchline reporting with a pen and soggy notebook and on more than one occasion with the rain teeming down, I found myself having to knock on the door of a nearby house to plead for the use of their phone.

My mother and I had moved from Putney back to Park West near Marble Arch, where we had lived when I was at prep school. It remains a large, red brick building just down the Edgware Road in what has now become a little

Beirut. Every restaurant and store seems to be Arab owned. I often wonder what my Mum would have thought about the change that has come over the neighbourhood. She wasn't racist but she was very proud to be British and despite her love of France and Italy which she knew so well – she had worked in a bank in Milan as a young woman – she enjoyed the English way of doing things and probably would not have been amused if Cooper's, our excellent grocery store (too soon for supermarkets) across the road had been turned into the ba'ala it is now.

My father, who had re-married and gone off to live in Bogota, Colombia with his wife who was an English teacher, was unable to increase the alimony because the Price Waterhouse pension never kept up with inflation, so money was tight and I didn't like the fact that my mother had to go out and find a job in her late fifties. For a while, she worked at Fortnum & Mason's in the dress department. With my army pay supplemented by the odd couple of pounds I was getting from Hayters at weekends, at least I was able to contribute to the housekeeping.

By this stage, of course, girls had come into my life and Diana, a curvy, voluptuous little brunette who was not averse to some serious activity on the carpet of her grandmother's living room across the street from Highlands Heath, was my first lover. She eventually went off with some spiv in a shark-skin suit and I was bereft for about five minutes. Nevertheless, my Mum thought it might be an idea for me to break free of the maternal nest for a while (this was when I was still at Hayters) so I decided to share a flat on Sloane Avenue, just down the street from the Royal Court Theatre, with a young man I had got to know called Mike Rowney. He was tall and a bit effete but, happily, he liked girls and we had fun knocking around town with another tall, gangling fellow called John Lloyd (not the tennis player who would become a good friend later). Like Mike, John had a wicked grin and not all our intentions were pure, but we stayed out of serious trouble. The Admiral Codrington became our local pub and I distinctly remember being able to get a half pint of bitter and a delicious slice of egg and ham pie with potato salad for three shillings and sixpence. Although nothing equates, that was about 30p in today's money. I suspect something similar today would cost about seven pounds.

Socially, the Sloane Avenue flat provided me with my first taste of true independence but, after six months, we gave it up when I went into the Army. At Hounslow there was a very nice girl called Lt Penny Jackson but we did little more than play a very bad game of tennis together. Later there was an exotic looking Nicaraguan with whom I spent an incredibly romantic evening dancing by the Mediterranean in Santa Margarita while a wonderful Italian band played 'Tu Sei Romantica' … heaven.

I suppose Judy Devitt was my first serious girlfriend, although we never slept together. In those days certain types of girl just didn't and Judy, someone I had met at a debutante ball, was much too serious to be led astray even though she was incredibly sweet and loving. After a couple of great holidays in the South of France and Malta with her family, who had a splendid house in Addison Road off Kensington High Street, we drifted apart.

The trip to Malta marked the end of my term serving Her Majesty. The Army made serious efforts to try to persuade me to stay on and become a regular soldier but there was no chance of that. I gratefully accepted the little present they gave you at the end of your two years – a paid week's holiday to any British territory – so I was able to join Judy in Malta. I was given tickets on BEA and, on the return journey, found myself boarding civil aviation's first jet airliner, the de Havilland Comet on its first visit to the island. I felt a bit of a fool when people back home asked me what it was like because the party Judy and I had enjoyed with a group of Malta-based Royal Marines the night before had been so splendid that, when I took my seat in the Comet, I just about managed to strap myself in and promptly passed out. I am sure it was a nice ride.

So that was the end of Captain Evans and what to do with the civilian version was a problem that fell into Reg Hayters lap. Under the law of the land he had either to give me my old job back or find me another one. It was a tricky situation because he had hired an excellent young reporter called Tim Brown – who went on the make a name for himself as a foreign correspondent in Madrid – and he could not afford to have both of us on the staff. But Reg, being the amazing man he was, always had a solution up his sleeve and he hadn't needed to go far to find it.

The Evening Standard was right next door and, as soon as he heard that their venerable 70-year-old rugby and rowing correspondent Hylton Cleaver was about to retire, he was over like a shot to talk to the sports editor, Peter Goodall. "I've g-got just the man for you!"

Like so many Fleet Street sports editors, Goodall, although a rather unsympathetic character, found it almost impossible to say 'No' to Reg and that was it – the next step in my career, onward and upward, was set.

Chapter 6
THE EVENING STANDARD

I was de-mobbed on Thursday 16th June 1960 and turned up for my first day's work, ostensibly as the new rugby and rowing correspondent, at the Evening Standard the next day. Immediately things took an unexpected turn. Unbeknownst to me, a discussion had been taking place between the editor, Charles Wintour, and his literary editor, Harold Harris, who, the previous year, had agreed to try something different and had ghosted Althea Gibson's copy at Wimbledon.

Obviously Harris was a tennis fan but he felt that one year was enough as he had plenty on his plate in the literary world, so he suggested Wintour find someone from the sports desk to take on the job. The Editor didn't have to think long. In another of those short sentences that changed my life, he picked up the phone to Goodall and said, "You've got this young reporter joining you today. Give him to Althea!"

So I was in the office about fifteen minutes before being dispatched to the Queen's Club, where the tennis world was gathered for the London Grasscourt Championships. Unlike today, there was no week in between Wimbledon and Queen's and this was Friday. No time to lose. I found the tall, elegant figure of the woman who had made history in 1957 and '58 by becoming the first black person ever to win Wimbledon standing on the steps of a clubhouse I would come to know only too well over the years, and introduced myself.

I received a warm smile and firm handshake and Althea couldn't have been more charming. I was walking into a world that was completely new to me and I was still a little star struck when I recognised faces in the club lounge that belonged to Roy Emerson, Billy Knight or Britain's golden girl, Christine Truman. But Althea quickly put me at my ease and on Monday we sat down next to each other on the world's famous Centre Court and went to work. Althea was perceptive and articulate and I wrote fast so there was no problem on that score.

However, there was a complication. My summer job – the prospect of which had not exactly thrilled me – was supposed to be rowing and Henley Regatta, the sport's equivalent of Wimbledon, was starting in a few days' time. I asked Goodall what I was supposed to do. "Forget Henley," he said. "You're doing Wimbledon."

Phew! What a relief that was. I had always loved tennis but had hardly ever covered it for Hayters and my most recent memory went back twelve months when I had watched Alex Olmedo, the great Peruvian, beat a very young Rod Laver on television. I remember I had been all dressed up in my uniform after taking someone to lunch at the Public Schools Club at 100 Piccadilly. Now the uniform and pips were gone and I was on Centre Court myself, working with a champion. It took me a while to digest all that.

But I was soon swept along by the excitement of Wimbledon and my new world. Writing for Hayters, most of my copy had appeared under a 'From our Correspondent' by-line or, occasionally, a nom-de-plume such as Hadley Stevens, which is what the Daily Mail called me on that trip to Eastern Europe. But from then on it would be Richard Evans on just about everything I wrote and have written since, and that's the way I like it. Nothing annoys me more than people offering strong opinions behind a cloak of anonymity which happens so often with today's 'bloggers'. The very name is inelegant and I abhor the trend.

But even though this was writing for someone else, I was no ghost. On Monday 16th June 1960, the Evening Standard carried a front page piece on the first day at Wimbledon 'By Althea Gibson with Richard Evans'. It was my first piece of writing on tennis. Little did I know where it would lead!

The press room, located on the first floor just above the South West entrance to the Centre Court back then, was populated by a few familiar faces like the pipe-smoking Roy Marshall of the Daily Express, whom I had met at Twickenham and other rugby venues, and the inimitable Geoffrey Green whose prose flowed as freely over tennis matches as it did at White Hart Lane. But there were people who had only been by-lines to me before, like the legendary Lance Tingay of the Daily Telegraph whose year-end rankings, in the absence of anything resembling a computer, were taken as gospel by the entire tennis world. You were No. 1 in the world if this studious looking fellow with a pair of spectacles perched on the end of his nose said you were. Other rankings were put out, of course, especially in America, but none carried the Tingay stamp of authority.

Then there was Frank Rostron, a larger-than-life figure who had boxed for his native South Africa and, as a war correspondent, had followed the Allied armies up through Italy, north from Monte Cassino. Always a man with an eye for a scoop, Rostron would break headline-making – and sometimes only partially true – stories on cricket and tennis for the Daily Express in the days when the paper was in its heyday of Beaverbrook ownership. Frank was a very good man to have dinner with, especially in Italy, where, spluttering over his cigar, he would wave away the first offering of a bill until a new one was produced which was more in line with what he felt the meal had been worth. Waiters tended not to argue with Frank.

Rostron was an enjoyable but exasperating colleague, none more so than during Roland Garros where the proximity of the Longchamp race course enabled him to disappear all afternoon to enjoy his favourite hobby. Then at around five o'clock, dog-eared newspapers and form guides tucked under his arm, he would re-appear, his brown trilby tilted at a jaunty angle and march straight into the unguarded locker room. Fifteen minutes later, he would emerge with some tit-bit of information that he would blow up into the 'scoop' we had all missed. Never having seen a ball hit.

Then there was David Gray of the Guardian who was a different personality. Soft-spoken and studious, David's breadth of knowledge and writing skills made him the editor's pick each year to stand in for Alastair Cooke in New York while the great man went on holiday. Cooke's 'Letter from America' on BBC Radio was part and parcel of Britain's listening habits for over 50 years, but many people forget that he wrote superbly for the Guardian as well.

Gray, who became a good friend, was an unsurpassed expert on women's tennis and it was a loss to the chronicling of the game when he accepted Philippe Chatrier's offer to become Secretary General of the International Tennis Federation in 1976. Tragically, he died far too young of cancer at the age of 68 just after returning from the US Open in September 1983.

Working with Althea turned out to be most enjoyable and by the time Neale Fraser had beaten Rod Laver in the men's final on the Friday and Maria Bueno had retained her Wimbledon title by defeating South Africa's Sandra Reynolds on the Saturday, I found myself asking Althea if she would like me to escort her to the Wimbledon Ball at the Grosvenor House on Park Lane. It seemed like a logical thing to do as we had been working together all fortnight and, to be honest, there weren't many young men at Wimbledon, American or British, who were going to ask her out.

Finding a doubles partner or even someone to talk to had been hard enough when she first played Wimbledon in 1956 and it took a Jewish girl from North London who was well versed in discrimination to offer to play doubles. Althea and Angela Buxton had the last laugh by winning the title and the pair remained friends throughout Althea's life.

Living so close to the Grosvenor House – you could walk from Park West in fifteen minutes – asking Althea round for a cocktail first was something I didn't think twice about. But it did make my mother a little nervous. It wasn't prejudice; just unfamiliarity. "I don't think I've ever met a black person socially before," she said with a worried expression. "I've certainly never had one in my home."

I assured her that Althea was a charming young lady and that she had nothing to worry about. And, of course, everything was fine. To say that we must have stood out amongst the LTA officials and their ladies as we descended the Grand Staircase at the Ball would be something of an under-statement. They had swallowed hard and got on with it when Althea won her first singles crown in 1957 and she must have opened the dancing with Lew Hoad, although I don't remember ever seeing a photo of them on the floor. But now she was just one of the crowd, being escorted by some young pup of a reporter, and I can well imagine what murmurings went on behind our backs. But we had a dance and a laugh and all was well.

I was sad, a year later, when Wintour and Goodall made the decision to drop Althea from their Wimbledon coverage and replace her with Jaroslav Drobny. They intended no slight on Gibson but the chance to sign Drobny, who had become a big favourite with the English public when he had finally won Wimbledon in 1954 at the age of 32, having lost in two previous finals in 1949 and 1952, was too good to pass up.

Luckily for me, I was still assigned to do the writing – lucky because Old Drob, as people called him affectionately, had become a real professor of the game and he taught me so much about tennis. Understanding exactly what he was saying in my ear with his heavy Czech accent against the noise of the Centre Court was not always easy but it needed greater concentration and that is a good thing if you want to remember what you have written. The tac-tical knowledge he was imparting, as the great Times tennis correspondent Rex Bellamy would have said, 'opened windows in my mind' as far as tennis was concerned.

By the time we started our three-year Wimbledon relationship, Drob had become a naturalised British citizen, having defected from Czechoslovakia and its suffocating Communist regime in 1949. Egypt was the first country to take him in and give him travel documents but he naturally gravitated to the UK as he had enjoyed so much success playing tennis there. He was a friendly soul although somewhat bitter about the fact that the LTA never asked for his services when it came to Davis Cup play. Miffed, and in need of some income, he was hired in turn by Italy and Sweden and, as the team coach, found himself handling players with very temperaments such as the incredibly charming Italians Nicola Pietrangeli and Orlando Sirola and those tall, blond Swedes, Ulf Schmidt and Jan-Erik Lundquist. .

Working with Drob became the highlight of my summer and drew me ever further into the wonderful world of international tennis. Being their age, it was easy to make friends with the players in those days when they were not closed off by an entourage of agents, coaches and physios. The Twist was all the rage in the early sixties and I remember parties at the Northern Club in Manchester when the fun-loving Welshman Gerry Williams, then with the Daily Mail, challenged players like Carole Caldwell, who was soon to marry Clark Graebner, South Africa's Marlene Gerson and a bubbly, bespectacled teenager called Billie-Jean Moffitt to a Twist competition. I think Gerry won at Twist, but Billie-Jean, on her first visit to England in 1961, grabbed the first of 16 titles in singles and doubles at Wimbledon by winning the doubles with Karen Hantze.

It was obvious Billie-Jean King, as she became after marrying Larry, was going to be something special but none of us could have foreseen how her incredible determination and pioneering spirit would turn her into a world-wide icon for the feminist movement. Without doubt she is one of the most remarkable people I have ever met and a true friend.

Despite the fact that tennis occupied much of my summers, I did not neglect rowing completely and I covered the famous Oxford and Cambridge Boat Race on the Thames throughout my years on the Standard. The actual race itself was fun and exciting and not without incident as I wrote in 1961 in this Page One report:

'In one dramatic moment fate switched the destiny of the 107th Boat race to give Cambridge a sensational victory by four and a quarter lengths in 19 min. 22 sec. today.

'As the crews approached Chiswick Steps, with Oxford a length clear, G.V. Cooper, the Dark Blues No 6, slumped. Ashen white, his head rolled forward and a mighty spray from his oar heralded the end of Oxford's hopes of gaining their first Boat Race hat-trick since 1913.'

It was April Fool's Day but this was no joke for poor Cooper. There was more drama another year when the Cambridge boat sank, which gave that great BBC broadcaster John Snagge more material to describe with his sonorous voice. But it was not the race itself that made rowing my less-than-favourite pastime. Covering the practice sessions by Putney Bridge or even up on the Cambridge Fens in February was a thankless, not to say freezing, task.

The job was made easier by the company I frequently kept. For a couple of years my closest colleagues were John Bromley of the Daily Herald and Michael Grade of the Daily Mirror. Brommers was one of the brightest and most amusing people I have ever worked with and I am sure people who spent far longer in his company than I did will concur. Peering through his glasses, with a funny comment never far from his lips, Brommers went on to a great career as Head of ITV Sport when it was just starting to give the BBC Sport some competition. With flair and wit and a keen sense of how to get a deal done without making too many enemies, he took charge of six World Cups and five Olympic Games for ITV. He was writing an excellent column for the Daily Telegraph right up to the time of his death from liver cancer at the age of 68 in 2002.

Ironically Grade, later to be knighted and then elected to the House of Lords, went into the same profession and, of course, became one of the great movers and shakers of British television. Coming from a theatrical family, Michael went into the business when his father died in 1966 and proceeded to enjoy an astonishing career that saw him take over Channel 4 in the late eighties and then become Chairman of the BBC from 2004 to 2006 before switching to be Executive Chairman of ITV from 2007 to 2009.

All that was unimaginable as the three of us repaired to the ancient Putney Boat Club in search of a warming noggin on some sleet-washed day in March before hunger forced us to eat the excruciating lunch provided by a chef who never dared showed his face. Or maybe it was a she. In the gloom of that dreary establishment with its brown walls and brown drapes, it would probably have been impossible to tell. But, boy, did we have some laughs.

Rugby consumed my winters but before we talk of the oval ball, let me offer a portrait of the best paper I have ever worked for. Under Charles Wintour, the Evening Standard was in its pomp in the 1960s. The Evening News sold more – about a million copies a day – and The Star came a poor third amongst the trio of publications which were sold all day, six days a week throughout the capital by vendors shouting, "Star, News, Standard – PAPER!"

It was the best because some of Fleet Street's finest writers were being guided by a man who remains the best editor I have ever worked for – a fact I was happy to relay to his daughter, Anna Wintour, when I met her at Roland Garros (she's a besotted Roger Federer fan) a few years ago.

Charles Wintour looked, and often acted, like a Cambridge don. Tightly combed grey hair, rimless spectacles and a straight-backed gait, he would move through the chaos and clatter of his editorial floor in a bubble of intellect and quiet contemplation. He was overseeing no less than nine editions a day, beginning with the racing special which came out at 8.00 am, but it was not until 'The West End Final' was being prepared in mid-afternoon that he left his office for any length of time to join his editors on the back bench. From there, he could survey the entire operation as subs marked copy and reporters bashed away on large and very unportable type-writers.

To his left, he could observe Ronnie Hyde, one of the Street's legendary News Editors, whose Savile Row suites and laundered striped shirts were as impeccable as his language was foul. Woe betide any poor reporter who phoned in without the story. In front of him, at the far end of the vast room, Wintour could see Peter Goodall with his Hitler moustache, occasionally giving in to his dictator's instincts and driving his sub-editors on the sports desk mad with unreasonable demands. Luckily he had one of the best subs in the business in Don Simpson, a small, bald figure whose serene temperament and skill at re-arranging errant words made him supremely suited to the madness that raged around him. And those words were not just arranged on paper. Downstairs, amidst the heat and odour of great clanking machines and printing press ink, sub-editors like Simpson really earned their corn, cutting and adding back-to-front words laid out in metal to ensure that they fitted the page. It is now a lost art but an art it was. Don always treated my copy with respect and it was a pleasure to work with him.

On Wintour's right one could find The Standard Diary, made up of bright young things who beavered away finding interesting quotes and bits of gossip about figures in London society. There was a young lady straight down from Cambridge on the Diary when I joined the paper called Glenys Roberts, and you will be hearing more of her later.

Wintour had an eye for talent far beyond his newspaper. The austerity of his countenance masked an intuitive if somewhat unlikely understanding of what made a story in the popular context, a fact that was brought into sharp relief when he called his young music writer into his office one morning. As Maureen Cleave peered out at him from under her perfectly cut fringe of brown hair, she was probably wondering what she had done wrong. However it was not a reprimand but a suggestion. "That group at the Palladium last night," Wintour said in his upper-class drawl. "Seemed to cause a bit of stir. Come from Liverpool, don't they? Go up there and see what they have to say."

And so it was that Maureen became the only reporter The Beatles would talk to for several years because she had been the first, because they liked her, and because Charles Wintour's quivering antennae had picked up the vibe before anyone else. That's what makes a good editor.

Something else that makes a good editor is letting your staff know that they are appreciated. Wintour, for the most part, seemed very unapproachable. The thought that he might be following your work and or even know who you were was remote indeed. Except, that is, for something that happened four or maybe five times a year. You would sit down at your desk in the morning, open the draw and find a half sheet of white paper. I can quote the notes from heart.

'I enjoyed your piece on the Harlequins match on Saturday. I think your writing is improving.'

Or, 'Congratulations on your prediction that Cambridge would win the Varsity match. It gave me great kudos in my family circle.'

Underneath was a great scrawled 'C'.

That's all you needed. That was enough. No fake back slapping and matey jokes in the pub that a reporter might get from some of the other editors around town. Just a couple of sentences from the remote figure who was quite liable to walk past you in the street without a flicker of recognition. Except he recognised you all right. He read your copy. That's what counted.

I presume we all got those notes, even established Fleet Street stars like that great feature writer Anne Sharpley; or Tom Pocock with his unrivalled knowledge of all things military, especially those with a naval twist, and young Jeremy Campbell who tested Wintour's judgement by creating a fictitious debutante, on whom he could pin amusing quotes, for the society diary he wrote. Many editors would have fired Jeremy. Instead, Charles sent him to Washington. And there, for the next 30-odd years, Campbell became recognised as one of the shrewdest observers of American politics. He also wrote several highly intellectual books such as *A Liar's Tale – A History of Falsehood*. Which might or might not have been inspired by his fictitious debutante. But he was another Wintour success story. From The Beatles to Jeremy Campbell, Charles could pick 'em.

But, as far as the foreign staff was concerned, there was no one to rival the legendary Sam White in Paris. Someone needs to write a book or make a film about Sam and I will try to paint some sort of portrait of this doyen of Beaverbrook foreign correspondents in a later chapter.

We had great sports writers, too, like Bernard Joy who will remain one of my heroes for some very good reasons. Apart from being a charming gentleman, Bernard had been one of the few 'gentlemen' (to use the old-fashioned term to denote an amateur sportsman) to play regularly for Arsenal. He was a commanding centre half for the Gunners just before World War Two and will go down in history as the last amateur to play for the full England team when he turned out against Belgium in 1936. But, on a more personal note, he cemented my role as the Standard's tennis correspondent by admitting that the increasing demands of summer football tours meant that he saw less and less tennis which was supposed to be his second beat. So, after I had been deputising for him at various tournaments for a couple of years, he suggested to Goodall that I take on the role full time. Thanks, Bernard.

Walter Bartleman, a cheery, burly, rosy-cheeked Cockney who was loved by all, wrote a lot of boxing for the paper but no one could compare with George Whiting, another one born within the sound of Bow Bells (which makes you a cockney) with the accent to go with it. However George wrote mellifluous English once he got behind his typewriter. Take this example when he was sent to interview Floyd Patterson in Chicago in September 1962:

'Petunias in the breeze and marigolds dancing round the mission hall may not normally be associated with the art of scientific savagery yet it is in just such an atmosphere of rural piety that Floyd Patterson, heavyweight champion of the world, is preparing to dispatch, dismantle and dismember Sonny Liston here next Tuesday.'

How's that for an intro? The thing about George's copy was that the next paragraph was usually as good as its predecessor and he was one of the leading examples of why reading the Evening Standard made the rush hour journey to Ealing, Chingford or Putney fly by on the tube home.

And then there was the story of how Wintour relented when faced with an unusual request from one of his best young reporters and, in so doing, helped change the way golf was written. Mark Wilson worked as a reporter under Ronnie Hyde, but such were his dynamism and writing skills that he soon found himself being sent off on foreign stories, not least to Cyprus where he distinguished himself with his reporting on Archbishop Makarios and the independence struggles there.

But Mark's passion was golf. And, after sitting himself down one day and thinking about it, he decided that he really wanted to spend his life on a golf course. So why not write about it? The Standard, of course, did have a golf correspondent but it was not working out for the young man and as soon as word got out that he might be leaving, Wilson asked to see Wintour. "I want to write golf for you," he said.

Hyde, having got whiff of what Wilson was after, was thunderstruck while Wintour was merely querulous. "Are you sure you want to be a golf writer?" he asked. "You have a great career ahead of you as a foreign correspondent if you want it."

Mark didn't. He wanted to write golf and, making another good decision, Wintour let him. I was not privy to how golf was being written in America at the time but, I can assure you, Mark changed the lingua franca of the sport in Britain. From a stroll down the course, he turned it into a race to the pin. Players were suddenly 'charging' down the fairway and drives 'clattered' onto the green. He made it exciting. He made a slow, deliberate sport come alive. He loved golf and it showed.

So the Standard, as we used to say in the trade, was a bloody good read and I was proud to be part of it. I was also surprised by how readily I was accepted as part of the rugby community. At 21, I was young to be doing any sort of job but being rugby correspondent of such an influential paper carried a certain responsibility and I quickly realised that anything I put under my by-line was scrutinised, digested and, on occasion, criticised.

Unlike tennis, I had been covering the sport on and off for four years so I had a bit more confidence about voicing my opinion, which I did every week in my column Ruggerfront. Reading some old cuttings today, I find that I was not always as forward thinking as I would like to believe. I did, for instance, support those who were against the introduction of substitutes! If someone broke a leg in the 1960s – tough. You played with fourteen men. I felt that it would be too easy to fake injuries and just replace an off-form player. Not in the spirit of the game, old boy! How things change.

I did, however, rail against absurd implementation of the strict amateur codes. While not envisaging the day when rugby would become professional (totally unthinkable at the time) I went to task on rules that said players could not wear track suits at Twickenham while warming up or standing in an icy wind for national anthems to be played. And I said this about another ridiculous rule: 'Last Thursday, England's captain Dickie Jeeps and his half back partner Richard Sharp were wary of being photographed together because they thought they might be breaking the rule which says it is against the spirit of amateur rugby for players to train together more than 48 hours before an international.'

I know, I know, you have to read it twice to believe it, don't you. But in those days the guardians of the game lost sight of reason and it cost everyone money to play for their country. I remember the great Irish front row forward Ken Kennedy telling me how his claim for a cup of tea at the hotel on match day was queried and often rejected. They were a miserly bunch, those Rugby Union officials. And mean, too. Any former union player who 'went north' and joined a professional Rugby League Club (the thirteen-a-side game) was immediately ostracised and couldn't even buy tickets to watch his old team. It was really incredible.

Having said that, there were a lot of great people in the game, too, and I made good friends with the likes of David Brooks at the Harlequins; Budge Rogers, the Bedford and England wing forward; and Mike Weston, England's tall and talented centre. I got to know England's fly half Richard Sharp quite well, too, and marvelled at his ability to drift away from the flailing arms of the open side wing forward as he stretched his long legs and went in under the posts. But I had no bigger pal than Johnny Williams, a mercurial scrum-half who remained loyal to the Old Millhillians a little too long for his own good before moving north and playing for Sale. I did my best to point out the error of their ways to the selectors when they refused to pick him for England and he ended up with a paltry number of caps. But, as usual, they went for the safety of someone like the admirable Dickie Jeeps, who would never lose you a match, instead of Williams who could win you one with his lightning quick breaks from the base of the scrum and his long, bullet-like passes. Johnny possessed the handsome good looks and seemingly shy personality that girls find irresistible. I hope he found the right one in the end but I lost touch after he moved to Sale and I went abroad.

Not wanting to be caught out like I had been in Bucharest, I decided to join Richmond and do some proper training on Wednesday evenings under the yellow lights at the Athletic Ground. After a while I found I could keep up with most people and I was chuffed when Iain Laughland, the brilliant London Scottish and Scotland centre three quarter, called out, "Hey, laddie, you're getting as fit as the rest of us."

London Scottish shared the Athletic Ground with Richmond and they had a star-studded team at the time, full of internationals such as Laughland, Franz ten Bos, Norman Bruce, Jim Shackleton and that slightly eccentric scrum-half Tremayne Rodd. Tremayne was far too intelligent and independent to see eye-to-eye with the Scottish Rugby Union and never got as many caps as his talent deserved. He was kind enough to ask me to play for his XV that travelled down to the West Country to play his old school, Downside, and this time I fared a little better than I had at football. But it was still daunting to have to tackle some of these top rank players. Later in life, Tremayne became involved in tennis and sponsored a couple of junior players. The last time I saw him before he died was at Wimbledon. He was a lovely fellow and carried no airs and graces despite assuming the imposing title of Lord Rennel of Rodd, bequeathed by his father.

Richmond had its personalities, too. Nim Hall, who needed a ciggie at half time when playing full back for either Richmond or England; Brian Stoneman, our massive prop-forward who could put away eighteen pints of bitter in the bar between 5.30 and 10.30 and still walk; Ted Wates, a member of the huge family construction firm who took over the captaincy from Bill Munks, whose dedication to the club made him something of a legend at the Athletic Ground. Rather than seek an interview, Bill was the sort of avuncular figure I could go to for advice and he taught me a lot about the game and London rugby.

And then there was the slightly mysterious figure of Tony Holmes whose life and persona would have tested Sherlock. A lightning quick fly half who moved to full back before leaving to play for the Harlequins, Tony used his maternal name because his father was a well-known actor called Henry Ainley who had died right after the war. For reasons he never fully explained, I think he wanted to keep his rugby life separate – but only for so long. When he entered his father's profession, he called himself Anthony Ainley and went to make a name for himself as The Master in the *Doctor Who* television series as well as appearing in films like *Oh, What a Lovely War*.

When he died in 2004, I was amazed to see the total absence of any reference to his rugby prowess in any of the obituaries. It was as if Tony Holmes and Anthony Ainley were not the same person. Such was his private nature, I am not sure Tony would thank me for it but I wrote to IMDb and had them insert a paragraph detailing his rugby career in his biography. It was, after all, not insubstantial. He not only played with much flair for two of the country's leading clubs but also turned out for Middlesex for many years.

He was an unforgettable character with handsome, swarthy features and deep set eyes. His manner was theatrical and I was never sure what the other players thought of him. But he was charming and amusing and enjoyed acting out his dreams. One evening, after an International at Twickenham (this was before he had played there for Harlequins) he came up to say hello as I was finishing off a report in the press box and whispered, "Watch this," and disappeared.

Within a few minutes, a figure in a business suit emerged from the tunnel clutching a rugby ball. The pitch, surrounded by the towering empty stands, was almost in darkness but I could follow him as he raced away, zig-zagging and side-stepping imaginary opponents before triumphantly planting the ball between the posts.

"I've always wanted to do that," he said when we met for a beer later. Sadly, I lost touch with him when I went to the States but our last time together was memorable. "Richard," he said fixing me with those dark, brooding eyes. "Would you like to join me for dinner at the Garrick and maybe we could play a little snooker afterwards."

And that we did. The Master. He was indeed a master, at rugby, at cricket which he played later in life; at acting and at disguise. Few people have been so prominent at two very public pastimes, with so few people realising that Holmes was Ainley or Ainley was Holmes.

The highlights of my years as a rugby writer were covering the Springbok tour of the British Isles which Avril Malan captained in 1961 and the 1963-64 All Blacks tour under the inspiring leadership of Wilson Whineray. Encouraged by a certain young lady who typed a lot of it, bless her, I took the plunge and decided to write a book called *Whineray's All Blacks*. I don't think it was too bad for a first effort and it sold reasonably well despite some stiff opposition from the engaging and whimsical Andy Mulligan, the Irish international scrum-half who went to become a foreign correspondent for BBC television.

It was a wonderful tour to cover and the Kiwis were certainly a more amusing bunch to be a round than the South Africans, virtually all of whom save for Keith Oxlee and John Gainsford were dour Boers. The All Blacks squad included those two mercurial Maoris, Waka Nathan and Mac Herewini, and Whineray himself was an imposing but always very approachable figure who finished off the tour in style with that famous try of his against the Barbarians at Cardiff Arms Park.

A small spin off from that tour was the 45rpm record Keith Turner and I produced. We had the idea of going to the BBC and asking them if we could take snippets of commentary from their radio coverage of the tour and package it as a record. When they said yes, we had the cheek to ask for a recording studio and a sound engineer and they said yes to that, too. You will never believe what they charged us. Twenty-five pounds for everything – the sound tracks, the studio, the lot. They were very naïve and I suspect their whole philosophy changed once it dawned on them just what they had given away.

So I wrote a blurb for the sleeve and recorded linking passages to go in between bursts of commentary from the likes of Rex Alston and Wynford Vaughan-Thomas, Robert Hudson and New Zealand's Bob Irvine. It sold quite well in New Zealand, I think, but now we only have one precious copy left!

Even during those seasons without a team visiting from overseas, the home Internationals were always the most fun to cover and I began to get used to taking the Royal Scot sleeper up to Edinburgh, check into the North British Hotel which was built right over the station and then walk to Murrayfield. Presumably one can do the same today.

Trips to Dublin were amongst my favourite and it was a delight to stay at the Shelburne or the Gresham near O'Connell Street where Irish hospitality was at its finest. Never an early riser, my constant fear in hotels has always been being told I was too late for breakfast but there was no problem with that at the Gresham. Rushing down at 9.50 one morning, I asked if breakfast was still being served. Drawing himself up to his full height, the elegantly attired maître d' announced in his lyrical Irish accent, "Breakfast, Sirrr, is when you want it." I could have kissed him.

But this being Ireland, not everything went to plan. The press box at Lansdowne Road was constructed like no other. The seats allocated to the three London evening newspapers represented by Ross McWhirter (of Guinness Book of Records fame) for the Star, Steve Roberts for the Evening

News and me for the Evening Standard had holes in them. In other words, they were lavatory seats. But with a different purpose. Although some people might suggest our copy deserved to be stuffed down the toilet, the idea was that we shoved our, er, running copy between our legs and it would then be caught by a scruffy little Irish lad who would rush to the phone and dictate it to London. With all of us wanting our scribbles sent off every twenty minutes, he was under a bit of pressure but seemed very willing.

With Ireland's match against England finishing before 4.30 we were able to make a dash for the airport and catch the last flight to London. In those days, the final edition of Saturday's evening papers all over the country were called the Classifieds, detailing all the scores and reports from the afternoon's football and rugby games. So our papers were on sale at Heathrow when we arrived and we all eagerly grabbed them to see what kind of a 'show' our reports have been given. They were all prominently displayed, 600 or 700 words of hastily written but readable prose. But there was a problem. On reading our copy we discovered we didn't recognise it. To do that we had to swap papers because our poor lad in Dublin had sent Ross's copy to the Evening News, mine to the Star, and Steve's to the Standard! "Oh, shit," was probably an apt reaction.

I was fortunate that, during my second season on the rugby beat, E.W. Swanton of the Daily Telegraph did not have a cricket tour to cover. Rugby was his second sport and this eminent figure in British sporting journalism decided to take me under his wing. Now, there are those who will tell you that Swanton was impossibly grand and arrogant and had been known to treat subordinates like serfs. 'Jim', as he was known, could certainly cut a swathe through a press room, with his large frame crowned with a heavy thatch of greying black hair and all dressed up in attire that would not have looked out of place on Oscar Wilde. It had been his habit to take on young aspiring journalists and mentor them for the job and he was certainly successful with John Woodcock who went on to become a celebrated cricket correspondent of the Times.

Swanton had survived a ghastly war as a prisoner of the Japanese and contracted polio but, on his return, he soon joined the Daily Telegraph and, building on a career that had started on the Evening Standard back in the thirties, became a formidable figure in cricket journalism. Apart from his writing, he turned into an expert analyst and commentator on BBC radio and his clipped vowels offered a striking contrast to the Hampshire burr of his colleague John Arlott. For Swanton, Denis was always 'Cumpton', an affectation that reflected his pre-war upbringing.

As I intimated, Swanton was not everyone's cup of tea but I always take people as I find them and he could not have been kinder to me. On the train down to Cardiff for the match against Wales, he reserved a table in the restaurant car and invited me to join him. When we went to Paris to watch England play France at Stade Colombes, he found this local bistro, probably recommended by Sam White who joined us for lunch before the match, and again, insisted I join the party. I listened and learned and, of course, became a huge fan of everything he wrote, not for the style but for the content. He championed West Indies cricket and, to the horror of some of his Telegraph readers, sided with those who wanted to boycott South Africa over apartheid. Instinctively, he was a good man. Old age did nothing to affect his mind and he wrote his last weekly column for the Daily Telegraph a matter of days before he died at the age of 92.

Mathew Engel, one of his successors as editor of the Cricketer Magazine, wrote this in his Guardian obituary: 'His genius was that, whether he liked change or not (and usually he didn't) he adapted to it, understood it and was able to comment pertinently on it. He kept this up for 70 years. It was a breathtaking performance and he will be remembered with awe.'

Talking of larger than life figures, Richard Harris appeared one Wednesday evening at the Athletic Ground for our training session. Harris was needing to get fit for the forthcoming film that would establish him at the forefront of the new wave of British (or, in his case, Irish) actors like Albert Finney and Tom Courtney who would bring a new, tough realism to British films. *This Sporting Life*, a story of a professional Rugby League player in the north of England, would go down as a classic and Harris and his co-star Rachel Roberts had much to do with that.

Being the extrovert he was, it was easy to get to know Richard, especially as he never let a yearning for fitness get in the way of a couple of pints at the bar. He became a friend, someone I would bump into on numerous occasions in Los Angeles or London over the years and I was very fond of him. Behind the bluster and wild behaviour, there was a sensitivity and even shyness that was very appealing. When he finally returned to the London stage for Pirandello's *Henry IV* in the early nineties, for which he won the Evening Standard Best Actor Award for his stunning performance, I went back stage at the Wyndham for a long chat afterwards. He was mellow and introspective and may have had more than an inkling that his life style would ensure he did not have long to live. That, however, did not prevent him from returning to the screen for memorable character parts in *The Unforgiven*, *Gladiator* and the first two *Harry Potter* films.

I saw him once more by chance. He was standing outside a pub near Drury Lane, having a beer with Gary Muller, the South African tennis player who had formed a relationship with the lovely Ann Turkel, Richard's second wife. Richard was not a petty man. There was no room for animosity and, for a while, the three had been good buddies, with Richard coming to cheer Gary at Wimbledon with Ann.

Harris was living at the Savoy by then. With the great wealth he had accumulated from his movies as well royalties from 'MacArthur Park' and *Camelot*, Richard could afford a suite at the Savoy on a permanent basis. "Nothing like room service," he used to say.

When the end was near, and he was carried through the lobby on a stretcher to be taken to hospital, Richard lifted his head off the pillow and hissed at a couple of tourists checking in, "It's the food!"

The Savoy probably forgave him. Richard Harris was an incorrigible, funny, talented man with plenty of faults and a huge heart. He's one of the people I miss most.

Glenys and I went to see Richard in *The Diary of a Madman*, Nikolai Gogol's one-man play at the Royal Court in 1963 and if we weren't quite married then, we soon would be. Glenys Roberts was the girl on Londoner's Diary who had caught my eye soon after I joined the Standard. We didn't meet for a while but eventually began seeing each other in the pub or at some office do and I plucked up courage to ask her out. I don't know what attracted me to her most – her reddish blonde hair, freckled face and lovely figure or her quick, biting wit and obvious intelligence. She had got the job on the Standard very soon after coming down from Cambridge, where she had been involved in the Footlights.

There, Glenys was surrounded by as much talent as one university has any right to enjoy at one time. Peter Cook, Jonathan Miller, Michael Frayne, Andrew Sinclair, Bamber Gascoigne and David Frost were eventually augmented by Dudley Moore and Alan Bennett who came over from Oxford to collaborate with Cook and Miller on *Beyond the Fringe*, a satirical review that lifted them all to stardom.

You will have to ask Glenys why she thought marrying me was a good idea, but we became swept up in our romance and enjoyed happy evenings at her little flat in Old Compton Street in Soho which led us to believe marriage was a good idea. We were too young, of course, both 24 and both Aquarians, born within a week of each other. It all seemed to fit and we were married at All Souls, the church which stands right outside the entrance to Broadcasting House just off Oxford Circus. Keith was my best man and the service was conducted by the Rev Roy McKay who, not coincidentally, had been my Chaplain at Canford. A powerful orator in the pulpit, this beak-nosed, stern-looking man had gone on to become Head of Religious Broadcasting at the BBC and, remembering that I had been one of his bell-ringers, kindly agreed to marry us. It was all very convenient because my sister Margot and her new husband, Frank Melville, then with Newsweek but later Time's political correspondent in London, were living in a flat at 50 Harley Street, less than five minutes' walk away. It was there that I spent my last night as a bachelor.

The reception was at the recently opened Carlton Tower in Knightsbridge and we spent our first night as man and wife at the venerable Mayfair Hotel. It was a September wedding and the weather was still beautiful in Greece and Turkey, where we enjoyed a lovely honeymoon looking at ruins and bartering in the bazaars of Istanbul. We stayed at the new Istanbul Hilton and I can still remember the fresh-pressed orange juice that was served with breakfast on our balcony with the Bosphorus in the distance. Sounds silly now, but those sorts of minor luxuries were not part of one's life in England in the early sixties. World War Two's cloak of austerity and minimalist living was only just starting to drop away and we were still young enough to be wide-eyed at little pleasures.

Marriage to Glenys opened my mind to a new sort of intellectual life. I have never been quite sure at what stage of one's education a person can describe themselves as an 'intellectual'. Is there a sort of scoreboard, enabling you to achieve a certain number of points in the thinking department so as to qualify? Is being an intellectual just thinking harder and deeper than the rest of us? Can you be a bit clueless about daily life and still be an intellectual? I would think the answer to that is 'yes'.

I have never remotely thought of myself as an intellectual even though my thinking did reach further than the outfield of a cricket ground. As an avid reader of newspapers, I followed world events in great detail and some of the leading foreign correspondents of the time like Sefton Delmer and

Christopher Dobson of the Daily Express, Sam White in Paris, and my journalistic hero James Cameron who wrote so brilliantly and provocatively for the Express and the News Chronicle, instilled a yearning to be part of this illuminating profession.

But my opinions were still naïve. Starting work at seventeen, I had missed the stimulation of university life where arguing and exploring ideas with one's peers has always seemed to me to be as useful as anything learned in the lecture hall. Glenys came to my rescue in that respect. Cambridge had provided her with a range of friends who were at the sharp end of intellectual life in the sixties and suddenly I found myself grappling to follow the barbed, witty and provocative conversations that flew across our sitting room as people like Bamber Gascoigne and Andrew Sinclair dropped by for a drink.

Although we didn't see that much of him, Andrew was welcome any time because it was his flat we were living in at No. 17 Soho Square. Sadly – or perhaps not, considering the uneven nature of the floors – it is one of the buildings that have been torn down and rebuilt in that little square that has long been home to publishers, movie companies and even the Football Association. Sinclair had just published a successful book called *The Breaking of Bumbo* and was expected to go on to great things. He certainly had a successful academic career but never managed the dizzy heights of Peter Cook, a true genius who, with Nicholas Luard of Private Eye, had opened The Establishment, a satirical hotspot, just across the square in Greek Street a couple of years before.

Winston Churchill was one of the targets for these irreverent satirists but I could never get my head around any mockery of a man who, I firmly believed, had saved the civilised world from Nazi domination. I still do. With a weaker, less defiant Prime Minister in 1940, no one can be sure just how Britain would have reacted to the yapping of Hitler's hounds, salivating across the Channel, almost within sight of the White Cliffs of Dover. But with the heroics of the hopelessly young and ill-trained Spitfire pilots lifting the spirits of a beleaguered nation by winning the Battle of Britain, the gravel voice of the nation's new leader blared out from our radios and echoed across the airwaves to Berlin. "We will fight on the landing fields, we shall fight on the beaches, we shall fight in the hills – we shall NEVER surrender." Hitler hesitated and never came.

As Churchill had admitted on assuming office when the well-meaning but ineffectual Neville Chamberlain resigned, "I felt as if I had been walking with destiny, and that all my past life had been but a preparation for this hour and this trial ..." He was a war leader, possibly the greatest war leader of all time, and he saved us.

He died on the morning of Sunday, 25th January 1965 at the age of 90. For the first time since Gladstone in 1898, a non-royal personage was afforded the honour of having their coffin lie in state in Westminster Cathedral. Glenys was one of the Standard reporters assigned to cover the funeral and I accompanied her as we mingled with the crowds in Whitehall. They were there in their thousands, liberally sprinkled with survivors of the Blitz, grief and pride etched across their faces, paying a final tribute to the man who had got them through those nights when the bombs came hurtling out of the sky – night after night after night. He had been amongst them at the height of the fear and disaster, stomping through the rubble in Whitechapel and Wapping while the fires still burned, cigar firmly between his lips beneath the Homburg hat, the very epitome of the defiance of which he spoke. No wonder Hitler looked elsewhere.

Our intellectual friends, less given to any form of hero worship, pointed to Churchill's faults which were plentiful but one could not argue that, when it came to the moment of greatest crisis, he was right and had been right all along. Throughout the thirties, his was often the lone voice in Parliament warning of the dangers of Hitler's re-armament in Germany but he was dismissed as a war monger. Incredibly, the nation dismissed him, too, when the Conservative party was voted out office in the first General Election after the war. After all he had done! But soldiers returning after years away were frightened about their futures and wanted the extra security that Clement Attlee's socialist policies would provide.

The Great Man was cut to the quick but he never murmured against the process. Of all the things I admire about Churchill – this bombastic, arrogant figure who had all the makings of a dictator – it was his subservience to the democratic ideal that struck me most. A few years earlier, while addressing a joint session of Congress in Washington just after Pearl Harbor, he laid out the principle on which he based his career and from which he never wavered: "I owe my advancement entirely to the House of Commons, whose servant I am."

He refused to accept a peerage because that would have sent him to the House of Lords. The House of Commons was his home. He wanted no adornment to his name and only accepted a Knighthood when it seemed churlish not to. But the name on his twelve-foot statue which towers, with appropriate pugnacity, over Parliament Square bears just one name. 'Churchill'. If you pass by, doff your cap. The twentieth century knew no greater man.

It was an emotional moment yet different, of course from the night eighteen months earlier when Glenys and I heard the cries of newspaper sellers as we crossed Shaftesbury Avenue on our way home from the cinema. It was always possible to buy the next day's papers in the West End after midnight but normally the vendors didn't shout about it and, anyway, it was only 10.30.

I remember turning to Glenys and saying, "What's happened? The Daily Express doesn't normally have an edition out this early."

President Kennedy had been shot in Dallas, that's what had happened. Like most people, we were shocked to the core. No leader had caught the imagination of the world like this young, vibrant, charming man who had ushered in the age of Camelot, an unattainable fantasy, to be sure, but one which had allowed a new generation to dream dreams that their parents never could. I recalled Jack Kennedy's inauguration which I had watched on a black and white television in the lobby of the Angel Hotel in Cardiff before a Welsh rugby International.

It was his youth that struck me most. For me, Presidents and Prime Ministers had always been old men, some obviously none the worse for that, of course, yet here was a man who could be viewed as an older brother, asking not what your country could do for you but what you could do for your country. From afar, I loved the look of the man and I loved his rhetoric, polished as it was by Ted Sorenson. But now he was gone and the violence which lurks behind too many shadows in American society had reared its head and the world was aghast.

Even though Glenys and I had been talking about America, I could never have imagined that there would be more political assassinations to follow and that I would be called upon to report on them for a British audience. In 1963, in the first few months of our marriage, such thoughts were far from our minds but a year later, we started asking each other some hard questions. On the face of it, we had everything two 25-year-olds could want. Apparently secure jobs on a great newspaper under a great editor. Surely we would be crazy to give that up? But Aquarians are hopelessly independent people, always tugging at no matter what kind of rope might be restricting their freedom. I think I might have been the one who broached the subject first when it dawned on me that I was probably set for life. Hylton Cleaver, whose job I had taken, had been 70. Was I to be rugby and tennis correspondent of the Evening Standard for another 45 years? Was that the limit of my ambition? Inevitably, the answer was no. Both of us had already made one brief trip the United States and we were intrigued by the place. We had a yearning to understand what made it tick; we wanted to find out how much was a Hollywood façade and how much was real.

I suppose it was a person who remains unknown to me to this day who helped me take the plunge. Back in 1961, when I was covering Wimbledon for only the second time, I got a message to contact the CBS News bureau in London. Charles Collingwood, a World War Two colleague of the great Ed Murrow, and a very young Dan Rather were the correspondents assigned to London around that time. But I only got to speak to a secretary who told me that a programme called 'Worldwide Sports' which went out nationwide at 7.15 EST every evening was wanting daily reports from Wimbledon. Could I help? "Of course," I said, even though I had never sat in front of a microphone in my life.

They wanted a minute's worth and they wanted it live. That meant a post-midnight trip to Broadcasting House in Portland Square to use a studio CBS rented from the BBC. On the first night, I was almost trembling with nerves but I think I managed to keep the quivers out of my voice and reel off the day's happenings, always remembering to name the home towns of the American players – Carole Caldwell (later Graebner) from Santa Monica, California; Kathy Harter from Seal Beach, California; they trip off the tongue even today.

But after a while I settled down and the producer in New York, a lovely man who would become a good friend called John Chanin, seemed to accept that my British accent gave a report from Wimbledon an air of authenticity. So the reports became routine but finding the right studio in that rabbit warren of a building was an on-going nightmare. I usually arrived with about five minutes to spare and the night time Commissionaire would check his roster and say '3 B' or '2 A' or '4 C'. You would have thought they would have been easy to find but it would have been simpler to get out of Hampton Court maze. '3 A' wasn't necessarily on the third floor and I will always remember charging up and down endless, winding corridors looking for studios that should have been properly signposted and weren't. There was no sweeter sound, once I had jammed the headphones on, than the crackle of the ether and the American voice asking, "You there, London?"

It became a regular gig each year, a nice little money earner and a useful introduction to the world of American radio. So as our madcap scheme formed in our minds, I clung to this one solid and viable source of income that might materialise if we decided to reach out across the Atlantic on the most wobbly branch imaginable. John Chanin said he would talk to the boss and word came back that, yes, CBS Radio would be able to use me on a reasonably regular basis if I pitched up in New York.

Glenys, of course, had plenty of contacts in Fleet Street and was sure she could sell some freelance articles but a lot of people thought we were out of our minds, not least Charles Wintour who was not at all happy at the thought of losing a young lady he was obviously grooming for big things on his paper. Me? Well, he could always find a rugby writer. But he took it very well and even had a little farewell gathering for us in a Fleet Street pub. He was a strange man, Charles, so capable of genuine warmth behind that frosty exterior.

And so the die was cast and the decision made. Two really good jobs were cast aside and off we went to Southampton one fine day in May 1965 to board the SS *France* and set sail for New York. We barely had a bean between us.

Chapter 7
AMERICA

Taking the boat instead of those new-fangled jet planes was still a normal way to travel to the United States in the mid-sixties, even though it had been on a Pan Am 707 that I had made my very first visit to America a couple of years before. My brother Tony was working for Pan Am by then and had got me a ticket called Sublo 3 which was airline speak for 'We'll take you if there's room'.

All airline employers fly off duty on something similar today and Tony, being the wanderer he was, considered it one of the best reasons for working for an airline. Strangely, for a man who had flown RAF fighters right at the end of the war, he never wanted to become a commercial pilot. He always told me he loved the feeling of being up there alone, untethered to mother earth, feeling as free as a bird. But I think the idea of having the lives of scores of people in his hands was something he didn't want to contemplate. So he spent his life in the sales department first of Pan Am and, later just because they offered him a job in San Francisco which was where he had always wanted to live, with United.

Rugby School, Oxford University, the RAF – Tony had the credentials to run United Airlines but he never got anywhere near senior management. He was never diplomatic in expressing his opinions and never mastered the skill of greasing his way to the top. It was a waste of a great education even though I think, with his small stature and lack of prowess at games, Rugby did little for his self-confidence.

Nevertheless, he certainly let me ride on his coat tails on several occasions and it was by grabbing the last available seat with my Sublo 3 ticket that I climbed aboard the first of innumerable Pan Am jets that I would take in the coming years and flew straight to San Francisco. Although not living there yet, Tony knew the city well and it was not hard to see why he loved it so much. It was a good if brief introduction to America, but now, in April 1965, Glenys and I were going to take a long, hard look at this amazing country.

Luckily, the Atlantic was behaving itself for our voyage and I was able to put sea sickness out of my mind and thoroughly enjoy the meals served up by the French chefs. SS *France* was the longest liner in the world at the time and remained a magnificent ship until it was sold to Norway and eventually scrapped in 2008. Glenys and I did little but eat and loll around for five days before the Statue of Liberty hove into view.

I think New York comes as a shock to any first-time visitor and I am sure the rough edges can be smoothed for anyone enjoying the luxury of a stay at the Plaza, Pierre or St Regis. But we weren't. We had chosen a cheaper establishment on East 44th Street right off Broadway – interesting, stimulating even, but far from luxurious. The biggest shock was the television in our room which flickered on and off and, even when working, offered a far inferior picture to what we were used to at home.

There was a sound technical reason for this. Being first with mass produced television sets, American had gone with the 525-line system. Europe, arriving later to the game, had benefited with more lines, especially in France where 819 lines took it close to what was to become High Definition, making the picture much sharper. But the disappointment went further than that. The cinemas – the Broadway cinemas no less – were dirty, strewn with popcorn and obviously employed projectionists who didn't know how to show a movie without the audience being aware of every reel change. Every so often, the movie jumped and even changed tone. I was shocked. Wasn't this supposed the Broadway, the epicentre of entertainment? In my eyes, it wasn't a patch on Leicester Square.

And then there was *The Ed Sullivan Show*, the legendary CBS production on which every performer dreamed of appearing. Any time an English singer made it onto *The Ed Sullivan Show*, it was headlined as a badge of honour back home in the UK, far greater than appearing on *Sunday Night at The Palladium*. Yet the latter was a slick, fast moving production compered by the wise-cracking, singing and dancing Bruce Forsyth or Des O'Connor – real talents who could carry any variety show by themselves. Yet when we eagerly switched on one evening to watch Ed Sullivan we were confronted by this barely articulate newspaper columnist who had to peer at the prompter before mangling the name of the next act. I was in shock.

First impressions! I must admit, as far as New York was concerned, they weren't great. I found the place noisy, dirty and rude. New York humour, which is real and funny, is an acquired taste and it wasn't mine. So many people seemed to be on the make; trying to get somewhere too fast and not caring how they did it. I soon learned that, if you wanted anything done, you had to raise your voice, if not actually shout, to make yourself heard. It was exhausting and it changed me. I had no option. Less of the 'please' and 'thank you' and more of the 'get it done, buddy!' It was the only way to survive. Fight your corner or get shoved into the gutter. I grew up fast and it didn't make me a nicer person.

It was, of course, not all bad. New York is a magnificent, thrilling city in so many ways and we were determined to make the most of the opportunities it offered. After a couple of weeks in our dingy hotel, we found a one bedroom walk-up on East 76th Street right off Lexington. It faced the side entrance to the Carlyle Hotel, "Where President Kennedy used to stay," said the real estate lady pointedly.

"That's another 30 bucks on the rent," I murmured to Glenys. I was getting cynical already. But the location was ideal and we had a roof over our heads. Now to work. I had my CBS connection but Glenys probably had more introductions to the British press corps in town and, in those days, they were numerous. Every Fleet Street paper had at least two permanent correspondents in New York and another in Washington. Again by-lines came to life as we met Jeffrey Blyth, the Bureau Chief of the Daily Mail; Ian Ball at the Telegraph; John Gold of the Evening News and the Standard's celebrated representative Lady Jean Campbell, whose appointment to the job was not wholly unrelated to the fact that she was Lord Beaverbrook's granddaughter.

When we met her, she was just a couple of years out of a brief and highly combustible marriage to Norman Mailer who, so legend has it, once hung her out of an apartment window two flights up by her ankles. It was one of their numerous rows that somehow ended up with neither of them dead. In later life they became quite supportive of each other.

If Lady Jean's prose left something to be desired, her contacts, using every sense of the word, were to be envied. Gossip had it that President Kennedy, Kruschev, Castro and the owner of Time Magazine, Henry Luce, had all been her lovers. Luce, for whom she worked as young girl, was a definite runner in the 'Who has Slept with Jeannie Stakes' but Kruschev is a bit far-fetched and it would have been difficult to have made love to Castro as she never visited Havana. And JFK? Well, there were so many at the starting gate that it would have been hard to tell, wouldn't it?

She was charming when we met her, a very attractive woman with wild dark hair that flew all over the place, a fine example of the eccentric British aristocracy.

Thankfully, my one American contact bore fruit. John Chanin was as good as his word and I received a warm welcome at the CBS Radio studios. John was a large person with a ready grin and slightly world-weary line in humour. With the typical hospitality that Americans show to newcomers, he invited me out to his home in New Jersey for dinner with his pretty and almost equally large wife. Telling me to get a beer from the fridge, I remember opening the door and being confronted by more food than I had ever seen in a home in my life. Again, it just emphasised the vast disparity in life style and disposable income that existed between America and Europe for several decades after World War Two. Buying steaks so big that they fell off the edges for your plate was routine for Americans. In England rationing was a recent memory.

I was privileged to find myself working with a top rate team at CBS. Pat Summerall, a great American football star who ended his career with the New York Giants, was the original presenter for Worldwide Sports and he was soon joined by another Giant, Frank Gifford, who was at the height of his fame, having retired only a few months earlier. There were no airs and graces with Frank. He knew he had a lot to learn about broadcasting and was humble enough to admit that he was prone to mangling some of Chanin's well-constructed prose when he got behind the microphone. Gifford could have come on strong with the Big Star act but there was never a hint of that and he couldn't have been nicer to me. Happily, he went on to enjoy a long career as a member of ABC's *Monday Night Football* in partnership with Howard Cosell. During those early days in New York, I was lucky enough to get to know two other terrific guys in the broadcasting business, Chris Schenkel and Jack Whitaker.

Occasionally one of them might take me to lunch at Toot Shor's, the legendary watering hole for New York's sports stars off Sixth Avenue. Still trying to get over the way people splashed money around in the States, I was stunned when my host tipped the maître d' $20 just to get us a good table. It seemed like a fortune to me at the time and was evidence of America's tipping culture which far outstretched anything we had in Europe. Nothing brought this home to be better than one morning when I was in a coffee shop on Third Avenue and a tramp was at the counter having a 99-cent breakfast of two eggs and a coffee. When he got up to leave he left a quarter on the counter. A quarter! More than 25% of the check! It was probably his last quarter, too. But he had to tip. Obviously it was a matter of pride or an unbreakable habit from his more affluent days.

Chanin thought it would be a good idea if I went to some of America's traditional sporting showpieces to offer a 'Limey's View' so I found myself reporting from the Preakness and the Belmont as well as a Yankees baseball game and a visit to Dallas to watch the Cowboys.

It was a great introduction into American sporting life but a passion for football, baseball, basketball and hockey just never took hold. I have no idea why. They are great sports, offering fabulous entertainment but cricket, soccer and rugby had so filled my heart with a love of all things sporting that there was no room for anything else, I suppose. I can think of no other explanation.

Tennis, of course, was the great common denominator and it was not long before I found myself covering those longstanding US summer grass court tournaments at the Longwood Cricket Club in Boston and South Orange, New Jersey. And, if I needed a few introductions, there was no one better than the self-styled Mr Communicator, Ted Tinling.

I think the best way I can introduce Ted, or Teddy as many people called him in the early days, is to quote from the foreword I wrote to his book *Sixty Years in Tennis*, which was a sort of updated version of the one he had originally published with Rod Humphries, the popular Aussie and sometime WCT PR man. Of Tinling I wrote:

'The man is copyright; stamped, sealed and delivered from above as one of a kind. There has never been a head that shape, encompassing a mind that sharp, a wit that witty or an eye so perceptive that it can analyse and strip bare the human condition at a glance. Anyone who leaves a conversation with Ted Tinling not knowing more than when he entered into it has to be deaf, because he could not possibly be that dumb.'

Tinling was bald and wore a diamond earring in his ear. He stood 6' 7" and had the largest hands I have ever seen. He was not a great tennis player but, nonetheless, had done something no one else had achieved – at tournament level he had played Bill Tilden in the thirties and Lew Hoad in the sixties, Wimbledon champions of completely different eras. And that was not the only unique thing he achieved. I doubt if there are many people who have been asked to do exactly the same job for exactly the same reason 50 years apart. But Tinling was. In 1928, after he had got a foot in the tennis world by umpiring for Suzanne Lenglen in the south of France, he received a letter from the Wimbledon Committee suggesting he become a sort of liaison officer between the players and themselves, "Because we are having trouble communicating with the modern day player."

Tinling, of course, leapt at the chance and continued to work for Wimbledon until the storm over the panties he designed for the lovely American star Gussie Moran in the 1950s caused him to stand down. "You have drawn attention to the sexual area," thundered the Wimbledon chairman Louis Greig in what must go down as one of the great sporting quotes of all time.

Tinling continued to design divine dresses for Billie Jean King, Margaret Court, Maria Bueno, Ann Jones, Virginia Wade, Chris Evert, Martina Navratilova, Evonne Goolagong and just about every female star of the 50s, 60s and 70s but it was in 1978 that he received a letter from the then Wimbledon Chairman, Sir Brian Burnett, which read, "We are having trouble communicating with the modern day player and were wondering ..."

So, 50 years after first being appointed, Ted became the go-between once again between the players and the committee. By then he was only two years off his 70th birthday. It mattered little. He knew the players and the committee didn't. I watched in amusement as he marched Sir Brian around the old players' restaurant and solemnly introduced him to Chris Evert, Bjorn Borg, Tracy Austin and Peter Fleming amongst other stars who were making Sir Brian's tournament such an on-going success.

Always quick to spot a newcomer, Tinling did not take long to introduce himself during my first Wimbledon in 1960 and I was soon integrated into the tennis family as a result of his generosity. If he liked you, he made you feel part of everything and, in 1962, I found myself being asked round to dinner at his flat on the Gloucester Road along with those two delightful South Africans Sandra Reynolds and Renee Schuurman and a dozen other players to discuss the topic of the day – should Ted abandon the pink under-garments that had flared from under Maria Bueno's skirt whenever she served and go to all white for his stable of players? Reluctantly, most players agreed that it was the best thing to do if one wanted to douse the salacious headlines and keep the Wimbledon committee off their backs. It turned out to be an historic meeting. Wimbledon has been white ever since.

By the time I arrived in New York, Tinling was as well known in American tennis circles as he was in Britain and Europe. You could hardly miss him. Happily, he had lost none of his ability to draw people together and I soon found myself being introduced to one of the most extraordinary women I have ever met – Gladys Heldman. Married to Julius Heldman, a Shell Oil Vice-President, she had been ranked as the No. 1 player in Texas and was the mother of two daughters, one of whom, Julie, reached the semi-final of the US Open. And, offering a great service to the game in America, Gladys published, edited and produced a monthly magazine called World Tennis. In 1965, Gladys was relying on such big name players as Gardnar Mulloy to write for it and did most of the editorialising herself. So, when Ted sang my praises as a leading tennis writer, that was it. Would I cover Forest Hills for her? The deal was done and I became a regular contributor with my Roving Eye column for the remaining life of the magazine.

Few people have succeeding in getting things done in quite the way Gladys managed. When, in 1969, she saw that the US Open, then played on grass at the West Side Tennis Club at Forest Hills, was suffering badly from lack of overseas participants, she hired a plane which flew about 90 top European stars over to New York from Amsterdam. How did she pay for it? By phoning up twenty of her best friends and demanding $2,000 for 'a good cause'.

It was the same when she founded the women's pro circuit in 1970. Having signed up nine players, including Billie Jean King and Rosie Casals, for a token dollar, she got on the phone to her great friend Joe Cullman, who just happened to be chairman of Philip Morris, and suggested his company sponsor the tour. A tobacco company sponsoring athletes? It was no problem in those days and the Virginia Slims circuit was born. With Philip Morris trying to crack the women's market, it turned into a partnership that was hugely successful for both sides, no matter what it did to people's lungs.

Billie Jean, of course, went on to become so much more than a tennis player. Her defeat of Bobby Riggs in "The Battle of the Sexes" became a landmark for the women's movement and, amazingly, her spirit and enthusiasm shine as brightly now as they did when Gerry Williams introduced me to the bubbly little Billie Jean Moffitt at Wimbledon when she was seventeen. She has been a dear and supportive friend ever since.

So eventually writing for World Tennis magazine and covering the odd tournament for various British newspapers brought in a little money but it was tough going at first – tough on our nerves and tough on our marriage. After three months, Glenys started to get homesick and decided to fly back to London for a few weeks. I battled on but before Gladys Heldman came to the rescue I remember taking a peek at my checking account at the Bank of

New York and seeing the princely sum of $50 sitting there. Savings account? No, didn't have one of those.

When Glenys returned we decided it was a good idea to take at a larger look at the United States so, after I covered my first US Open in September 1965 (the year Manolo Santana beat Cliff Drysdale in the final) we grabbed an interesting opportunity. Somehow we heard of an elderly couple who wanted their Oldsmobile driven across the country to Los Angeles. It was too far for them and, in typical American fashion, they were trusting enough to let two young strangers do the driving for them – alone. They took the train.

The timing was a little difficult as I had an assignment to cover the US Amateur Golf Championships at the Southern Hills Country Club in Tulsa, Oklahoma. But driving wouldn't get us there in time, so I flew to Tulsa, which is situated right in the middle of the US while Glenys, bravely, volunteered to meet me half way. She made it without mishap and we had enjoyable trip along Route 66 through the desert landscape of New Mexico and Arizona seeing cacti growing in profusion by the roadside. Earlier we had passed through strange, sparsely populated towns like Elk City, Oklahoma. "Looks like a one Elk town," I muttered, and Glenys laughed. Maybe I didn't make her laugh enough.

My brother Tony was living just at Poinsettia Place, just off Sunset Strip, and he was kind enough to put us up. Los Angeles was so different to New York and much more to my liking. I am a sucker for palm trees but it was more than that. It seemed so different to everything on the East Coast. I felt it as soon as we got west of the Mississippi. Here was a land that had nothing to do with Europe – vast, expansive and still a little wild. I had been brought up on those Western comics like Roy Rogers and Gene Autry that Tony had sent me every month as a child as well as film magazines called Silver Screen or some such name, adorned with covers of Jane Russell or Veronica Lake. This was the America I had dreamed about – guys with big hats driving long, sleek limousines with the top down in the sunshine. A restaurant on the Strip was called Dino's because it was owned by Dean Martin and everything seemed very glamorous. And more so than in New York, we encountered the expansive generosity for which Americans are rightly known. Someone we were introduced to, with connections to an automobile company, asked if we had been to Las Vegas. When we said we hadn't got that far yet, he offered to lend us a car for a long weekend. It was a Buick Electra. "Just take it," the man said. "Need it back on Monday."

Somewhere in Nevada on one of those long, straight highways, I was cruising along at what I thought was a reasonable speed and, to my horror, discovered we were going at 100 mph when I glanced at the speedometer. I had never driven a car that powerful or that quiet before and quickly decelerated. Luckily there was no sign of the Highway Patrol.

Las Vegas was absurd, even then. It was the days when you could find a hotel for 30 bucks a night even at upmarket joints like the Flamingo, Desert Inn or at the Rat Pack's hang out, the Sands. We didn't get to see Sinatra but took in a couple of other shows, dabbled very modestly in a couple of casinos and tried not to get blinded by the huge, flashing neon signs that almost made street lighting redundant on the Strip. Caesar's Palace had yet to be built and a guy called Andre Agassi who would revolutionise the city's education programme, was not born.

With the connections she had established through Peter Cook, David Frost and others in England, Glenys was well placed to start writing some show business articles and it was fascinating to visit the studios at Paramount or MGM and see how the dream factory actually turned out the subtle, and sometimes not so subtle, propaganda that gave America its image in the world. Even the gangsters seemed glamorous in Hollywood movies and the lifestyle, for better or worse, was polished, glittery and very seductive, even in black and white. Not until James Dean came along with *Rebel Without a Cause* and Bill Haley started rocking in *Blackboard Jungle* with Sydney Poitier did a little modern day reality start to infiltrate the façade.

It must have been on the set of that ultimate Western comedy *Cat Ballou* that Glenys introduced me to Jane Fonda, who was known then as much for being Henry Fonda's daughter as a great actress in the making. Just then it would have been difficult to visualise her as the wife of Roger Vadim or a highly controversial anti-Vietnam war activist. She was very beautiful and now, 55 years later, she still is.

Hollywood was just about everything it was cracked up to be as far as I was concerned, but the nasty little realities of American life kept popping up to shock me. I was away on a brief trip somewhere when Glenys, who was feeling the pressure of our financially fragile existence more than I was, fell ill at Tony's house with severe stomach pains. She was so incapacitated that Tony had to call the ambulance. They found her lying on the floor, crying with pain and promptly demanded $100 before they would touch her. Tony came up with the money, thank God, but if I had been there I might have lost it and hit someone.

I know Americans would find this an extreme reaction but they were familiar and strangely accepting of the way the US health care system worked. Money first, treatment afterwards. For me it was outrageous. Now, with Obamacare having received such detailed exposure, most people are aware that the United States is the only industrialised nation on earth not to guarantee its citizens automatic free healthcare. I still find it appalling. And while I am grateful that I receive Medicare benefits now as an American resident who has worked long enough in the country to qualify for them, that does not do anything for the 40 million US citizens who live in fear and dread of falling ill. I write as Donald Trump has been elected President. What hope for them now? We shall see.

I am not sure some Americans quite grasp the fact that, in Europe, whether or not people should receive free, state-subsidised health care such as we get in Britain is no longer a subject for discussion. The question is how to pay for it, not whether it should be dismantled. Yet Americans allow billions of dollars a month to be spent on foreign wars while, apparently, not being able to look after the health of its own people.

It infuriates me to this day and I get very angry thinking about it. To lighten the mood, I always remember Torben Ulrich's typically alternative solution to the problem. Torben, a Danish Davis Cup player and father of Metallica's Lars Ulrich, used to say in his slow, deliberate manner, "The thing to do with doctors is to pay them to keep you healthy. Then stop paying them when you are ill."

Unworkable, of course, but the logic is hard to refute. It wouldn't be too far different from an insurance policy. Healthy people would be paying a monthly fee to their doctor and would resume paying once they got better. If nothing else, it would concentrate the doctor's minds.

Anyway, Glenys recovered but our marriage was in trouble and she decided to go back to her parents in East Sheen for Christmas. That left me to roam California and wonder what I would do on Christmas Day. Richard Harris turned out to be the unlikely solution by being kind enough to invite me to his Bel Air mansion. He was in the midst of filming *Camelot* and did his best to live up to the fairy tale with the kind of Christmas party one does not easily forget. Peter Ustinov and the British comedy actor Terry-Thomas were just two of the other well-known actors I remember being there as well as scores of kids from the large British community which always seems to be in residence in Hollywood. Ustinov, a raconteur like no other, had two of his children with him and he tried to entertain them with some funny stories. But all he got was the 'Oh, Daddy!' look of kids who had heard it all before. They were brushing off what millions would have paid to witness.

We all ate from a lavish buffet off our knees in the living room while Richard sat the fourteen kids down in the dining room at a long table groaning with food. I remember him bursting in and saying, "Hands up for more Christmas pudding!" Sticky hands shot in the air.

But there was no problem washing them. Someone lacking in foresight had given one of the children bubble soap as a present. And, of course it went in the pool. The results were nothing if not frothily spectacular.

I eventually got myself back to New York and resumed an uncertain married life with Glenys. But things were about to change and, professionally if not personally, 1966 turned out to be a very good year. I had started to do the odd freelance job for John Gold. He was a one man band as far as the Evening News was concerned in North America and, occasionally, needed to travel out of town.

I remember one of the first pieces I did for him was on a press conference given by Britain's Foreign Secretary George Brown at the United Nations. Brown was a small man with huge eyebrows and a brilliant mind. He was probably the cleverest man in Harold Wilson's cabinet and summed up whatever the problem of the moment happened to be (if in doubt put down the Israel-Palestine crisis and you will have a fair chance of being correct – plus ca change) in a way that revealed a first class brain. Yet within 45 minutes, he had downed two large gin and tonics at the official cocktail party; was pissed as a parrot and was pinching the waitresses' bottoms. And I mean pinching. I saw two of them nearly spill the drinks as they flinched. It was a tragedy that Brown could not hold his liquor, because he could have made a fine Prime Minister.

I was mulling over how to infer all this with a bit of subtlety for the Evening News back at the apartment when Glenys suggested I get a move on or we would be late for dinner. "It's all very fine!" I shot back, feeling the pressure of the moment. "Harold Wilson is going to read this tomorrow!"

He probably wouldn't enjoy it, either, even though I had only hinted at the inebriated state of his Foreign Secretary. But it was beginning to dawn on me that the pen I was starting to wield carried a little more weight than a proposed change at fly half for the Harlequins. I was moving into a bigger league.

Like Reg Hayter and Charles Wintour, John Gold became the third guardian angel to enter my life and, in this case, probably save it. I have no idea how long I could have existed on scraps of freelance work and a column in World Tennis Magazine. But a combination of fate and Gold's faith in my ability to do the job on somewhat flimsy evidence led to him offering me his position when he was recalled to London to become editor of the paper. Suddenly, out of nowhere, I was the resident North American correspondent of the Evening News and its one million readers. Talk about a leg up!

THE EVENING NEWS

The miracle behind my surprising appointment lay in the fact that it was almost unheard of for a foreign correspondent to be appointed editor of a major newspaper straight from the field. A few had returned home and spent time as deputy editors before moving into the hot seat but to be dumped straight into it was rare indeed. It could possibly have been a first.

So I was lucky on that score but in many other ways, too. One of the obvious benefits lay in having an editor back in London who was going to understand everything I was writing about and give it the space it deserved. Another was purely technical. The Evening News first edition came off the presses at 8.00 am London time which was 2.00 am in New York. So any US based story was fresh for London from the previous afternoon or evening, making a front page splash all the more likely.

And then there was John Gold himself. In New York I had got to know him as a sharp, industrious fellow with a ready smile who was always business-like but friendly as he peered at you through his spectacles. He was an old New York hand; happily married (and still is to the devoted Bertha) and not one who spent hours drinking with the British press pack. Largely, he kept to himself, worked his US contacts and got the job done.

How does one do the job of a foreign correspondent? There is no blueprint. I had it easy to the extent that I was already living in New York and knew a few people, although not nearly enough in political circles. But being dumped in a place like Moscow, Budapest or Bangkok with no knowledge of the local language is a far more daunting task. Often there will be some local agency guys around who are not in direct competition and they usually ease a newcomer through his first weeks. It helps, too, if there is (or, more likely, was) a Foreign Press Club like those which used to exist in Rome, Paris and Hong Kong where you could pick up the drift of what was going on.

But I found the biggest asset is to have a nose for who is writing the most sense in the papers one had to read every day. Opinions were coming at you from all quarters but picking out great journalists like Walter Lipmann, James Reston, Murray Kempton and, particularly in New York, Jimmy Breslin and Pete Hamill set you on the right track in forming your own opinions.

And there was Walter Cronkite offering as balanced a view of America as one could wish for on the CBS Nightly News, not to mention various radio stations that allowed the voice of the people to filter through on their talk shows.

Happily, I think John Gold and I were on the same page about what was right and what was wrong about America, even though that might not have always gelled with the opinions of our right-wing publisher Vere Harmsworth. But only once was I ever censored and that was after Gold left the editor's chair. The problem with political viewpoints when comparing the United States and Europe could be summed up in one word: Communism. To Americans, Communism is the evil to end all evil and, in their minds, socialism is closely aligned to it. The very concept hits at the bedrock of the American way of life – free enterprise, a life free of government interference, freedom itself.

Many American's jaws dropped when told that, for several years after World War Two, Italy, a country close to their hearts, was under the control of a Communist government. How could that be? This thinking affected one's own political alignments and, whereas I had been brought up as a Churchillian Conservative, I found myself being pushed to the left by the right-wing extremism that was so prevalent in the States. You could say that Barry Goldwater was not my cup of tea.

Glenys had decided to try her luck in Hollywood by this time, both as a writer and, very briefly, as a bit part actress. The unravelling of our marriage had not been fun but we remained friends and tried to make things work as best they could. With a guaranteed income, I was able to upgrade my living arrangements and moved into a reasonably modern block on East 57th Street, right on the corner of 3rd Avenue. It was a not very attractive blue bricked building which still stands today. But the cinemas do not. I counted eleven within four minutes' walk of my prime location when I lived there in 1967. I think there is one small complex left. And Schraffts, the coffee shop on the corner frequented by old ladies, has gone with them.

My apartment was just close enough to Rockefeller Plaza to allow me to walk to work most mornings. John Gold had shared an office with the Daily Mail, the paper's Harmsworth stable mate, and it was everything one could have asked for with a view of the skating rink and restaurants galore. Geri Elrod, a warm, attractive American lady, was in charge of the office and looked after us very well. Being of the right temperament, she learned to ignore the occasional explosions of anger and frustration that blew up as deadlines approached and London was screaming for copy. Like John before me, I tried to mind my own business as Jeffrey Blyth, a stickler for detail and punctuality, kept his troops in line. Iain Smith, a gregarious Scot, was one of them and others came and went, including Charlie Wilson who became a good friend when he surprised himself by ending up as editor of the Times many years later.

Taking a story out of sequence, let me give you an example of Blyth's professionalism. It was the time of the 1968 Olympic Games in Mexico and the Daily Mail Group was assembling a major task force to cover it. Blyth, who could speak Spanish and knew the city well, was sent down to mastermind the arrangements. After a few days, the story about Aristotle Onassis marrying Jackie Kennedy broke. The telex machine – our means of instant communication in those days – started chattering. London wanted 800 words on Onassis from Jeffrey and, as usual, they wanted it pronto.

It was our lunch time and Geri didn't need to be told that Jeffrey would be washing down an enchilada or two with at least one tequila. A lunch time snifter was routine for Blyth. When at home base, he would walk across to the 21 Club almost every day, order a Scotch and soda, and see who of interest there was to talk to. Contacts were made with people like Onassis.

So, after a few frantic phone calls, Geri got hold of her bureau chief who, luckily, had been eating just round the corner from whatever office, probably Reuters, he was using in Mexico City. "Bugger," was his reply. "How much, 800? OK, watch the telex."

And we waited. But not for long. After about fifteen minutes, the machine started spewing out 800 well written, informative words beginning, "When I last spoke to Onassis …" Right off the top of his head. It was an example of the journalist's skill. You make contacts; you store knowledge; you remember salient quotes and you develop the ability to put it all into printable words anywhere, at any time. And, one could add, pissed or not pissed. Jeffrey Blyth was the consummate professional.

Our Rockefeller Plaza office was a great learning experience for me. I was able to witness in close up how a busy foreign bureau functioned and, of course, all the reporters working there were top-of-the-line operatives. The work was incredibly varied and you needed to keep your pulse on everything that was going on and make judgments on which particular story would interest your readers. I was fortunate to have an affable Foreign Editor back in London called Fred Colbert who was always ready to offer advice and tried his best not to disturb me in the middle of the night when the late London editions were going to press.

Part of my working day took place at home where I had installed the all-important telex machine. I retired there after dinner every night, clutching the next day's New York papers, and made final decisions on what I was going to file. I usually finished around 1.00 am and went to bed hoping the phone wouldn't ring or the telex wouldn't chatter. When it did, I managed to snap to fairly quickly and I always made sure I sounded reasonably awake and ready for action if Fred called. After a while he became a bit bewildered as to my sleeping habits. "It doesn't SOUND as if I've woken you – when, actually, do you sleep?" he asked on more than once occasion. The answer was through the early hours of the morning. I never had a problem sleeping through to 10.30 am if I needed to.

The days and evenings were filled with every imaginable activity from covering an Emile Griffiths fight at Shea Stadium; following Mayor John Lindsay around the city; finding out why London cabs couldn't survive in Manhattan (the suspension couldn't handle the pot holes) or covering the entertainment scene when the likes of Shirley Bassey sang at the Waldorf Astoria or Nancy Wilson at the Plaza. Once, when I was attending a big fund raiser at the Plaza, I was phoning over a bit of copy from a phone near the kitchens and a waiter jumped into the booth next to mine and phoned his wife. "Honey, you won't believe it! Frank Sinatra just tipped me $100!"

He had reason to be excited. One hundred bucks was a lot of money back then and Old Blue Eye's generosity added a nice line to my story.

Later that year I attended the post-premier party for *Camelot*, which was glittery and star-studded even by Broadway standards. Most of the cast was there, of course, headed by Richard Harris, Vanessa Redgrave and Franco Nero. The latter may have provided the link for an Italian connection because it was the appearance of *Dr Zhivago* producer Carlo Ponti and his wife, Sofia Loren, that stands out in my memory. Everyone knew the stunning Sofia would be coming so New York's most glamorous society ladies got out their best jewels and were draped from head to foot, not wanting to be completely upstaged. But, of course, the great Loren trumped them by turning up in a long black dress with a square neck, cut just low enough but not too low, and nothing else. Not an earring, not a bauble or bangle in sight. She left the competition for dead.

All this was the fun side of the job. But there were plenty of moments that were not amusing at all. As soon as the heat of summer began infiltrating the crowded, litter strewn ghettos of New York, Philadelphia and Newark, just across the Hudson in New Jersey, disenchanted black youth started getting agitated. And when two white cops pulled over a black Newark taxi driver and started beating him up, the touch paper was lit and the shooting started.

I rented a car and crossed the George Washington Bridge to see what was going on. I reckoned the offices of the Newark Daily News was the best place to head for but before I could get within a couple of blocks, I was flagged down by a policeman who warned me to go no further. "They're shooting from the rooftops," he said. "It's not safe."

I flashed my press badge and told him, sorry, but I couldn't turn back and hit the gas. The huge neon sign made the News Building easy to spot and, as firing erupted somewhere in the vicinity, I parked the car right outside the front door, and made a dash for the entrance. I heard the crack of 'incoming' as I sprinted up the steps but whether someone was aiming at me or just firing into the night, I have no idea. I looked up and the door was being held open for me. It was only when I was half way up the staircase inside that it dawned on me that the man who had held the door open was black. The incongruity of the situation typified America's confusion. This was a race riot but there were blacks who were shooting at whites and blacks who were holding doors open for whites so they could get out of harm's way. It took me a while to sort that out.

The unrest went on for a week and it was bloody. By the time it subsided into a sullen truce between Newark's huge black community and the authorities, 26 people were dead. It turned out to be just a presage for what was to come.

The Detroit riots have gone down in American history as a benchmark in race relations in the inner cities because the riots that erupted on the 23rd July 1967 were barely believable in their intensity and ferocity. By the time it was all over, 33 blacks and 11 whites had been killed, no less than 1,189 people had been injured and 7,200 had ended up in jail. The estimated cost of the damage was $32 million but you can't put a price on what that kind of internecine war does to a city's soul.

It got so bad that the Governor had to call in the National Guard and, by the time I arrived and started walking around the deserted streets, troops from the 82nd Airborne, who were stationed nearby, were on patrol. They brought badly needed order to the situation because, once a civil disturbance gets that bad, a regular police force is simply not trained to deal with it. Especially when it comes to white cops trying to quell a black riot. We saw that so clearly in 2015 when a young black man was shot to death by a white cop in Ferguson, Missouri, reportedly when he had his hands in the air.

Race relations and the possibility for African-Americans to improve their lot have improved immeasurably since 1967 but the resentment lingers and lessons still have not been learned. Black folks are no longer prepared to be bossed by a predominantly white police force and the citizens of Ferguson showed just how militant they could become by demonstrating – for the most part peacefully – for more than a week.

The Governor, slow to react at first, was sensible enough to find a black captain from the Missouri Highway patrol who had grown up in Ferguson and put him in charge. He talked to the people, gently and sensibly – what a concept – and he probably saved lives. No one was killed. And there, too, the National Guard were eventually called in. Quite understandably, several American commentators abhorred the fact that American troops were needed to confront American citizens but, in the long run, it is better for everyone. The Ferguson police had revealed themselves to be unpredictable and under-trained. With the Army you know what you are going to get, as I had discovered walking down Michigan Avenue in Detroit at midnight all those years before.

A soldier had stepped out of the shadows of a burnt-out office building and shouted, "Halt." Maybe because I had been in the Army myself, I knew what that meant. When a soldier in a helmet with a rifle says, "Halt!" you halt. There is no room for discussion. I showed my press badge, he saluted and I went on my way, eventually finding a public phone box that worked. Within no more than a minute of asking for a collect call to London, I was dictating copy. Another front page story for the early edition. I was getting a lot of space.

I was at the Village Vanguard in Greenwich Village a few weeks later to listen to that great black comedian Dick Gregory whose wit always reflected, often with bitter irony, what was happening amongst his people.

"Black people don't have a voice unless they do something to get whitey's attention," he said. "And then just a little ole' riot won't do. They only got the white man's attention in Detroit because the fires got too near the Mustangs, baby."

It was one of those phrases you don't forget. Detroit was, and is still thanks to President Obama, the great motor city, home of Ford, GM and Chrysler, and if some politicians were prepared to let it collapse when the financial crisis hit in 2008, it was unthinkable in the sixties. The automobile was the backbone of American life and the Mustang was its new star. They would have used more than the 82nd Airborne to protect that.

So, in a few short weeks, I had received a close up of the nation's underbelly. One of the most amazing aspects of the United States is its ability to hide poverty. You can drive across the entire nation, as we had, and never be confronted by anything more than a hobo or some people sleeping on the streets. Suburbia seems to stretch endlessly from the centre of any city with row after row of nice houses with their manicured lawns. If you don't happen to turn that particular corner which takes you to shantytown you would never imagine that millions of Americans (40 million at the last count) live below the poverty line and that children go to bed hungry.

And the poverty can be really close. Coconut Grove just outside Miami is a popular tourist spot with a thriving area of top class restaurants and boutiques, with high rise hotels all around. I was with a girlfriend one evening and, as she lived locally, she was driving her own car. Seeking a short cut to Dixie Highway, she turned down a street no more than four blocks from the centre of Coconut Grove. Suddenly we were confronted by the sight of a bare chested black man with a bandolier draped across his shoulder and a machine gun in his hand. He was sitting on an oil drum like some sentry to No Man's Land.

I don't know what would have happened if Alison Blake had not been Jamaican. I think he saw her first, hesitated for a second, and by the time his eyes alighted on me in the passenger's seat, Alison was starting a rapid U-turn and we were out of there. It was not the moment to stop and ask if we were welcome.

So it's all around you but so few middle class Americans, let alone visitors, get to see it. Only when someone gets shot and the riots start does the world get a glimpse of the America Hollywood, back in those days, rarely wanted to show you.

On so many levels the job was fascinating and I was learning so much.

But it was good to get home occasionally and, even though he was not a huge sports fan himself, John Gold was understanding about my close ties to the tennis world and allowed me to cover Wimbledon every year, as well, of course, as the US Open which was still being played on grass at Forest Hills.

I had missed the Wimbledon of 1965 but the following year I was back to see my friend Manolo Santana become the first Spaniard ever to lift the crown when he beat Dennis Ralston in the final. Santana had won Forest Hills the year before, proving that Europeans could play on grass – but only if you were as talented as this little son of a Madrid groundskeeper.

Winning the US Open was big but it was his triumph at Wimbledon that opened up tennis to the masses in Spain. On his return to Madrid, Santana was embraced by Franco and people started rushing out to buy tennis rackets – not that there were many places to play unless you belonged to the upper-crust country clubs that had reserved tennis for the rich.

But before Franco got his paws on him, we had some serious celebrating to do. First there was a big reception at the Spanish Embassy where, by some weird chance, the Ambassador, Pepe de Santa Cruz, and his charming wife Casilda, had been friends of my parents during the war. I believe they bought a house from us when we moved to Shropshire.

After that, Manolo and his great friend Edison 'Banano' Mandarino, a Brazilian player who lived in Spain, and the elegant Nicola Pietrangeli, who had been friends with Santana ever since losing his title to him at Roland Garros in an epic five set final five years before, and I repaired to The Saddle Room on Park Lane. It was London's first discotheque. I have this memory of us drinking champagne out of the Wimbledon Cup but I can't believe the club would have allowed us to take it off into the night so it must have been the small replica they give to the champions to keep.

Anyway, we had plenty to drink and watched everyone dancing The Madison, which was the latest craze, led by the club's famous hostess Helene Cordet, who spent much of her life denying that she had been Prince Philip's girlfriend. In fact they had known each other since childhood in Greece and he gave her away when she married her first husband just before the war.

He's a fine man, Manolo Santana, and, as all the players that followed him will attest, he really is the father of modern tennis in Spain. It was good to share his great moment of triumph.

Returning to the States, it was back to news reporting apart from the US Open which was won that year by my old mate Fred Stolle after he had been infuriated by not being seeded. He felt he deserved to be, which of course he did, and just to prove it went out and won the whole thing, beating the much-fancied John Newcombe in the final.

The variety of the job continued to stimulate me and, occasionally, I found myself covering stories that were truly bizarre. One day news came through that Martin Bormann, one of Hitler's top deputies who had vanished without trace as Berlin fell, had been found in Panama. It must have been a slow news day because most Fleet Street editors told their men in New York to get on a plane and fly down there. Mine was no exception.

So by the time we got ourselves on the late afternoon Pan Am flight – it was so easy in those days, you pretty much just turned up – the midnight arrival in Panama was way out of morning paper time in London. So, once again, whatever story there was fell into my lap for the Evening News first edition.

The police station was the first port of call but before we got there I remember telling the taxi to stop at a roadside fruit stall – still open at 2.00 am – and asking some bewildered Panamanian if he had ever heard of the Nazi, Martin Bormann. He'd heard something on the radio, he said, but otherwise looked blank. I wasn't surprised.

The police chief was more forthcoming and said they had picked up this German-speaking beggar who was wearing some sort of military cap. If there was some other reason to connect him to the long lost Bormann, it was not readily apparent. And the likelihood of it being Hitler's chief operative became even less likely when the poor wretch was produced for our perusal. Thin and morose with nothing coherent to say, the man looked far more like an ex-German army corporal, which I think was what he turned out to be, than a fearsome Nazi leader. Harry Benson, the brilliant Daily Express photographer who went on to take great pictures of truly famous people, snapped away and, after we had all run out of anything more to ask a man who was obviously of absolutely no interest to anyone, most of us repaired to a nightclub calling itself The House of Love and tried not to spend too much more of our newspapers' money. By the standards of Fleet Street's wild goose chases, it ranked right up there.

Unhappily, there was nothing even faintly amusing about the next two major stories I covered. They changed the history of the world, as well as the United States – and not for the better.

Chapter 8
AND THE SHOTS RANG OUT ...

On Thursday 4th April 1968, the entire Associated Newspapers bureau was invited to cocktails at the Fifth Avenue apartment of Lord Harmsworth, our boss in all but name. It would be three years before Vere Harmsworth succeeded his ailing father as Chairman of one of the world's most prominent newspaper groups but, in the meantime, his hands-on approach to the business left us in no doubt as to who was in control.

For a man who had been considered a bit dim at Eton and served as a private for four years in the British Army during National Service without ever getting a commission, Vere had come alive during the final part of his education at Duke University in North Carolina and emerged as a Lord in every sense, tall, charming, witty and very much in charge.

But it was not Vere who greeted Jeffrey Blyth, Iain Smith, Geri Elrod and the rest of us when we were ushered up to the sprawling apartment. In all things social Pat 'Bubbles' Harmsworth ran the roost. The nickname was totally apt. Bubbles was a small, vivacious and often hilarious woman whom the Independent described as 'a brilliantly dotty, shimmering, exotic figure frequently dressed in the gallimaufry of 18th century costume'.

If I recall correctly, her long, cream gown was relatively sober that evening but the smile was broad and we were soon made to feel at ease as a flunky served champagne. Inevitably, the conversation turned to newspapers and it soon became obvious that even Jeffrey Blyth, whose blood was the colour of ink, did not know as much about the industry as his Lordship. He was a proprietor who was in the habit of calling the Daily Mail office two or three times a day – not to interfere but simply to keep abreast of what was going on.

He would do so from any of his homes in Paris, New York, Jamaica or Kyoto where he spent time with his mistress, Maiko Lee, a Japanese woman he married in 1993, a year after Bubbles died. The liaison was quite open and Vere was lucky to have a wife who not only stuck by him but, realising the necessity of producing a male heir after giving birth to two daughters, agreed to try for another child when she was 38. As a result Jonathan Harmsworth was born in December 1967. Bubbles, in fact, must have been pregnant when we met her.

Once Vere took over the group, he immediately installed David English, who I had got to know during his days with the Daily Express in New York, as editor of the Daily Mail. English went on to become one of the great editors in the history of Fleet Street and, after the initial shock had worn off, masterminded one of the biggest revolutionary acts of that age in newspapers – turning the Daily Mail from a broadsheet into a tabloid. It was Vere's idea, as was the decision to buy 50% shareholding in the company that owned the Evening Standard and, in 1980, merging it with the Evening News which, effectively, ceased to exist. It proved to be the turning point for the age-old rivalry between Beaverbrook and Northcliffe newspapers. Until then the Daily Mail had always been the poor relation to the Daily Express but all that was to change as Vere used his intuition to appeal to a broader market and start running competitions like 'Win a Pub!'.

"I learned from my time as a private in the army that the working man would like nothing better than to own a pub," Vere told the writer Nicholas Coleridge. The Lord who had visited the other side of the tracks was right about that as well as many other things that swung the pendulum between his newspapers and Beaverbrook's.

All this lay in the future on that April evening in New York but, no matter how fascinating the conversation, Jeffrey was not about to forget his habit which closely mirrored that of his proprietor – check with the office. As his entire staff was at the party, Jeffrey called his usual contact at Reuters just to make sure the world was still on an even keel. It wasn't.

Emerging from the little alcove from where he had made the call, Blyth, looking a little pale, brought all conversation to a halt by announcing, "They've shot Martin Luther King."

End of cocktail party. Jeffrey started making his apologies but they were waved away by his Lordship. He knew exactly what we needed to do and, as Geri Elrod commandeered the phone to make our bookings, we made the last flight out of LaGuardia to Memphis on Braniff. With half an hour of landing we found ourselves outside a nondescript motel in a Memphis suburb, surveying a scene that showed blood on the second floor balcony and groups of stunned people telling what they knew.

The Rev Jesse Jackson, less well known in those days, was amongst those describing what had happened. Dr King had been chatting to friends. "He had just bent over," Jackson told us. "If he had been standing up he wouldn't have been hit in the face."

Solomon Jones, Dr King's chauffeur who had been standing beside the car looking up to the balcony, said, "He had just come out of his room. I told him 'It's getting chilly, why don't you put on your top coat?' He said, 'OK, I will,' and he smiled. He had just finished smiling when I heard the shot. I ran up the fire escape. When I got to him he looked dead."

As the police, reacting immediately to the gunfire, came running, a white man rushed up with a hotel towel to try and stop the blood pouring from King's face. But another, craven white man had already done his work and it was too late. Rumours were flying but one report said that the sniper had dropped his rifle and suitcase and fled in a white car.

All these quotes and observation appeared in my report that covered the front page of the Evening News a few hours later. I finished it with these paragraphs:

'Dr King was a sitting duck for his assassin. That much was readily evident when I stood on the balcony of the Lorraine Hotel where Dr King met his death.

'With the lime green door of Room 306 at my back, I looked across the road over the tops of the sparse, leafless trees to the row of downtrodden buildings that included the dosshouse the sniper used as his vantage point.'

Seconds before the shot rang out, Martin Luther King had said to a colleague, "My Man, be sure to sing 'Blessed Lord' tonight and sing it well."

For the next few hours at least, the singing was stilled. Dr King had been shot at 6.00 pm and, as darkness fell, black communities across America in Chicago, Baltimore, Detroit and Washington DC erupted in angry cries of despair. Troops with bayonets were immediately deployed around the Capitol as fires broke out and riots were numerous in ghettos all over America – with one exception.

Senator Robert Kennedy, running for President, heard of the assassination as his campaign plane left Muncie, Indiana. Unsurprisingly, he gasped at the news. Gun shots … a leader slain … it was all too close and familiar to this man who had been affected like no other by the assassination of President Kennedy. But Robert Kennedy's reaction allowed his nation to see, maybe for the first time, exactly what sort of man he was, exactly what sort of man he had become.

When the plane landed in Indianapolis, he went directly to a pre-arranged rally in a black section of the city. The large crowd that had gathered there had not heard the news. There was no extra security, no way of knowing how some 1,000 people might react to what this white man was about to tell them. But Kennedy, a small, hunched figure wearing a black overcoat against a chill wind, climbed the platform and began to talk:

"I have bad news for you," he began. "For all of our fellow citizens, and people who love justice all over the world, and that is that Martin Luther King was shot and killed tonight."

The crowd cried out in shock and pain but, as Jack Newfield of the Village Voice describes it in his brilliant biography of Robert Kennedy, 'Kennedy, speaking extemporaneously, near tears himself, and inevitably thinking of Dallas, gave a talk that all his skilled speech writers, working together, could not have surpassed.'

His was not a powerful voice, with its Boston accent and scratchy tones, and he was not known as a great orator but the moment seized him and here is what he said:

"Martin Luther King dedicated his life to love and to justice for his fellow human beings, and he died because of that effort.

"In this difficult day, in this difficult time for the United States, it is perhaps well to ask what kind of nation we are and what directions we want to move in. For those of you who are black – considering the evidence there evidently is that there were white people who were responsible – you can be filled with bitterness, with hatred, and a desire for revenge. We can move in that direction as a country, in great polarisation, black people amongst black, white people amongst white, filled with hatred toward one another.

"Or we can make an effort, as Martin Luther King did, to understand and to comprehend, and to replace that violence, that stain of bloodshed that has spread across our land, with an effort to understand with compassion and love."

The crowd, restless, unsure, waited for more.

"For those of you who are black," Kennedy continued, staring down at this sea of black faces, "and who are tempted to be filled with hatred and distrust at the injustice of such an act, against all white people, I can only say that I feel in my own heart the same kind of feeling. I had a member of my family killed but he was killed by a white man. But we have to make an effort in the United States, we have to make an effort to understand, to go beyond these rather difficult times.

"My favorite poet was Aeschylus. He wrote: 'In our sleep, pain which cannot forget, falls drop by drop upon the heart until, in our own despair, against our will, comes wisdom through the awful grace of God.'

"What we need in the United States is not division, what we need in the United States is not hatred, what we need in the United States is not violence or lawlessness but love and wisdom, and compassion towards one another, and a feeling of justice toward those who still suffer in our country, whether they be white or whether they be black.

"So I shall ask you tonight to return home, to say a prayer for the family of Martin Luther King, that's true, but more importantly to say a prayer for our own country, which all of us love – a prayer for understanding and that compassion of which I spoke.

"We can do well in this country. We will have difficult times. We've had difficult times in the past. We will have difficult times in the future. It is not the end of violence; it is not the end of lawlessness; it is not the end of disorder.

"But the vast majority of white people and the vast majority of black people in this country want to live together, want to improve the quality of our life and want justice for all human beings who abide in our land.

"Let us dedicate ourselves to what the Greeks wrote so many years ago: to tame the savageness of man and to make gentle the life of this world.

"Let us dedicate ourselves to that, and say a prayer for our country, and for our people."

And they went home, just as he had asked. And Indianapolis was one of the very few cities in America that night which did not suffer from violence in its ghettoes. And the reason was clear. A small, rich, privileged white man had spoken from his heart about his love and his hopes for his nation to a deprived crowd and, while never allowing an inflammatory thought to escape his lips, had asked for compassion and understanding. And they accepted his plea. They accepted it because they felt he was sincere – sincerity coming as a surprise to a crowd like this because so few politicians appear to possess it.

Considering the circumstances and the timing and the audience, and the fact that he was a controversial figure, this speech has to rank as one of the greatest off-the-cuff pieces or oratory in the history of American politics. It brought honour to a night of shame.

In its special way, it did justice to Dr King's memory. The speech did not have the rising cadence of fire that led to the preacher's exhortation of, "I have been to the mountain top … And I've looked over. And I've SEEN the promised land."

But, on this cold evening caught in the fires of anger and frustration, that was not what was needed. A quiet, sincere understanding of their pain was what was required and that is what Robert Kennedy was able to give them. Because he cared. He cared because of what his family history had done to him; what his country had done to him and how it had changed him.

When Newfield asked him when he had started reading poetry, he had replied, "Oh, sometime towards the end of 1963." In other words, right after Jack was killed. It was where he sought solace and here he was, quoting Aeschylus.

The timing of this transformation was backed up by Frank Mankiewicz, Bobby's press officer, a charming, witty man whose father had helped Orson Welles write *Citizen Kane*. "We were on the campaign plane one day and began talking about capital punishment which Bobby said he was against. I reminded him that he had not been against it during his time as Attorney General. He agreed that was true but in answer to my question of why he changed his mind, he replied, 'After Jack died, I read Camus.' I was amazed. How many politicians do you know who read Camus?"

The way in which we dig deep enough to find our true selves, to find our souls, is what defines us. Bobby had a compassionate soul but it had been masked throughout his early life by the need to be the tough little brother, dedicated to doing the dirty work of politics for Jack who was running for President. He was the tyke in the shadow of the glamorous sibling and he didn't have time to examine his own feelings, which were being suppressed for the greater good of the man who would be king. But the king was dead and the younger brother had agonised for months over whether he was prepared to reach for the crown himself.

I was fortunate enough to be able to observe quite closely how those months unfolded from the end of 1967 to the moment the dream died. My reporting was helped by the fact that I was already friends with some people very close to the Senator, like Donald Dell and his law partner Lee Fentress, who both became advance men for Bobby when he finally decided to hit the campaign trail. I dated a couple of his assistants, too, like the lovely red-head Peggy Cuthbertson who worked in his Washington office. But it was not pillow talk I was after. I found the scene that was unfolding, which centred on a belea-guered Lyndon Johnson in the White House desperately trying to deal with the Vietnam war; RFK dithering about whether to run and Senator Eugene McCarthy, the smooth intellectual from Minnesota entering the race, totally absorbing. It was a story that could have played out a hundred different ways because moods, feelings, ambitions and decisions were being buffeted on a daily basis, not just by polls and the changing fortunes of politicians at home but by the echo of the ever-escalating war in faraway Vietnam.

It is no exaggeration to say that the future of the world hung on the timing of the decisions that were made during those politically fraught early months of 1968. From a personal perspective, I have never covered, and will never cover, anything as important or absorbing or ultimately tragic. Nor will I have the opportunity of observing a politician as unique as Robert F. Kennedy run for high office.

TO RUN OR NOT TO RUN

I first set eyes on Robert Kennedy when some bright staffer decided that CharleyO's, our local watering hole at Rockefeller Plaza, a block from my office, would be a good place for the Senator to drop in at lunch time and say a few words to the customers. As the clientele of this popular bar and restaurant always included a heavy sprinkling of media people from NBC, as well as numerous foreign news bureaus such as ours and the London Daily Telegraph, his brief appearance probably carried above-average impact.

What that impact was did not become readily apparent to this reporter nor, I think, to others. If I had expected any resemblance to John F. Kennedy, whose stature, smile and sheer handsomeness illuminated any room he entered, I was soon disillusioned. The first adjective that sprung to mind as we watched this small, tentative figure appear, nervously sweeping a recently grown forelock of brown hair from his forehead, was 'frail'. It looked as if one good puff of wind would blow him back into the street. Instead, two well-muscled minders lifted him bodily onto the bar which had been rapidly cleared of beer mugs and martinis.

The smile was fleeting and the voice thin. This, I thought, is a deeply shy man no matter what his record or reputation. He spoke of why he had decided to run, of the need to challenge the President's policies and find a way to end the war in Vietnam. There was an edge of passion in his voice but it was not great oratory and barely memorable. And with that he left.

The complexities and contradictions associated with Robert Kennedy can fill a book and have, indeed, filled many. But there is a theme that runs through the assessments and Arthur Schlesinger, in his Pulitzer Prize winning book *A Thousand Days* put it succinctly: 'I do not know of any case in contemporary American politics where there seemed to me a greater discrepancy between the myth and the man.'

This observation was echoed by the great Vietnam war correspondent David Halberstam, writing in Harper's magazine: 'His reputation was for ruthlessness, yet in 1968 there seemed no major political figure whose image so contrasted with the reality; most politicians seem attractive from a distance but under closer examination they fade ... Robert Kennedy was different. Under closer inspection, he was far more winning than most ...'

This mirrored exactly my own impression of the man as I began to cover his campaign and I saw others – experienced, hard-nosed political writers of every stripe – go through a similar conversion. Within days of joining him on the campaign trail, they were scratching their heads, challenging their original assumptions and muttering, "This guy's different."

And he was. As we shall see.

To take you through the course of events in some kind of sequence, let me backtrack to 30th November 1967, the day Eugene McCarthy declared that he was going to challenge President Johnson for their party's nomination. McCarthy was an elegant, silver haired man who, of course, had no connection to the notorious Joe McCarthy, the Senator who conducted the odious Communist witch hunt hearings and for whom a young Bobby Kennedy had once worked. Eugene McCarthy had spent many years in Congress and then the Senate for Minnesota and was, mostly, a liberally-minded Democrat who came out early against the Vietnam war.

By declaring his candidacy, McCarthy threw Kennedy's mind into even greater turmoil. Bobby had agonised over whether to speak out against LBJ's war policies for fear of causing even more disruption within the Democratic party. But if that was the primary motivation for his hesitation, it was not the only one. His brother's assassination played on his mind and, generally, he wondered if he would eat up political capital by charging into a race that would be doomed to failure against as powerful a sitting President as Lyndon Johnson.

He was surprised by McCarthy's move. A few weeks before he had told Jack Newfield, "I don't believe he'll run. He is not that sort of fellow. And if he does run, it will only be to top up his lecture fees."

Despite both being Irish Catholics, Kennedy and McCarthy had little else in common. After a few weeks of seeing him fleetingly at campaign rallies and following what he had to say, I found McCarthy to be somewhat superior and supercilious, a man who seemed to enjoy the limelight in as much as it would enable him to expound his theories on the war and other matters. I thought he had entered the race as an intellectual exercise and had no more real expectation of winning the nomination than any other detached observer of the political scene.

At any rate, it was clear Kennedy didn't like him and that only increased Bobby's feeling of frustration and helplessness. He knew his legions of supporters were desperate for him to run just as his numerous detractors were hoping he wouldn't. Groups of advisers held meeting after meeting. Ted Sorensen, the man who had crafted JFK's speeches, Pierre Salinger who had been JFK's Press Secretary, and Ted Kennedy himself were all against him running. They felt he could not win in the primaries or even change the Vietnam policy and that any failure of a Kennedy would only help the cause of Richard Nixon, who was almost certain to win the Republican nomination.

Richard Goodwin, another of the Boston mafia under JFK, was not so sure but was unwilling to counsel against Ted Kennedy. However Arthur Schlesinger had started to change his mind in early November and wrote Bobby a private memo. In part it read: "I have feared that your candidacy would result in making Nixon President. I am now having second thoughts about this argument ... I think that events are moving faster than one could have supposed three months ago and that events could become highly fluid in another three months. I think you could beat LBJ in the primaries and that you have unexpected reserves of strength in the non-primary states."

All these assumptions were based, of course, on LBJ accepting a second term. For most people it was inconceivable that he wouldn't. For reasons I cannot remember I picked up the faint whiff of a different wind. On 19th December, I wrote a piece about the surprise decision of Bill Moyers to step down as President Johnson's Press Secretary. That was his official title and it was a role Moyers performed impressively. But this young bespectacled Baptist minister, who went on to use his profound intellect and humanitarian instincts during a long television career at PBS, was more than just a press secretary to LBJ. As I wrote in the Evening News, he was as much of a 'son' to the loud-mouthed but emotional Texan as Bobby had been a brother to Jack.

Commentating on the fact that one columnist who had travelled with LBJ (and Moyers) to China wrote that 'only once did Moyers lie which is a fantastic average for a government press agent ...' I finished my Evening News piece like this:

'Now Moyers will soon be gone and the rickety bridge which spans that gap of credibility (between LBJ and his public) will sway unguarded. Next year, a nation disillusioned by false promises over an insoluble war may bring it crashing down.

'But then again, it is the 1968 election which poses another question – the mystery of why Moyers chose this moment to leave. Was it because he knew that he would not be wanted in two years' time for the simple reason that Johnson himself will not be running?'

I left the question unanswered but it turned out to be quite prescient. Moyers may well not have known LBJ's intentions and could have decided to leave for matters concerning his own conscience. Recently I have heard it said that Moyers, who came from a modest background and had a young family to support, needed to secure his future and felt unable to turn down an offer to become publisher of the well-respected Long Island publication, Newsday. Despite the deep-seated animosity which existed between the President and the Senator from New York, Moyers had maintained an excellent relationship with Bobby Kennedy and, indeed, went on to advise him on many matters the months that followed.

I continued to cover a wide variety of stories for my paper as the fateful year of 1968 unfolded, a year of seismic drama and tragedy that would alter the way peoples and nations viewed each other. In the spring, there would be student riots in Paris and Russian tanks in Prague while, in America, the question of who would run for the highest office in the land continued to dominate the news and grab the attention of people far removed from the incestuous little world of Washington DC.

Much of it centred on Robert Kennedy. Would he or would he not throw his hat into the ring? He had already stirred up real hatred amongst disappointed followers or those who hated him anyway by allowing smooth Mr McCarthy to have the field to himself as an opponent of the President and 'his' war. And still the Senator and his advisers, who numbered amongst them the best brains in America, dithered. The reluctance was surprising given the collapse of the President's popularity after the devastating Tet offensive in January, which had blown apart any notion that the United States was winning the war in Vietnam.

But slowly Kennedy began to realise that he could not live with himself if he stayed out. Being a Kennedy demanded participation. The family was not into spectator sports. The extent to which he agonised and fretted is laid out in intimate detail by Jack Newfield who was given extraordinary access to the Senator during the days building up to the announcement.

And he was not the only one. The way in which many American politicians admit journalists into their inner sanctums is something few in Europe would countenance and Kennedy provided an example one evening by inviting not only Newfield, who had become a closer friend than most, but also Roger Mudd, a famous face from CBS television, and Sylvia Wright of Life Magazine to dinner at his home in MacLean, Virginia. And not any old dinner, but one pre-arranged for 25 small-town editors who were in Washington for a convention. Despite the imminent declaration to run, there was no thought of putting them off.

Ethel, the wife who could handle any situation, no matter how strange or awkward, had them sitting at tables dotted around the large dining area. Kennedy was at an adjacent table to Newfield who was talking about legalising marijuana to Mrs Renee Carpenter, the wife of astronaut Scott Carpenter. The Senator overheard the conversation and scribbled a note which read: 'Can't you talk about something else? You're going to cost me the election before its starts!' He signed it 'Timothy Leary'.

So the sense of humour had survived but, as Newfield reveals in the following passage from his book, Kennedy was far from at ease with himself.

'Mrs Wright and myself were the last to leave. It was after midnight and very cold. Kennedy walked us out onto his porch; he was shivering and his hands were jammed into his suit pockets in a pose reminiscent of John Kennedy.

'"You think I have a right to run, don't you? Tell me if you think I am being unfair."

'We said no, and he continued his monologue, looking like a parody of all the ruthless cartoons of himself.

'"I've thought about it. I want to do the right thing. I want to do what will help end the war, and what will be best for the country. If others can run, why can't I run, too?"

'It was a remarkable tableau. Kennedy silhouetted by the house lights, the wind blowing his hair. His teeth chattering, his face a mask of pleading, begging to be reassured. I reminded Kennedy that I had favoured his running since last September and that I still preferred him to McCarthy. He nodded and, without responding, went back into the house.'

The next morning, Friday March 15th, 1968 Robert F. Kennedy declared that he would become a candidate for the presidency of the United States. And signed his own death warrant.

On March 31st I was invited to the theatre by some friends. My first reaction was to accept, even though I knew that President Johnson had scheduled a national television address for that evening at 9.00. I could be back in the office, just a couple of blocks away, by 10.00 and pick up everything I needed from the wires and late TV bulletins, right? The speech would be about Vietnam and some slight deviation from current policy. Nothing too sensational surely. Right? After some contemplation, my better instincts kicked in and I told my friends I couldn't make it. A quick bite to eat across the road and a cup of coffee from our machine in a deserted office (Jeffrey and the Daily Mail gang had gone home as it was out of their edition time) and nothing quite as stimulating as a Broadway play to look forward to.

I was beginning to regret my decision as LBJ droned on. He did make a major concession to the idea of luring Hanoi to the table for peace talks by halting the bombing of North Vietnam, which was certainly newsworthy, and I consoled myself that this would make a good front page piece for the first edition.

Then, after almost 40 minutes, Lyndon Johnson said this: "I shall not seek – and I will not accept – the nomination of my party for another term as your President."

That cleared the front page. Holy Cow, as they say in Texas. As I wrote: 'With these words, Lyndon Baines Johnson delivered one of the most shattering and totally unexpected statements in the history of American politics.'

It was, I suggested, the ultimate grand gesture. Johnson had been viewed by his enemies as a supremely ambitious and self-serving leader but, as I wrote: 'If, as one must assume, LBJ means what he says, he will have proved himself capable of making the politician's ultimate sacrifice.'

Obviously it was not a decision he came to lightly and he had, in fact, been thinking of it for some time, even to the extent of having the words he had just uttered waiting in his pocket when he made his State of the Union address to Congress back on January 17. But he never read them.

Now, having had his devoted wife Lady Bird help him with the wording, Johnson had made his feelings public and there was every reason to believe that his motivation was altruistic as well as offering him a way out of the terrible impasse on Vietnam that was tearing the country apart.

After the speech, Lady Bird Johnson told reporters, "We have done a lot. There is a lot left to be done in the remaining months. Maybe this is the only way to get it done."

Unhappily for the millions of Vietnamese who would be killed under American bombs and the American and South Vietnam soldiers who would sacrifice their lives in the coming years, LBJ's sacrifice was not enough. There was probably only one man on earth who could have shortened the suffering and he was not going to be allowed to live.

Bobby Kennedy heard of Johnson's decision at 9.50 pm, according to Newfield, as his plane landed at JFK International after a campaign trip to Phoenix. As soon as the doors opened, Dall Forsythe, a young member of Kennedy's New York staff and the son of actor John Forsythe, burst into the cabin, shouting, "The President withdrew; the President withdrew."

Kennedy, half out of his seat, promptly sat down again, trying to digest the news and what it meant to him, his campaign and to the country. His team were elated but Bobby quickly became aware, as he sat silent and brooding on the way into Manhattan, that the news had delivered him a two-edged sword. Obviously, at first glance, Johnson's elimination from the race had hugely enhanced his chances of getting the nomination. And yet … LBJ's withdrawal deprived him of his two great weapons – the war and the President's record. And from his own perspective it made the campaign simply a campaign rather than an emotional crusade. It made Johnson a figure of sympathy and enabled the McCarthy supporters to remain loyal to their man without the feeling that, in order to get Bobby elected, they might have to switch horses.

There was much to ponder and, by the time Kennedy got back to his apartment at 870 UN Plaza, almost the entire team were assembled – figures that would, and had, played such a huge part in the saga of JFK's Presidency and RFK's search for it. Sorensen, Schlesinger, Fred Dutton, Frank Mankiewicz, speech writer Adam Walinsky, Jeff Greenfield, Carter Burden, Bobby's personal secretary Angie Novello and Donald Dell, who had been asked by Kennedy to escort Ethel out of the plane's rear exit, under the wing and away from the seething mass of media waiting for the candidate to appear.

"Ethel hated flying," Dell told me. "She was a nervous wreck most of the time which made her determination to go everywhere Bobby went all the more laudable. So I tried to shield her from the bedlam that was going on as much as possible."

With everyone gathered at the apartment, with phone calls being made to Democratic leaders all over the country, Ethel decided she, as much as anyone, needed a Scotch and promptly produced a bottle. She was the dream wife who instinctively came up with what was needed at any given moment but, for all the love she lavished on those close to her, she was also as tough as nails. Passing the drinks, she said, referring to her husband's arch-enemy, "Well, he never deserved to be President anyway."

There never was, and never would be, any warmth of feeling between the Kennedys and Lyndon Johnson.

The next morning was April 1st but LBJ didn't have that kind of sense of humour. He had meant what he had said and the American political landscape was never the same again.

With the likelihood of a second Kennedy in the White House now greatly enhanced, I tried to reveal a little of the man to my Evening News readers, excerpts of which ran like this:

'He was the tough little brother who wielded the machete; hacking his way through the political landscape so that John F. Kennedy could march towards the New Frontier relatively unscathed. It was a role for which Bobby was eminently suited.

'But now, as his chances his of attaining the high office his brother held with such grace grow day by day, it must be asked: "How suited is Robert Kennedy for the responsibilities of the Presidency?"

'From a practical standpoint his three years' experience as the president's closest adviser make him more than adequately qualified for the job … But Bobby would be a different type of President from his brother simply because he is a different type of person. Not that different, of course, because both are products of a closely-knit family brought up to adhere to the same rules and the same beliefs. But, while both wielded iron fists, Jack concealed his in a velvet glove while Bobby's knuckles glint, bare.

'The late President used a beguiling charm to get his way – Bobby commands respect through the driving, and often frightening, force of his personality.

'JFK absorbed knowledge from the written page and, although Bobby reads at an alarming pace, he prefers to listen and observe. Yet, the differences between Bobby and his dead brother have been narrowed by the very fact of

Jack's death. The loss of his brother left an indelible scar on Robert Kennedy. Never, previously, an introspective man, the tragedy turned him inward, and for months he brooded in despair. The process added new dimensions to his character, not the least of which was a tolerance and an understanding that had not been in evidence before.

'Yet for such an allegedly cold and ruthless man, Kennedy enjoys the complete and unswerving loyalty of his staff. Personally, I know of three people who have thrown up secure and lucrative jobs in the past two weeks to join the crusade. "He's just an inspiring man to work for," one of them said.

'Should he reach the White House, Bobby will not be a second JFK. But in his own differing way, he could be an inspiring president.'

We were never to know. That piece appeared one day before the nation was thrown into greater turmoil by the assassination of Martin Luther King, with the result that Kennedy found himself thrown into an even harsher spotlight. As we have seen, his calming speech in Indianapolis did much to reveal a side of his character few people at the time believed he had. Bobby had faced his first crisis as a Presidential candidate and had enhanced his frequently battered reputation. Every day from now on would be a disorientating whirl of take offs and landings; of crowds and handshakes and speeches, demanding emotional and physical strength of a type few people are asked to experience. It required diligent staff work, too, down to the last simple detail like, "Remember, this is Fort Wayne, Indiana," as the candidate stepped from the plane. Thirty minutes before it had been South Bend; in another hour, it would be Indianapolis. I have no knowledge of Kennedy having done so but I am sure more than a few candidates have whispered to a staffer, "Where the hell am I?"

I tested the water first of all with Richard Nixon. After applying through the Nixon Campaign Headquarters, I was accredited for a trip to Massachusetts which meant I could fly on the campaign plane – an Electra Turbo Prop rented from Eastern Airlines. I found it all very regimented. We were under orders from Ron Zeigler, the young Press Secretary whose dark good looks did not translate into a welcoming personality. Smooth, sleek and just slightly creepy, I thought. There were some Washington reporters who were known to drink with him but most did so out of duty. Zeigler was the barrier to the candidate and he was an effective one.

The actual design of the plane's interior offered physical evidence of Nixon's attitude towards the press. A wooden door separated the two cabins. And, while I was on board, it never opened. As we stopped in various small towns, Nixon appeared at the top of the steps at the front of the plane; addressed the relatively small crowds that had been allowed to gather on the tarmac; went through his jerky and completely uncoordinated arm movements, and with a smile smeared across his face, disappeared back inside the aircraft.

You did not have to be a liberal to find Richard Nixon a less than appealing personality. He had risen fast as a young politician to become Governor of his home state of California and then, on being defeated when running for re-election, came out with his famous quote, directed with a cynical smile at the media: "You won't have Dick Nixon to kick around anymore."

Most observers felt that the terse remark would stand as his political epitaph. But, recognising a sharp intellect, Dwight Eisenhower chose him as his running mate in 1952 and Tricky Dicky, as he became known, found himself Vice President of the United States.

A famous, sweaty television debate, which had left him looking dishevelled and uncomfortable alongside the elegant John Kennedy, ruined his chances of reaching the White House in 1960 but now, after the all the tragedies, false hopes and ever-widening war in Vietnam that the following eight years had brought, Nixon realised the door was open for him to try again.

Nelson Rockefeller, a back-slapping liberally-inclined millionaire and an actor called Ronald Reagan who was also using the Governorship of California as a launch pad, were his main rivals but Nixon, until paranoia overcame him in his last years as President, was a ruthlessly clever and adroit politician and it did not take him long to leave them behind in the primaries.

Towards the end of April, I switched candidates and joined up with the Kennedy campaign. He was already running behind because McCarthy had won a stunning victory over President Johnson (before LBJ decided to pull out of the race) in the New Hampshire Primary and was gathering support across the country. We were headed out of New York for Indiana where Kennedy would pit himself against McCarthy for the first time. It was do or die stuff and I expected some serious politicking. Yet when I put my head through the door of Bobby's Electra Turbo Prop – this one rented from American Airlines – I blinked. There seemed to be a party going on. An attractive American stewardess thrust a glass of Scotch into my hand and as I grabbed a vacant seat, I caught sight of a small figure moving up the aisle just ahead, white shirt sleeves rolled back, the inevitable Scotch in his hand, chatting and laughing with reporters. There was no door on Bobby Kennedy's plane.

The contrast was almost too much to take in. Here was a man on a mission who was clearly at ease in the midst of supporters and critics alike and was happy to take them along for the ride. And what a ride. For the next three days we were up and down all over the state of Indiana, roaring into towns like Richmond and Evansville in the south to Gary in the industrial north; crowds growing, clamouring; reacting to a new message of hope and determination and daring.

And Bobby Kennedy dared. He dared to say things no normal politician would have said while trying to garner votes, sometimes telling people things to their face that they did not want to hear.

One of the most remarkable speeches I have ever heard from a politician took place at the Indiana University Medical Center. I was sitting off to the side and immediately noticed what colleagues had told me; underneath the lectern Kennedy's hands shook. After I listened to what he had to say I was not surprised.

There were 500 medical students seated in the main body of the hall but it was a voice from the balcony that shouted out, "We want Kennedy!"

It was one of the hospital's black employees and the retort was swift. "No we don't," some white, middle class students shouted back. So the scene was set. Kennedy had just been reminded of who he was talking to and, of course, he was prepared for it because Indiana was a conservative state. In 1960 Nixon had carried the state against John Kennedy by a margin of 225,000 votes. In the 1964 Presidential primary, George Wallace, the right swing extremist of whom more later, had polled almost a third of the votes.

So Kennedy had no illusions but he was intent on saying what he had to say. He launched into the scandal that was and, until Barack Obama intervened, remained the American Health Care system. The discussion was heated from the start as Kennedy began taking questions from the floor.

The students wanted to know why Social Security benefits should be increased for the elderly; what was the point of running health services in the slums when everyone knew Negroes didn't make use of those facilities anyway and, finally, "Where are we going to get the money to pay for all these programmes you are proposing?"

"From you!" Kennedy snapped back. He was angry and his venom brought gasps from his audience. Was he crazy? Was this man asking for our vote and, at the same time, asking us to pay for poor people's health care? That's exactly what he was asking and now he was in full stride, all the pre-planned notions of how to campaign in Indiana thrown to the wind. He was saying it like he felt it, deep in his soul, and leaving the lectern, he strode forward to within inches of the first row of seats and continued:

"Let me say something about the tone of these questions. I look around the room and I don't see many black faces who will become doctors ... Part of a civilised society is to let people go to medical school who come from the ghettoes. I don't see many people here who come from the slums or off the Indian reservations. You are the privileged ones here. It's easy for you to sit back and say it's the fault of the Federal Government. But it's our responsibility, too. It's our society, not just our government that spends twice as much on pets as on the poverty program. It's the poor who carry the major burden of the struggle in Vietnam. You sit here as white medical students while black people carry the burden of fighting in Vietnam ..."

Hisses and boos broke out and for a split second I thought Kennedy was in danger. But he simply glared back, returned to the lectern and brought proceedings to a close. He knew he hadn't won any votes but he had made his point and made them think.

Nor did he let up. It was off to the city of Valparaiso where he was heckled by McCarthy supporters as well as conservatives when he spoke at the university. But people were starting to listen because the sincerity and honesty shone through as he kept asking the tough questions. "How many of you spend time over the summer vacations in a black ghetto or on Indian reservations? Instead of asking what the Federal Government is doing about starving children, I say what is your responsibility? What are you doing about it? As Camus once said, 'Perhaps we cannot prevent this world from being a world in which children are tortured. But we can reduce the number of tortured children'. And if you don't help us who else in the world can help us do this?"

These were difficult questions to answer but the message was getting across. Hatred of Kennedy was still rampant amongst the right wing and also unforgiving McCarthy supporters but it was clear that he was forming an unlikely alliance between black voters and blue collar workers – the working class whites who, otherwise, would be inclined to lean towards the bullying dogmatism of a George Wallace who had become hugely popular in southern states.

Kennedy, the rich liberal from New England, was starting to feel greater admiration for the working man he discovered in the poorer parts of Indiana than with his own kind back east. He was scathing about them when he talked to Jack Newfield. "I just feel those New York liberals are sick," he said. "They spend their time worrying about not being invited to the right parties or seeing their psychiatrists. I personally prefer many of the poor white people I have met here. They are tough, and honest, and if you help them, they remember it. They are not fickle."

He could look those people in the eye and they were starting to understand him. But it was a hard slog; a fifteen-hour-day slog and it was nearing midnight as we were preparing to take off from some city or other when, unannounced, the candidate slid into the seat next to mine, grappled for his seat belt as he handed the empty glass of Scotch to the flight attendant and began to talk.

"It's an endurance test," he said. "A physical one for us and a mental one for the people. Frankly, I don't know how they put up with it for eight months. They'll be sick of the sight of us by November."

The fact that his hands were raw and scratched and his lip large from having collided with the upraised arms of a well-wisher somewhere along the way as the crowds following the motorcades grew didn't seem to bother him. Bobby Kennedy seemed relaxed and ready to chat. I barely had to ask a question.

"Always, I get asked the same questions," he smiled. "Vietnam, the race problem, the cities – and one can only give the same answers. But it's the system we have and, if a candidate is sensible, he can learn a lot from coming into such close contact with the people."

As we had boarded the plane, some of those people included a group of young McCarthy supporters who were waiting for their flight. Kennedy had stopped and talked to them. Taken slightly off guard at being confronted by the man they were campaigning against, they stated their case about his being late coming out against the war; late declaring his candidacy and all the other things that had made Eugene McCarthy an early favourite to beat both Kennedy and the Indiana Governor Roger Branigin in the Primary. Kennedy listened and told them he admired their fervour.

"I do," he said as we continued our chat. "I understand completely why they went for McCarthy. They're young and eager and idealistic. I have nothing but admiration for them. But, you know, it's frustrating because, in the long run, I can do so much more for them."

But there was to be no long run. It was a sentence that came back to haunt me a few weeks later, because what Robert Kennedy had said to me was something that was clear by then to anyone who understood American politics. McCarthy was never going to become President. Once it came down to the basics of who was electable, there was only going to be one winner. Vice President Hubert Humphrey might have been the front runner for the nomination; McCarthy might have been a contender up to a point; but Kennedys won elections. Bobby was becoming certain that the unusual alliance he was forming between blacks and poor whites, as well as the Eastern liberals who would come round in the fullness of time, would give him an excellent chance of succeeding his brother as President of the United States. But time was not full, it was draining away and soon it would be empty. As the plane started its descent into Indianapolis where another Holiday Inn awaited us, Robert Kennedy was not allowing himself to think about the chances of having his life cut short and was full of optimism for what he could do for his country.

"In the long run, I can do so much more for them." What a tragedy that he never could.

After a few days, I was ready to fly back to New York and leave the candidate to his backbreaking schedule that included a gruelling nine-hour motorcade through northern Indiana cities. The only respite came with post-midnight suppers in all night diners and pick-up games of touch football on the lawns on Holiday Inns with staffers and reporters. In one, Richard Harwood, a Washington reporter who had been a severe critic of Kennedy before he joined the campaign, almost came to blows with Bobby after being fouled by the little guy who was always looking for an edge to compensate for lack of size and talent. Harwood, a Marine and a fine athlete, called Kennedy 'a dirty player' and the feud might have continued had not Bobby invited Harwood to spend the night in his private suite and talk late into the night. By the time the campaign moved out to California, Harwood's opinion had changed to such an extent that he asked to be re-assigned because he had come to like Bobby so much that he didn't want to be accused of bias.

Before I left, I witnessed another moment that will linger in my memory for ever. We had just paid a visit to the museum home of the famous Indiana poet James Whitcomb Riley and, as the next stop was a relatively short distance away near downtown Indianapolis, we set off on foot, Kennedy leading the way with some staffers, including the ebullient PR man Dick Tuck, all followed by a press corps of about 25 people. After a couple of blocks we came to a kindergarten playground, surrounded by wire fencing. Instinctively, Kennedy stopped and called over one of the women in charge to ask her about the place. After a few minutes' conversation, he asked if he could go in. So the gate was opened and in we trooped.

The kids were aged from about three to five. Imagine looking up at this invasion from their height. A mass of adults, some with cameras. It must have been daunting but amongst any group of kids there are always a bunch whose curiosity will overcome any apprehension and so, indeed, a few came towards us. And they all gravitated straight to Bobby. Inevitably, he picked one up while others clung to his trousers. And he started to talk to them. Not in a jokey, let's-take-a-picture sort of way but quietly, almost solemnly, like a father who had something serious to say.

And then something very strange happened, something I have never witnessed before or since. The press pack backed off. No one told us to. We just did. As we agreed amongst ourselves later, we just felt we were intruding on a private conversation. There was no other explanation. "That was the damnedest thing," someone said. And so it was.

I had long known the saying 'you can't fool animals or little children' and now I had seen the proof. The kids were too young to pick out a famous face they might possibly have seen on TV from a crowd this size. But they had been drawn straight to Bobby Kennedy as if guided by some magnetic power. They listened to him for a few minutes and kissed him and Bobby thanked the ladies and we left. It was the sort of moment that made you a believer.

Less prosaically, the cold, hard statistics of Primary voting offered more proof of the effect Robert Kennedy was having on the grown-ups. On the evening of May 7th, the candidate was in the shower at the Holiday Inn when the results started coming in. The atmosphere was tense amongst staffers like Walinsky, Dutton, Greenfield and Goodwin who had escaped from the dingy Sheraton-Lincoln campaign headquarters downtown to come and join their man, knowing that a poor showing vis-à-vis McCarthy would signal the end of the road.

But, as Bobby emerged dripping wet, wrapped in towels, Larry O'Brien, the old JFK hand, came in with the first precinct returns. They looked good. A poor, Polish district in Gary had Kennedy on 241, McCarthy 86 and Branigin, the Governor who was thought to be running as a stalking horse for Hubert Humphrey who had declared too late to enter Indiana, had 62.

In an all-black district in Gary, Kennedy was leaving everybody behind. He had 697 votes to McCarthy's 52 and Branigin's 16.

"Don't you just wish everyone was black?" Ethel exclaimed and everyone laughed. Maybe it was going to be OK. And it was. By 10.00 pm the result was clear. Kennedy had won the Indiana Primary with 42% of the vote to Branigin's 31% and McCarthy's 27%.

And just to confirm the potency of Robert Kennedy's candidacy, in the result from the District of Columbia where a Primary was also being held, Kennedy had left Humphrey trailing, winning 62.5% of the vote to the Vice President's 37.5%.

There was champagne and scrambled eggs on the flight back to New York next morning but within hours Kennedy was off again, this time to the sparsely-populated wheat fields of Nebraska, hunting down crowds by car and train. He had seen what was possible now, this emerging coalition of blacks and poor whites and it re-invigorated him. Although Newfield found him private and pre-occupied most of the time, he allowed the humorous side of his nature to shine through at odds moments.

In Bellvue, Nebraska, a man started heckling him during a speech at a shopping centre. The police moved in and arrested him, despite Kennedy's protestations. When the police refused to let the man go, Bobby raised a laugh and a round of applause when he said, "I promise that if I'm elected President of the United States, one of the first things I'm going to do is get you out of jail."

I didn't join up with the campaign until a couple of weeks later in California where he was swamped by crowds in the black Los Angeles ghetto of Watts and then flew south for another speech in a hall near San Diego Airport. At every stop, the media piled into a bus straight from the plane, listened to the speech and then had to rush back to the bus. Bobby soon came to realise that timing was crucial for everyone and sometimes it was difficult for the media to keep up when he was whisked out and bustled straight into his car by Rosie Greer, the former grid-iron football star, or one of his other minders. So he made a pact with us. He would save one of his favourite sayings, "Some people see things as they are and ask why? I see things that never were and ask, 'Why not?'" until right at the end of his speech and he promised to say nothing newsworthy afterwards.

So as he soon as he started, "Some people …" we all made a mad dash for the exit, often to the surprise of the unsuspecting audience. And, of course, he always kept his word. It wasn't like that on the Nixon campaign.

Despite the fatigue and the fervour and seriousness of what everyone was trying to accomplish, there was always a moment or two of silly humour to lighten up the day. On that occasion at San Diego Airport, Connie Chung, then a very attractive young reporter who would go on to the dizzy heights of anchor for the CBS Evening News, got left behind as we were leaving the meeting and she had to hitch a ride in a staff car. We were all crowded around the door of the plane when she emerged from the hangar in her mini-skirt and high heeled shoes and began a 200-yard sprint towards us, clutching her microphone and notebooks. Inevitably the skirt rose higher the faster she ran and, just as inevitably because boys will be boys, we cheered her on with ribald comments. Eager hands helped her up the steps and she was only blushing a little bit.

I had skipped Nebraska where Kennedy had won 51% of the vote to McCarthy's 31% but Oregon was going to be a tougher nut to crack. Oregon's population was only 1% black, 10% Catholic and was virtually devoid of Mexicans and Eastern European blue collar workers. So Bobby's message fell on deaf ears. When he said he wanted to 'turn America around' Oregonians thought, "Why?" He said he was good at helping people with problems but most people in this relatively affluent state didn't really have any.

Right from the start, Kennedy had refused to debate McCarthy on television because he knew the Senator was a smooth talker and, in any case, he felt he didn't have to. But as the obvious problems of Oregon loomed, some staffers started to urge him to change his mind. Adam Walinsky was so adamant about it that Kennedy became irritated and refused to listen. It proved to be a serious mistake.

Robert Kennedy became the first Kennedy in history to lose an election when, on May 28th, McCarthy polled 44.7% of the vote in Oregon to RFK's 38.8%. The defeat hurt but Bobby accepted it with good grace. "I lost," he said. "I'm not one of those who think coming in second or third is winning." The realism with which he accepted his new stature as a candidate struck me forcibly at the time. Suddenly, he accepted an invitation to debate McCarthy. His reasoning was stunningly honest. "I'm not the same candidate I was before Oregon and I can't claim that I am."

He readily accepted that the mistakes had been his own and apologised to his staff. Putting an arm around David Borden, his chief student organiser in Oregon, he said, "I'm sorry I let you down."

The much-hyped debate on June 1st turned out to be a lacklustre affair with neither candidate excelling themselves, although McCarthy did finish stronger when answering the final question of why each candidate thought they were qualified to be President. He was eloquent while Kennedy mumbled through a not very coherent answer. The excuse he offered Jack Newfield afterwards was amazing. "You won't believe it," Bobby grinned. "But I was day dreaming. I thought the program was over and I was trying to decide in my mind where to take Ethel for dinner when they asked that last question. I was lucky I didn't answer Joe DiMaggio's."

The fact was, Kennedy was exhausted. In California, his supporters had responded to his defeat in Oregon by turning out in ever greater numbers, grabbing at him; trying to jump on to the motorcade, tearing at his shirt; snatching his cuff links. It must have been a nightmare for Rosie Greer and Rafer Johnson, his big black football star minders who had to mix muscle with common sense while trying to keep the crowds at bay.

It was scary at times. Never more so than when his open convertible was threading its way through the packed, narrow streets of Chinatown in San Francisco. A fire cracker went off really close to the car and then five more. Most people cringed, including Ethel, but Bobby didn't flinch and merely asked a reporter, trotting alongside, to climb in and hold Ethel's hand. I wasn't there but colleagues told me that everyone's mind flashed back to Dallas. Bobby was riding in an open convertible because his brother had been killed in a convertible. He wasn't going to cower.

The extent of the toll the campaign was taking on Kennedy became apparent when he flew down to San Diego one more time on the eve of polling day and gave a barely coherent speech at the El Cortez Hotel, packed to the rafters by supporters of the great Mexican farm workers' union leader Cesar Chavez, whom Bobby had befriended. Kennedy staggered off stage and promptly sat down, head in his hands. He complained of feeling dizzy and Rafer Johnson and Bill Barry stood guard on the door of Men's Room while Ethel and Fred Dutton went in to attend to him. He didn't throw up and, after some water, seemed to revive, heading back out to give another speech.

That night, Kennedy accepted the invitation of John Frankenheimer to stay with Ethel and six of his children at the film director's Malibu home. He swam there next morning after a solid night's sleep and arrived at his suite in the Ambassador Hotel on Wilshire Boulevard early that evening. Newfield recounts that soon after Kennedy stuck his head round the door of room 516, across the corridor from his suite where reporters and staff had gathered, and said, "Do you want to hear about the Indians?" He was referring to the South Dakota Primary where polling had been going on that day, too. It transpired that an Indian precinct had given him 878 votes to 9 for the Humphrey-Johnson slate and 2 for McCarthy. In all, Kennedy would claim 50% of the vote in the state in which Hubert Humphrey was born.

As the California results started coming in at 10.30 pm, it was clear that Los Angeles, with its vast black and Mexican population, was adding the final touches to a state-wide Kennedy victory. Kennedy, upbeat and chirpy, started doing television interviews with Sandy Vanocur of NBC and Roger Mudd of CBS, both good friends. He was relaxed with both of them but winced when Mudd asked if he felt if any delegates leaning towards Humphrey were squeezable or solid.

"I don't like either of the expressions," he replied but added that he would make an effort with them as he looked forward to more difficult battles in Illinois and New York. Soon he would be heading downstairs to give his acceptance speech and, after he had thanked, "My dog Freckles and – I'm not doing this in any order of importance – my wife Ethel ..." reporters were told that the celebration party would soon be starting at The Factory, which was LA's hip discotheque at that time.

I was on the other side of the country, busily typing up my report on the California results at my apartment on East 57th Street. I had a telex machine not far from the bed but I generally preferred to dictate to one of our expert copy-takers in Fleet Street who came on duty at 5.30 am London time. I checked the latest polling results and turned on WINS, the 24-hour New York radio station which had reporters live in Los Angeles interviewing anyone they could get their hands on. I heard Kennedy talk, added a couple of paragraphs and dictated the piece.

"That should be it," I told my Foreign Editor Fred Colbert. "Let me know if you want anything else."

It was just after 1.00 am and I had my tooth brush in my hand when something odd started happening with the radio coverage from LA. I don't know why I hadn't turned it off but I hadn't and now there were voices shouting and sounds of mayhem.

Eventually, the screams were becoming intelligible. "He's been shot; he's been shot; someone shot Bobby Kennedy!"

I leapt for the phone and yelled at the startled sub-editor who came on the line. Absurdly, I used that old cliché, "Hold the front page! Scrap what I just sent you. They've shot Kennedy. Get me a copy-taker!"

The first ad-libbed story made the 8.00 am edition in London by a matter of minutes and the next two or three hours were spent adding details to the appalling story as it unfolded. In an attempt to avoid the huge crowds in the ballroom of the Ambassador Hotel, Kennedy had been guided through the kitchen and pantry area of the hotel. It was there that a 24-year-old Palestinian called Sirhan Sirhan, facing Kennedy, had pulled out a pistol and fired in the Senator's direction. His first shot missed and hit Paul Schrade, a long-time friend of Bobby's, in the forehead. Schrade had been walking six feet behind him. He then fired again before the maître d' Karl Uecker, who had led Kennedy into the pantry, and another waiter, grabbed him and pinned his arms while Sirhan managed to get off another five or six shots from his Iver Johnson Cadet pistol, which could fire eight shots. Uecker was immediately assisted by former FBI agent William Barry, Rosie Greer, Rafer Johnson and George Plimpton who were in close attendance. Meanwhile, Ethel had rushed to her husband's side and was cradling his head as blood spread across the pantry floor. Before he lost consciousness, Bobby said, "Is everyone all right?"

This is a fuller account of what actually happened than I had been able to piece together from the radio and wire stories, but I filed what I could and by 5.00 am in New York, it was time for me to catch a cab to Kennedy Airport – the name, at that moment, being an irony in itself --and get the first flight to Los Angeles. Kennedy had been taken to the Good Samaritan Hospital and none of the news we were receiving was good. I checked into the Beverly Hills Hotel – then affordable on a newspaperman's budget – and started making some phone calls. When I went down to the Polo Lounge for a drink, I ran into Gavin Young of the Observer, a tall urbane Englishman and a bit of a wanderer at heart who had written some wonderful travel books, including *In Search of Conrad*. We had mutual friends in Nik Wheeler and Pamela Bellwood so I had met him before.

Gavin had been invited round to Joshua Logan's house for supper. I had asked Carole Cole, daughter of Nat King Cole whom I had met when she was in a Broadway play, to join me for a drink and Gavin suggested we all go along to the director's house. It was not a night to sit around moping. Logan and his amazing wife Rosalind Russell did their best to be jovial hosts but we were all dreading the news from the hospital and, as my deadline for the early editions approached, I said goodnight and took a taxi to the Good Samaritan.

It was just before 2.00 am on the sixth of June that Frank Mankiewicz emerged to announce what we had all been dreading. His face a white mask of pain, Frank somehow managed to get the words out. "Senator Robert Francis Kennedy died at 1.44 am today, 2/6/1968. With him at the time of his death were his wife Ethel, his sisters-in-law Mrs Steven Smith and Mrs Patricia Lawford, his brother-in-law Steven Smith and his sister-in-law Mrs John F Kennedy." And then he added in a tone of bitter finality, "He was 42 years old."

I walked out into the misty California night and mingled with a small group of people who had been keeping a vigil outside the hospital. An elderly black man turned to me, his eyes full of tears, and said, "He was our last hope, you see. Bobby cared about us. We have no one now."

In his despair and dread of having to announce to death of the man he had served with such flair and good humour, Mankiewicz got the date wrong. He said 2/6/1968. He meant 6/6/1968. Coincidentally, it had been on the sixth of June just 24 years before that the Allied armies had landed in Normandy, taking the first major step to end Hitler's tyranny. One would have hoped that, two decades later, Americans of all races, colours and creeds who fought and died as brothers in arms that day would have been living in greater harmony; that it would have taken more than one Senator to fight for the minority's cause and win their battles.

But shots fired by someone obsessed with a faraway conflict, by someone who had no right to interfere with a great American drama, had cut down a good man and altered the course of history. Or had he? Despite the fact that, as I write, Sirhan Sirhan is still languishing in a Californian jail, long after a less celebrated murderer would have been released, there is considerable doubt as to whether the shots fired from his gun were the shots that hit Bobby Kennedy.

The autopsy showed clearly that all three shots which did strike the Senator entered his back and the rear of his neck below the ear. But Sirhan Sirhan, everyone agrees, was standing in front of Kennedy. As guns don't shoot round corners, he could not have killed him.

There is a great deal of eye-witness evidence concerning a girl in a white polka-dot dress who, the theory goes, was involved in hypnotising Sirhan beforehand and putting him back in a hypnotised state just before the shooting by touching his elbow twice. After examining him, Dr David Brown, a psychologist from Harvard Medical School who spent hours evaluating Sirhan many years later, concluded that Sirhan was very vulnerable to coercive social influence. Dr Brown has been quoted as saying, "Sirhan is one of the most hypnotisable individuals I have ever met." To this day, Sirhan insists he has no memory of having shot Kennedy or even firing a gun.

As recently as February 2016, the case came up again when Sirhan applied for parole and was refused. It had happened more than a dozen times before but, on this occasion, the parole meeting took on a dramatic turn when Paul Schrade, by then 91, turned up to plead on Sirhan's behalf. Apologising profusely for not having come forward before, Schrade insisted that Sirhan could not have killed Kennedy for the reasons I have given – that Sirhan had been in front of Kennedy when he fired and hit Schrade and that Kennedy had been shot in the back. Despite Schrade's emotional appeal, the parole board remained unimpressed and Sirhan is still in jail. There is, obviously, a great deal more to this story and still questions remain unanswered.

But to return to 1968: Obviously everyone wanted to know more about this young Palestinian who had emerged from nowhere to change American history, so I went in search of some details and found myself at a health food store in the nearby city of Pasadena. And this is what I wrote for the Evening News:

'A talk with John Weidner at the health food store he owns in Pasadena revealed a great deal about the nature and motivation of Sirhan Sirhan – the man accused of killing Senator Robert Kennedy.

'Sirhan, called "Sol" by his family and the few friends he had, worked for Wiedner as a delivery boy from September 1967 to March this year. At his desk at the back of his clean, impeccably-kept store, Wiedner told me how he and his wife had tried to befriend Sirhan and help him overcome the intense hatred he felt for Israel and United States.

'Wiedner is Dutch by birth and talks with the precise clarity typical of his race. "I offered Sirhan a job here because I had known his sister before she died and I also have a great regard for his mother who is a warm and wonderful person. Sirhan was always very polite and correct – not the sort of person to tell dirty jokes or anything like that. He was completely trustworthy, too. I would often send him to the bank with a thousand dollars. But I had to be very careful how I spoke to him because he did not like taking orders. He would get very upset when I criticised his work because he was insecure to the extent that he had this feeling of being an underdog. I think he had a longing to be recognised as somebody. Sometimes he would get very argumentative. He liked arguments and would often provoke them. He was an intelligent person but also childish and immature. He finally stopped working for me as a result of a silly misunderstanding. I sent him on an errand and he went to the wrong place first. When I started to tell him off, he told me that he had followed my instructions and that I must be wrong. After accusing me of lying, the conversation turned political and he went off about his hatred of Israel. I tried to instil some forgiveness in his heart. I told him that although I had been in prison and tortured by the Germans during the war, I did not hate the German people. Evidently I did not make my point well enough for he said, 'I would like to be like you but I cannot.' Ironically his hatred of America was based on the injustices dealt out to Negroes and other minorities and he felt that they could only get what they wanted through violence. He condoned riots in the cities."

'So it is clear from John Wiedner's account that Sirhan's blind, pathological hatred of Israel so consumed him that he went out and shot one of the few men in America who was capable of helping the poor. The irony of that is almost too much to bear.'

There was, of course, a great deal we did not know when I wrote that piece no more than 24 hours after Kennedy had died. But the conspiracy theories I have related burst to the fore twenty years later when all the police files relating to the assassination were released for public consumption. The most disturbing revelation was that no less than 2,410 photographs taken by a freelance who was in the pantry had been burned just a few weeks later by the police on 21st August 1968. Paneling and tiles had also been destroyed and the LAPD seemed very keen to close the case as quickly as possible.

At the time, it all seemed strangely immaterial. Robert Kennedy was dead and that was all that mattered. Too many people were grieving to worry about the whys and wherefores.

A couple of weeks later Eugene McCarthy, now running alone against Hubert Humphrey for the Democratic nomination, decided to try and reach out to the bereft Kennedy constituency and hold a rally in the epicentre of Harlem at 125th Street. I went along and was surprised to find a relatively small and muted crowd turn up to hear McCarthy speak. A middle-aged black man was standing on the sidewalk, outside his store, observing the scene.

I asked him why there weren't more people there. "McCarthy's views on race relations aren't that different from Kennedy's," I said. "Why are black people so ambivalent about him?"

"Look into his eyes, man," was the reply. "Look into his eyes."

And with that the man turned and walked back into his shop.

You can't fool the children and you can't fool the poor people. Despite everything his critics said about him, Robert Kennedy cared and it showed and he connected with those who needed him. It is why I remain convinced that he would have ended up as President of the United States had he lived. As we will see, there would have been serious obstacles for him to overcome but none of the other contenders, not McCarthy, not Humphrey and certainly not Nixon had that ability to connect with an electorate who were hungry for someone they could trust and believe in. He had been building a coalition that was unique in American politics and it would have carried him to the White House because he was a unique politician.

Chapter 9
JAMAICA, AUGUSTA AND MEXICO CITY OLYMPICS

Happily, there had been other things to do in the early months of 1968. As a relief from politics I covered a wide variety of stories that took me to Augusta, Georgia for The Masters; Pine Bluff, Arkansas to visit a notorious penitentiary; and Kingston, Jamaica to watch a cricket match. And in November, I could have been in the wrong place at the wrong time had I not been recalled from covering the pre-Olympic student demonstrations in Mexico City. But more of that later.

Let me start with Jamaica. For as a long as I could remember – or to be more precise from the moment I picked up Robert Louis Stevenson's *Treasure Island* – this image of a tropical island had formed in my mind and Harry Belafonte's songs only helped to make it a little more vivid in my imagination. Yes, once I had finally made it to the island of my dreams I did have a little girl in Kingston Town – more than one, if truth be told – and if I left, it hardly mattered because for years I was always going back at every opportunity to enjoy the richness of a very special nation.

Jamaica is special for many reasons but two make it indisputably so. I do not know of another nation that, in the 20th century, created its own music and its own religion. Reggae is purely Jamaican and so is Rastafarianism. Add to that the fact that their sprinters run like the wind; their bowlers bowl FAST, man; their artists create explosions of colour and their women are amongst the most regally beautiful, argumentative and alluring in the world and you have a package that, for me at least, becomes irresistible.

Unhappily, one cannot ignore the other side of the crown coin that the British left behind. Parts of Kingston are seriously dangerous as gangs rule and corruption reigns. Various governments have made faltering attempts to deal with the corruption but it has become endemic and it would take Haile Selassie to appear in person with Bob Marley at his side to change it which, unhappily, can no longer happen.

So one has to take Jamaica for what it is – an infuriatingly dysfunctional country with a charm and a spirit that enables it to muddle through, com-plainin', hollerin', laughin' and lovin' as each gorgeous sunset falls over the Caribbean Sea.

I think it was 1966 that I first set foot in the place and, thankfully, I had a friend to show me around. Richard Russell was, and remains, the most talented tennis player ever to emerge from the Caribbean, so much so that Harry Hopman, the stern and demanding Australian Davis Cup captain, thought it worthwhile to invite Richard down to Sydney to train with his team. The talent was not in doubt but the focus ... well, let's just say that Richard was easily distracted. Aussie girls couldn't keep their hands off him – it wasn't much different back in Jamaica – and he never fulfilled his potential as a player. More's the pity because he was seriously good.

At any rate, in February 1966, Richard suggested I join him for a couple of days in Kingston so that we could attend the Test match between West Indies and England at Sabina Park. I was due a few days off so I eagerly accepted. I had no intention of writing about the match as the Evening News cricket correspondent, a certain E.M. Wellings, was covering the tour. I can't remember whether Nancy or Virginia Burke were working my flight out of New York but they were both Air Jamaica stewardesses at the time and I would meet them soon enough through Richard, along with another friend of his, Maxine Walters, who was a good junior tennis player in Jamaica.

They all deserve chapters to themselves for the huge and loving parts they have played in my life but let me get on with the story of this particular visit. With his sporting contacts, Richard had got us tickets in the Pavilion at Sabina Park, a shrine to the game in Jamaica with its walls adorned with pictures of all the island's great cricketers from the incomparable George Headley to Allan Rae, Alf Valentine, and Collie Smith. Matches against England were always the highlight of any cricket season for the West Indies and, inevitably, the old ground was packed with noisy, but normally good natured, supporters.

But it doesn't take much more than a few sips of rum and a dubious umpir-ing decision to set things off and when England's wicketkeeper Jim Parks had scooped up a low catch which looked as if it might have just touched the ground, all hell broke loose when the umpire gave the batsman out. The verbal abuse of, "Cheat!" and worse was one thing but when the beer and rum bottles started flying in from the boundary, the situation looked as if it was getting out of control.

So the Constabulary, in their wisdom, decided to let off a little tear gas, not necessarily a bad decision had it not been for the fact that their wisdom had not taken into account which way the wind was blowing. And it was blowing straight towards the pavilion. The England captain, Colin Cowdrey, had already taken his players off the field before electing, in an act of alarming bravery, to go back to try and calm the crowd. No good. They weren't interested. So Colin returned to the dressing to discover his team coughing and spluttering with tears running down their cheeks.

Someone yelled out that it was better in the West Indies dressing room, so we all piled in there to discover cricketers grabbing wet towels and hiding under massage tables. Cowdrey, who had taken the full force of it, couldn't speak for about five minutes but Fred Titmus, the chirpy cockney, was still chattering on. "Three London bobbies – that was what we needed," said the little Middlesex off spinner. "They'd have taken care of that lot in no time."

That was a slightly optimistic assessment of what had become quite a problem for the local police but the teargas had done the trick, even at the far end of the ground, and, after about 45 minutes, play was able to resume. By then, of course, my reporter's instincts had kicked in and, realising that Wellings was stuck in the press box, which was situated on the far side of Sabina Park, I thought I might as well get on the phone to London and file a story. I described how the England dressing room had looked like a casualty clearing station and how the great Gary Sobers had sat motionless in a corner of his own dressing room, hunched over his bat, silent and apparently unaffected by the chaos around him. And I quoted the fast bowler David Brown who had told Parks, "It's all your fault, Jim. That'll teach you to take bloody brilliant catches."

It was a nice colour piece, the happy result of being in the right place at the right time, and it went down well with the desk in London. Less so with Mr Wellings. With his lean, unsmiling features, he was not a man to see the funny side of life at the best of times and was, by all accounts, furious at having been scooped by a colleague who wasn't supposed to have been there in the first place.

There was nothing remotely amusing about the story I covered in Pine Bluff, Arkansas. The lurid tale of bodies being dug up in the State Penitentiary came to light when the authorities decided to sack the Superintendent and install Thomas Murton, a qualified penologist who seemed more willing to stare down the 'trusties', a bunch of self-appointed prisoners who had virtually been running the place for several years. The extent to which this was true did not have to be spelled out to Winthrop Rockefeller, the Arkansas Governor, who, incredibly, had not been allowed inside the prison until his own guards had been disarmed by the trusties!

Flying into Little Rock where, years later, I would first set eyes on Rockefeller's successor, a chap called Bill Clinton, was something of an eye opener – a close-up look at the vast expanse of America which lies between the two coasts and, as far as life style and attitude is concerned, doesn't have much in common with either. But Pine Bluff was something else. A 75-mile drive through wheat fields and farmlands, it seemed to be situated in the middle of nowhere and as for Cummins State Prison Farm, to give the place its official title, well, one needed to pluck up a little courage just to make a visit.

Happily Superintendent Murton appeared to be a civilised, welcoming sort of fellow who quickly explained the problem. "This place has had bad times," he said. "Brutal, inhuman things have happened here."

Like torture and executions. A few months previously, evidence of what had gone on started appearing when some soggy turf at the bottom of a field within the grounds had started caving in, revealing skeletons encased in cheap coffins. "Going back to 1900, we have had 5,000 escapees from this establishment and all but 213 have been accounted for," Murton said. "It's possible some of those 213 were able to make good their escape but it's also possible that many of them are lying right here."

Murton was not only brave and humane but his revelations about exactly what had been happening at Cummins and another prison called Tucker – routine beatings, nail-pullings, crushing of genitals with pliers and electric shock torture – suddenly became a nationwide story and Rockefeller, to his shame, panicked. Less than a month after I had talked to Murton he was fired for encouraging bad publicity and told to get out of the Arkansas on pain of being arrested for 'grave robbing'.

There was, of course, a financial aspect to all this. Despite the fact that the prisoners were served disgusting food, the produce from the Prison Farms were raking in $1.4 million annually for the State, quite a nice little sum in those days. Putting any of that money towards better living conditions for the prisoners was not high on Rockefeller's agenda.

Murton's book, *Accomplices to Crime*, written a year later, did not spare Arkansas from further embarrassment. In it he wrote, 'Prisons, mental hospitals and other institutions are a thermometer that measure the sickness of the larger society. The treatment society offers its outcasts reveals the way in which its members view one another.'

It's the sort of observation that needs to be plastered over the entrance to every prison in America but there are simply not enough people in power with sufficient conscience to make that happen. Murton was ostracised by the prison service for his honesty but did spend time lecturing on penal reform at Berkeley in California and later at Oklahoma State University. By then he had, at least, been recognised as a man worth talking about and he was played by Robert Redford in the 1980 film *Brubaker* which was a partially fictionalised story of his attempts to clean up Arkansas's prisons. Bobby Darin also wrote a song about him called 'Long Line Rider'.

Thomas Murton was good man who died too young at 62 of cancer in 1990, leaving behind a wife and four children.

A few weeks later I headed south again on a more pleasant mission. I went to Augusta to cover the Masters golf. Visually, the famous National course was everything I had read about. Pink azaleas bloomed amongst the pine trees and along the borders of beautifully manicured greens. It was a pleasure just to walk around the course and, for a golfer, it must be heaven to play it.

I have often found Wimbledon's rules a little pernickety at times but you really had to mind what you were doing and what you said at Augusta. Poor Jack Whitaker, a fine broadcaster for CBS and the most delightful of colleagues, discovered this to his cost one year when he let the word 'mob' slip from his lips while describing a mass of people swarming onto a green. The word from on high announced that Augusta didn't entertain 'mobs' and CBS was told to eject Whitaker from the commentary box. No one argued. CBS valued their contract too much.

But in 1968, someone suffered from 'the rules are rules' syndrome more agonisingly than Jack. It was the year that went down in history – the year Roberto DiVicenzo handed the Green Jacket to Bob Goalby by failing to check if his playing partner, Tommy Aaron, had marked his card correctly.

The story, which echoed around the golf world like a thunderclap, began when DiVicenzo, a polite, affable and popular Argentine, began his 45th birthday by celebrating with a 7 under par 65, which should have drawn him level with Goalby on 277 for the tournament, thus forcing a play off. But something very unfortunate had happened on the 17th hole. DiVicenzo made a birdie but Aarons, simply through not concentrating, had put it down as a par 4 on Roberto's scorecard. And DiVicenzo, amidst the backslapping and the hubbub of congratulations, signed for it. Ignoring one of the basic rules which says you must be crazy not to check how your partner has scored your card, Roberto cost himself the play off with Goalby that he had so richly earned.

In one of the great broken-English quotes ever to be uttered in a sporting arena, a crestfallen DiVicenzo said, "What a stupid I am to be wrong here."

An alternative reaction might have been to throttle Aarons but that sort of thing isn't done in golf and minutes later Bob Goalby was being helped into the Green Jacket. There were murmurings amongst the golfing fraternity against Goalby, suggesting that he might have asked for the simple error to be waived and played a final round against the Argentine. But all Goalby would say was, "I couldn't have changed the rules," and, at Augusta, that is probably an undeniable truth.

Apparently, some of DiVicenzo's supporters, who might even have included a few of his fellow players, had a green jacket made for him with his initials on it. Roberto received it gratefully but never wore it. He loved the game too much to do that.

So, once again, I had been lucky enough to walk into a big story and, although I would never presume to call myself a golf writer, I grasped the essentials quickly enough to send a page-lead story to the Evening News.

In the meantime there was always something of interest happening in New York and sometime earlier I had got to know Michael Crawford after interviewing him for the paper. Making his Broadway debut, Crawford was appearing in Peter Schaffer's play *Black Comedy* which had an intriguing plot line. When the curtain went up, the set – a sitting room – was in darkness but the cast were behaving normally as if the lights were on. Then, after a couple of minutes, the script called for a fuse to be blown and, bingo, the lights went out – as far as the actors were concerned. But, for the rather obvious reason that the audience needed to see what the hell was happening, the lights were actually turned on, leaving the actors behaving as if they were in darkness. Cue all manner of mishaps and chaos with Crawford, in particular, proving himself adept at walking into the sharp edge of doors; falling down a flight of thirteen stairs and, in one hazardous trick that threatened to break his back night after night, treading on a telephone placed on a low table which jackknifed him backwards as it slipped from under his foot.

Crawford, of course, was incredibly adept and fearless about all this and, as his career developed, always insisted on doing his own stunts which required huge insurance premiums as producers anxiously bit their nails. Later, while he was filming the movie *Hello ... Goodbye* in the South of France, I watched him drive an open-topped vintage Rolls Royce into a swimming pool, stand up as it hit the water while releasing air tanks below the dashboard to regulate the time it took to sink, all the while delivering a few lines. After calculations with experts, Michael knew that he had to drive the car off the edge of the pool at between 21 and 23 mph, I think it was. If not there would be a calamity. Too fast and he would hit the far side of the pool and too slow ... kerplonk, he would turn the thing over. Not surprisingly, Crawford had made it very plain to the director and the cameramen: "This is a one take deal. I'm doing this ONCE!" And once was all it took.

But back in New York, a great deal of constant rehearsal was needed for *Black Comedy* to make sure everyone hit their marks because the piece demanded split-second timing. All went smoothly during the first six months of the acclaimed run until Lynn Redgrave, Crawford's co-star, got married and decided to leave the cast. To Michael's horror she was replaced by a not very experienced young English actress designated by the absent director John Dexter, who was in London and didn't bother to fly over for the extra rehearsals that Michael insisted upon.

Crawford had not been getting on too well with Dexter from the word go and this only made matters worse. "What does he want? To get us all killed?" he ranted one evening. Thankfully for all the cast, he insisted on having Redgrave's replacement in the theatre twice a day for two solid weeks of personal direction before he was satisfied that she could handle the very special demands of this unusual production.

No need to add that Crawford was a perfectionist, a trait that lifted him to rare heights during a hugely successful career. He went on to make a name for himself on British television as the hopeless Frank Spencer in the comedy series *Some Mothers Do 'ave 'em* but, of course, giant theatre roles in *Phantom of the Opera* and *Barnum* lifted him to different levels of achievement and fame.

We struck up a good friendship in New York and I spent some fun evenings with Michael and his lovely wife Gabrielle. Once, I took them to Basin' Street East to listen to Vic Damone, whose fabulous voice probably put him second only to Frank Sinatra amongst the great popular singers of the day. Damone was backed by the Woody Herman Band, if memory serves, but I well remember watching the change that came over Michael's expression half way through the evening. He was seated opposite me and, with little space between tables, was well able to hear the conversation going on behind him. You didn't need to be a private eye to discern that the four gentlemen with their dark glasses and sharkskin suits were members of the Mafia that ran New York's night life, and the look on Michael's face told us all we needed to know about the gist of their conversation. I can only assume that someone was on their hit list and that they were not being particularly quiet about it.

"Christ, can we leave?" Michael asked as Vic Damone launched into his lovely rendition of 'Stardust'. Whatever he had heard – and he never explained it to me in precise terms – was evidently a bit too rich for a young man born in suburban Salisbury and schooled at Bexleyheath. It was time for a cab and home.

A couple of years later, the Crawfords moved back to England and took a house on Marryat Road which happens to lead straight down the hill from Wimbledon Village to the All England Club. Michael and Gabrielle were kind enough to invite me to stay during the Championships and I have never, before or since, had more convenient or congenial lodgings while covering Wimbledon.

Unhappily, the marriage didn't last but by the time they split up in 1975, Emma and Lucy had been born and, in the following years, I was a frequent visitor to Gabrielle's new home in Fulham. A person of no small ability herself, Gabrielle took up photography and used her close, life-long friend Jane Birkin, the English actress who went to Paris and never came back, as her model. She produced a concert called *Arabesque* which uses the songs and music of Jane's late ex-husband Serge Gainsbourg and which has played in cities from Paris to Algiers to Tel Aviv (despite the Arab make-up of the orchestra). Recently, in 2014, Gabriella edited a book, *Attachments*, of her photos of Jane, cementing in print a loving and long-lasting friendship.

As if everything else that was going on in the world wasn't enough, 1968 was a momentous year for the game of tennis, it being the year when All England Club chairman Herman David threw open the gates of Wimbledon to any player of sufficient standard, amateur or professional and thus forced the birth, kicking and squealing, of Open Tennis. It was the old, reactionary, amateur officials of numerous national associations who did most of the squealing because they knew their power was being eroded, never to return.

The story is so pivotal and important that I will deal with it in a separate section but, suffice to say, I was there as the whole tennis world gathered at Wimbledon; professional outcasts like Lew Hoad, Ken Rosewall, Rod Laver and Tony Trabert being welcomed back into the fold like long lost brothers. It was a happy, even euphoric, moment for those of us who had championed the cause for so long and there was no doubt that Herman David, an emotional silver-haired Welshman, was the hero of the hour.

But, having watched and reported on Laver retrieving his crown after a six-year hiatus, it was time to fly back to America and face the final months of a fateful and frequently chaotic Presidential campaign which I will cover in some details in the next chapter.

But before Nixon had completed his resurrection in American politics by becoming the 37th President of the United States, I was sent down to Mexico City at the end of September to take a look at student unrest which was building on the eve of the Olympics. Gustavo Diaz Ordaz was proving himself to be an unpopular President amongst those who were sensitive to the needs of democracy, the poor and free speech and, as is so often the case, it was the young who were most indignant. They felt that the prestige Mexico would gain from staging the Olympic Games was an insufficient excuse for the huge amounts of money being spent to run and promote them when swathes of this large nation lived in abject poverty. So they formed an organisation called CNH (Consejo Nacional de Huelga) from around 70 universities and began demonstrating. In late August almost half a million people had gathered to demonstrate in the centre of Mexico City. President Diaz Ordaz's first response was to form a Brigada Olympica – ostensibly an Olympic police force – to try and prevent the movement from growing. It was a fateful decision.

After making a few inquiries, I was directed to a café in downtown Mexico City where I was told some of the more militant students hung out. I needed to find the leaders of this movement and soon the name of someone called Raul was being offered by a few of the young people I spoke to. "There is a demonstration at the Plaza de la Tres Culturas in the Tlateloco district this evening," one young man told. "Go up to the balcony on the 10th floor of the big apartment building. You will find him and our leaders there."

I discovered later that I was looking for Raul Alvarez Garin, who was the most prominent member of the organising committee and, sure enough, he was to be found exactly where my informant had suggested. The balcony, which reflected others in the building, was indented so in fact it was more of an open space at the front of a few of the apartments. After introducing myself, Raul spoke briefly about the need to make their voices heard against the government who were ignoring the needs of the Mexican people at the expense of international acclaim. "This is how we can make them take notice," said the good-looking, dark haired student. "Whether they will listen to us … who knows. But what we do have, as you can see, is a lot of support."

One only had to look out over the large square for evidence. About 4,000 people were gathering as darkness fell and, after listening to speeches for more than an hour or more, they rolled up newspapers and lit them, holding them aloft as torches as they drifted home. It was quite a moving sight because it was all done peacefully, in a totally unthreatening way. Which, I thought, was a good thing because like everyone else on that balcony I had observed the figures of armed police – maybe members of the Brigada Olympica – silhouetted against the darkening skyline as they stood on the rooftops of neighbouring buildings.

I filed a piece, mentioning the peaceful nature of the rally along with the omnipresent threat of authoritarian force and had a chat with the desk in London about what to do next. It was a Friday night and I had learned that another demonstration had been scheduled in the same place for the following Wednesday. I wanted to stay but the final decision was that I should return to New York as a big team from Associated Newspapers was due to arrive that weekend to cover the Olympics, including Bob Trevor, the sports editor of the Evening News who was a good friend of mine.

"We'll have a lot of people there and they can take care of anything that comes up," I was told. "You go home and keep an eye on Mr Nixon."

So I did and, without being melodramatic about it, the decision may have saved my life. There is not the slightest doubt in my mind that I would have gone straight back up on that balcony in the Plaza de las Tres Culturas on Wednesday, 2nd October had I remained in Mexico City and, like virtually everyone else who did, I would have been shot. Soon after another big crowd assembled in the square, a few members of the Brigada Olympica fired some shots in the general direction of the police who immediately thought they were being shot at from the crowd and retaliated with a fusillade of fire. Raul and his friends on the balcony were the prime targets but the rifle fire was also aimed at the helpless crowd below and, inevitably, panic ensued.

Officially, 44 people died but many observers spoke of piles of bodies being carted away and the death toll was probably much higher than that. Many of the student leaders were killed although Raul survived. He was imprisoned for several years and died in 2014. Oriana Fellaci, the very prominent Italian journalist, was on that balcony and she was hit three times and then dragged down the stairs by her hair as the police came storming into the building. I am fairly certain no one on that balcony escaped unscathed. Luckily I had not spoken to Bob Trevor so had not had the chance of telling him about it. But he was down in the crowd and reported the carnage as people tried to protect themselves from the hail of bullets raining down from the rooftops.

It was, of course, a scandal that the Olympic Games began a few days later as if nothing had happened. The Games should, in the opinion of many, have been scrapped but Avery Brundage, the imperious President of the Olympic Committee who had been an overt Nazi sympathiser at the time of the 1936 Berlin Games, was never going to allow that to happen and would have dismissed the protesters as riff-raff. Those that were still alive were either in hospital, where many died of their wounds, or in prison. Just how long they remained in prison is something that has never been properly documented. They became non-persons as one poor, grieving mother discovered when she asked for information about her son at a police station and was told, "You don't have a son," before being pushed out of the door.

It was not until Vicente Fox was elected President of Mexico in 2001, all of 33 years later, that anything was done about it. A proper investigation of the appalling incident was set up and, the following year, ex-President Luis Echeveria, who had been Interior Minister in 1968, was charged with genocide. But in 2009 the charges were dropped. For many Mexicans, the massacre is too painful a memory to be re-examined.

Strangely, the Mexico City Olympics will be remembered for a protest of a different kind. The black American sprinters Tommie Smith, who won gold, and John Carlos, who took the bronze, raised their fists in what appeared to be a Black Power salute during the playing of the Star Spangled Banner. The pair wore human rights badges on their track suits, as did Peter Norman, the Australian who had won silver. He was heavily criticised in the Australian press but it was nothing compared to the vilification suffered by Smith and Carlos, who, despite protests by the US Olympic committee, were thrown out of the Olympic Village on the explicit orders of Avery Brundage.

In his book *Silent Gesture* Tommie Smith denied it had been a Black Power salute but a gesture of solidarity with all oppressed peoples. Both Smith and

John Carlos were so indebted to Norman for his support that they were pall-bearers at his funeral in 2006.

There is little doubt that the silent gesture, Black Power or not, had a huge impact and is remembered to this day. Symbolism can sometimes have a more lasting effect than gestures of sheer atrocity and while the names of Smith and Carlos live on, Raul and his brave friends have disappeared under that sombrero which Mexicans use to shield themselves from the hot sun along with moments in their history which blind them from reality.

Chapter 10
MIAMI & CHICAGO 1968

After the pleasant sojourn in Europe, played out amidst the familiar sights and sounds of the Queen's Club and Wimbledon as we welcomed old friends back from exile with the advent of Open Tennis, it took a moment or two to re-adjust to the hot and sweaty world of American politics.

And Miami, where I headed for the Republican Convention on 5th August, was, as far as the heat was concerned, suffocating. A few minutes' walk between the Fontainebleau and Eden Rock hotels, where the Nixon staff were staying, left one drenched in sweat and, just for once, yearning for the refrigerated air of the vast Miami Convention Hall. There the mood was jubilant. Former Vice President Richard Nixon was the party's nominee and the proceedings were little more than a coronation. King Richards have had a notoriously uneven time governing over the past centuries and Nixon would fare no better. By the end of his 'reign' in the White House, there was serious evidence that he was viewing himself as a medieval king rather than a democratically elected President and acting accordingly. Unhappily for him, Nixon had to deal with the Fourth Estate, something that King Richard the Lionheart and his successors hadn't needed to worry about.

But the outcome that befell the Nixon Presidency was unimaginable to all of us gathered for this ritual of hyperbolic bravado, streamers and straw hats during that steamy week in August and it was left to reporters to work sources and build relationships for the coming campaign. So I took a deep breath and hung around the bar at the Eden Rock, eavesdropping and sometimes even participating in conversations with various Nixon staffers, the most prominent of whom was the Press Secretary Ron Ziegler. This youngish Californian had the smarmy good looks and smirky smile that did something to the hairs on the back of your neck and I frequently fled to find solace in the company of NBC's John Chancellor, Roger Mudd of CBS and the young rising star at ABC, Peter Jennings. Apart from being congenial company, their opinions and insight were invaluable to a young foreign reporter still trying to grasp the nuances of American politics.

With its lack of political conflict and an inevitable outcome, there was nothing in Miami to prepare one for Chicago. In contrast to the Republicans, the Democrats were in chaos. Any chance of Vice-President Hubert Humphrey being denied the nomination had vanished with Bobby Kennedy's death but that did nothing to prevent the rancour from spilling out all over the convention floor. The anti-Vietnam war movement was in full voice and Chicago Mayor Richard Daley, probably the second most powerful political figure in the country at the time, was ready for the hordes of demonstrators descending on his city.

Bunting and flowers may have been draped along some of the avenues but the stockyards one had to pass on the way to the International Amphitheatre had been fenced off, eliminating the sight if not the smell of slaughtered beasts. The hall itself was surrounded with barbed wire atop the steel partitions and the entrance door was bullet-proofed. It looked as if Daley and his police force were expecting trouble and they got it.

The shouting matches between delegates went on till 3.00 am but it was the clamour and chaos that developed in Grant Park, right opposite the Conrad Hilton Hotel, which echoed around the world. Hippies and yippies and alternative voices of all sorts – some 10,00 of them – had gathered to scream their displeasure at their President, his Vice President and the traumatic political year America had endured. Inevitably, a minority pushed dissent too far and maybe there were a few rocks thrown at the blue-helmeted police but, having observed the proceedings in close up, I can assure you that what developed was nothing short of a police riot.

Wielding their billy sticks, they waded into the crowd, beating, tear-gassing and Macing young and old alike in a manner that brought disgrace to Mayor Daley and his great city. One of the best reporters of the time, Haynes Johnson of the New York Times, writing for the Smithsonian a while later, said, "The 1968 Chicago Convention became a lacerating event, a distillation of a year of heartbreak, assassination, riots and a break down in law and order that made it seem as if the country was coming apart."

That was no exaggeration but, being there in the heart of it, one struggled to stand back and grasp the wider picture because stuff was happening on an hourly basis with little time for sleep. You will find in reports of what happened that week the fact that no one was killed, which was true as well as being a miracle, although hundreds were quite badly injured. But it is not true, as was reported at the time, that no shots were fired.

I was in the lobby of the Conrad Hilton, where most of the media and many delegates were staying, when Peter Jennings grabbed my arm and shouted, "Come on, something's happening on the other side of Grant Park – let's go see!"

So we jumped in his ABC TV News car and drove off in search of something – we did not know what. A separate demonstration seemed to have developed in a residential neighbourhood and we were standing in the half-shielded entrance of a local store when shots rang out. Peter and I took a step back but there were only three of them and we never discovered who fired them. Meanwhile, in Grant Park, the beatings went on.

When I got back to the hotel I went to the line of public phones behind the lobby to get a call through to London. Before I picked up the receiver, the conversation which was going on in the next booth caught my attention. A boy of fourteen or fifteen was pleading with his mother.

"But you don't understand, Mum, you have to let me stay. This is history happening here. This is important. I'll get the train back tomorrow. Yes, I'll be careful. I promise. Please, please ..."

What a kid, I thought. He understands; he gets it and he wants to be part of it. If I had been his mother, watching what she must have been watching on TV, I would have insisted he get the next train out but I think he won and stayed. I hope he wasn't hurt.

Max Hastings, the future reporter and editor of the Daily Telegraph who was studying in the US at the time, was lucky not to get assassinated. That evening, I was in the hotel bar when Hastings' voice began to rise above others from a discussion he was having with a group of American reporters at a nearby table. Suddenly, Max leapt to his feet and from his massive height of 6' 7", began berating his listeners and the entire United States of America with what he thought of their politics, their way of life and their country. The voice was stentorian and flush with every upper class vowel that can be bestowed on those who attend British public schools like Charterhouse. For a moment, I really thought he was going to be set upon by some true-blue Yankee reporters who were already into their third martini. Luckily, a couple of British colleagues hushed him down a bit and dragged him off to safer pastures. No wonder Max was the first man into Port Stanley as the British Marines liberated the Falklands some years later. He was not afraid of sticking his neck out, and it was a very long neck.

Even before the riots turned Chicago into such a huge story, John Gold had decided to enlist the services of Winston S. Churchill to help me cover it and the late Prime Minister's grandson was due to join me a couple of days after I got there. I had never met young Winston who had been busy following in his grandfather's footsteps as a foreign correspondent, covering Middle East conflicts and writing a book with his father, Randolph, on The Six Day War.

I was looking forward to his arrival but was anxious that he would not have any trouble with hotel reservations as every hotel in the city was sold out, not least the Conrad Hilton. So I thought I had better confirm his booking for the following day and dutifully joined the line in the Hilton lobby as journalists from all over the world checked in. Peter Younghusband, a giant of a man who was normally based in his native South Africa for the Daily Mail, was just in front of me and we chatted until I reached the front desk to be greeted by a camp young man who made no attempt to hide his sexual orientation.

Hopelessly, I had decided to try and circumvent the inevitable looks and questions that would follow the name I was about to offer up by just saying, "Churchill," when he asked for my colleague's identification.

"First name?" he snapped back, hand firmly on hip. I took a deep breath and muttered, "Winston."

Swinging around to fetch a ledger behind him, the clerk paused for a second and, with an over the shoulder toss of the head, retorted, "I had a friend called Robert Browning."

Not bad, I thought. As a comeback, it wasn't bad at all.

So Winston got his room and we set about working together when he turned up the next day with a happy grin and easy charm. He did not remind one instantly of his great ancestor, but there was enough of a steely glint in those blue eyes to suggest that he carried his heritage with pride. It was frequently said that carrying the exact name of his grandfather was a terrible burden to bear and he admitted that it was a bore on occasion but he was proud of it and tried his best live up to it. That, of course, was impossible and it was sad that, when he was elected to the House of Commons as MP for Stretford in Lancashire two years later, he was never able to convince Margaret Thatcher or John Major that he was Ministerial material.

Unlike the old man, who had switched sides to spend many years as a Liberal MP is his youth, young Winston was a hard-headed and sometimes hot-headed right winger who espoused policies based on strong defence spending, echoing those of his grandfather in the 1930s. But there was no Hitler lurking this time and his views frequently seemed ill-judged.

Jokingly, I told friends at the time that I could have turned him into a liberal if I had spent another couple of weeks with him dodging the Chicago police because, by the end of the week, he was beginning to lose faith in blind adherence to uniforms and 'law & order', not least because he himself was set upon by two burly cops just outside the Hilton. Despite protests that he was staying at the hotel, he was clubbed to the ground when he told them his name.

"They lacked a sense of humour," he said wryly when he joined me in the lobby, having managed to take the blows of their billy sticks with his fore-arms rather than his skull.

We worked well together, compiling enough material each day to write a composite piece under a joint by-line which, inevitably, ended up splashed all over the front page of the Evening News. Back in London, I'm sure John Gold was checking the circulation figures with a wicked grin on his face. The Churchill name was not hurting sales. For us in Chicago, it kept cropping up at awkward moments. Once, when we attended a campaign reception at another hotel, the inevitable name cards were waiting and poor Winston had it pinned on his lapel by an insistent hostess. The 'oohs and aahs' as we moved round the room became a little tedious. Winston was endlessly cour-teous but I really don't know how he put up with it.

In the meantime everyone was having to put up with the troubling and sometimes frightening atmosphere of a police state. Mayor Daley had 11,900 police at his disposal augmented by 5,000 of the National Guard. As soon as he saw the size of the opposition, he had 6,500 Federal troops flown in. It was an occupation and the violent behaviour was not confined to the streets. One evening inside the convention hall, Dan Rather of CBS was moving round the floor, in constant contact with the booth where the avuncular figure of Walter Cronkite fronted the network's coverage in a great glass-walled studio. Cronkite's position as the most respected voice in American journalism had been cemented earlier in the year when President Johnson, having listened to his critical report from Vietnam, was reported to have said, "If I've lost Cronkite, I've lost the country."

But the police and muscled 'minders' on the floor weren't interested in reputations and Rather, while pressing a Humphrey supporter for a quick interview, found himself grabbed, roughed up and frog-marched towards the exit. Somebody must have hissed in their ear to lay off as the scene was being broadcast live on CBS and, when he was finally let go, Cronkite, not a man given to hyperbole, said, "I think we've got a bunch of thugs here, Dan."

Amazingly, not everyone in the country agreed. In fact a poll found about 60% were in favour of the police action. In those early days of alternative politics, it was too much to ask conservative, small town America to side with a bunch of long-haired hippies. Today, unhappily, Trump supporters would agree.

By Friday it was all over bar the shouting and there was still a lot of that going on. But it didn't matter because Hubert Humphrey, the garrulous, generally well-liked Vice President who had not made much effort to dis-engage himself from LBJ's Vietnam policy, had carried the vote by 1,567 delegates to a combined total for those voting for someone else of 1,041. Individually, Humphrey had received 1759 votes to Eugene McCarthy's 601 with George McGovern, who had only put his name on the ballot eighteen days before, getting 146.

It was during the hours following his inevitably sombre acceptance speech that Humphrey ruined his chance of ever becoming President of the United States. The speech was OK although it must have been galling for such a nat-urally ebullient, upbeat figure to have to spend much of it decrying the scenes that everyone had been witnessing on the streets. But it was a moment to show courage and real leadership and to tell America that it was not accept-able for police and guardsmen to club people indiscriminately and that the right to demonstrate was an American right that had to be observed. But that would have meant criticising Mayor Daley and Humphrey felt that he needed Daley's machine to get elected – just as John Kennedy had done eight years before. He was probably right, but there were others ways Humphrey could have shown some understanding of what all the fuss was about.

And lying around his hotel suite, soaking up the adulation of his cro-nies as he watched re-runs of his speech on television while, a few floors down, McCarthy campaign workers were being hauled out of their rooms and beaten, was not the way to do it. It was a shocking lack of judgement on the part of a man who career had been built on better instincts.

The immediate result of the police action in the Conrad Hilton Hotel on the final night of the convention became immediately apparent to me as I walked into the lobby at 5.00 am. Along with a small handful of reporters and Winston, who soon joined me following his own altercation with the constabulary, I was confronted by the sight of at least a dozen young McCarthy people who had been pushed and frog-marched downstairs by the eleven policemen who had been sent up to the 15th floor to investigate reports of Coke cans and ashtrays being thrown out of a window.

They would have been thrown bodily into the street had not Richard Goodwin, the former JFK staffer who had joined the McCarthy campaign, intervened. Just a few minutes before I arrived, Goodwin had angrily confronted the police and informed them in no uncertain terms that they had no right to eject people from a hotel in which they were registered.

"Are you arresting these people?" Goodwin demanded to know. "Because if not, they are staying exactly where they are."

Goodwin told the McCarthy kids to form a semi-circle and sit down. The sight is etched in the memory. Each young person had a Chicago cop standing behind them, smacking their billy sticks in the palm of their hands, just itching to give the kids another whack. Already there was blood pouring from the head of John Warren, a 24-year-old from Lansing, Michigan, whose skull had been hard enough to snap the club that hit him. A couple of others were obviously hurt as well. Heaven knows what would happened had Goodwin not been there, especially as the level of antagonism was raised a notch when one of Goodwin's colleagues, Philip Friedman, came charging out of the elevator and, observing the scene, called the police "Mother fucking pigs."

This was documented in the extensively detailed Walker Report which examined the happenings of Chicago '68 and came to the accurate conclusion that there had been a 'police riot'.

However, I have to take issue with another of their findings which stated, 'Soon afterwards (referring to the arrival of the McCarthy people being herded into the lobby) Senator McCarthy arrived, comforted his followers and suggested they disperse in small groups.'

I don't know what the Walker Report meant by 'soon afterwards' because there was nothing 'soon' about it. We waited and waited for the man who was supposed to have picked up the hopes and aspirations of Robert Kennedy and use them to turn his own campaign into something meaningful. But the minutes ticked by as Goodwin held the fort, staring defiance at the cops, and it was almost an hour before McCarthy appeared, looking as cool and unflappable as ever. And perfectly groomed. This is what hit me the most as he emerged from the elevator. This champion of the oppressed had obviously been more concerned about how he looked – suited up with tie tied and not a silver hair out of place – than he had about what was happening to his kids. He had been doing his toilette.

I have rarely been so disgusted with a politician and that is saying something. Bobby Kennedy would have been down there in his pyjamas; getting Mayor Daley out of bed; ordering the police out of the hotel. But Bobby was dead. And the altruistic young people who had sided with McCarthy because Kennedy had dithered were being shown their hero in his true colours, a preening professor who was big on thought and very short on action.

But at least McCarthy had shown up, which was more you could say for the new standard-bearer of the Democratic party who must have heard what was happening as he partied on up in his suite. Shots of Humphrey doing so were shown on TV and they left his campaign dead in the water, possibly costing him the election. He and Daley had to share the blame. With passions running so high over the Vietnam war and Kennedy's assassination, it was never going to be easy but Bobby had shown how courage, leadership and oratory can calm a crowd with his Indianapolis speech following the assassination of Dr Martin Luther King. However there was no one left of remotely similar stature and America's image in the world took a heavy hit. Anthony Carthew, an acerbic writer for the London Daily Mail, summed up the atmosphere in one short sentence. 'We descend for breakfast at the Conrad Hilton,' Carthew wrote, 'to the smell of tear gas and policemen's feet.'

The odour lingered and eventually suffocated the chances of Hubert H. Humphrey.

Quite recently I had a long talk with a man who was just starting out on his own political career in 1968 – Senator George Mitchell, a future Majority Leader of the Senate, who, at the time, was an aide to Senator Edmund Muskie of Maine, Humphrey's nominated running mate. I wanted confirmation of my impressions of all those years ago and I knew George was just the man to talk to. He had become a good friend ever since meeting his future wife, Heather MacLachlan, a dear and close friend of mine going back to the time she worked as a secretary at the ATP Paris office in the Tour Montparnasse.

"It's true that from the moment the convention ended in Chicago at the end of August through virtually all of September, our funding dried up. Most Democrats were so shocked and disappointed by what they had witnessed that none of them wanted to offer up a dime until they realised it was costing them the election."

It had also taken President Johnson an entire month to actually endorse the candidacy of his Vice President and poor Hubert was like a train left in the station for several weeks before picking up steam in October and roaring down the tracks for what turned out to be a close finish, boosted largely by Humphrey's belated decision to break with LBJ's Vietnam policy and McCarthy's eleventh hour endorsement.

The final results showed what might have been but for the disaster of Chicago. Although Nixon won a clear majority in the electoral college, 301 to 191, the popular vote was very close with Nixon winning 43.42% to Humphrey's 42.72% – a margin of just 500,000 votes.

Muskie, who helped Humphrey carry Maine, had some influence on that because he was a much better campaigner than the gaff-prone Spiro Agnew, Nixon's running mate, and some of that success was due to George Mitchell's ability as a fledgling politician. "Muskie called me as soon as the votes were in and told me to head for Washington and set up a campaign headquarters. We had little money and no time but somehow I managed to hire enough staff to get something going."

It was interesting to hear that there had been a small core of Kennedy supporters in the Maine delegation before Bobby was killed, backing my assertion that, had he lived and become the Democratic nominee, there would have been a groundswell of support from all quarters.

"Bobby's ability to draw support from two normally disparate sections of the electorate – blacks and working class whites – would have put him in a very strong position because he also had the backing of large sections of the East Coast liberal community," said Mitchell. "He could have put together a strong coalition."

Maybe George was not quite as convinced as I was that Kennedy would have made it to the White House but he agreed that it would have been a distinct possibility. My premise is based on several factors. If Humphrey, hamstrung by his direct link to a largely unpopular President and shorn of money for the weeks following a calamitous convention (which would have been completely different in tone had RFK been alive) had been able to run

Nixon as close as he did, I don't think there can be much doubt that Kennedy would fared decisively better. As I have referenced in the previous chapter, the more people who got to see Bobby and know him a little bit, the more they liked him. He would have been a tireless and convincing candidate and would have been helped by Nixon's unlikeable persona.

But none of that mattered on the eve of polling day in the first week of November. Having watched the year unfold with a mixture of bewilderment and disgust, I sat down at my desk amidst the towers of mid-town Manhattan and wrote this for the Evening News. Looking back, I don't think I'd change a word.

'It began with Robert Kennedy, Eugene McCarthy, Nelson Rockefeller and cautious hopes of peace abroad and unity at home.

'It is ending, ten tragic and tumultuous months later, with Richard Nixon and Hubert Humphrey and a record of political as well as the ultimate sacrifice; of violence, disgust and disunity and just the barest glimmer of hope for that long-sought end to the war.

'It has been a bad and expensive political year for the United States of America. One has watched a nation writhe in anguish as it cried out for change and finally subside into brooding apathy as outdated political machines snubbed and clubbed a protesting generation and then arrogantly offered men of the past to deal with the problems of the future.

'As the enlightened and ever-growing minority know, it is the system that is at fault and it is the system that must – and eventually will – be changed.

'George Wallace is a somewhat unfortunate example of why this is so. For Wallace is the only one amongst the three candidates who is not qualified to be President. Yet he is the only one who will receive votes from people who believe in him, who admire him and who will vote for him because THEY want to and not because a political party is telling them they must.

'Millions of other Americans who – and let us be thankful for it – have a little better understanding of the unpalatable realities of life will be voting, either for Humphrey because they can't stand Nixon, or for Nixon because they are either die-hard Republicans or dissident Democrats. Very few will be supporting the two major candidates out of a true conviction that one of them is the man they really want. Why? Because Nixon and Humphrey are not the choice of the people but of the Party politicians who once again found it expedient to put their own careers and the well-being of the Party that gave them those careers, above the general good.

'Last January, Bobby Kennedy and Nelson Rockefeller were unquestion-ably the most popular politicians in the country. Yet both, for very different reasons, did not want to run for the nomination of their respective parties – Kennedy because he quite rightly felt the time was not right for him and Rockefeller because he had genuinely lost the incentive.

'By March the Tet Offensive which converted many hawks into doves, and the arrival of Eugene McCarthy as a growing political force, had altered everything ...'

I went on to describe much of what I have written about in the preceding pages and ended the piece like this:

'And so two old party pros from yesteryear were thrust upon a stupefied electorate and under the circumstances, it was not surprising so many flocked to Wallace. In fact his boom – which is on the wane now as people regain their senses – really started with Kennedy's death. For not all the people who have voted for Wallace are bigots and racists. Many belong to the bewildered, unhappy lower-middle classes who are frightened by the crime wave; fearful of long-haired hippies and 'uppity' blacks and distrustful of liberal intellec-tuals who do not have quite the same respect for God, the flag and apple pie.

'All these people want a change because they feel anything would better than the last four years. There can be no greater indictment of the Republican and Democratic Parties and the outmoded systems that run them than that.'

I don't know whether our lord and master Rothermere enjoyed that piece taking up a full page of his newspaper but with John Gold in the editor's chair, he wasn't going to interfere and it stayed in all nine editions that November day.

A word, perhaps, on George Wallace who I may have subconsciously tried to air-brush out of this story. He was a truly dreadful man but that is not a good enough excuse. Even discounting the time his wife, Lurleen, was Governor of Alabama (she died of cancer eighteen months after succeeding her husband) Wallace spent a total of sixteen years in the state's Governor's mansion and ran for President on four occasions. He was a fire-brand segre-gationist whose excuse for riding rough-shod over the democratic ideals of his party was summed up in this offering for political expedience: "I tried talking about good roads and good schools and things that have been part of my career and nobody listened," he was quoted as saying. "Then I started talking about niggers and they stomped the floor."

So he knew where to find his votes and, in the 1960s south, he found plenty of them. I decided I better go and have a look and flew down to Montgomery, Alabama to attend one of his rallies. It was a truly terrifying experience. At least a couple of thousand bellicose rednecks packed into one steamy hall, hollering and clapping every racist epithet that fell from the Governor's lips, was not a pretty sight. To my amazement I found myself sitting next to a small, very young black reporter from a local radio station. She was the only black person in the place. "Are you OK?" I asked her. "Aren't you scared?"

"Only a little," she replied with a smile. "I'll be OK. I'm used to them."

She should have received a journalistic medal for bravery.

I got the last plane out of town and have never been back, although I am sure it has changed a great deal in the intervening years. George Wallace changed – after he was shot. A man, whose diaries revealed he wanted political fame, shot Wallace five times as the Governor campaigned for the Presidency in a shopping mall in Laurel, Maryland in May 1972. He was paralysed from the waist down and spent the rest of his life in a wheelchair. I don't know how much that affected his attitude to his fellow man but he did recant in later life and apologised for his attitude towards blacks. He even appointed two of them to high level positions in Alabama in the last years of his Governorship. No matter what his views, he left his mark on American politics.

Soon after the election, I got a call from John Gold asking me if I wanted to stay on in New York or move to Paris. "It's your call," John said. "Simone French is going to leave Paris and I have Stephen Claypole ready to take over from you in New York. What do you think?"

The decision was easy on several counts. Had Bobby Kennedy lived and become President I would have stayed in America because the country would have embarked on a new and exciting adventure and, with the contacts I had made amongst his staffers, I would have had a front row seat. Conversely, the thought of having to write about Nixon for the next several years was exceedingly unpalatable. And then there was Paris. For me, of course, it would be like returning home. My father still lived there; I had friends there and it offered so much that I had missed in New York.

So Stephen Claypole, a tall, friendly and quite serious young man of about my age, arrived in January 1969 and we flew down to Washington together to cover the inauguration of Richard M. Nixon and traipse around the six Balls that were being held by his bejewelled followers all around the capital. It was a triumph for the man who had said, "You'll never have Dick Nixon to kick around anymore," on losing the governorship of California but he still couldn't manage to speak the truth.

Towards the end of a wearying evening, Nixon told the enthralled crowd at the Sheraton Park, "We're not going to let you down."

Wrong again, Mr President, wrong again.

Chapter 11
PARIS: A NEW BEAT

I was returning home. Although my French was far from perfect and my memories of actually living in the city were those of a child or adolescent, Paris enveloped me in a joyous embrace that uplifted the spirits. No matter that the trees were bare in the depths of January or that grey skies left wisps of cloud swirling around the turrets of the Sacre Coeur high on that hill in Montmartre. It was home and being able to spend the first couple of months with my father at his new flat just off the Avenue Henri Martin, the broad road that leads from the Trocadero to the Boise de Boulogne, made it feel even more so.

That, obviously, made things so much easier as I searched for a place of my own and settled into running my one man bureau, once again closeted next to the Daily Mail. Simone French, my predecessor, bequeathed me a delightful secretary called Dominique Fouchez who was very French but worldly and efficient and immediately made my life so much simpler by staying on top of things I might have missed in the French media.

I have always struggled to understand why I find New York and Paris so hugely different in style, rhythm, humour, taste and feel. For me they might as well be on different planets. There were many things I came to like about New York – and many more whenever I went out west – but the French way of life was so familiar to me and therefore so simple. It was 'Merci, Madame', 'Bonjour, Monsieur' whenever you bought your newspaper from the local kiosk or sipped your coffee over the zinc-topped bar and watched the 'garçon' flick ashes off the tables on the terrace with an unerring crack of his large white napkin.

No, you didn't get a smile but you didn't get wisecracks either and it didn't take long for you to be recognised and accepted in a 'quartier' as one of them. The bonjour became 'Bonjour, tout va bien?' and even on the tourist-saturated Champs-Elysees the fellow with the pencil-thin moustache at the kiosk on the corner of the Rue Marignan, where my mother had lived in the early 1930s, would reach under the counter to produce the last copy of the Evening News that he had saved for me.

I probably picked up on the way things work in Paris quicker than someone who was completely new to it but, even then, the penny only really dropped when, after a few months working at the old Continental Daily Mail building in the Rue du Sentier, a little side-street off the bustling Boulevard Poissoniere, I got a late invitation to a formal dinner and needed a white shirt. There was a men's clothing store on the corner of the Boulevard which we passed two or three times a week to go to a little brasserie next door. The proprietor was often standing in his doorway and we would exchange 'Bonjours'.

That's the place, I thought. I'll go and see our friend on the corner. But when I walked in and asked to buy a shirt, the proprietor looked slightly shocked.

"Ah, non, Monsieur, pas ici! Pas ici pour vous. Je suis trop cher."

He went on to explain that his prices were for the passing trade because the Blvd Poissoniere was a sort of Frenchman's Champs Elysees beginning at the Place de l'Opera and leading all the way down to the Place Republique. He told me go back down the Rue du Sentier and turn right. There I would find a shop selling shirts at prices suitable to local clientele.

So that's how it works, I thought. I had suspected something of the sort every time I saw workmen in overalls tucking in to the most enormous meals at lunchtime, their plates laden with food that would have cost a week's wages at the smart restaurants. And all washed down with plenty of rouge. Parisians look after their own.

On a personal and professional level, I found myself in a very different culture to New York. There had been a certain camaraderie amongst my foreign correspondent colleagues in Manhattan, but nothing compared to what I discovered in Paris. These were the long lost days when British newspapers each had two or even three correspondents in their main overseas bureaus. And in the late sixties and early seventies there just happened to be a bunch of reporters in Paris who formed a happy band of ex-pats, rivals but friends who enjoyed each other's company and spent a lot of time together.

The list is long but the core of the drinking, lunching, dining and even roulette-playing society we formed included David Leitch of the Sunday Times; Alexander Macmillan of the Sunday Telegraph, grandson of the former Prime Minister; Pat Chapman, a British freelance who worked for

ABC News; Jack Starr of the Daily Mail; John Ellison and Richard Killian of the Daily Express along with their resident photographer Reg Lancaster; Peter Stephens and Paul Hughes of the Daily Mirror, soon to be augmented by Roy Rutter and Don Cooligan; and before he disappeared to South-East Asia, Jon Swain who started on the Agence France Presse English desk but was later picked up by the Sunday Times in Vietnam. And there was Mark Ellidge, a fine photographer whose beautiful young wife died at a tragically early age from cancer after giving him two children. Mark was related to Robert Wyett of the Soft Machine, far more popular in France than they were in England, so we got tickets to some good concerts.

Then, always available for a drink and a chat in the corner of the Hotel Crillon bar at lunchtime but otherwise somewhat removed from our social activities, there was the doyen of all Paris correspondents, Sam White.

A Ukrainian Jew by origin, Australian by birth – and known as a Communist during his time at college in Melbourne – Sam had been sent into Paris with the liberating Free French and American forces in 1944 for the Sydney Daily Telegraph and had returned two years later on Beaverbrook's ticket for the Evening Standard. He never left. He was an acerbic, droll, intuitive reporter who quickly established himself as a figure of some repute in the capital while building the kind of contacts with General de Gaulle's people that would prove hugely beneficial several years later when de Gaulle was finally elected President. Sam's reporting on the conflict in Algeria became legendary.

The strength of White's personality – charisma, if one wants to use a word he would probably have hated – enabled him to achieve something I have never seen any other reporter manage to do in any city in the world. Realising that his regular Friday column needed to be filled by juicy tit-bits of gossip, he let the gossipers come to him in a public place because he knew they would never go to his office or even pick up a phone.

So, from noon to about 2.30 every day, his office was that corner of the bar at the Crillon. The American Embassy was right across the street; the fashion houses were lined up along the Faubourg St. Honore 50 yards away and if the great and the good were heading for lunch at Maxim's just around the corner, why not drop off for an aperitif at the Crillon first?

So it was that all manner of people with all manner of little secrets would sidle up to Sam and drop something in his ear. In return, Sam would massage their curiosity with a little information of his own and everyone was satisfied.

With his thick, greying hair; a low brow hiding a high intellect; a hooked nose and gravel voice, White exuded the kind of masculinity that had ladies all of a flutter especially as he was always perfectly turned out in a dark suit, brightly striped shirt with white collar and coloured 'kerchief falling out of his breast pocket. Journalistically, Cole Porter would have called him The Top ('You're the top; you're Napoleon brandy …') and that, for me, made him a somewhat daunting figure because he was the Evening Standard and I was The Evening News – his direct rival! Trying to make sure I was not The Bottom was going to be seriously difficult.

I quickly set up my own weekly column called 'Paris On the Line' but it never was and never could be compared to 'Sam White's Paris'. It was fun trying, however, and one could not have asked for a more amenable rival. In his gruff way, Sam was always charming to me and never slow to offer a piece of advice.

I believe White's idea of setting up shop in a bar of a major hotel began at the Ritz soon after Ernest Hemingway declared Paris free by storming into the bar on the Rue Cambon and demanding champagne. It was a sort of Hemingway thing to do but, for reasons I have forgotten, Sam found the Ritz not to his taste and moved to the Crillon. Heaven knows how much business he took with him over the years but let no one say the management was not appreciative. When Sam finally retired in the 1980s, the bar was undergoing renovation and the hotel gave him that corner of the bar to put in his flat on the Left bank. They must have known he (or at least Beaverbrook Newspapers) had paid for it a thousand times over.

Before Roy Rutter arrived to set himself up as the focal point of late night carousing on the Left Bank, we often gathered at our various residences for an evening of roulette. Someone, I think it was Pat Chapman, had a wheel and all the necessary pieces and we all drank too much while somehow managing to gamble within our means. If memory serves, Reg Lancaster, a tall red-headed northerner with a wide smile never far from his lips, did much of the winning but it didn't really matter.

These sorts of nights made up for some fairly tedious reporting I was required to do covering the Vietnam peace talks, which took place at a building on the Avenue Kleber just off the L'Etoile. I had an extra need to pay attention to the often unfathomable arguments because I had received a request from Newsday, the much respected Long Island newspaper of which Bill Moyers was then the publisher, to write some features for them. John Gold had no objection and it provided a little extra pocket money.

With sorties across the street to a little café that must have made a fortune out of the Peace Talks, those of us assigned to the task would stand behind the barriers on the pavement whenever rumour had it that someone might emerge to say something interesting. They rarely did, because Henry Kissinger and his North Vietnamese counterpart Le Duc Tho continued their verbal sparring at other locations. In Paris, David Bruce, an elegant New Englander who had served his country in numerous ambassadorial posts, was the designated head of Nixon's negotiating team but it was his opposite number, the chic and lovely Madame Nguyen Thi Binh, who attracted most of the attention.

Madame Binh's feminine appearance did not fool anyone. Having spent time in prison during the last years of French colonial rule, she had been a revolutionary fighter from way back and greeted us with a smile that only just managed to hide deep-seated resentment. Her signature was on the final document that was supposed to bring hostilities to an end once Kissinger and Duc Tho had settled their differences, but not before Nixon had ordered more bombs to be dropped on North Vietnam and Laos over Christmas 1972 than fell on Europe during World War Two. The laugh was that the pair were then awarded a joint Nobel Peace Prize. The award raised furious protests around the world but the American comic Tom Lehrer had the most crushing response. "It has," he said, "made political satire obsolete."

Duc Tho had the decency, if one can call it that, to refuse it. Kissinger, his conscience finally getting the better of him, eventually returned the award and the one million dollars to Norway. Unsurprisingly, Madame Binh went on to become Vice-President of Vietnam in the 1990s.

Some time later, an extraordinary story developed under our noses and we missed it. One of our group who I have not yet mentioned was a tall, attractive Canadian photographer in her mid-twenties called Patricia Roxborough who was freelancing in Paris, working mainly for the Sunday Times. She used to join us for lunch at our hole-in-the-wall bistro next to the Daily Mail and Reuters offices on the Rue du Sentier and was convivial company.

She became close friends with Jack Starr and Paul Hughes and his wife and frequently had some of us around to her apartment just behind La Maison de la Radio near the Trocadero. A couple of times she threw full blown cocktail parties for around 30 people and we noticed how many Jordanian and Lebanese diplomats attended.

"Very good contacts," Patricia explained, while telling us of an assignment she had managed to get herself in Amman riding with King Hussein in his car. She had a German boyfriend called Wolfgang who didn't seem to be around that much and one got the impression that the occasional night in the company of a young Jordanian attaché fell in the category of 'making a good contact'.

I think I used Patricia when I needed a photograph of Countess Albina du Boisrouvray, a women of rare beauty and wealth on whom I was doing a story and who will re-appear in this narrative as one of the closest friends I made in Paris. At any rate, all seemed to go well for Miss Roxborough until she started complaining of lack of work. "I think I may have to re-locate," she said, hacking into a tough steak over lunch one day. "There is too much competition here. Maybe Rio or some other place would be better."

So she threw a farewell party at her apartment, kissed all of us goodbye and disappeared. Paul Hughes received a postcard from her from Toronto a few weeks later saying she was visiting her family while on the way to Rio. And then silence. "Wonder how Patricia's getting on," we would ask each other over a glass of rouge.

About two months later, we found out. The headline across the front page of Le Figaro left us gasping. There had been a shooting in Norway. A Palestinian waiter had been killed. And 'Patricia', or at least one of her accomplices, had shot him.

She wasn't Patricia Roxborough and wasn't Canadian. She was a South African Jew called Sylvia Raphael and she was a member of a Mossad hit-squad. She had never left Paris but had sequestered herself in the suburbs while helping to train the squad before leaving for Norway. To make a tragic story worse, they got the wrong man. He was just a waiter working in the ski-resort of Lillehammer who wasn't even Palestinian but a Moroccan called Ahmed Bouchikhi whose brother was a famous singer and whose wife was pregnant. He had been mis-identified as Hassan Salameh, the PLO intelligence chief who was wanted for master-minding the death of eleven Israeli athletes at the Munich Olympics.

To say we were gobsmacked would be putting it mildly. Jack Starr, who was Jewish and, I think, secretly in love with her, was in tears. Our 'Patricia' was now a confirmed terrorist and safely locked up in a Norwegian prison. After a couple of years, she was released and married her defence lawyer with whom she lived in South Africa until dying of cancer in Israel in 2005.

Deception is a common occurrence but rarely does one run into it in such a personal way. Inevitably, it makes you a little less trusting and a little more wary but it is not my nature to be suspicious and I could be accused, on occasion, of being fairly naïve, so I can't say that this incident radically changed the way I viewed people. You just have to assume that most of them are not Mossad spies.

A couple of years before, David Leitch had co-authored a book on the spy Kim Philby with Bruce Page and Philip Knightley. It was an amazing tale and I always remember some of those correspondents who had been with Philby when he was working as the Observer's man in Beirut telling of how they frequently had to carry him upstairs to bed, literally legless after another heavy night in the hotel bar. And he never dropped the mask; never dropped a hint; never offered a clue as to who he really was. I find that extraordinary, this ability to succumb to alcohol while closing off that part of your brain you don't want anyone to see. 'Patricia' used to have a few but she never got that drunk.

Dear David Leitch was not a man to keep secrets and actually wrote a fascinating book called *Family Secrets*, one of two that covered his extraordinary and unfortunate beginning in life. The other was called *God Stand Up for Bastards*. He wasn't technically a bastard but his parents had sold him when he was eight days old in the lobby of the Russell Hotel in Bloomsbury. Really. Obviously it was not something he was afraid to talk about and a more endearing and amusing companion it would be hard to find.

In our Paris days, he was living with an ethereal and faintly erotic Australian poet called Jill Neville in one of those dark, cavernous apartments that can be found near the Luxembourg Gardens in the shadow of the Pantheon. By then he had made his name through his exceptional coverage of Vietnam for the Sunday Times and was recognised as one of the most perceptive foreign correspondents of his time.

Later he married Rosie Boycott, who would go on to edit the Independent and Daily Express after their marriage collapsed. They had lived in a book-lined flat in Little Venice overlooking the canal before too much weed and wine and resulting bad temper had broken things asunder. David moved into a little flat nearby and one day I saw him walking towards Lords to watch the cricket, a lonely figure in his raincoat, clutching a bag of sandwiches on a grey day. I wanted to call out but the lights changed and I was swept on into the gridlock of the Edgware Road. I never saw him again and I have felt guilty ever since.

One evening at a restaurant a year or two before, he had wept on my shoulder and called me his best friend. I am not at all sure I deserved the accolade but it is not something you forget and, near the end, before he died in 2004 at 67, I did not act like a best friend at all. Sorry, David.

But back to Paris. After a few months living with my Dad, I found a one bedroom flat to rent in a modern building on the Rue Jean Goujon. It was affordable but, more than that, its location was very appealing. From my little balcony at the back I could look across a couple of courtyards and actually see 6, Rue Francois 1er, where I had been born. It was like returning to the womb.

My father, being the good chartered accountant he was, helped me with much of the paperwork required to rent an apartment in Paris – after 50 years living in the city he knew the ropes! – and my mother came over from London to help me choose some furniture and make the place look like a home. Daddy came round one day when she was there and they met for the first time in decades. After a while they decided to go off and get a sandwich together and I have this image of them walking with the uncertainty of old age, my mother holding on to my father's arm, as they disappeared round the corner into the Rue Bayard. It was a sight I had never expected to see again and it caught me with more emotions than I can describe.

The job was going well and it was a fun time to be a reporter in Paris, not least because Britain and the United States had both assigned ambassadors to France who were not your average envoys. Christopher Soames was a large man with a personality to match who also happened to be Winston Churchill's son-in-law, so once again I found myself interacting with members of Britain's leading political family. His style of ambassadorship befitted his extrovert personality and he and Mary Soames certainly kept the champagne flowing as they worked at maintaining the entente cordial.

The Ambassador did, however, find the need to call on the assistance of his teenage daughter Emma when he tried to get into Castel's one night. Castel's was the leading discotheque of the time, situated down a side street just off the Boulevard St Germain, and was not open to the average night clubber. There was a lady who sat behind a little guichet just inside the front door and, if she didn't recognise you, she didn't press the buzzer to let you in. She had no idea who Christopher Soames was and wasn't interested in his status. "Pas possible." So Soames had to ask to use a telephone and call his teenage daughter Emma, who was, of course, tres connu at Castel's, and she persuaded the lady to let her father in.

The American Ambassador was none other than Sargent Shriver, brother-in-law to the Kennedy clan who had been posted to Paris by President Johnson just a few months before I arrived. It was a master stroke by LBJ because Franco-American relations had frozen to the point of zero contact between Shriver's predecessor and President de Gaulle and Sarge, with his warm, boisterous, upbeat personality, could de-frost a fridge at a glance.

I had met Shriver in America because he was not only a tennis fan but had employed Donald Dell as one of his young assistants at the Office of Economic Opportunity in Washington DC, a role he took on after founding the Peace Corps. But LBJ's decision to pick Shriver for the role was not simply based on his social skills. Unashamed, for once, to use a Kennedy-link, Johnson had taken into account the fact that President de Gaulle was besotted with Jackie Kennedy and would take kindly to having her brother-in-law in Paris. And so it proved. Despite an excruciating accent, of which more in a moment, Sarge would throw caution to the wind and march up to Le Grand Charles at formal receptions where de Gaulle would often stand around looking lonely because people were terrified of approaching him and say, "Bon jour, mon General – comment ca va?"

The General might have winced but he appeared to be quite amused by Shriver's bravado and the thaw quickly set in. Suddenly everyone found the Elysee easier to deal with.

Shriver explained the language problem to me one day when he called me up ("Comment ca va, Dick" – eek) to invite me over to the Embassy for a chat. "The request to take this post came right out of the blue," he explained. "And although I felt I couldn't refuse, it left me with a problem. All through my days at the Peace Corps I had Iaid down the law about no one being allowed to go to a country unless they spoke the language, no matter if it was Hindu or Swahili. I couldn't break my own rule so I had a six-week crammer course in French before getting on the plane!"

I teased him about his accent but it was an impressive effort nonetheless. We rattled on about politics and tennis and various things way past the allotted time which did not amuse the person next in line to see the Ambassador that morning. As I left through the little ante-chamber, I caught sight of a slightly cross-looking Billy Graham waiting to go in. I asked the Lord's forgiveness.

The move to Paris had done nothing to diminish my involvement with tennis, which, thanks to an understanding editor, I was able to maintain by covering the major tournaments. I had missed the drama of the 1968 French Open, played out against a backdrop of riots on the Left Bank, but, of course, it became my local tournament from 1969 onwards and I was there to see Rod Laver progress towards his second Grand Slam – winning all four majors in one calendar year – by beating his long-time rival Ken Rosewall in the final. For the following two years Jan Kodes, a stiff-limbed Czech with a stern countenance who went on to do great things for tennis in his country, totally dominated Roland Garros, winning back-to-back titles in 1970 and '71.

Being the same age as many of the top players it was inevitable in those free and easy days that I would become good friends with some of them – none more so than Pierre Barthes, the French No. 1 of the time, who had recently married Carolyn, a long-legged, ethereal blonde beauty from Canada whose grandfather happened to be Leslie Howard, the British actor of *Gone with the Wind* fame amongst numerous other starring roles. Tragically, Howard had been killed when a plane he took out of Lisbon during the war was shot down, the rumour being that the Nazis thought Churchill was on it.

Howard's genes lived on his granddaughter whose delicate, finely chiselled features bear a striking resemblance to the actor. Carolyn had gone to all the right schools in Toronto and had moved in social circles that included Conrad Black. I am not quite sure what her parents thought about their very eligible daughter falling for a French tennis pro, but if you knew Pierre you would know why. Handsome was only the half of it. The young man from Bezier exudes a Gallic charm that has made him friends everywhere, some in very high places. The Chinese Ambassador to Paris for many years was so taken with him that Pierre has been working on some major development projects in China. There is hardly a President of a major French corporation that he does not know from Peugeot to Gaz de France to Air France. His colleagues on the tour in the sixties used to call him 'Spacey' because of his fractured English and tendency to forget things but, with Carolyn's help, he started his business career by creating the largest tennis camp in Europe at Cap d'Agde near Montpellier long before the likes of Nick Bollettieri got started. That smile and Pierre's infectious enthusiasm are difficult to resist.

But back in 1969, he was a newly-wed who used to spend all his prize money on calling Carolyn if she was not travelling with him and, for one reason or another, he could not be with his wife when she delivered their first child. Nicolas Barthes was born in Toronto and his father was alone in

Paris – until, that is, I heard my apartment doorbell ring. Pierre was standing there with a silly grin on his face. "Richard, I am a Papa!" he giggled. "We must celebrate!"

And, indeed, we did. Pierre drove us across the river to the aforementioned Castel's where, as was the case at Regine's and other top night spots, regular customers could order a bottle of Scotch, have their name put on it, and imbibe whenever they returned at a later date. Jacques Renevand, the genial host of Castel's at the time, just happened to be a former French Davis Cup player and naturally made sure that the tennis fraternity always received a warm welcome. With some other friends, he helped us celebrate the far-away arrival of little Nicolas. So much so that we decided to buy a bottle of Scotch and put his name on it.

"Then, in eighteen years' time, we can come back and help him drink it!" exclaimed Pierre as we all raised a glass. Unhappily I was not present when the moment arrived but Nico did, indeed, have a glass from a well-aged bottle that had been sitting patiently on the shelf, and more toasts were in order. And plenty more are now. The younger Barthes has grown past his father by several inches and risen through the ranks of Nike to become a senior executive after several years looking after the tennis division. It's all about getting the proper start in life.

A few months later, Pierre said to me, "I am crazy; I have bought this 'ouse. It is very large but very beautiful. I think I have spent all my money."

He pronounced the word like the artist's name and the house he had bought at Vaucresson, a few miles down the road from Versailles, was certainly worth a canvas or two. It is built in the mould of a classical French chateau with a swimming pool in front of the terrace and proved to be a beautiful home for Carolyn, Nico, Sybilla and Emma, as well as a long line of Labradors who have always been part of the family. Thanks to Carolyn's unending generosity, I have stayed at Vaucresson during Roland Garros and the Paris Indoor at Bercy for more years than I dare think about and, of course, owe them more hospitality than I could ever repay.

Albina du Boisrouvray came from a very different milieu. We met soon after I had been posted to Paris at a very formal, incredibly buttoned-up dinner party at a grand apartment just off the Champs Elysees. I have no idea why I was invited but, thank heaven, I found myself seated next to this raven-haired beauty with a wicked smile who was obviously as bored with the starchy formalities as I was. We soon found ourselves chatting away happily about movies which was easy as Albina was a fully-fledged producer at the time and would go on to make films like *Police Python* with Yves Montand and Simone Signoret and, some years later, *Fort Saganne*, which was shot with in the middle of the Mauritanian desert with Gerard Depardieu and Catherine Deneuve.

She spoke flawless English; had a terrific sense of humour and enjoyed the economic luxury of being directly related to the Patino tin-mining family in Bolivia. We became intimate friends – intimate to the extent that we shared hotel bedrooms together in Rome, Porto Ercole and Phnom-Penh but never became lovers. That was the way she wanted it and I valued her friendship too much to argue.

She had a son by a Swiss Alpine pilot who was as blond as she was dark and Francois-Xavier took his father's genes, growing up to be a tall, lanky young man with a mop of flaxen blond hair. He was called Truffi by the family and, when he was away at school in Switzerland, Albina sweetly let me use his room while I was working on the Ilie Nastase book at her apartment overlooking the Seine on the Cours Albert 1er, just a few hundred yards from my own place. I had rented it for a time to a South African model and, although she shared it platonically with me on and off, it was difficult to get the peace and quiet I needed to write a book.

So the years passed and Albina remained a great friend. Truffi went on to get an engineering degree at the University of Michigan and when he returned we occasionally played tennis at the Polo Club on the edge of the Bois de Boulogne with his mother's second husband, the film producer Georges Casati. I saw Truffi one night, having a great time with some young friends – ex-princes of Yugoslavia, I believe – at a party at the Meridien Hotel at the Porte Maillot. He could have developed into an aimless party man with too much money, but Francois-Xavier was far too intelligent and committed for that. Following in his father's footsteps, he became a helicopter pilot and flew some 300 rescue missions in the Alps. Helping people was in his DNA.

In 1986, I disappeared on one of my longer trips to Asia which finished with a few days spent with the England cricket team, then captained by Mark Nicholas, in Colombo. I took an Air Lanka flight back to Paris and we stopped at Zurich where I got off and bought the Observer in the lounge. Settling back into my seat my blood ran cold. At the bottom of the page there was a small item which read 'Helicopter pilot dies in Dakar Rally crash'. It was Francois-Xavier.

Apparently, he had been ordered to take off in a sandstorm and had crashed in Mali, dying along with his three passengers. He was 24. Horrified at his death, my first thoughts fled to Albina. As soon as I landed, I tried phoning her at the apartment and then her office but the accident had happened three days before and it was too late for me to help even though there was little I could have done. Albina disappeared in a cocoon of grief and when I eventually reached Georges he told me that she was inconsolable and would not see anyone. Later, I learned that she had considered suicide.

But Albina was a stronger woman than that. Recovering her strength she decided to build a monument to her son by helping others. She founded Francois-Xavier International, FXB, a development organisation that, in the thirty years since Truffi's death, has helped some 17 million families whose lives have been devastated by AIDS in places like Colombia, Rwanda, India, Burma and Thailand. She did it by divesting herself of much of her wealth, auctioning off jewellery, real estate and her late father's paintings and raising about $100 million.

The extent of the work she had achieved was brought home to me in 1999 when I was driving to the Longwood Cricket Club for the Davis Cup Centenary celebrations – the US was playing Australia – and looking up, I found myself passing a large building on Huntingdon Avenue emblazoned with the name Francois-Xavier Bagnoud. Albina had donated $20 million to build the FXB Centre for Health and Human Rights at the Harvard School of Public Health. No wonder she was made a John Harvard Fellow, just one of innumerable awards she has received over the past two decades including the Legion d'Honneur and receiving a Lifetime Achievement Award in India for her work in 35 states in that vast nation.

Mark Honigsbaum told her story well in a piece in the Observer in March 2012 and you can see Albina talk about her life's work on YouTube by watching a Plum TV clip from 2008. "Children who had parents with AIDS don't have their parents anymore," she said. "I don't have my son anymore so it seemed a natural thing to do."

She is insistent that FXB is not a charity because, rather than just giving handouts, its aim is to help people stand on their own feet and lead their own lives without constant help. "We are below micro-aid," she says. "We give the poorest of the poor $345 over three years to buy a cow and then pigs and chickens so that they can start to build a life."

Albina embarked on a new life and I was not part of it. We exchanged letters and, once, several years later, spoke on the phone. But the only way she was able to cope in the early years following Truffi's death was to block out the past and I was part of that past. I hadn't been there the instant she would have needed me most and, as I keep saying, life is all about timing.

Albina has proved herself to be a remarkable woman who has given life and hope to so many and I am so proud of her. She lost a son and I lost a friend. The two are not comparable but both are very meaningful to me.

Charles de Gaulle was still President of France when I arrived in Paris in January 1969, but not for long. He had pulled one of the great political sleights of hand by campaigning in 1958 on the basis of supporting France's colonial aspirations in Algeria and then pulling the rug once he got into the Elysees in January 1959 after a brief stint as Prime Minister. The wrath of the French right wing, and, in particular the Army generals, at the thought of Algeria being given independence was considerable and led to attempts on his life. But the man obviously had nine lives. He had defied German snipers by marching up the Champs Elysees unprotected at the head of the Free French Forces in 1944 and then, in 1962, he and his wife defied all the laws of probability by surviving an ambush, carried out by eleven OAS extremists, as he was driven from the Elysee Palace to Orly Airport. No less than 140 bullets were fired at his Citroen DS, mostly from behind, killing two police outriders and puncturing all four tires. Due to the Citroen's advanced suspension system which was way ahead of its time, the chauffeur was able to pull out of a skid and drive on. De Gaulle was a very large man but, by divine guidance or otherwise, not a single bullet touched either him or his wife.

Rather than becoming afraid for his life, I believe it was a general weariness about the attitude of the country he was trying to lead which prompted the decision to hold a referendum on decentralisation in the spring of 1969. The student riots of the previous year had shocked him and the failure of the French people to live up to his visions of grandeur left him in despair. He wanted France to be the greatest country on earth but the French didn't seem to get the message. So, to all intents and purposes, he committed political suicide. He knew the people were getting a little weary of him after ten years of Gaullism and he knew the risk of losing the referendum was high. But he insisted on going through with it and, on the 28th April, duly lost. A remarkable decade which had transformed France in so many ways had come to an unnecessary end. De Gaulle, as haughty and unbending as ever, gave a final speech and retired to the solitude of his house, La Boisserie, in the little village of Colombey-les-Deux-Eglise, 160 miles west of Paris.

After I had been in Paris for just over a year, I was approached by Erik de Mauny, the veteran BBC Paris bureau chief, who told me he was looking for a back-up reporter to cover for him when he was out of town. John Gold didn't seem to mind me indulging in a little more freelance work so I started doing the odd radio piece, drawing on my experience with CBS in New York.

I had barely woken up on the morning of 9th November 1970 when the phone rang. It was a frantic Janine, the BBC Office Manager. "It's De Gaulle!" she yelled. "He is dead. And Erik, he is on a plane. You must come!"

So I threw on some clothes, jumped in the little red Triumph Vitesse which I was driving at the time, and raced across the Champs Elysees to the BBC studios at the top of the Rue St. Honore. And there, catching my breath, I went live on air to announce the death of one of the great military and political figures of the 20th century. He was a hard man to love but Charles De Gaulle loved France and he died with the nation in his debt.

Again, life is all about timing and I would never have had the chance of making such an historic announcement had not Erik de Mauny taken a 9.00 am flight to Rome that morning to attend some conference or other. Of course, he turned around and flew straight back but by then I had done a couple of more considered pieces and everyone at Broadcasting House seemed grateful that I had been available to fill in.

By the end of 1970, I was starting to hear rumours from London that the Evening News was in financial trouble. As it was still selling close to one million copies a day, this seemed difficult to believe but reality set in when I got a phone call from John Gold telling me that the bean-counters were insisting he cut costs and the Paris bureau was going to be one of the savings. He offered me a job on the subs desk in London, the thought of which did not appeal to put it mildly, although had I been more patient, it might have led to something worthwhile.

A couple of people had sent word through the grapevine that my work in the field had inspired thoughts of future editorship of the paper, following the precedent Gold had set. It was flattering and, I thought, somewhat far-fetched. Even if I had returned to London and moved in the direction of the editor's chair it would have done me little good because about six years later the Evening News was effectively shut down, merging with its arch-rival, the Evening Standard in a complicated deal that saw Northcliffe newspapers buy the Standard title from Beaverbrook. For while The Evening News name remained on the masthead but no one was fooled. The Evening Standard survived and does so today – as a free sheet, which tells you where the newspaper industry has got to in this digital age.

So, once again giving in to my instinctive inclination towards independence, I turned down the London offer with the assurance from Gold that he would use me from time to time as a freelance. This turned out well, even after John left to be replaced by Lou Kirby and, in 1972, I found myself back in America covering the Nixon re-election and subsequent debacle.

But, in the meantime, I remained in Paris, searching for work which, happily, was always available in the tennis world, and continuing to broadcast pieces for the BBC. Soon, I was forced to reveal just how stubborn I could be about refusing to be tied down. Erik de Mauny called me in one day and offered me the position of his full-time deputy. He said he wanted to travel more and spend time at his country retreat in Normandy and he was sure I could fill the role.

Again it was flattering and again, deary me, I said, "No." I would have been at the BBC's beck and call night and day with little chance of ever leaving Paris. I could see myself tugging at the strings in order to get free for Wimbledon and Forest Hills and anything else I wanted to do. Security? Never a word that interested me much. I was still young, quite experienced, unmarried and still able to buy a few airline tickets.

So I did and set off on a strange double assignment which, possibly, only I could have thought up. I had been invited to cover the Seiko Classic, a big indoor tournament on the ATP tour in Tokyo in those days and, on the way back, I would drop in for a third visit to Vietnam. I had a personal reason for wanting to return to Vietnam, but then, my Indo-China travels deserve a whole chapter to themselves.

My mother, Mary Evans, adding a little glamour to post-war Paris.

My father, Harry Evans, in his early days as Price Waterhouse partner in Paris.

Dad with one of his pre World War Two cars.

My beautiful sister Margot, now in her nineties and then about 85, making a mockery of the passing years.

Private Evans and a fellow Warley Barracks inmate lean on Brian Henderson who later played rugby for Scotland.

This suggests I am about to do something brilliant in Philippe Chatrier's Press v Players Am rugby match. Wrong. The chap who is about to flatten me – and did – is Jean Prat who captained France & was called "Monsieur Rugby".

Two great friends, Pierre Barthes and Roy Emerson, early in their careers.

To Richard
With Sincere Regards
Althea Gibson

Having written her copy through Wimbledon in 1960,
I get to dance with Althea Gibson at the ball.

Richard Russell, the Jamaican No 1 who showed me
how to make the most of life, Caribbean style.

Donald Dell working out another contract for his client Stan Smith during a tournament in Jamaica. Could have been the Adidas shoe contract which is still selling in its millions today.

. The ever effervescent Billi Jean King who won titles galore and, with Larry King, founded World Team Tennis which she sold recently to the great entrepreneur Mark Ein of the Washington Kastles and San Diego Aviators owner Fred Luddy.

John McEnroe always wanted to be a rock star. Much later he ended up marrying one, Patti Smyth, who really could sing.

THE **WORLD**
WCT CHAMPIONSHIP of TENNIS

14th leg in the 20 tournament one million dollar series

NAME		POINTS		TOURN WINS
OHN NEWCOMBE	AUST.	5	8	4
OM OKKER	NETH.	5	4	2
FF DRYSDALE	S.A.	5	1	1
D LAVER	AUST.	4	6	1
RTHUR ASHE	U.S.A.	4	5	
6 KEN ROSEWALL	AUST.	4	5	3
7 MARTY RIESSEN	U.S.A.	3	5	1
ROY EMERSON	AUST.	2	1	
ANDRES GIMENO	SPAIN	1	8	
BOB LUTZ	U.S.A.	1	7	
DENNIS RALSTON	U.S.A.	1	5	
JOHN ALEXANDER	AUST.	1	4	
RAY RUFFELS	AUST.	1	2	
CHARLES PASARELL	U.S.A	1	2	
OGER TAYLOR	G.B.	1	1	
MAIL EL SHAFEI	U.A.R.	1	1	
B MAUD	S.A.	1	1	
CKI PILIC	YUGOSLAVIA	1	0	
Y ROCHE	AUST.	1	0	
K COX	G.B.		8	
STOLLE	AUST.		7	
			6	

Cliff Drysdale has a laugh with WCT boss Mike Davies at the Colonial Country Club in Fort Worth. Davies sent all those guys on the leader board all over the world, setting the standard for pro tournaments in the early 1970's.

When he lived at Rancho Mirage in California, I got Rod Laver to produce all four of his Wimbledon trophies. Later he sent two to the International Hall of Fame.

A young Yannick Noah captured at Gstaad by photographer Roxanne Francois
whose sister Diane was a great friend and later formed her own law firm.

I was always happy to spend time with the great Jack Kramer, 1947 Wimbledon champion and godfather of professional tennis who taught me so much.

Chic as always – the lovely Carolyn Barthes.

Mike Hurst, a fine Australian track & field coach and former Sydney Telegraph sports writer and I visit Ted Tinling, a true original, at the Rembrandt Hotel in Knightsbridge.

At Lord's, my spiritual home, with Maxine Walters, a loyal friend over so many years and her Chloe, my god daughter.

On the campaign before it all came to a tragic end – Senator Robert. F. Kennedy.

Our paths did not cross in Vietnam but Nik Wheeler, one of Newsweek's top photographers during the conflict, and his wife Pamela Bellwood have been dear friends for decades.

At the Kremlin Cup, Gene Scott said, "I'm going to be late. Can you make my speech for me?" So, at a half hour's notice, I found myself addressing 200 Russians inside the Kremlin. Just to annoy them, I talked about the integrity of professional sport.

At a refugee camp outside Da Lat, I finally get to meet my Vietnamese foster child, Truong Van Manh.

The brilliant Mel DiGiacomo catches Arthur Ashe in a
typical moment of reflection at a change over.

After his first historic visit, Arthur Ashe returned to South
Africa to oversee the building of courts in Soweto.

Soon after we met, I took Gayle Hunnicutt to Cairo for a tournament.
Mike Estep, long time coach of Martina Navratilova and John
Feaver, a big figure in British tennis, were glad to meet her.

Ilie Nastase wafted his racket as a magic wand. But tying his black tie? Henri Leconte had to provide assistance in Monte Carlo.

In Fiji, where we were guests at John Newcombe's Tennis Ranch, a local village welcomed Carol Thatcher in traditional style.

Three great Grand Slam champions, Fred Stolle, Manolo Santana and John Newcombe enjoy the Barthes hospitality on the terrace at Vaucresson.

Ingrid Lofdahl Bentzer and former Italian No 1 Lea Pericoli who both played rather well at the Monte Carlo Country Club. It says so – carved in marble.

Gene Scott (right) pictured here with Graeme Agars and myself. Graeme, equally at home in the worlds of golf and tennis, was PR for the ATP tour many years. Gene played more roles in tennis than is possible to describe. We miss him so much.

John McEnroe and Ingrid Lofdahl Bentzer, who makes you laugh on
any occasion, react to Peter Ustinov's wit at the Arthur Ashe Memorial
Dinner that Ingrid and I staged at the Grosvenor House.

Orville Brown, who helped me
create the Grassroots Challenge in
Brockwell Park, later won the ATP
Humanitarian Award. Here he is
with the wonderful Pidge Spencer,
then Miss Hutton of the ATP.

Patrick McEnroe and Cliff Drysdale
on duty for ESPN, waiting no doubt
for another tit-bit of information
from Lynn, who worked as their
Stage Manager for a while.

. The sporty and incredibly bright Lee family always make me feel at home. Here, in their Ealing garden: Kate Lee, her daughter-in-law Gael; Richard Lee and Jeffrey Lee. The beautiful Tessa lives in Italy. Their father Marshall lives in our hearts.

At Monte Carlo's Night of the Stars gala, Lynn and I sit next to the legendary J.P. – John Parsons, tennis correspondent of the Daily Telegraph.

Lynn shows how carrying a two year old across the terrace of the Monte Carlo Country Club can be achieved with style. Ashley is now 6ft 5". No more carrying.

At the age of 83, E.W. (Jim) Swanton still on active duty, checking Wisden in the press enclosure of the Kensington Oval, Barbados during the 1990 England tour. Geoffrey Dean seems to be on deadline.

I got to know Lew Hoad properly in Spain but every Australian Open I get the chance to say 'Good'day, mate' as I walk past the statues at Melbourne Park.

Relaxing and growing – Ashley in Florence.

George and Heather Mitchell chat to Ilie Nastase during the
Monte Carlo Open. The Bernard Noat, who was a good friend
and tournament director at the time, is in the background.

Risking life & limb, I took this photo of Dell's boys in the middle
of the Champs Elysees. L to R: Tom Gorman, Donald Dell,
Charlie Pasarell, Stan Smith, Arthur Ashe and Bob Lutz.

My family gathered in New Jersey for the 1995 wedding – l to r: brother Tony, Andy Scholz, my nieces Elizabeth Campbell & Claire Scholz, sister Margot. Seated l to r: Alan Campbell, sister Pat and Margot's husband Frank Melville.

Wedding guests: Back row: l to r: Maxine Walters, Chloe Walters who was a beautiful Flower Girl, Nancy Burke, Kevin O'Keefe. Front: Betty and Tommy Tucker, Bridget Byrne, Linda Pentz Gunter.

Chapter 12
VIETNAM

It's the air. The moment you breathe it, moist and faintly scented, impregnated with the perfumes of orchids and frangipani – then you know you are in South-east Asia. The scent even won out when competing with the greased up mechanical horror of Tan Son Nhut Airport as I climbed down the steps from the Pan Am 707 to be confronted by more military hardware than I have ever seen. It was 1965 and America's involvement in the Vietnamese war, which pitted Communist North against the supposedly democratic South, was reaching its peak.

Everywhere you looked there were trucks, jeeps, hulking Hercules cargo planes and troop carriers, helicopters and – screeching against your eardrums – the noise of F-4C fighter jets flashing down the runway. At the time, it was the busiest airport in the world.

It was the first of three visits I would make to Vietnam, Cambodia and Laos between 1965 and 1972 and let me make an early disclaimer. As I write there have been unfortunate incidents of American TV personalities trying to bolster, or maybe even justify, their fame and importance by embellishing stories about what they did in the war, be it Vietnam, the Falklands or Iraq. I was saddened when Brian Williams of NBC was found to be claiming to have done things he never had and I found it shocking that the egregiously smug and self-satisfied Bill O'Reilly on FoxNews tried to maintain he had been at the sharp end of the Falklands conflict when he had barely left his Buenos Aires hotel room. Williams' career at MSNBC was put on hold for a while and, happily he is now showing his skills as a late night political anchor. However, FoxNews, which believes a fact is something to be manipulated and bent out of shape for one's own ends, allowed O'Reilly to continue lecturing his audience like the schoolmaster he used to be, glibly maintaining that 'the spin stops here'. No, it doesn't, Mr O'Reilly. It begins with you. Take a bet on much of what you hear on FoxNews being distorted or plain wrong and you'll win money.

All that is by way of saying you're not going to hear too many tales of der-ring-do from me. I wanted to go to Vietnam because it was THE story of my early years as a foreign correspondent and I did want to witness war, not only to see if I could take it, but also because I felt it important to tell the story accurately which was something the American military singularly failed to do.

It wasn't just a case of journalistic cynicism that resulted in the 5.00 pm press conference held each evening in Saigon by the MACV spokesman being dubbed the Five O'Clock Follies. There were no dancing girls but if brazen manipulation of the truth was your bag, it was almost as entertaining.

So I wanted to find out what was what without trying to become a hero. When I got to Saigon, I discovered there were plenty of young guys hell bent on trying to become just that. Someone offered me a bed at an apartment being rented by a group of photographers – an American, a Cuban and an Argentine as far as I can remember. But the most celebrated resident was not there that week and it was his bed I slept in.

I have still not met Tim Page. There were a lot of genuine journalistic heroes to come out of the Vietnam war and Tim was probably near the top of the list. He was a pot-smoking adventurer who became a photographer as he moved through the Far East, ostensibly on his way to Australia. He never got that far because the war lured him to Vietnam where he got himself wounded four times, putting himself in harm's way; doing everything the US Marines did and getting some amazing photographs for UPI who had hired him initially as a freelance. In his brilliant book *Despatches*, Michael Herr referred to Page as 'the most extravagant of the wigged-out crazies run-ning around Vietnam'. But Page earned the respect of the Marines to such an extent that, when he landed on a mine jumping out of a helicopter and had part of his skull blown away, he became the first civilian to be treated at the Walter Reade Army Hospital in Washington DC. They flew him there and paid for it. Quite a statement and it may have saved his life.

Looking around the apartment, I felt I was living with a few other crazies. Opening up a cupboard I was faced with a small arsenal of weaponry – pis-tols, hand grenades and a machine gun. The Cuban, in particular, looked as if he was trying to emulate Che Guevara and it was obvious they were all acting out some wild schoolboy fantasy. I made a mental note to stay away from the guns and I never carried one during any of my visits – especially not in Cambodia, where your last chance of survival if the Khmer Rouge captured you would be ruined instantly if they found a weapon on you.

But let's backtrack a bit because the journey out to Vietnam from Los Angeles in 1965 was not without incident. I was flying on one of Tony's Pan Am Sublo 3 tickets again and our first stop was Honolulu. I had never been to Hawaii and the thought of wasting a four-hour stopover sitting at the airport was too much to bear so I hailed a cab and gave him the only name I had ever heard of on Waikiki Beach – The Beachcomber.

It was everything I expected, bamboo furniture and an open-air bar surrounded by heavy tropical foliage. Literally the first person I saw as I walked up to the bar was Roger Taylor, British's No. 1 tennis player at the time, who was on his way to Australia. He was already a good friend and we clasped each other in surprise.

After a few minutes we fell into conversation with a couple of well-dressed young Americans and time started to pass quickly. Looking at my watch, I said, "Oh my God, I'd better get going. I don't want to miss my flight to Manila!"

"Pan Am 1?" one of them answered. "Don't worry, we're on that flight and you can hitch a ride with us. That plane's not going to leave without us."

It was not an idle comment. It turned out that we had fallen into the company of two US Congressmen, John Culver of Iowa and John Tunney of California, who were on their way to Vietnam to link up with a close friend to both of them, Senator Edward Kennedy.

Tunney, who was the son of the famous heavyweight champion Gene Tunney, had been a roommate of Ted Kennedy's at Virginia Law School while Culver had played on the same Harvard football team as the youngest Kennedy brother. All three remained lifelong friends and Culver was one of the speakers at Kennedy's funeral in 2013.

Tunney and Culver had both just been elected to Congress but they would go on to become Democratic Senators in the early seventies and would serve their country with distinction throughout long careers. But they were young and boisterous when we met and, for me, the chance meeting was fortuitous to say the least.

"We're meeting Teddy in Manila so come and join us!" Tunney exclaimed. "Maybe we can get you on some of the fact-finding missions out in the country when we get to 'Nam."

He was as good as his word. I remember watching a sunset of many colours settling over Manila Bay as we partied in their hotel suite and then, on arrival in Saigon, working through a bit of red tape to get myself accredited as a journalist so that I could fly down to the Delta with Kennedy's party. We dropped in on various US outposts and, finally, an Australian encampment. The Aussies were in the Vietnam War while Britain stayed out, geographical proximity being one of the reasons. It was no secret that the US Marines and Cavalry units struggled a bit in the early years of the war because, unlike the Australians, who had fought against the Communist-insurgency in Malaya, they were inexperienced in jungle fighting.

"The Yanks have still got a bit to learn," I remember one Aussie captain telling me. "When we go out on patrol for ten days, no one opens their mouth. The jungle has ears. Everything is done with hand signals. We don't leave Wrigley chewing gum wrappers behind us, either."

There is always rivalry between allies while fighting a war and there was obviously plenty here. I didn't get to talk to Ted Kennedy too much but it was a wild ride, not least because I had my first experience of flying in a Huey, the helicopter that, more than any other piece of equipment, allowed the US Forces to at least hold their own in a war that was proving more than a little difficult.

The thing about flying in a Huey, especially if you are on the end of the line of four seats behind the pilot, is that you listen very carefully when he tells you to strap yourself in. There is no door. As he banks away and tilts the thing at an angle there is nothing between you and the carpet of jungle below except nice, warm tropical air. You only need to be told once.

Back in Saigon, I stayed at the fabulous Continental Palace Hotel with its veranda overlooking the square and, inside, a garden courtyard where breakfast was served by white-coated waiters. I remember the coffee and papayas with that skin texture, so velvety, moist and pink. Saigon was a sensual place, even when overrun by GIs and Marines and army trucks. Somehow the slender Vietnamese, their women dressed in those beautiful 'ao dais', with the silk of the leggings fluttering as they weaved their bicycles in and out of the traffic, managed to survive the heavy-handed invasion. There was no more incongruous sight than a 6' 4" broad shouldered GI walking down Tu Do Street, clutching the tiny hand of his 4' 10" Vietnamese girlfriend. One wondered how she survived the nocturnal embrace.

Tu Do Street, formerly Rue Catinat in the days of the French, was the street for restaurants and bars with their alluring hostesses who may or may not have been in the pay of the Viet Cong. Some of the bars had money changers at the back and I noticed that, almost without exception, the person changing your dollars was an Indian.

I made a couple more trips out of town, once to Cam Ranh Bay, one of the great natural deep-water ports of South-East Asia which was chock-a-block with US navy supply ships, merchant vessels and the odd Destroyer. There was a lot of work going on as they needed a runway and I remember talking to one large Sergeant who told me, "We're doing fine. Once we get rid of that hill over there, we'll be able to make the extension."

Just move a hill. The air of optimism; the feeling that there was nothing America could not achieve, still pervaded the whole operation in 1965. Reality had yet to set in.

I returned to the reality of the United States, a new job and the policies and politics that were so affected by everything that was going on in Vietnam. One of the basic problems for the American people in trying to understand what was happening lay in the conflicted reports from the battlefield. The wire services like AP, UPI and Reuters were duty bound to report what was said at the Five O'Clock Follies because it was official. And, true or not, those reports found their way into 90% of the newspapers across America who did not have their own correspondents in Vietnam. So, depending on the diligence and bravery of the correspondents assigned at great expense by the New York Times, the Washington Post, The Baltimore Sun and Los Angeles Times, to name some of the few rich enough to have their own reporters in the field, readers found themselves reading about a very different war – a war that was not so gung-ho and glorious.

Peter Arnett, a New Zealander who gave AP's reporting a different slant no matter what his colleagues were forced to file, Morley Safer of CBS, and the New York Times pair, David Halberstam and Neil Sheehan, were at the top of a list of brilliant reporters who slowly started to open the public's eyes to the truth. In contrast, for too many others, The Five O'Clock Follies was preceded most days by nice lunches on the terrace of the Continental or in the air-conditioned comfort of the Caravelle on the other side of the square. But that was not the way to cover the war. To do your job properly, you needed to go out and find it.

The great irony of the whole media operation was the way the US Military co-operated totally in helping you get out into the countryside to monitor what was really happening and then lied through their teeth to you by the time they got you back to Saigon at five o'clock. It was really weird.

'US casualties were light while over 100 Viet Cong were killed' might have been the official report of the day which flatly contradicted what Arnett or Sheehan had seen as they watched a fleet of Hueys climb away laden with dead or wounded Marines. And 100 Viet Cong dead? No one had gone out and counted the bodies.

The problem of two different wars being presented to the American public had become so acute while President Kennedy was in office that he finally picked up the phone to Arthur Sulzberger, publisher of the New York Times and demanded that David Halberstam be recalled.

"He's lying," Kennedy raged. "His reports totally contradict what Secretary of State Dean Rusk and my generals tell me."

Kennedy was right in one aspect. There was a severe contradiction because Rusk was not being told the truth – a fact that was hammered home to him, I heard, by a reporter at a Washington dinner party. Rusk, a quiet, somewhat aloof figure, was hugely embarrassed.

But the facts were clear. Good news was exaggerated and bad news watered down. It was human nature. If you were in charge of one of the villages that the US Army had been sent to protect under the pacification programme and it was attacked in the middle of the night by swarms of little men in black pyjamas, the report sent back to MACV headquarters in Saigon for the perusal of the US Commander, General Paul Harkins, would play down the extent of the damage. Picking up on the least bleak aspects of the attack – the village had triumphantly survived etc. – the report Rusk and Defense Secretary Robert McNamara would receive in Washington would reveal even less of the bloody mess the Viet Cong had left behind. Harkins' pride was at stake and nothing much changed when the celebrated General William Westmoreland took over. Long after he was removed following the Tet Offensive in 1968, Westmoreland sued CBS for a documentary which alleged he had boosted the number of Viet Cong troops he was facing so that he could persuade the Pentagon to send him more of his own. CBS apologised and the suit never came to trial.

This is what always tends to happen in times of crisis when the centre of operations is far from home. Sargent Shriver spelled it out for me one day. "When I was running the Peace Corps, I always had half a dozen young people travel around to where we were operating on the ground in Africa, Asia or South America and report straight back to me. No complicated bureaucratic lines of communication. They just got on a plane and walked in to this office to tell me the way it was – good or bad."

That was one reason why the Peace Corps was such a success. But Vietnam, of course, was a much more serious and dangerous situation. And, for me, the lure of it was undeniable. By the time, I got to Paris and became immersed in covering the peace talks, it was three years since I had made that initial trip to Saigon and I was itching to go back. By the end of 1970, the Evening News was about to close the bureau and I was doing more and more freelance work for BBC Radio. Peter Jennings had provided a contact at ABC Radio in New York, as well, so when the opportunity arose to head east, I grabbed it.

The Tet Offensive of 1968 had changed America's feelings about the war and, on the ground, the atmosphere amongst the US military had changed. The 'can-do' attitude had been tempered by the blood and loss of so many men and there was a realisation that the US commitment to Vietnam had to be finite. Nixon was looking for a way out but he was demanding that Kissinger save face in the process and so the bombing and the killing went on.

Back in Saigon, I took a room at the Continental, where the overhead fans were still whirring and the staff still bedded down in the corridors, and settled into the unchanged routine of heading for the MACV headquarters at the Majestic Hotel at 6.00 am and asking where the action was. "Take me to the war!" It was absurd really but all a lot more organised and therefore considerably safer than what was happening in Cambodia. As most of the work I did was for radio, my cuttings and points of reference are sparse but I do remember being flown up to Da Nang and spending a bleak night in the press HQ, where we slept under a blanket, side by side on thin, damp mattresses, listening to disturbing thump of Nixon's bombs exploding a few miles to the north. After a chopper flight to Pleiku the next morning to take a look at the last stages of a nocturnal fire-fight with some Viet Cong elements, I remember hitching a ride back to Saigon with Air America, the CIA airline that ploughed the skies of Indo-China carrying out all manner of clandestine missions.

They flew old prop Dakotas, the work-horses of World War Two, although I think the plane I took was a good deal smaller than that. I remember sitting just behind the young pilots who clearly had a sense of humour. "No, that's not right! You sure? Hell, we're way off course!" They kept this up for a couple of minutes while we peered out at the carpet of green jungle below us, wondering how many Viet Cong were tracking our journey. Eventually the couple of whackos up front burst out laughing. "Scare you, did we? It's OK, we know where we're going. Could fly it blindfold."

They probably could have, too, because those Air America guys knew their stuff when they weren't trying to be funny.

Saigon was swarming with every imaginable kind of correspondent and photographer, from the highly legitimate, like Morley Safer, who filled me in with a few 'do's and don'ts' tips over a coffee on the terrace of the Continental, to a rag bag of unqualified freelancers searching for glory.

I decided to head for less congested pastures and took a flight to Vientiane, the capital of neutral Laos, which was, at the time, the spy capital of the world. On the surface, it was a sleepy little place compared to the buzzing mayhem of Saigon but the chatter on the diplomatic cocktail party circuit or at the bar of the Constellation made up for that. Everyone remotely involved in the Indo-China conflict was to be found at one place or another. The Brits, the French, the Russians, the Chinese and, of course the Americans – they were all behaving with forced civility when invited to each other's embassies. There was even a Pathet-Lao colonel who leered politely at everyone as he clutched his Scotch and soda while his pals were killing people about 25 miles out of town. The Pathet-Lao were the rough equivalent of the Viet Cong, communist insurgents nibbling away at the status quo.

I decided to make a call on the North Vietnamese ambassador whose residence was a typical Asian-style villa situated in a residential neighbourhood of the city. He came out into the courtyard to talk to me, a sweaty, nervous little man who was obviously at his wits' end.

"They watch me all the time!" he exclaimed in a high-pitched voice using serviceable English. "Look! Look! They have cameras, every move we make is recorded!"

He was pointing to a couple of windows from a nearby house which did not seem to be especially festooned with monitoring kit but, no matter, this poor man was obviously not sleeping well and he was in serious need of repatriation.

The Ambassador was right in as much as everyone was observing everyone and trying to make out what was, and wasn't, the truth. Mostly it was a pack of lies. There was a Graham Greene novel in every conversation and some of the characters one ran into at the Constellation, run by an amiable but obviously very savvy Frenchman called Maurice Cavalerie, could have filled volumes. Although frequently bloodshot eyes offered tell-tale signs of opium addiction, Maurice was a handsome man who had been born of a French botanist father and upper-class Chinese beauty. Fleeing the fighting in the north, Cavalerie had brought his family to Vientiane and set up this far from upper class hotel with two floors of rooms that reeked of marijuana and a bar downstairs which opened onto the main street. People flocked to it because Maurice knew everyone and could fix anything, especially for the correspondents who drank quantities of his Heineken for which he owned the franchise. There were plenty of flies around in this hot, sticky city but none on Maurice.

There were Brits and Aussies; Czechs and Argentines; Italians and Poles, hippies and wanderers, some of whom really were scribblers or snappers of some form or another and many who were not. Everyone had a story and the majority, probably, were just doubling up – a bit of journalism and a nice little bit of cash in the hand from some embassy official or another for anything they heard.

The gossip continued through the night at the White Rose, one of the more notorious brothels in South-East Asia where, for the duration of a song on the juke box, the girls danced naked on your table for a dollar. Outside the mighty Mekong flowed on through the night with the twinkling lights of Thai villages clearly visible from the opposite bank.

It was late December and I spent Christmas Day at the home of a very nice young English couple. He was second secretary at the British Embassy and, from the inside, their home might have been situated in Surbiton. As we made small talk over a sherry, it became clear he was either being very wary or really didn't have a clue about what was going on. As Indo-China did not seem to have marked him in any visible way, I suspect it might have been the latter. But the kind, if slightly prim, hospitality was welcome on a day when one was thinking of family far away.

New Year's Eve was even more bizarre. I had travelled down to Pakse, one of the larger Laotian towns on the Mekong. I am sure not what I expected to find but the answer was nothing much, except a couple of Polish lorry drivers who were ensuring that whatever else one lacked in that part of the world, it wasn't going to be a Heineken. They obviously worked for Maurice. I chatted with them for a while at an open-air bar with a corrugated iron roof, sipping the inevitable beer, and then headed off to the boarding house I had found.

Sitting on the steps was a young Lao girl of about twenty, dressed in bulky army fatigues with no insignia. She smiled and when I opened the door, she followed me in. Just like that. Communication was purely by hand signal because she spoke not a word of English. I think I offered her a beer, my pals at the bar having been liberal with their cargo, and then we lay down on the bed. At no stage did she take off a stitch of clothing. It had been a long day and I fell asleep quickly. In the morning, she wakened me with a kiss, massaged me in all the right places and left. Had she just been looking for a place to sleep or was she just curious about round-eyed men? I have no idea. But I welcomed 1971 secure in the knowledge that I was unlikely to spend a more bizarre New Year's Eve.

Phnom-Penh was the next stop. It was a city I had always wanted to see, ever since my sister Margot had returned from Cambodia with tales of her time there as the wife of the British Charge d'Affaires. She had married George Littlejohn Cook in Stockholm towards the end of our time there when George was already in the Foreign Service. He had spent almost the entire war in a German prison camp.

A posting to Santiago, Chile followed and before they left for Cambodia, my niece Elizabeth was born. I still remember the old style telegram my mother and I received announcing her arrival on the other side of the world. As head of the British Legation, George had a far more prominent position in Phnom-Penh and Margot found herself being invited to tea with the King. At the time, Norodom Sihanouk was, apparently, a charming, clarinet-playing jazz fiend – a round faced little man with a good sense of humour who was, as yet, years away from being pushed into the arms of China and its communist ideology. He had an extraordinary life. Born in 1922; he became King in 1941 under Japanese and, subsequently, French rule but in 1955 during my sister's time there, took the extraordinary step of abdicating and making his father King! For a while he became Prime Minister and then took the throne again on his father's death. Striving to keep his country independent, Sihanouk was forced into doing deals with North Vietnam, allowing their troops to infiltrate South Vietnam by using a convoy corridor just inside his border and, for that, his Cambodia was mercilessly bombed by the United States. There is little doubt this helped to create the Khmer Rouge. "How would your attitude be towards Americans be if the only thing you had knew about them was the bomb which came through the trees and blew your village to bits?" an old Indo-China had asked me one day. There was only one answer.

Margot described the city as many had done before – a Paris of the East with its wide boulevards and sidewalk cafes. I found a slightly shabbier version but still a place clinging to a certain charm, populated by smiling if wary people. Sihanouk had fled to Beijing; the guerrilla movement calling itself the Khmer Rouge had grown up in the countryside and the smiles were on the wane. A General called Lon Nol had seized power, ousting Sihanouk while he was away in Moscow. Lon Nol was desperately trying to elicit more help from Washington but Nixon insisted on pretending that the US would not get involved in yet another country's problems. I use the word 'pretending' advisedly as we shall see.

In the meantime, I had Jon Swain to show me around. I had first set eyes on Jon when he walked into my Evening News office one morning in the Rue du Sentier. I thought he was still at school. Lightly built with fine, chiselled features and a mop of brown hair, he looked more like a college kid than an Agence France Presse reporter or, indeed, the hugely admired war correspondent he would become. But, like me, he had started his journalistic career at a young age and, on assignment for AFP's English desk, he had been sent to Cambodia. Most people are affected by South-east Asia but Swain fell in love with it – a love embellished by real, heart-felt love for a Eurasian girl of great beauty called Jacqueline whom he met a little while later in Saigon. You will find no finer or more evocative account of covering the war in Indo-China than his book *The River of Time*.

Now, I found him ensconced at the Hotel Royale where the majority of the guests were either foreign correspondents or Air France crew; the lovely young stewardesses arousing illicit thoughts as they displayed their bikini-clad bodies by the hotel pool.

Swain quickly filled me in on what one needed to know about covering the Cambodian conflict. There was no US military to chopper you in and out of a battle zone. You had to go and find it. Unless you had a car of your own, the only way to do this was to pay some highly reluctant and often terrified driver $100 to drive you out of town for as far as you both dared go in the hope of finding some action. The problem, for as many as one hundred reporters in the preceding months, was that the Viet Cong or Khmer Rouge found them first and shot them. Or, at the very least, frog-marched them off into the jungle.

When I arrived, Jon, like all his colleagues, was still hopeful of finding Sean Flynn, the photojournalist son of the great swashbuckling actor Errol Flynn, and Dana Stone, who was on assignment to CBS. Instead of taking the cars made available for them to drive to Saigon for a news conference, Flynn and Stone chose to ride their motor bicycles. On the way back, they took Route One and ran into a Viet Cong road block. Some say they were deliberately searching for a chance to photograph some Viet Cong and, if so, it was a fatal mistake. There had been no trace of them since.

It is possible they did not adhere to the rules which kept their more cautious colleagues alive. If on-coming traffic suddenly stopped, you should, too. It suggested that an ambush had blocked the road ahead. If no children rushed out to swarm happily around your car as you drove into a village, get out. They had probably been told to stay indoors by the Viet Cong or Khmer Rouge. And if you wanted real information from a local, it required patience. Talk to him first; ask about his crop and his family before getting to the serious questions. It was easy to scare them off.

I listened to all this advice, knowing my life probably depended on it and then agreed to accompany Jon when he suggested we drive east along Route One, in the direction Flynn and Stone had taken and see if we could find any trace of them or news about their disappearance. It had been months by now and the rumours were swirling. Some said they were still alive (later information suggested that, at this stage, they well might have been); others that they had been killed immediately, including one or two particularly unpleasant stories of crucifixion.

We were to travel in Swain's little blue Toyota sports car which he had bought deliberately because of its height. "It's got such a low profile on the road, it presents a much harder target to hit," Jon said with a wry smile. His humour was already tempered by the harsh experiences he had been through in his comparatively short time in the field. On one journey back to the city, he had been speeding down a darkened road after curfew and hit a bomb crater which sent his Peugeot tumbling into a paddy field. He spent the night shivering, half submerged, fearing he would not survive. The kid I had met at the Rue du Sentier was already a battle-hardened correspondent.

So we set off, heading east towards the Vietnamese border, checking for tell-tale signs of Viet Cong activity along the way, never knowing what the next bend in the road would bring. It concentrated the mind. Eventually we got to Svay Rieng, not far from the border, and started to ask questions as we stopped for an ice cream at a local café. Children, laughing and pleading, surrounded the little car but we didn't mind. It was a good sign. Not so our attempts to glean any information. Yes, some people had heard of Sean Flynn, the actor's son. They had heard he had been captured. Just the looks on people's faces told you what they thought had happened to him and his companion. Sean, who had already made a few movies before becoming bored with his father's profession, was 24 when last seen.

Life in Phnom-Penh was surreal. You spent the day searching for war and the evenings trying to get your copy or photos out through the over-worked post office and its lifeline telex machines. The nights were for dining, drinking and smoking while you tried to decide whether or not to accept the offer of the girls on their cyclos or rickshaws who slid up alongside you, laughing and shouting out, "Mange La Banane! Mange La Banane!"

They had been taught how on an actual banana by one of the well-known Madames who resided in the city at the time. It was probably the owner of one brothel where a sign on the door, spotted by the legendary Daily Mirror correspondent Donald Wise, read 'Cunnilingus Spoken Here'.

There were opium parlours, too, and it became routine for reporters to ignore the 9.00 pm curfew and head for 482, a little house on stilts off a main road which was run by Chantal who had set up her own 'fumerie' after working for Cambodia's Opium Queen, Madame Chum, who had her own place for 30 years before her death in 1970.

I was always told not to smoke opium with any regularity because it is seriously addictive but, like all our colleagues, Jon seemed to partake on a fairly regular basis and he certainly did not become an addict. Sex, opium and, of course, marijuana were readily available in Phnom-Penh and for anyone whose days were spent flirting with death they became an almost essential means of relaxation, even of staying sane.

Chantal's house was divided into four rooms, each furnished with little more than pillows and rattan matting. Stripping naked, you put on a sarong and lay down. A girl would come and mix a pipe for you. Sometimes she would do more but often not. Sex was part of the equation but not essential. What one needed was quiet conversation and the blissful feeling of total relaxation as the opium seeped into your system. Chantal offered a refuge from reality.

Albina du Boisrouvray came to visit me for a few days while I was in Phnom-Penh. My presence offered her the excuse to give vent to her adventurous spirit and she was up for trying everything – including a visit to Chantal's. She took a pipe and although she did not avail herself of one of the girls, she quizzed me on their techniques, seeking knowledge to put to her own use. Not, unhappily, with me despite the fact that we were sharing a bed but we had plenty of fun together exploring the city. She was quite a girl, Albina.

Marijuana amongst the press corps was a story in itself. At the Hotel Royale, one British agency reporter, a large fellow called Robin Mannock and nicknamed 'Bunter', had turned his room into a gin distillery, fermenting marijuana with it through pipes and all sorts of weird equipment that looked as if it belonged to a chemistry lab. I think the weed was officially illegal in Cambodia but that did not stop an excellent French restaurant called La Pagode from offering marijuana soup if you called in the morning to order it.

As one might be aware, marijuana ingested stays in the body a lot longer than if you merely smoke it and, on one memorable occasion, Denis Cameron and another photographer, took full advantage of a situation which presented itself. Two high ranking Congressmen arrived from Washington for an important meeting with General Lon Nol. So the clandestine phone call to La Pagode was made and the two Americans were invited by our colleagues to join us for dinner. About ten of us sat with the visitors at a round table and the soup was duly served. Unsuspectingly, the two officials slurped it down and commented on its excellent, if different, taste. One of them took on the look of a man who suddenly realised he had done something silly but soon both were too happy to care. And, of course, they were still both in a fine old state of euphoria the next morning when they had to present themselves to Lon Nol. No matter if you could spell his name backwards. They were barely in a state to know what a palindrome was … pal … pa … panic … oh, what the hell. I am sure the meeting was a great success. Apparently one of the Congressmen saw the funny side but the other did not. I hope Henry Kissinger got a nice coherent report.

I had been doing numerous pieces for ABC Radio, New York under the guidance of Mort Perry, one of their South-East Asia staffers who was helpful in letting me know what he was filing and what else they might be looking for. One morning Jon Swain said there was something happening down Route 4 towards the Gulf of Thailand. To get there you had to travel through the Pich Nil Pass and that was where the problem lay. Some Cambodian armour was being held up by Viet Cong and the battle had been going on all night. So we jumped in Jon's car and went to have a look.

Sure enough, we eventually came upon a few tanks and infantry just at the entrance to the Pass and, after parking the car, we moved alongside the troops to see what was happening. Suddenly the staccato sound of machine gun fire opened up and, as we dived into a ditch, Jon hardly needed to tell me, "Get your head down – that's incoming!"

Bullets started pinging about above our heads, ricocheting off tree trunks and, short of burying it in the ground, I kept my head as low as I could. After a while I looked up and saw one of the numerous Aussie TV cameramen working for CBS strolling down the side of the road, happily filming whatever he could find.

"Jesus, you'll get yourself killed in a minute," I called up to him.

"Can't get any action film from down there, mate," he replied cheerily.

They did it every day on month long assignments, most of them Aussies and Kiwis working for the big American networks, and then went off to Bangkok for a week to blow most of their considerable pay packets and return to risk their lives again. An amazing bunch.

After a while I noticed a Cambodian Army major chattering away into his walkie-talkie whenever a Cambodian helicopter flew overhead. He spoke in French but I had been told from people who seemed to know about these things that there were American military personnel aboard those choppers. If so, it would contradict everything coming out of Washington, where the Nixon Administration were adamant in stating that no American ground forces were involved in the Cambodian conflict other than crews operating the high altitude bombing raids.

So I kept an eye on the major as the Cambodian mortars soared over our heads. They were intended to flush out the last Viet Cong machine gunner who had been left behind by the main force to delay the tanks as long as he could. Unhappily, he was doing a fairly good job. More than one Cambodian soldier was carried back past us, bleeding from serious wounds, and Jon did nothing to lighten the mood by observing that Cambodian mortars had a great reputation for being unreliable with some alarmingly high percentage falling short of their target which, in this instance, would mean on us. Thankfully none did.

The choppers were still circling above us, trying to pinpoint our persistent little adversary and the Major was still yapping away. I had started a few casual conversations with him during the course of the afternoon so he had become used to me lurking around with my microphone and Sony tape recorder. Finally just as the sun was starting to dip behind the hills, I heard him switch language and start talking in English. That was what I had been waiting for! I jumped up and jammed my microphone right up against his ear piece. I thought I could hear an American accent replying to him and when I played it back a few minutes later, I had proof of what I had suspected.

"OK, buddy, I got you loud and clear! Over and Out!"

The accent was straight out of Ohio or Illinois and my little fifteen-second clip would be part of the undeniable evidence that forced the State Department to admit that 'in certain circumstances … blah, blah, blah.'

The Major wasn't best pleased at having his conversation taped but we didn't give him time to think about it and got the hell out of there. By six o'clock I was at the Post Office where, with Mort Perry's help, I fed the tape down the line to New York. It served as a useful backup to the more obvious evidence of American involvement in Cambodia that had emerged about 24 hours before by way of an agency photo of a US Army officer running to board a Cambodian helicopter.

The next day was to be my last in Cambodia and, after contemplating another sortie out of town, I decided against it. Why? I wasn't sure then and I'm not sure now. I seem to have a sort of in-built gauge which tells me how far to push my luck. I wasn't particularly afraid, although I had come to realise I didn't like being shot at, but I just couldn't persuade myself that, having got my story, another trip into the unknown was going to be worth it.

So I spent the day doing some work at the hotel and chatting to Stanley Cloud of Time Magazine and some other correspondents, said goodbye to Jon, and took a cab to the airport for a late evening flight to Bangkok. But minutes before I left, a group of reporters who had been back down the Pich Nil Pass, in an area I would have been had I decided to go, returned with the news than an NBC cameraman had stepped on a mine and had his foot blown off. Had someone been trying to tell me something?

Neil Sheehan happened to be aboard my flight and when we got into town we decided we deserved an enormous Thai meal which we duly enjoyed. I think the New York Times paid for it.

It was only when I turned on the TV in the hotel the next morning that I learned how lucky we had been. A few hours after our plane had taken off, the Viet Cong launched a massive raid on the airport, blowing up planes and buildings and killing scores of people. Have to say it again – life is all about timing.

My third visit to Vietnam was motivated for a personal reason. Anyone who has seen me around the tennis circuit will know I carry a brown briefcase out of which I live. Few will know that one of the photographs I carry in that briefcase is of Truong Van Manh, who was six when the picture was taken. He was my foster child.

Soon after I started working for the Evening News in New York I signed up to become a parent with the Foster Parents Association – an organisation based in Newport, Rhode Island. They seemed to be legitimate because all parents received photos of the children they were supporting, whether they were in Africa, Asia or South America. I opted for a Vietnamese child because I already felt an affinity to the country and soon received documentation for a little boy called Truong Van Manh whose parents were refugees from Cambodia. Tens of thousands had been killed as the Cambodians turned on their previously accepted and integrated neighbours. Manh's family was lucky in at least they escaped with their lives. Now they were living in a refugee camp just outside the hill city of Da Lat in Vietnam's highlands.

I had made inquiries about the possibility of visiting him on my previous visit but ran into too much red tape. Having applied through the proper channels in Newport when I returned to the States, I eventually received permission to visit Manh.

"It's an unusual request," I was told by a rather prim lady. "Very few of our parents actually visit their foster children."

Well, I was going to be one of them and I worked out a schedule that took me back to Saigon in 1972. By that time, Jon Swain been thrown out of Cambodia by nervous government officials who didn't like something he had written and had been re-assigned to Saigon by the AFP. (He would later be picked up by the Sunday Times, for whom he did his most memorable reporting.)

I told him about Truong Van Manh and he agreed to drive me to Da Lat to see if we could find the refugee camp. It wasn't difficult. The Foster Parents office had given me good directions and we found it a few miles outside the cool, pleasant city which had been a popular tourist resort in peace time.

An administrator was expecting me and was obviously proud to have someone to show around. Families lived in little thatch-roof houses and I was delighted to see that Manh, when he was presented to me, seemed to be a little bit better dressed than other children. Was it just for the special day when 'Uncle' would arrive from America? I have no idea. But the fact is that Manh's family – he had a couple of brothers and sisters I seem to remember – were happy to see me and seemed appreciative of the pathetically small amount of money I had been sending them every month. I really can't remember the exact sum but I would guess it was about $25.

I chatted to 'my' little boy through an interpreter and Jon took snaps of us, one of which travels with me round the world. We spent about an hour at the camp and then checked into an old colonial hotel with dark, cavernous rooms that could have housed about three families each. It doesn't do any good to dwell on the inequities of life.

I kept up my payments for the next three years and received quarterly messages from the camp, including a few handwritten notes from Manh. But I never saw him again. When the North Vietnamese won the war, overrunning the south and sweeping aside all the old institutions I am sure Manh's family were re-housed and re-educated and, for all I know, he grew up to be an upstanding young Communist. Only a small part of me believes that the family had the ingenuity and the means to make another escape and get to Hong Kong or somewhere in the west.

The Foster Parents Association were unable to help. They told me all connection with Da Lat had been lost and all pleas for information had fallen on deaf ears. There was nowhere to send another twenty bucks. On one of my numerous trips to Hong Kong in the eighties and nineties I trawled through the names of Vietnamese refugees listed in the camps that had sprung up there but I could never find the exact combination of names reading Truong Van Manh. He would be nearing 50 now. I hope he is alive and I hope he hasn't suffered. Hope is all that's left.

After a couple of days in Saigon, I decided to try and get into Hanoi. I knew it was virtually mission impossible but I reminded myself of all the old clichés about getting nowhere if you don't try and booked myself on a flight to Vientiane and, from there, on the weekly Aeroflot flight that came in from Moscow and journeyed on to Hanoi. Of course, I didn't have a visa and had no means of getting one. You needed to be terribly important to get officially invited to Hanoi – Jane Fonda had managed it – and I have no idea why Aeroflot allowed me on the plane. But they did – accepting my flatly stated assertion that I would get one on arrival, which was a load of rubbish.

Arnaud de Borchgrave looked at me as if I was mad when we found ourselves boarding the plane together. Before he became a celebrated Newsweek correspondent, I had met Arnaud a few times in London because my brother in law, Frank Melville, had been with Newsweek before transferring to Time Magazine. Arnaud, a fascinating character who was some kind of Belgian aristocrat, had been working in the London Bureau.

"They'll never let you in but good luck!" he smiled. Arnaud had worked all his exceptional diplomatic contacts to secure his own visa. Not having a clue what kind of reception I would receive, I busied myself recording 'voicers' into my Sony – 40 second reports on what I saw – as we drifted into Hanoi's Noi Bai Airport over paddy fields and the Red River. I described a crumpled bridge that had obviously been hit by the US Air Force and then, as we landed, the lines of North Vietnamese fighter jets parked outside their hangars.

When we landed, the doors opened and a couple of uniformed, helmeted military customs officers came aboard. They demanded visas and passports from everyone as they filed past. I didn't move as De Borchgrave bid me farewell with a knowing look on his face.

"Visa!" one of the soldiers snapped.

"I have a British passport," I replied with as much authority as I could muster. Technically Britain was not at war with North Vietnam, although I was under no illusions as to how much ice that would cut.

"No visa – you stay on the plane!" And that seemed to be that. Everyone else got off and, while the crew cleaned up, a solider stayed on board to guard me. I sat there for about half an hour and decided to try a different tactic. "I'm getting hungry – could you at least let me into the terminal building? I promise not to go anywhere!"

Perhaps he was as bored as I was because, to my utter surprise, he agreed and I made a dash for the airport lounge before he could change his mind. The only seat that seemed to be available was at the end of a brown, tattered couch. The other places were occupied by four North Vietnamese officers. Looking at me quizzically, they asked me who I was – in English. They were very friendly and said they were sorry that it appeared I would not be able to see their lovely city.

"But you must have a drink," one of them exclaimed. "You must try Bia hoi, our local beer. The water comes straight from our Ho Tay lake, right in the centre of Hanoi."

The beer tasted good and soon some food arrived in the form of a very large round pie. On biting into it, I found it was filled with every piece of nutrition you could think of – nuts, dried fruit and ham and heaven knows what else. And then it suddenly struck me. I had discovered one of the great secrets of their war. Give a soldier one of these and he could march on it for days down the Ho Chi Minh Trail. As far as I was concerned, it certainly took care of lunch.

When I offered a dollar in an attempt to pay for it, they laughed. "No, no … much too much. And we don't have any change to give you."

So I accepted their hospitality as graciously as I could and got back on the plane. I hadn't made it into Hanoi but I had spent a couple of hours in North Vietnam and that was better than nothing!

Back in Vientiane, I switched planes and flew straight on to Hong Kong and caught the first available flight to Los Angeles. Rather than try and feed stuff down dodgy airport telephone lines, I thought it better to pitch up at the ABC News studios in LA and give them everything first hand. I wasn't the first Western reporter into Hanoi but I was one of very few and they were fairly amazed when I related my tale. I did numerous voicers, fresh ones as well as those I had recorded on the plane, and then spent much of the day being interviewed by Michael Jackson – no, not the singer, but a very well-known LA radio host of the time who was actually English. He was a small, chirpy character who, I think, married Alan Ladd's daughter. I had been on his programme a couple of times before during reporting stints in California and he was delighted to talk to someone who had been in Hanoi little more than 24 hours before – even if it was only the bloody airport!

It was a long time before I returned to Saigon. By 1992, the war was but a memory for the middle aged and simply history to the kid who was selling the International Herald Tribune outside the Continental Palace. The city seemed strange without American military uniforms confronting you at every corner but it was no less busy; motor scooters and bicycles competing on every street with hooting cars and trucks. A couple of friends whisked me off to see the tennis facilities at the restored Cercle Sportif and it was an invigorating experience. Clinging to my friend's back as he weaved through the traffic, our scooter was literally within six inches of people and machines every yard of the way, no matter the speed. The precision in judging distances on those machines was quite extraordinary and more than once I was so close to some lovely lady in her ao dai that the silk of her sleeve fluttered against my skin and a waft of her perfume overcame the smell of exhaust.

I went to some formal reception at the Town Hall and met the Mayor. Cheekily I told him how I had just been to Singapore to witness the birth of a sky-scraper city bereft of its old charm. "Don't let that happen to Saigon, will you?" I said. I knew what a futile remark it was and I smiled when the Mayor assured me, even though it was now called Ho Chi Minh City, that Saigon would always be recognisable.

It's been twenty years now and I am afraid the Saigon we knew has gone. But out in the countryside, life continues much as it always did, as I was able to show Lynn in 1995 just before we were married. Indo-China, once it has you in its embrace, has a lure that clings forever.

Thousands who spent more time there than I did will attest to that; Jon Swain and his Jacqueline foremost amongst them. I don't think he ever used this Japanese poem in his book but it seems appropriate and rings so true:

'Though on the sign it is written
Don't pluck these blossoms
It is useless against the wind
Which cannot read.'

Chapter 13
NIXON: A SHORT LIVED TRIUMPH

Tennis was in political turmoil in 1972 but it mattered little compared to what was happening at the Presidential level in America, where the Vietnam war continued to tear the country apart. The Democrats needed to produce a powerful alternative to Richard Nixon if they were to unseat an unpopular but politically shrewd President, but with Robert Kennedy dead and Ted Kennedy unwilling to run, they never found one.

George McGovern, an affable, dedicated Senator from South Dakota, eventually emerged as the chosen candidate but, for reasons that I will explain, ended up losing the November election by one of the biggest land-slide defeats in American history.

I was there to cover both Presidential Conventions by virtue of John Gold agreeing that I was the best choice to cover American politics even though I was no longer a staff writer on the paper, as Stephen Claypole had left for other pastures. We worked out a deal whereby I would spend a few weeks in New York and Washington, return for Wimbledon, and then hot-foot it to Miami in time for the Democratic gathering which was due to start the following week. Deadlines would be tight and, although that posed no prob-lem for an ex-Hayters man, this one did actually require some fast footwork.

On Sunday 9th July 1972 I was sitting in the press box at Wimbledon watching Stan Smith seize the title from the talented hands of Ilie Nastase by a score of 4-6, 6-3, 6-3, 4-6, 7-5. It was a match won in the mind. Smith, with his big serve and volley grass court game, had the tools to beat the mer-curial Romanian but Nastase, as he was to prove by defeating Arthur Ashe on grass at Forest Hills two months later, had the skill and flexibility to adapt to any kind of surface. What he lacked was the calmness of mind. Fretting about his rackets and string tension, Ilie allowed his concentration to fly all over the place and, after a duel that included much drama and fascinating tennis, Stan emerged as a deserving champion.

From a personal point of view, I could have done with him managing to do it a bit quicker. I was booked on a 6.30 pm Pan Am flight out of Heathrow that evening. My brief was to produce a pre-Convention piece for the Evening News first edition the following morning and I needed to be in New York, if not Miami, to do it.

The last moments of the match remain a blur. I had my little red Triumph Vitesse parked across the street and I had a girlfriend lined up to take it off me at Heathrow. And I was trying to calculate the timing. What was the last moment I could leave? Come on, Stan, finish this thing! Eventually I knew I had to go. Tapping my good friend Gerry Williams on the shoulder, I asked him to cover for me if anything truly dramatic happened after the match and was making a dash for the exit just as Smith was raising his arms in triumph.

Beating the crowds out of the ground, I proceeded to make the most of the more lenient speeding restrictions that existed at the time and, after literally throwing the car keys to my understanding friend, swept through immigration and onto the Pan Am 747. Flying in those days was actually that easy. Security lines didn't exist.

Being the bachelor that I was, I had another good friend meeting me at JFK and offering a bed for the night. Mala Jennings had a basement apartment a block from Central Park West which reeked of cats, but she was delightful in every other way and put up with my somewhat distracted greeting. I rushed out to grab the first editions of Monday's New York Times and Daily News which are always on sale by midnight while she made the coffee and, after turning on the radio (I wasn't about to forget how WINS saved me over the RFK shooting) I pulled together a piece on what was about to happen in Miami and, at 2.00 am, dictated a story to London as soon as the copy-takers came on duty at the Evening News at 5.00 am UK time. I suppose anyone who had seen me at Wimbledon at 5.00 pm the previous day must have looked at the New York by-line on my story with some skepticism.

I think I managed a few hours' sleep before kissing Mala goodbye and catching a morning flight to Miami. By lunchtime I was back in the world of American politics, as suffocating in its way as the August heat which left you dripping in sweat after a two-minute walk. Everywhere you turned in the lobbies of the Fontainebleau, Eden Roc or Doral hotels, there were groups of delegates, aides or reporters rubbing shoulders, trying to pretend they weren't listening to the conversation going on two yards away. I had done the political rounds of press conferences and lunches with contacts during the weeks

I spent in America before Wimbledon but this was everything and everyone thrown together in the great melting pot of a giant Convention.

Unusually, both political parties would be convening in the same city that year as the Republicans had made a late switch from San Diego after some skulduggery came to light over bribes and other irregularities in the bidding process.

Irregularities! Hah! How minor they turned out to be compared to the huge story that was just starting to simmer under the already boiling pot of Presidential politics that summer. On 17th June, six men broke into the offices of the Democratic Headquarters in the Watergate complex in Washington, setting off a chain of events that remains one of the most remarkable stories in the history of any nation's politics. At the outset the headlines were mostly confined to Washington, with few people outside the Beltway taking much notice. Certainly it played very little part in the proceedings at the Democratic Convention where, after the usual in-house battles, the Democrats had emerged with George McGovern as their likely candidate to run against the President.

Back in the spring, Edmund Muskie, who had been Hubert Humphrey's running mate back in 1968, seemed to be the hot favourite and, at one stage, had 47 delegates in his pocket to McGovern's 17. But, as I wrote at the time, Muskie, while likeable, failed to inspire the young and fervently anti-war group that the Democratic party needed. The hard-core of that group were laden with former disciples of Robert Kennedy and Eugene McCarthy, and they preferred McGovern.

By the time the Convention got under way, McGovern's main concern was finding a running mate. A last-ditch attempt to persuade Senator Ted Kennedy to join the ticket was left dead in the water when the last remaining Kennedy brother pre-empted McGovern's intended phone call with one of his own. Calling the candidate in his 17th floor suite at the Doral Hotel on Miami Beach, Kennedy said that he could not run. "For very real personal reasons, I cannot accept," he said. A disappointed McGovern issued a statement which read, "The Kennedy family, I know, have already made great sacrifices to the nation and I fully understand what you are telling me."

An alternative – and an extreme one – would have been to reach out to the wheelchair-bound George Wallace but, in fact, McGovern had given up any idea of trying to placate the south and was left with a list of possibilities which hardly engendered enthusiasm amongst the faithful. Eventually he came up with a little-known Missouri Senator called Thomas Eagleton and, in retrospect, it was a decision that probably killed off his last chance of beating Nixon.

Within a matter of weeks, it was revealed that Eagleton had suffered from 'severe depression' and 'suicidal tendencies' and, some time earlier in his life, had undergone electrical shock treatment. Despite resisting the call to resign for a few days after the medical record – which had been missed during the vetting process – came out, Eagleton did eventually step down.

McGovern then made an inspired choice by calling on Sargent Shriver, who was back from his assignment in Paris and was willing to serve. Shriver, with his ebullient personality, injected vim and vigour into the campaign, not to say a welcome touch of humour, but it was too late. McGovern's image had been damaged by sloppy staff work which suggested ineptitude and his ratings plunged.

We obviously knew nothing of this as the politicking continued in the Convention Hall, strewn, as ever, with bunting, paper hats and slogans. By the Monday evening, just over 30 hours after leaving Wimbledon Centre Court, I was able to file this piece (abbreviated here) to the Evening News.

'Senator Hubert Humphrey and Democratic Party chairman Larry O'Brien played pool at the pink marshmallow edifice called the Fontainebleau Hotel on Miami Beach last night.

'But the real hustler of this potentially wild and unorthodox Democratic Convention which opens tonight – Senator George McGovern – ended up the winner of the first skirmish to be played out amidst the hot and sticky settings of this middle-aged sun lover's paradise.

'And it was O'Brien, a one-time aide to President Kennedy, who ignored the pleas of his pool partner to give McGovern his first tentative, inconclusive success.'

I went on to describe, in the kind of detail that must have bewildered strap-hangers on the District Line heading for a day's work in the City, the complications involving 151 delegates that McGovern won in the California Primary and which the Stop McGovern group – headed by Humphrey – felt he should be deprived of through some technicality. O'Brien decided they should stay with McGovern, which considerably smoothed his passage to the nomination.

I made reference to George Wallace later in the article, oblivious to something that I have only just discovered through reading far more recent articles in Washington Post, the paper which, under the leadership of editor Ben Bradlee, played such a decisive role in the eventual downfall of the President.

On May 15ᵗʰ 1972, Wallace was shot while campaigning in a parking lot in Laurel, Maryland. His would-be assassin was a young man called Arthur Bremer who eventually served 35 years of a 53-year sentence for harming Wallace and three other people. If Bremer's intention was to kill Wallace, he failed but, weirdly, he played a fascinating role in a chain of events that led to the demise of Richard Nixon.

Anyone who has read *All the President's Men* by Bob Woodward and Carl Bernstein (played by Robert Redford and Dustin Hoffman respectively in the award-winning film) will be aware of the remarkable journalistic story that unfolded and the presence, lurking mysteriously at odd hours of the morning in underground parking lots, of the man called 'Deep Throat'.

It appears that, had it not been for the Wallace shooting, Woodward and Deep Throat might never have met. It would have been impossible to deduce this until 2005 when Vanity Fair published an article which finally revealed the true identity of Woodward's informer. The man, then 91, was W. Mark Felt, who had been No. 2 at the FBI when the legendary J. Edgar Hoover died just two weeks before Bremer tried to kill Wallace. Felt, it transpires, was hoping to get Hoover's job and was furious when another Nixon lackey, the Assistant Attorney General L. Patrick Gray, was appointed instead.

Felt already had a reputation for being someone who was prepared to talk to journalists and Woodward, an eager young reporter on the Washington Post, thought it might be worthwhile contacting him to get the FBI's take on the Wallace shooting which had occurred in nearby Maryland. It was as a result of that contact, and a few subsequent phone conversations, that Felt decided to reach out to Woodward later in the year when it became clear that he and Bernstein were digging for material on the mysterious Watergate break-in. Still smarting at being overlooked for the top job, Felt was becoming increasingly incensed at the politicisation of the Bureau and resented what he called, according to Woodward, "a strong-arm takeover of the agencies (of Government) by the Nixon White House."

In later years Woodward and Bernstein were at pains to point out that Deep Throat was not their only source and that they collected at great deal of other evidence which eventually led to the uncovering of Nixon's attempted cover-up of what, initially, was little more than a stupid and relatively minor crime. But Felt, with his nocturnal whisperings, played a significant part and got his revenge. By April of the following year Gray had been forced to resign and was lucky not to join some of Nixon's senior aides in prison, so close had he been to the cover up.

But back to Miami Beach, where two political worlds were attempting to exist side by side – and failing. The Republicans were ensconced – or perhaps one should say barricaded – in their plush hotels along the sea front while in nearby Flamingo Park various segments of the anti-Vietnam war movement were sleeping rough, mostly untroubled by the 3,000 National Guardsmen who had been called in to ensure the delegates' safety. For everyone's safety, it was a good thing they decided to stay out of Flamingo Park. Perhaps someone remembered what had happened in Chicago's Grant Park four years before.

That, however, did not completely eliminate the rough stuff, as I will relate. But first I filed a report to the Evening News which attempted to explain a few of the differences between America's two political parties. It read:

'Apparently oblivious of the demonstrators gathered in Flamingo Park and of North Vietnamese advances on the battlefield, the Republican Party prepared for the opening of its convention in Miami Beach today on a note of harmony and optimism.

'With most opinion polls giving President Nixon a 25% lead over Democratic nominee George McGovern, the reasons for that optimism are obvious enough. The harmony is a little more contrived. Any chance of dissenting voices being heard at this convention has been successfully eliminated by the party committee. Paul McCloskey, the anti-war Congressman from California who was one of only two Republicans to challenge Nixon in the primaries, has been refused permission to speak.

'Party leaders want nothing to mar the mood of euphoria. This is just one of many ways in which the Republican gathering differs sharply from the Democratic convention last month. Republican leaders have been talking enthusiastically about their party embracing a broader cross section of the nation but statistics show they still have a long way to go. The delegates are older, whiter and richer than their Democratic counterparts.

'The Republicans have also been trying to deny that their convention is more secretive and private. They have not helped their cause by sealing off the luxurious Doral Hotel to the public. During the Democratic convention Senator McGovern stayed at the Doral and, on one occasion, came down to the lobby to speak to a group of anti-war protestors who had demanded to talk to him.

'Now it is impossible to get as far as the front door without a pass. At any hour of the day or night there are 80 security guards on duty, some of whom patrol the roof with M-16 rifles. President Nixon will not be staying there when he arrives on Tuesday but members of the White House are already installed along with Nixon aide Herbert Klein and his secret communications centre. Some of the communications are so secret that one paragraph of a memorandum issued to the staff reads: "While at the hotel you are requested to put all sensitive paper into the 'Confidential Burn' bags found in every office. A paper shredder is available in the security office."

'Meanwhile, the Miami police have had the good sense to stay out of Flamingo Park where a slightly less harmonious but somewhat more open mood prevails. While leaders of various anti-war groups who have formed the Miami Convention Coalition to try and convince more militant factions of the need for non-violent action, rock music blared, marijuana joints were passed from hand to hand and scores of young men and women swam naked in the pool.

'Tourists gaped at the strange scene as they wandered around, stepping gingerly over sleeping bodies sprawled on the grass. There are signs and posters everywhere including one next to a picture pf Richard Nixon which says: "Get your nausea bags here".

'Apart from the ejection of a group of youngsters from the American Nazi party, all has been peaceful so far….'

Well, there were demonstrations and, reacting to provocation, the police ensured that they were not exactly peaceful, as I can testify. Trying to keep close to the action, I joined the end of a long line of anti-war marchers on the road leading to the Convention Center. Suddenly tear gas canisters were thrown by the police and, trying to avoid the awful stinging, burning sensation that invades one's nostrils, we were forced into a side alley, away from the television cameras. And it was there that the police went to work. Charging after us, they began clubbing the first people to come within reach – and I was one of them. The blow caught me behind the right ear and the lower part of my neck. I managed to stay upright and race away out of danger but many demonstrators were not so lucky and were clubbed to the ground.

To be fair, the Miami police were not nearly as brutal as their counterparts had been in Chicago in 1968, but the mayhem was fairly extensive for several hours before proceedings eventually subsided, weighed down by the knowledge that nothing was going to prevent the inevitable re-affirmation of Richard Nixon as leader of the Republican Party inside the convention hall. Three thousand delegates acclaimed Nixon as the hero they perceived him to be, ignoring the clamour outside; ignoring Vietnam and ignoring the nagging, nasty little stories that the Washington Post insisted on printing about a burglary at Watergate. Few, if any, could have conceived that the gates would open and the flood would sweep their man away.

After a period back in Paris, I returned to the States to cover the remaining days before the November election. The polls had Nixon leading Senator George McGovern by hopeless margins and, as I wrote in one of my reports: 'Obviously Nixon now feels he can say "No" to everything and get away with it. He says "No" to McGovern's demand for a TV debate; "No" to requests for press conferences and "No" to eleven Bills – including one to ease financial burdens on the elderly – sent to him for ratification by Congress.'

McGovern had been forced on the defensive in the face of the usual Republican counter-attacks over Watergate – accusing the Democrats of espionage, which was exactly what they had been doing themselves – and, in doing so, the Senator had started to lose the support of his idealistic young supporters who had been drawn to him as a result of his willingness to speak out against the Vietnam War and other issues close to their heart.

Sargent Shriver, with his endless enthusiasm and bonhomie, provided the only spark of hope and optimism for the Democrats. Flying out to California, I joined his campaign and, soon after his plane took off from LA, he walked down the aisle and, spotting a familiar face, greeted me with his slightly wicked smile. "Can you believe this, Richard? I got my own plane! Welcome aboard! It's been rough but we're still fighting."

And so he was. Sarge was the life force the Democrats desperately needed, but it had all happened too late after the fiasco of Chicago and Eagleton and all he could do was use his sharp wit and quick brain to lash back at Nixon and his cronies. But by the time the first results started coming in on election night, he knew it was all over. I had been invited to join in the gathering at his lovely Virginia home just outside Washington and it was a desperately sad occasion for a man who believed deeply for the cause he had been fighting for. Everyone had been fearing the worst but Shriver, Donald Dell and all the rest of his supporters gathered around the television in the living room were aghast at the extent of the Democratic disaster. By the time the final results were in, the McGovern/Shriver ticket had captured just one State – Massachusetts – and the District of Columbia. The embarrassing disparity in electoral votes was Nixon 520, McGovern 17. Eighteen million more Americans voted for the incumbent President than for the challenger – the widest margin in the history of American politics.

McGovern, a good man, an effective public speaker but, according to George Mitchell, very timid when asked to put his case in a one-on-one situation, at least came up with an honest parting line: "It hurts too much to laugh but I'm too old to cry."

So was Shriver, who put as brave a face on it as was possible when I interviewed him that evening for BBC Radio. Despite realising he was fighting a losing cause, Sarge had enjoyed campaigning immensely and one could only wonder if it might have been a bit different had he been the original pick – or, indeed, the nominee.

But the hard fact was that the American people had been duped. For the second time they had voted for a deeply scarred and chronically insecure personality who saw shadows at every turn; enemies in every corner. He was also corrupt. George Mitchell put it succinctly in our recent conversation: "Nixon was a crook."

None of this might have become public had not, for reasons that are probably too complicated to analyse, Nixon decided to tape every word uttered in the Oval Office during his Presidency. Once Ben Bradlee and his Washington Post reporters had prised open the can of worms, it was the tapes (and the missing eighteen minutes) that brought him down and proved what kind of a man he really was. Not just because they revealed the extent to which the Watergate break-in had emanated from the President's desk, but because of the almost total disregard he showed for the state of the country or the people he was supposed to be leading.

I confess I did not read all the Oval Office tapes – I simply didn't have time. But I did read or listen to over an hour's worth and was appalled at what I heard. Not one statesmanlike sentence was uttered. Not one mention of a policy that might do something for the country. It was all about Richard Nixon and his survival. It was all chat between himself, Bob Haldeman, John Ehrlichman and Ron Ziegler about how to get 'them' – all those Americans who opposed his policies and his plans and whose names were on his famous Enemies List. Frequently it sounded like the rantings of a paranoid man who had completely forgotten what he was supposed to be doing with the priceless position he held.

There were stories of people who were on that list having dinner interrupted as FBI agents burst through the front door of their suburban homes and ransacked the places, looking for God knows what. Others had their tax returns scrutinised or were woken by threatening calls in the dead of night.

It was no use appealing for justice because the head of the Justice Department, John Mitchell, was enough of a crook himself to end up in jail when all was revealed. At the FBI, Patrick Gray, as we have seen, was another loyal Nixon appointee. People on that Enemies List – academics, lawyers with a conscience, liberal professors, Democratic functionaries – had nowhere to turn. Nixon was turning the world's greatest Democracy into a police state.

I remember dining at Frank Melville's house in London when my brother-in-law was Time's much respected political correspondent at Westminster. Frank and my sister Margot frequently had cabinet ministers round to the house and numerous visiting American journalists were often invited, too. One Washington correspondent was there on the evening in question – I'm afraid I can't remember his name – and when he asked me my opinion of Nixon he seemed shocked by the severity of my condemnation of the man. I told him that, judging by what I had seen and heard, Nixon was working his way towards asking Congress for a third term. It wouldn't have been easy because, despite the Presidential landslide, the Democrats still controlled the Senate 56-42 and also held a majority in the House of Representatives. But otherwise Nixon had all his generals in place and I was delighted, years later, when I found a leading political figure who agreed with me. Ed Koch, appearing on a TV talk show several years after he had stepped down from being Mayor of New York, threw this line, almost casually, into the conversation. "Well, Nixon was just trying to create a coup."

Of course he was! That's exactly what he had in mind. As the years went by, having managed to stay out of jail only because his successor, Gerald Ford, came up with an undeserved pardon, Nixon tried to re-invent himself yet again as a political sage and elder statesman in New York. His supporters pointed to his brilliant mind and his success in foreign affairs – referring to his meetings with Mao Tse-tung and ignoring the fact that his bombing raids had slaughtered hundreds of thousands of Vietnamese civilians. But why should one be surprised that he found the Chinese dictator such amenable company? Dictators think alike. Extreme right wingers and extreme left wingers do not disappear into the distance. They simply circumvent the political globe and meet round the back. They understand each other perfectly. Dissent? Crush it. Democracy? Pah! It took a man of Nixon's political instincts to be able to have a fruitful conversation with Mao. The old monster would not have understood what a liberal President was talking about, no matter how well it was translated.

The story I filed for the Evening News on Wednesday, 8th November 1972, was written, of course, long before I knew the outcome of the saga that was unfolding before a stupefied electorate. Woodward and Bernstein had yet to complete their work and King Richard still seemed relatively secure on his throne despite mounting evidence of wrongdoing. But, looking back, I think it is something of which I can be proud. Peter Jenkins of the Guardian, regarded as one of the best political analysts of the era, was the only other British correspondent to write an anti-Nixon piece after the landslide election. Every other newspaper went with the numbers and ignored the man. 'Triumph!' 'Greatest Landslide in History!' The headlines revealed the extent to which many, if not all, of my colleagues were prepared to go with the flow and praise Nixon as a cunning, wily and brilliant political operator. All that was true. But he was also a crook. And he did not serve his country.

I have mentioned before that Lord Harmsworth was a publisher who almost always allowed his editors to print what they saw fit. But my piece, evidently, was too much for him. As a staunch Conservative, he couldn't stomach such a critical evaluation of a right wing American President who had just won an outstanding victory and the piece you see here was yanked out of the day's final edition. But at least it got a run earlier in the day and for that I am eternally grateful to John Gold and his editorial team back in London.

Covering the US Presidential campaigns of 1968 and 1972 was an exhilarating experience and taught me so much about the United States, the good, the bad and the ugly. The great regret, of course, was that both ended up with a bad man being elected to the position of the most powerful person in the world. Tempering that is the pride one feels in being part of a profession that cut the tyranny short. America's debt to Ben Bradlee, Bob Woodward and Carl Bernstein is immense. Without their courage – real courage determination and skill, Nixon would have got away with it and his country would have been in peril. There has never been a more important reminder of why a free country needs a free press – and why we can see, all these years later, that it creates disaster when it doesn't do its job.

Donald Trump was a very famous real estate magnate and TV personality

4-3   TWENTIOS NEWS, Wednesday, November 8, 1972

Four more years of Nixon the Slick

"FOUR MORE years," has been the Republican cry in this campaign, and now they have got it.

Four more years of Richard Nixon—a Nixon free of the need ever to win another election; free of the will of the American people; free to do as he chooses with the power that now lies in his hands.

It is a sobering thought. Many millions of people in this country — and let us not forget that there are millions of them, even if they are a minority — find it more than that. They find it sickening and frightening.

Self criticism

Long before George McGovern said it, an Englishman who has lived in America for 22 years told me: "The choice this year lies very clearly between good and evil, between the selfish and the unselfish, between the bigoted and the unbigoted."

That is not to say that everyone who voted for Nixon yesterday was evil and bigoted. But it is a sad fact that millions of basically decent Americans—weary of self-criticism and fearful of sudden change —were sold a sleek, slick political package of lies, innuendoes and manufactured truths by a cynically calculating salesman. This may seem harsh judgment to those who view America from afar. The world has watched, with justifiable admiration, as Nixon flew off on his truly historic

Why I fear for America under this cynical salesman—by

RICHARD EVANS
in WASHINGTON

missions to Peking and Moscow.

It is absolutely correct to say that no Democratic President could have pulled off coups like these without being branded a little pink. But, of course, no one was going to accuse Nixon of being soft on Communism.

What so few people realised was that Richard Nixon has much in common with the Kosygins, Brezhnevs and Maos of this world. Although they stand at different ends of the political spectrum, they speak each other's language.

The past four years

They are all tough, cruel, cynical men who believe that any means justifies the end—men who admire political power-play and sheer brute force on the battlefield when the occasion demands. They are like heavyweight boxers who clasp each other in sickly sentimentality after they have bashed each other to pulp.

No one even pretends that Brezhnev and Mao believe in the democratic system. The

joke is that many people believe Nixon does. How that is possible after his behaviour over the past four years is difficult to comprehend.

He expended 20,000 American lives and systematically brutalised a sub-continent and its helpless people with the heaviest air bombardment in history under the pretext of supporting the cause of democracy.

Yet, who, in fact, has he been supporting at such incredible cost? A nasty little dictator called Thieu who jails political opponents; closes down opposition newspapers; and forbids free local elections.

Could not lose

When his re-election committee is presented with well documented charges of espionage, sabotage and deliberate disruption of the political process, Nixon hides behind his Press secretary, issuing either unspecific, unsubstantiated denials or throwing out that revealing little phrase that cancels a multitude of sins—"No comment."

When an albeit naive but thoroughly sincere opponent was nominated to run against him and proceeded to discuss the issues that really needed to be discussed in America—welfare, poverty, tax loopholes, pollution and, of course, the war — he put on his carefully constructed Presidential air and refused to campaign.

The ethics if not the rules of campaigning in a democracy demand that an elected leader standing for re-election take his case before the jury; that is, the people, and discuss his plans for the future.

But Nixon is more interested in polls than ethics and the polls told him that he could not lose. So he confined his campaigning to a few carefully selected and brilliantly orchestrated forays into areas where he would be assured of a tumultuous welcome.

During the 23 minutes he spent campaigning in New England—Providence Airport, Rhode Island, was his only venture into the New England state—Nixon did not even leave the steps of Air Force One and shook hands only with a section of supporters who had needed invitations to get that close to him. And they call that democracy.

What is far more serious, however, is the way Nixon has attempted to reduce the influence of Congress by limiting its spending powers and by vetoing no less than 11 Bills after Congress recessed that

A light-lipped smile from President Nixon as he acknowledges applause from campaign workers in Washington after his victory.

were designed to help the elderly and the poor and to fight pollution.

Nixon claimed there was not enough money, but he always has enough money for bombs and never vetoes anything that might assist vast corporations who dodge taxes.

After trying and failing to get a third-rate judge on to the Supreme Court, Nixon continued his assault on that vital body which Earl Warren once led so wisely, by appointing men of narrow-minded reactionary views.

The Nation is now facing the prospect of an all-Nixon court by 1976—a court that will be more likely to reflect the views of the '20s more than the '70s.

It is not a pretty prospect for people who had hoped for a steady advancement of human dignity and decency.

But one can only pray that some of the better elements of the President's character will also prevail. Presumably, the war will finally be brought to

a close—hopefully before too many more peasants have to die in order to satisfy Nixon's ideas of honour—and presumably inflation will be brought under control.

But, for the jobless, the blacks, the American Indians, the poor, the elderly and the idealistic youth, four more years of Nixonism do not raise much hope for a better America.

219

when he decided to run for the Republican nomination in 2015 and, as a result, fed the cable TV stations' insatiable hunger for ratings. But, like so many of the people who ultimately voted for him, they became blinded by his fame with the result that any hope of candidates being offered equal air time was doomed.

For months, beginning in the autumn of 2015, Trump was virtually never off the air if you turned to CNN, MSNBC or FoxNews. It was to be expected of Fox with their right-wing bias but I was shocked by the extent to which CNN, which usually tried to be balanced, and MSNBC which is openly Democratic in its leanings, sold their souls to the money crunchers and handed over their airtime to Trump. The networks are, of course, owned by corporations who are only interested in profit.

The CBC, NBC and ABC Evening News hours were no better. A study of a six-week period in October revealed that ABC had given a total of 86 minutes on its show to Trump and one – just one – to Bernie Sanders. The independent Senator, who was gathering huge crowds at his rallies as he tried to offer an alternative to Hilary Clinton as the Democratic nominee, would surely have come a great deal closer to causing a huge upset within the Democratic ranks had he been given 50% of Trump's airtime.

The imbalance – quite extraordinary in its severity – continued through-out the campaign, enabling Trump to grab the nomination and, eventually, the Presidency. Everyone can change, as we have noted with Robert Kennedy, but, as I write during his first, chaotic the weeks in the White House, it seems highly unlikely that Trump can turn himself into the kind of President the United States so desperately needs at this time in its history.

The rating-chasing media was not wholly responsible for the rise of a bigoted demagogue whose campaign rhetoric was, frankly, terrifying but it played its part and it cannot escape collective blame. Neither, of course, can the system. For the second time in five Presidential elections, the Electoral College allowed a person who did not gain a plurality of the vote to become President. It had been relatively close between George W Bush and Al Gore in 2002 but 2.8 million more people voted for Hilary Clinton than Trump. And she lost. That makes a mockery of democracy.

There are many lessons to be learned, not least by my profession, but the scars of 2016 will linger, leaving, I suspect, a more troubling legacy than Nixon and Watergate.

Chapter 14
I JOIN THE ATP

I returned to Paris in an uncertain frame of mind. I had enjoyed being part of one of the biggest stories of the year and working with such august colleagues as Charles Wheeler, one of the great BBC foreign correspondents, but autumn had faded by the time I got home and the trees along the Seine were no longer golden. I began to wonder about the colour of my own future.

I had burned my bridges as far as a permanent job was concerned with the BBC; the thought of returning to London to work inside as a sub-editor on the Evening News did not seem a very good idea, especially as the paper was obviously starting to have financial constraints, and other options were limited. All the major London papers had well established tennis correspondents like Lance Tingay at the Daily Telegraph, Frank Rostron at the Daily Express and Roy McKelvie at the Daily Mail. And Barry Newcombe had slipped smoothly into my role at the Evening Standard so there was no chance of going back there.

What to do? There was enough freelance work in those days to survive and I had a little money in the bank, but my mother needed financial help, which was a responsibility I couldn't ignore.

Then, one fine day when they were in town for a winter tournament, Jack Kramer and Donald Dell asked if they could have a chat. I had a feeling they wanted to talk about the ATP – the Association of Tennis Professionals – which had been formed after numerous failed attempts during the US Open at Forest Hills the previous September, and I was right. In between covering the elections, I had managed to attend Forest Hills, not just as a reporter but, clutching my trusty Pentax, as a photographer as well. Incredibly, when you look at the courtside throng today, Russ Adams and a couple of agency snappers and I were the only photographers sitting out on the grass in 1972 as Ilie Nastase scored the greatest victory of his career by shocking the tennis world with a five-set victory over the former champion Arthur Ashe. World Tennis used my photographic efforts and I actually got the cover a few times

– pictures of Ken Rosewall, Bob Lutz, Marty Riessen and a few others if I recall.

Anyway, I was still to be found around the tennis world in a variety of roles and I had managed to get to the US Open by the second day of the tournament that year after charging back from a campaign trip to the midwest with George McGovern. It had been one of those absurdly early morning flights and I was seriously lacking sleep by the time I climbed the stairs to the clubhouse locker room, eyed the large sofa which members of the West Side Tennis Club used to enjoy year-round, and collapsed into a deep sleep. When I opened an eye I remember seeing the tall figure of Stan Smith peering down at me. "Rough night, Richard?" he smiled.

When I got my act together I realised some serious political manoeuvrings were taking place amongst the players and that, finally, a player's association might become a reality. After an historic meeting in the US Open Club tent, which formed one corner of the large stadium, Jack Kramer agreed to become the first CEO of the ATP and, with such a huge and respected figure on board, the leaders amongst the players – Ashe, Smith, Cliff Drysdale, John Newcombe, Charlie Pasarell, Jim McManus, Ismael El Shafei and Jaime Fillol – found it easier to persuade the rank and file to sign up and show the solidarity needed to give the people who went out there and actually hit balls a proper say in the running of their sport.

Within ten months of its existence, the ATP became embroiled in one of the great scandals and, ultimately, the great turning points in the history of the sport. As a result of desperate efforts by the International Lawn Tennis Federation to flex its threatened power by banning the Yugoslav player Nikki Pilic because had refused to play the Davis Cup, the players cried, "Enough!" and refused to buckle when the amateur establishment deliberately dragged Pilic's ban into the Wimbledon fortnight.

"You chaps will boycott anything but not Wimbledon," Walter Elcock, the USLTA President told Dennis Ralston. How wrong he was. Eighty players boycotted Wimbledon on the Friday of the Championships, forcing referee Mike Gibson to re-do the draw.

It was front page news in the British press – and indeed, world-wide – and much of the stuff that was written was wrong. Unable to contemplate going against Wimbledon, a British institution, the media turned on the players, calling them a money grabbing bunch of greedy pros. But even that gave the editors pause because Arthur Ashe, John Newcombe, Rod Laver, Ken

Rosewall and Cliff Drysdale (the first ATP President) were hugely popular sporting stars who did not fit the image the press was trying to create.

So Kramer became the fall guy. The man who had kept pro tennis alive in the dark days, prior to Open Tennis in 1968, was portrayed as the cigar-chewing American wheeler-dealer who was obviously goading these nice fellows into doing something dishonourable. It was not one of Fleet Street's finer moments.

Kramer was not the instigator. Drysdale, Newcombe, Ashe and Pasarell were the people who had come to the correct conclusion that the moment had arrived to challenge the stifling authority of the ILTF and its smooth and supposedly smart Danish President Allan Heyman. And, after polling the locker room in Rome and Paris, they found a very militant group of players itching to take Heyman on and call his bluff.

The tennis world was appalled when it happened and poor Herman David, the hero of 1968, found himself having to defend his tournament against his former friends as Wimbledon suddenly became very far from the best tournament in the world for that particular year.

Kramer, who had conducted the midnight meetings in the basement of the Westbury Hotel in Mayfair, was, of course, fully supportive of his players' wishes but nerves were frayed and doubts lingered in the minds of a few Board members, particularly the English duo of Mark Cox and John Barrett – the latter a former Davis Cup captain and All England Club committee member. Understandably Barrett abstained when it came to the final vote and he was not alone.

The pressure from all sides was incredible. Roger Taylor, not a Board member but obviously a prominent figure as Britain's No. 1, was being pulled every which way. The media was screaming for him to break ranks and play while his father, a Sheffield steelworker and a solid union man, was telling him not to become a scab. In the end, poor Roger made himself hugely unpopular in the locker room by electing to play. Obviously, with a second-rate field taking to the courts, made up of lowly ranked players along with a bunch of top Eastern Europeans who were not allowed to be ATP members, Taylor had a big chance of grabbing the title. But the pressure got to him in the end and the powerful lefthander succumbed to the eventual winner, Jan Kodes of Czechoslovakia, in the semi-final.

It is difficult now to grasp the magnitude of the story. The Pilic Affair ended up in the high court when the ATP decided to take out an injunction against the ILTF knowing that, if it was granted, it would take so long to settle that Pilic would have to be allowed to play Wimbledon. But, it wasn't. Kramer, Heyman, David, Drysdale and an increasingly embarrassed Pilic had gone to the High Court Chambers and watched Mr Justice Forbes read through each ILTF rule and cross-question counsel at length, before refusing to grant the injunction. Mr Forbes did not, however, voice an opinion as to whether Pilic was guilty or not. The media didn't care about that. 'Players' Case Thrown Out of Court!' screamed the headlines.

But Drysdale, the articulate South African mature beyond his years, was not about to give up and sought a meeting at Westminster with Eldon Griffiths, the Minister of Sport. Griffiths, a Welshman who had returned to the UK to become an MP after several years as a celebrated Newsweek columnist, knew exactly how things worked on both sides of the Atlantic and, after assessing the facts, asked Drysdale and Heyman to return the next day. But time and again the ILTF President was letting his true colours show. Drysdale agreed to the meeting. Heyman refused.

When the ATP Board reconvened in the basement of the Westbury, the pressure was mounting to an unbearable degree. What transpired changed the history of professional tennis forever. The first vote on whether or not to boycott Wimbledon passed in favour of a boycott. But the players were acutely aware of the seriousness of that decision and of how tired and pressurised everyone felt so, at the instigation of Arthur Ashe, they decided to sleep on it and return the next day. Drysdale then made two decisions that probably proved decisive. Firstly, to broaden the discussion, he invited Ken Rosewall, Charlie Pasarell and Cliff Richey to attend. "Looking back, I am still not sure whether I was right to let Charlie or Cliff into the meeting. They were not Board members so, of course, they did not have a vote but they certainly made their presence felt and might well have influenced the others."

Pasarell and Richey were militantly in favour of a boycott. In the end, the second vote was split when Barrett, Cox and Smith, the defending champion, voted to play while Kramer, Ashe and McManus voted to boycott. A majority was needed under the by-laws to overturn the previous night's vote. The deciding vote was Drysdale's. And he abstained.

Kramer nearly fell off his chair. "It was brilliant," he wrote later. "What a politician the kid turned out to be!"

And a very cool one in the heat of the moment but, as I got ready to drive him over to the newly-opened Gloucester Hotel, where the majority of the players were staying, the façade cracked and there were a few expletives flying around the car.

"What the fuck was I supposed to do?" he asked. "I knew by abstaining we would have a boycott but I also know I am going to have to lead the entire association in the next few months and try to keep the whole thing together."

Cliff knew all too well that, if he had voted against the boycott, about 25% of the membership, including Newcombe and Pasarell, would have walked out and the fledgling ATP would have been dead.

So, despite huge pressure being put on European players like Adriano Panatta and Paolo Bertolucci of Italy and Manolo Orantes of Spain by their national federations, 80 players withdrew from The Championships. The media screamed blue murder; the British tennis public were shocked and appalled in equal measure because they only knew one side of the story and showed up in droves to show their support for Wimbledon. "Who needed the dirty pros?" was a prevalent attitude. It was all very sad but, for the future of the game, very necessary. Against all odds, a bunch of athletes who played a very individual sport had produced a show of solidarity of which any union would have been proud. In the most dramatic way, it emphasised a basic truth – if they work together and stand solid, players can achieve anything because without them there is no game.

Donald Dell seized on the ILTF's unwise tactics and, with his lawyer's expertise, grabbed the moment to set up a structure that would radically alter the way in which the game was governed. The ILTF had lost the battle and never again would exercise such authoritarian power over the way tennis was run.

In partnership with Philippe Chatrier, the visionary President of the French Federation who would eventually become a long-time President of the ILTF, Kramer and Dell set up the Men's International Professional Tennis Council, consisting of three player reps, three tournament directors and three from the ILTF (soon to drop the 'Lawn' and become the ITF).

Inevitably it was not a harmonious group and the squabbles and battles continued through the next two and a half decades. Marshall Happer, the strict but affable lawyer brought up to New York from North Carolina to run what became known as the Pro Council, had a pretty torrid time over the next decade as power struggles, often involving Lamar Hunt's WCT which was now run by the former South African player and promoter Owen Williams, flared up at regular intervals. The story, and what followed in 1990 when the ATP broke away to form its own tour, deserves a book in itself and that is one reason why I am not going to go into detail here.

My book *Open Tennis* covers much of it up to 1992 and there is a great deal to add. But doing so here would not only make this tome far too long, but would create an imbalance to the story I have told so far. From this point onwards, I am going to concentrate mainly on my personal life away from tennis and push the sound of ball on racket strings into the background as far as detailing matches are concerned – although politics will intrude!

So, for the sake of cohesion and continuity, let me tell you what Kramer, Dell and Ashe had in mind when they asked for a meeting. "We really need to get our act together on the PR front," said Ashe, who was on the verge of taking over from Drysdale as the second President of the ATP. "We suffered a lot of bad press during the Wimbledon boycott, as you know, and we feel you could help us turn the image around a bit."

They wanted me to become the association's first PR Director and this time, I could not find a way to refuse. These were two friends asking for help and it was a job I felt myself well qualified to do. The salary was small and it only got marginally bigger when, six or seven months into the job, Dell came back to me and offered the post of European Director. Pierre Darmon, the former French No. 1, had been in that role from the outset but he wanted to pursue his own business interests and it was thought I was capable of handling the job.

So suddenly, I found myself in a reasonably influential position in the world of tennis at a very critical time in the game's development. Basically my job was to professionalise the old amateur circuit. Most of our tournaments, which were, by then, grouped together as the Grand Prix circuit, were still being played in the traditional country clubs from which they had sprung decades before.

The old order was quaint and completely out of touch with the evolving professional circuit. There was a classic example at the lovely Real Club de Barcelona where the tournament was run by a charming Spanish gentleman called Miguel Lerin. Ever since he had been tournament director he had been of the mind to charge players for practice balls and the use of towels. I suggested we have a coffee. Sitting him down, I tried to point out as gently as possible that the players were reasonably well paid now and would not steal the towels. And that they really shouldn't have to pay for practice balls. There were a few other details reflective of an amateur viewpoint which I have forgotten and, by the time I had finished, Miguel was looking a little flushed in the face.

"You have made me very cross but I will go away and think about it!" he said before disappearing into his office at the top of the stairs which were, and indeed still are, lined with honours boards, listing every champion to have played at the Real Club since its inception in 1899. But he said it with a twinkle in his eye and it did not take him long to realise that the march of progress was inevitable and that he would to survive without towel money in his kitty.

It was a fascinating time to be involved with the game and I saw myself as something of a protector of the players, who were having to deal with the incredibly terse and high-handed attitude of some of the amateur officials who were still filling the roles of referee and umpires at many tournaments. I remember one incident at the Club di Circolo in Florence where the South African John Youill had just come off court after an exhausting singles in the blazing Italian sunshine. He was sitting in the club house, red in the face, sipping a drink and trying to cool down when the grey-haired referee, adorned in his blue blazer and airing an attitude of pumped up authority, came up to Youill and spat out, "You, Youill, you have no time for that. You are on Court 3 for your doubles – NOW!"

I don't think he was prepared for what followed. Grabbing him by the shoulder, I spun him around and thundered, 'Don't you dare to talk to one of my players like that ever again! They are professionals and deserve your respect and as long as I am around I will ensure they get it!"

Just the look on his face was worth it. He had never been spoken to like that by anyone connected with a professional tennis player, whom he obviously viewed as a species who could be ordered around. Youill was allowed to finish his drink.

The thing that used to annoy the players most in those early days was the ignorance of so many amateur officials. Many of the umpires barely knew the rules and sat in the chair barking out orders like little martinets. But there were some funny moments and, inevitably, Gordon Forbes recounts one of the best ones in his hilarious and brilliantly written memoir, *A Handful of Summers*.

Checking in to verify his practice court at Forest Hills one year, the tall, lean South African with the ginger blond hair answered the request for his name by saying, "Forbes."

The elderly official looked up at him and replied, "You're not Forbes, you're Emerson. Court 17."

"Oh, that's strange, I thought I was Forbes," said Forbes and wandered off, wondering how he could have been confused for the shorter, muscular Roy Emerson with his jet black hair.

So it was a process, a very long process as the far-flung, very cosmopolitan tennis world tried to work out who was who and how it should all be organised. What we needed was a proper ATP rule book which would free itself of some of the prissy and outdate minutiae of ITF rules. Ashe, a scholar at heart, took it upon himself to collect the views of various players and, with the help of Dell's legal mind, write the rule book that would become the ATP bible as the years unfolded. On a couple of occasions Arthur came round to my extremely cramped office on the Rue du Colisee just off the Champs Elysees and work on it with me.

The ATP's European 'office' was really nothing more than a cupboard at the back of Benny Berthet's ladies dress store. Benny, a jovial character with a sudden, explosive temper, was an ex-player and prominent figure at the French Tennis Federation and was kind enough to offer us this space for free. That made it just about bearable. There was room for my secretary and me sitting side by side and one visitor – providing the person was not too broad in the beam. No problem there for Arthur but we still preferred a bit more space so, at lunchtime, we adjourned to the little bistro on the corner of the Rue Ponthieu to continue our work. It is still there to this day, oblivious no doubt to the part it played in the writing of the rules for the men's pro tour.

We were all on a big adventure, learning, proposing, testing and finding out just what would enable the game of professional tennis grow to its fullest potential. Sadly, I don't think it ever has. Despite enormous growth in popularity and exposure, to a degree we could never have envisioned in 1974, the sport has remained fragmented with too many governing bodies – the ATP, WTA, ITF and the Grand Slams – all guarding their own nests and jostling for the limelight. Compared to golf, which is not as international and simply not as popular a sport as tennis, and basketball which also has limited appeal internationally despite its growth, tennis has never managed to make the most of what it has to offer. In the words of Charlie Pasarell, who had the vision to build Grand Champions and then the Indian Wells Tennis Garden as sites for what is now one of the best tournaments in the world, "Tennis does not punch its weight in the market place."

Indeed it doesn't and it continues to be a source of huge frustration to those of us who believe a great game could become greater still. But, back in the seventies, we were ploughing on, doing the best we could and I was thrilled to be part of it. As far as I was concerned, it didn't last long because Jack Kramer, with whom I had worked so well, decided he had had enough and a very large, amiable but limited Texan called Bob Briner took his place.

Briner was Donald Dell's man and was backed by Ashe but he was the wrong man for the job. He started making promises he couldn't keep which caused me huge embarrassment with people like Len Owen, the Benson & Hedges executive who ran the big winter indoor event at Wembley's Empire Pool in London every year. It was a showcase event for the ATP in Europe, attracting sell out crowds of 9,000 virtually every night, and deserved our wholehearted support.

When a new contract was signed under Briner's signature, it stated that no other ATP event would be scheduled against it. Within a year, a tournament in South America was inserted into the calendar that same week, depriving Owen's event of top names like Guillermo Vilas and Jaime Fillol. Owen was, quite rightly, furious and I was left squirming at our next tournament meeting, unable to offer anything but a meek apology for not having lived up to our word.

The fact was decisions were being over my head in Briner's newly established headquarters in Garland, Texas and I was powerless to do anything about it. Europe, as has always been the case, had the most top players and the most tournaments, bringing in the most money, but it was the Americans who called the shots. There was a moment when I had sufficient backing from European stars such as Adriano Panatta, Paolo Bertolucci, Hans Kary, Rolf Thung and Georges Goven to lead a breakaway movement, divorcing Europe from the United States. But my heart was never really in that idea. We had worked so hard to create the ATP as a global entity and I was loath to destroy that.

But it was becoming obvious that I could not work with Briner and when he ordered me to stay at my desk in Paris during August 1976, waiting for the phone to ring – something that might happen twice a week at best as Europeans hit the beaches – it was time to make a stand. Briner had no clue about Europe or how it worked and used this piece of insubordination to fire me.

Happily I had the last laugh. A year later, during the US Open, I was elected to the eleven-man ATP Board over which Briner presided. It was a huge embarrassment for him and he must have resented having to answer some sharply worded questions about his conduct from the two British Richards on the Board – myself and Richard Lewis, who is now CEO at the All England Club. John Newcombe was President of the ATP by that time and did a good job but Briner continued to squander ATP funds and make himself so unpopular with a large number of players that he dared not enter the locker room – a ridiculous situation for a players' leader. He managed to get me off the Board by reducing the number of Board members – clever trick that – but I continue to cherish my two years as a rare species, a non-player elected by the players to serve them.

And so I returned to freelance journalism and a period when a personal relationship allowed me a peek into a different world.

But, first, let's talk about Africa.

Chapter 15
ASHE IN AFRICA

I spent many memorable moments in the company of Arthur Ashe and saw him react, in his understated way, to many situations, some funny, some complex and some hateful. But I shall always remember one in particular.

It was the moment he walked down the gangway of a British Airways 707 to greet an Entebbe dawn and set foot on African soil for the first time in his life. His face carried an expression I cannot begin to describe. All one could tell was that a variety of emotions were welling up inside this controlled and private man and that the moment would become a stepping stone in his life.

Ashe's heritage was that of an Ashanti, a tribe from Ghana, and he had delved deeply into his roots. His curiosity knew no bounds and it came as no surprise when he invited me to join him in visiting the author Alex Haley when we were at a tournament in San Francisco. At the time, Haley was in the middle of writing a book he was calling *Roots* and he had no idea that it would turn into a bestseller. It was a work that had required him to examine Africa and the slave trade in intricate detail and Arthur was fascinated by everything he had to say.

Obviously Ashe had been champing at the bit to get to Africa but the continent had few tennis tournaments in those days, a fact that remains unhappily true today. So Donald Dell, using his Washington DC contacts to the full, set up a couple of State Department sponsored tours to the continent. The first, in 1971, would send Ashe and his US Davis Cup colleague Stan Smith to English-speaking countries such as Uganda, Kenya, Tanzania, Zambia, Ghana and Nigeria while, the following year, Ashe, with Charlie Pasarell, Tom Okker and Marty Riessen – all Dell clients at ProServ – as companions, would visit French-speaking Africa – the Ivory Coast, Cameroon, the Gabon and the Congo.

I was lucky enough to get invited along and the experiences were those of a lifetime. In a way it was like being on the campaign trail again in that the journeys became a blur of airports, hotels and greetings with all manner of people from President Gowon of Nigeria, who received us as peacocks strutted on his lawn, to tennis officials and, most importantly, the hordes of young players and kids who turned up for the clinics and exhibitions.

Lagos, then the capital of Nigeria, remains in my memory as the most suffocatingly humid, over-crowded shambles of a city that I have ever visited. The huge, gleaming smiles of welcome had to make up for the absence of sun during the two days we were there – just a low, thick layer of cloud that hovered above like a wet blanket pressing on your head. Even Arthur looked hot when he played and I vividly remember Stan Smith having to wring out his socks at changeovers to prevent himself swimming in his over-size shoes. (The Stan Smith Adidas model which, amazingly, is still selling in its millions today.)

Further west along the coast, Ghana seemed a complete contrast. Accra is a city of wide boulevards and boasts one of the world's largest outdoor markets – the only one, I believe, to be run entirely by women. All colourfully clad in their long robes and turbans, these well-built ladies strode around balancing everything from fruit to chairs on their heads, clamouring for you to buy their goods. They took the whole thing down at night and put it up again next morning. I can only presume that it remains as stimulating today. I hope so.

Coincidentally or not, we arrived in Nairobi on Kenyatta Day and, almost before we had a chance to check in to the hotel, we were whisked off to the giant Parade to celebrate the father of modern Kenya. Like many others who had opposed British rule during the colonial era, Jomo Kenyatta had spent a decade in jail or detention before the MauMau terrorist crisis was brought under control in 1960. Kenyatta, born of an illiterate Kikuyu family in the late 1880s – he never knew his birthdate – somehow got enough of an education to go to a Quaker college in Birmingham and spent World War Two working on a farm in Sussex. He married an Englishwoman, returned to Kenya and immediately became involved in politics. As he proved on his release, he had never been the firebrand terrorist the media of the day had tried to paint him, and after a period as Prime Minister, became his country's much loved President.

The parade was as colourful and joyful as one might have expected and, looking back now, it is fun to speculate whether there might have been the father of a future United States President celebrating somewhere in that vast crowd.

In 1972, we started in Abidjan, capital of the Ivory Coast, which was another attractive city, exuding a French feel with gendarmes waving their arms around at traffic stops on Parisian-style boulevards. It was there that we heard one of my favourite stories about how panicked we get about pigmentation.

This newly-arrived and very white French wife of a government functionary was trying to find her way around as she drove her husband's car in the city and apparently misread the signal given to her by a gendarme holding one of those signs with 'Go' in green on one side and 'Stop' in red on the other. Whistling her to stop, the policeman strode up to the car and sticking his large, round, sweaty head half in the window, bellowed, "Madame, quelle couleur je suis? Quelle couleur?"

Terrified at this confrontation which seemed pregnant with awful racial over-tones, the poor woman gripped the wheel in terror as she searched for the most diplomatic answer. After a few seconds, the gendarme put her out of her misery.

"Je suis ROUGE, Madame, je suis ROUGE."

Arthur used to chuckle at these stories for, no matter what he was feeling inside, he always gave off an air of sophisticated amusement at the tangle some people used to get into over the fact that his skin was a different shade of brown. I was guilty of exacerbating that fact the following year in South Africa, but I will leave that story till later.

On arrival in Yaounde, the largest city in Cameroon, the guys continued to give clinics for large numbers of local kids, and Bud Collins, who was still with the Boston Globe in those days and already making a name for himself in his ebullient style as a TV commentator for WGBTV Boston – the public broadcasting station that pioneered coverage of tennis on television – proved his extraordinary ability to remember names.

These, of course, were French African names, some easy and many a bit complicated. But Bud would line up twenty kids, ask their names and as they filed past a second time to hit a ball with Arthur or Tom or Marty, he would call each child by his or her name and get it right. Amazing. Although this tour was doubling as Charlie and Shireen Pasarell's honeymoon – they had been married a few weeks before – the main purpose was to fly the flag for tennis and see if we could unearth some promising talent from all the hundreds of athletic youngsters we would meet.

As it turned out, we did – but in entirely fortuitous circumstances. I have told this remarkable story many times but let me document it now for posterity. On our second night in the Cameroons we were invited to the Yaounde Tennis Club for dinner. After you get left off at the gate, there is a path leading up to the clubhouse steps which, halfway along, is divided in two by a clump of palm trees. You can either go left or right. I was with Arthur and Charlie and, for absolutely no particular reason, we went left. If we had gone right, you would almost certainly never have heard of Yannick Noah. And, for you American basketball fans, that means Joakim Noah would never have been born.

Adjacent to the left-hand path, there was a tennis court which at the time we arrived was illuminated by yellow lighting which cast a strange opaque glow. The first thing I noticed was that the leggy young boy about to serve to the man at the other end – it turned out to be his uncle – had to sweep large, moth-like creatures off his baseline before he could do so. Once he got the ball in play, the level of tennis made us stop and pay attention.

The boy, who was eleven, was extremely athletic and agile and was not afraid to come charging into the net. After a minute or two, Arthur indicated his approval by calling him over as he unsheathed one of his gleaming Head graphite rackets, which were the latest thing in racket technology at the time.

"Here!" he said to the boy, "try this."

"Oh, merci, monsieur, merci beaucoup," the boy replied, eyes wide in wonder. Dropping his old battered wood Maxply, Yannick then ran back to the baseline and played the most important point of his life. Kicking in a big first serve, he raced to the net and put away a clean backhand volley winner.

Arthur was not given to hyperbole so when he turned to Charlie and me with his cocked eyebrow and said, "Mmm, kid can play," we knew he was impressed.

So we watched for a few more minutes and then went into the clubhouse. Arthur enquired of a local official as to the identity of the boy we had been watching and was told that his father was standing a few feet away. Zacharie Noah had played soccer for the Cameroons and was keeping that option open for his son. Until this moment. Suddenly confronted by Arthur Ashe telling him that his son had serious potential as a tennis player changed all that.

"He could become a player but not here," Arthur said bluntly. "He will need to go to France or the United States."

"If you really think so, that shouldn't be a problem," said Mr Noah. "His mother lives in Nice."

Ten days later, when we had flown back to Paris, Arthur spoke to Philippe Chatrier, President of the French Federation and a good friend of us all, who took Ashe at his word and made arrangements for young Yannick to join the training academy the Federation had recently opened in Nice. It was the first one they had established outside Paris and timing was perfect. Six years later Noah had progressed sufficiently to be able to partner Ashe in the doubles at Wimbledon. I watched them walk out together on the Centre Court with a bit of lump in my throat. Certainly, the kid could play.

After Cameroon, we flew down to Libreville, capital of the Gabon, after which the guys were due to head off to the Congo. But that was where we parted company because I could not get a visa. No journalists allowed.

So I grabbed the opportunity to explore something completely different – the hospital that Dr Albert Schweitzer had established near the little town of Lambarene. Dr Schweitzer had died seven years before but the hospital was still operating, run, I was told, by a group of Belgian and Swiss doctors and nurses employed by the Schweitzer Foundation.

The man himself had been a person of so many talents and contradictions that any attempt to characterise him would inevitably be left wanting. Schweitzer was a theologian, an organist specialising in Bach's religious works, a philosopher and a doctor. He was also a Lutheran who wrote extensively on Jesus. In electing to disappear into the African jungle and tend to the natives in 1912, he gave up a life of acclaim and rewards in a gesture that seemed wholly praiseworthy. Once in Africa he spoke out against the cruelty of colonialism. Yet while treating Africans who trekked miles to attend his hospital, he never gave any of the ones he employed positions of authority and, staggeringly, never once invited an African to sit at his dinner table.

My opinion of Dr Schweitzer was, inevitably, coloured by an account of a visit to Lambarene in the 1950s by James Cameron, who wrote scathingly about what he found in his brilliant biography *Point of Departure*.

Cameron wrote: 'The hospital was a shock. I had been prepared for some professional unorthodoxies, but not this glaring squalor. The Doctor had fenced off all mechanical advances to a degree that seemed both pedantic and appalling. The wards were rude huts, airless and dark, plank beds and wooden pillows; every one infested with hens and dogs. There was no running water but the rain; no gas, no sewerage, no electricity except for the operating theatre and the gramophone. [...] I said then that the Hospital existed for him rather than he for it. It was deliberately archaic and primitive, deliberately part of the jungle around it, a background of his own creation which clearly meant a great deal more philosophically than it did medically.'

Cameron had some interesting conversations in French with Dr Schweitzer during his stay but admitted that, on balance, he preferred the company of three chimpanzees. 'They would sit for hours on the floor by my doorway, embracing each other, with their six dark, sorrowful eyes fixed intently upon me. If I turned a page or crossed my legs, they would stir quietly, nudging each other [...] There was one genuinely startling moment: I was working beside the window, grinding out from the typewriter whatever contemporary nonsense was required, when I glanced round and there they were in a row, by the doorway, beating out a ragged tattoo with their fingers on the floor; a very reasonable imitation [...] I could have nearly cried: two more typewriters were all I needed for the conclusive experiment: given time WOULD they have written the first two acts of Hamlet?'

With Dr Schweitzer dead, I was anxious to know who was now in charge of the hospital and asked around some diplomatic contacts in Libreville at the receptions we were invited to. There seemed to be one unifying answer: "Find Madame Joan."

It was made clear to me that Madame Joan, whoever she might be, was not the official head of the hospital. But, I was told, she made it tick. So, making a note of that, I set off and flew down to Lambarene and inquired as to how I could get to the Schweitzer Hospital. By boat was the answer, and so I made my way down to the Ogowe River and, for a modest sum, negotiated a ride in a thin, long craft that carried about a dozen people. Petrol fumes soon mingled with the thick, humid air as the motor sprung into life and off we went – deep into the jungle. It was both picturesque and desolate and the journey seemed to go on forever. But in little over an hour, if memory serves, we turned a bend in the river and there, on the bank, was this settlement of corrugated iron roofs covering buildings that ran down to the water.

I had sent word ahead of my pending arrival and I was greeted, after walking up a damp path, by a blonde nurse wearing a starched white uniform. She was Belgian like almost all her colleagues, doctors and nurses alike. After being shown to my quarters, a room with bare essentials, presumably not unlike the one James Cameron had occupied, I was invited to dinner and found myself being introduced to Madame Joan. She sat opposite me near the end of the table, which had a vacant high-backed chair at its head. It was Dr Schweitzer's chair.

She was a woman in her late forties with long brown hair and a long black dress. No starched uniform for her. She greeted me warmly in fluent English but the accent was faintly foreign. Even Professor Higgins might have struggled to place it. With her bearing and personality Madame Joan, in fact, gave off an aura of faint mystery. I had never met anyone quite like her before.

After dinner, she invited me to walk with her to the leper colony which was located a few hundred yards from the main encampment. The crickets chirped in tune with the hum of the jungle and the temperature dropped from stifling to almost bearable. When we reached the lepers, Madame Joan stooped to pick up a young man and immediately started rubbing his stumps in the soothing manner of a faith healer.

"They are wonderful people," she said. "Leprosy used to carry such a stigma but it is getting better now as we understand more about it. I spend a lot of time here. They need company and reassurance. I will be staying most of the night so we can continue talking in the morning."

With that I was dismissed and I left her there in the blackness, amidst the quiet crying of the lepers as they tried to find sleep.

It was clear that Madame Joan was the mover and shaker of the place. When she had arrived a few years before, mosquitoes presented a huge health hazard but she quickly identified the problem and had a large, stagnant pool, bypassed by the river, drained and cleaned out. Overnight, the mosquito population was decimated.

One wondered what the autocratic doctor would have made of her. It can be safely assumed that he did not spend his nights in the leper colony and would probably not have enjoyed some of Madame Joan's dogmatic and progressive thinking. It was probably just as well that he was lying peacefully at rest in a grave dug out of the little slope that ran from what had been his office window down to the river.

The doctors and nurses spoke reverently about him, which was only natural, and pointed to the thousands of lives he had extended by simply offering basic treatment and medicines to the hundreds of people who literally walked out of the jungle to find his hospital.

There was no much to admire about what Dr Schweitzer had done and yet, as Cameron noted, so much to query. Having made such an effort and turned it into his life's work despite having so much to offer European civilisation in so many ways, why had he not done more? When I was there the facilities were still basic even if the care was good.

Now, I believe, there has been a great deal of modernisation and the hospital handles 6,000 in-patients and some 35,000 out-patients a year, thanks to money provided by the Schweitzer Foundation. It has obviously saved thousands of lives and for that, one can only be grateful. But …

After I left, I wrote a piece about the hospital and Madame Joan for a British magazine – one of those supplements that used to arrive tucked into your Sunday newspaper. About three months later, I received a letter that had been forwarded to me from the magazine. It was postmarked Weymouth in Dorset. Its contents shocked me.

From memory, it began, 'We were extremely interested to read your article on "Madame Joan" because she is our mother.'

Apparently, the letter was written by three of her children whom she had deserted when they were in their teens. They were asking me if I knew how to contact her. I replied by saying that they should write to the Schweitzer Foundation in Brussels and refrained from adding that I was surprised they hadn't done so already.

From what I could gather after a little more research, Madame Joan, who was part Russian which explained the accent, had simply walked out one day and gone to India where she worked with the poor. From there she made her way to Lambarene. Quite clearly, she was someone who had an urge to succour people in need and, as they grew up, one can only assume she felt her children were not going to need all the love she had to give.

But who knows? We all have our reasons and motivations for doing things and many are inexplicable. I never heard from her, or the children she had left behind, again.

I have lost count of the number of flights I have taken in my life – at one point in the seventies and eighties, I was averaging about 80 or 90 separate flights a year – but the one I took from Lambarene remains in the memory as one of the most unique.

It was the daily Air Gabon flight that began in Libreville and did a circular tour of the country – down to Port Gentil, then Lambarene and on until, about a dozen stops later, it landed back in the capital. There was a slight delay as we waited for the DC 6, its propellers whirring, to land from Port Gentil. To pass the time I had started chatting to the captain and his crew, inspired, possibly, by the fact that the sole stewardess was a stunning

Gabonese who wore her uniform with all the flair she would have picked up from French fashion magazines.

The cockpit crew were French and, from what I could gather, Air Force veterans of the war in Indo-China. Once the plane arrived, they wished me bon voyage and I settled back in greater comfort than one finds on most 737 jets today.

After about an hour, it was announced that we would be stopping for lunch. Yes, that's right, we would be landing at some God-forsaken air strip in the middle of nowhere to eat. As we circled, I looked down on a jungle clearing that offered nothing except a hut with some smoke emitting from a pipe and a long table laid out in the sun with a white table cloth and place settings. To one side there was a sort of corral with a table laden with sandwiches and bottles of Evian.

As we prepared to leave the aircraft, it became clear to me that the corral and the sandwiches were for the passengers while the crew would be seated at the table. Luckily, I caught the captain's eye. "Venez avec nous," he said surreptitiously.

And so it was that I found myself tucking into a properly prepared French three course meal, washed down by some excellent wine decanted from the bottles that lined the table. One was a whiskey bottle if I remember correctly.

The meal was being produced by a thin African who appeared to have no help. "We trained him in Vietnam," the captain smiled before taking a swig of Scotch. "He cooks the French way."

And indeed he did. It was all delicious and slightly surreal. Half way through the meal a single engine plane appeared out of nowhere, wiggling its wings before settling down a few yards from us. The young bush pilot, his cap at a jaunty angle, greeted the crew in familiar fashion and sat down, tucking in with gusto.

After about an hour, coffee having been served, the crew stretched themselves and the young stewardess went off to lead the passengers back onto the plane. I tried to feel guilty about not partaking in the sandwiches but passed out before I could bother. The heat and the wine had ensured that I was unconscious as we hopped our way back to Libreville, the pilots apparently still sufficiently in charge of their senses to ensure that we negotiated a few more dicey landing strips in one piece. I'm all in favour of Air Gabon.

Chapter 16
ASHE AND APARTHEID

On Friday, 16th November 1973 Arthur Ashe boarded a BOAC 707 and flew to South Africa. It was a big deal; a front page story with numerous connotations.

Ashe was going to play in the South African Open at Ellis Park in Johannesburg but, of course, it was the subplot that was causing all the interest and controversy.

Although he had yet to win Wimbledon, Ashe was already an international celebrity, having caught the attention and won the admiration of people all over the world for the manner in which he had handled himself as a black man in a white sport and the intelligent things he had to say on the subject.

One of them might not have been so intelligent but even a low key, patient man like Arthur had his limits and when he found himself being peppered yet again by questions at a press conference as to whether he would continue to apply for a visa to play in South Africa, he tried to deflect the intent behind the questioning by saying, "Hell, we have a great tournament at the River Oaks Country Club in Houston where I am not welcome, so what do you do?"

The follow up was quick. "So what would you do about South Africa's problems?"

"Oh, I'd drop a hydrogen bomb on Johannesburg!" It was said light-heartedly, partly in exasperation, and Arthur quickly tried to laugh it off. But the quote was in reporters' notebooks and as this was not some little post-match gathering at a small tournament somewhere, the news was on the wires in no time. Ashe was, in fact, talking in Paris where Donald Dell's victorious Davis Cup was stopping on the way back from Australia. Donald had taken the team to the American Embassy to see his pal, the Ambassador, and, of course the ebullient Sargent Shriver had given them a big welcome with a press conference to follow – right there with every Paris-based foreign correspondent in attendance. And Arthur Ashe suggested bombing Johannesburg. That tested Sarge's savoire faire.

Back in South Africa, Owen Williams groaned. The former South African No. 1 who had turned himself into the country's biggest and most flamboyant sports promoter was desperate to get Ashe to play in the South African Open which he ran. But, despite having quite good contacts with the Afrikaaner government – rare for an English-speaking liberal – attempts to get Ashe a visa had failed time and again. Now, it seemed, the last chance had gone.

But Williams didn't totally give up hope and, more importantly, neither did Gladys Heldman, that feisty creator of the women's tennis circuit who believed that hurdles were only made to be jumped. When Owen visited the Heldmans at their Houston home, the subject of Ashe and South Africa came up and Gladys immediately started to insist it was not a lost cause. In his book *Ahead of the Game*, Owen describes what happened.

'We were chatting by the pool on a very hot day … As the conversation developed, I found my inner voice agreeing with her but my outer voice said, "Hell! No – it won't happen!". Then Gladys provided the vital prop – a large yellow legal pad on which she suggested, with a steely edge in her voice, I could write to Prime Minister John B. Vorster. You got the full treatment from Gladys. The sweet smile and the cold stare – a Gladys speciality – and the flip comments. Oh, I was such a glib fellow, she suggested, I could persuade anyone to do anything. Eventually, she reached my inner voice and I began scribbling the draft of a letter that would create a little bit of history.'

As a result of that meeting, Williams, on his return home, found himself in the Prime Minister's office doing exactly what Gladys had told him he could do – persuading Vorster that Ashe would cause no trouble; that he would be far more afraid of them than they should be of him and that he would be with Arthur every step of the way.

Surprisingly, Vorster agreed and, with Donald Dell pulling all the right strings in Washington, this unlikely trip was arranged.

Once again, I was lucky enough to be invited along. Bud Collins and Frank Deford, who was in the process of helping Arthur with his fascinating diary, published later by Houghton Miflin as *Portrait in Motion*, were also with us. My role was to help Arthur write two or three long pieces for the London Sunday Times.

Later, when we met South Africa's most celebrated author, Alan Paton, who wrote *Cry, the Beloved Country*, he had told Ashe, "We are an odd country." Speaking to me, Paton used the word 'complex'. There was proof of that before we even left the plane. A small man came up to Ashe just as we landed

241

and said timorously, "Mr Ashe, I am one of those horrible South Africans – and I just wanted to wish you the best of success. I promise you we're not all as bad as we're supposed to be and, you mark my words, three fourths of the people will be pulling for you."

Did he mean white people or ALL the people? Understanding the divisions that existed in South Africa at the time was not just a question of black and white. There were political categories for Indians and Coloureds, too, each having limitations placed on their ability to live as free individuals.

And so it started – the complexities and incongruities, the ignorance and the simple unfairness that one met every step of the way. In those days, so many people had opinions about South Africa, gleaned from what they had read or heard. But none of it made much sense even when you got there and you certainly couldn't even BEGIN to understand unless you set foot in the country. That was why Ashe went. He needed to see for himself.

Arthur didn't have to wait long for the first piece of shock and embarrassment. Along with Donald and Carole Dell, he was being billeted in a wealthy Johannesburg suburb at the splendid home of Brian Young, a Jewish real estate broker. Brian's wife had left him so he was living alone with his servants. When lunch was served, Arthur asked the maid for a cold drink. She dropped her eyes and answered, "Yes, Master."

Arthur's reaction is spelt out graphically in *Portrait in Motion*.

"FOR GOD'S SAKE! So here is little Artie Ashe, the skinny black kid from the capital of the old Confederacy, all set up in a mansion, carrying on jes' like the white folks, and getting' hisself called Master!"

That's what Ashe was thinking to himself as he gently tried to deal with the situation. Ashe wasn't going to let himself be called Master by anyone, let alone a black servant, but eradicating a lifelong tradition of blacks calling whites 'Master' with all its implications wasn't going be achieved by the commands of a tennis player who had been in the country five minutes. I think, after a persuasive conversation, they settled on 'Sir'.

Although Ashe had plenty of ulterior motives for wanting this trip to happen, ostensibly he was there to play the SAB Open at Ellis Park, the nation's main tennis centre, situated next to the famous rugby ground where the Afrikaaner nation displayed its manhood to the world in the form of its mighty rugby union team.

On arriving at Ellis Park to practise, Ashe was confronted with large signs for toilets, saying 'Whites' and 'Blacks' – just in case he didn't know where he was. It had been stated, in the press releases before the trip began, that one of the concessions Ashe had been able to win was integrated seating at Ellis Park. That was not strictly true. The Government had never agreed to it, but there was another colour that played its daily part in South African life at the time and it was called grey. Today we might associate that colour with the pornographic novel *Fifty Shades of Grey* and, looking back, one might say that, in a non-sexual sense, everything happening in South Africa in the seventies was a pornographic bastardisation of how people should live together.

But grey was everywhere. Hard and fast, black and white rules were implemented, or not, depending on the situation and who knew who. If you were as canny and commanding as Owen Williams and fully aware of just what shade of grey you could aim for, you could get away with quite a lot.

So although it had not been officially sanctioned, Owen and his wife of the time, Jennifer, who worked tirelessly for the liberal cause, handed out 'whites only' seating to blacks, Coloured and Indians they knew and, providing they were brave enough, the people used them. In previous years, Williams had continuously broken the colour barrier by inviting leading members of all communities to sit with him in the President's box. The men from BOSS, the apt name for the Bureau of State Security, watched, silent and unsmiling, but did nothing. On balance Owen Williams was too important to the image of South Africa to interfere. In just one year, since taking charge back in 1966, Williams had lifted the South African Open to the second most attended tennis tournament in the world.

In retrospect the figures are extraordinary. In 1965, Wimbledon had drawn a total attendance of 250,000. The US Championships at Forest Hills drew a paltry 32,000. And South Africa? No more than 4,600! No wonder Williams was asked to take over. His first year produced figures of 62,000 and by 1967, that had doubled to 126,000.

The Government could be block-headed but it wasn't stupid enough to nit-pick that kind of success so, to an extent, seating at Ellis Park was integrated but Ashe was still disappointed to see the vast majority of blacks penned into their own corner of the stadium.

In the first round, Ashe defeated the Texan, Sherwood Stewart, in what most people viewed as a historic encounter as it was assumed it was the first time a black player had played in the South African Open. For the record that is not quite true. A couple of years earlier, a very black Frenchman from New Caledonia called Wanaro 'Bill' N'Godrella had slipped through the net

– probably on the evidence of his French passport – and had been allowed to play. He lost in the first round and split before anyone took note of his pigmentation. And, of course, the hugely popular Evonne Goolagong, a light skinned Aboriginal, had not only played the tournament but been acclaimed as champion in 1972, having lost in the final to Margaret Court the previous year.

But, nevertheless, Ashe's win over Stewart did provide a notable milestone and the loser was delighted to have been part of it. Sherwood Stewart, a smart, humorous man who thought life was there to be lived, had deliberately entered the tournament as soon as he had heard Ashe was going to play. He had wanted to observe history being made. By the luck of the draw, he discovered he had become part of it!

On the fourth day of his visit, Ashe met with Don Mattera, a coloured poet who worked as a journalist for the Johannesburg Star. His work had been seen by Nikki Giovanni, the famous American poet when she visited South Africa and she had admired his ability to be creative in such a restrictive atmosphere. So did Arthur, who was quickly sharpening up his diplomatic skills.

When he was introduced to Jim Fouche, the President of South Africa whose role was purely ceremonial, Fouche asked the visitor how he liked South Africa.

"How are you enjoying the tennis?" Ashe answered.

The tennis player was learning on the job just how to become a diplomat and an ambassador for his country and his race. He needed to sharpen his wits still further when Mattera told him that he had arranged for Arthur to hold a meeting with black journalists two days later. Arthur steeled himself for the occasion, knowing that opposition to his visit would be expressed quite vocally.

But, on the morning of the meeting, Ashe picked up the paper at breakfast and read that Don Mattera had been banned. A banning order was reserved for people who were starting to get on the Government's nerves but hadn't done anything quite so serious as to warrant jail. It meant that the banned person could not meet in a public place with more than one individual and could not have more than one person at his home. In other words, as a journalist, he couldn't function. His life was simply put on hold.

When we all arrived at the downtown headquarters of the United States Information Service where the meeting was to be held, we saw Mattera on the pavement outside. Stepping aside from the two BOSS agents hovering close to him, he went up to Arthur and apologised. Mattera would not be able to attend the meeting that he, himself, had organised. He was banned.

The situation was both sad and hilarious. The Afrikaaner Government was bending over backwards to ensure that their high-profile visitor saw only the best aspects of this beleaguered nation and through bureaucratic stupidity they had allowed him to be presented, personally and in close up, with the worst.

The order to ban Mattera for writing things they didn't like had gone into the slow-moving state machine two weeks before and was moving relentlessly through the pipeline, popping out bang slap in the middle of Ashe's visit. Did anyone think to halt its progress until their visitor had left? Of course not. So there we were, standing in the street, watching Ashe being given a face-to-face example of how South Africa treated one of its most talented citizens. The apartheid regime in all its glory.

The hall was packed when Ashe walked up to the podium to talk and answer questions. In *Portrait in Motion*, Arthur described the scene this way:

'And so, as Don watched us go, we climbed the stairs to attend his meeting. I agreed to speak in the auditorium, so long as I could ask questions as well as answer them. There were about 75 of us jammed into this small, windowless room – counting the man from BOSS and the predictable number of informers. The atmosphere was charged with fear and passion, and the place was as hot from the tension as from the crush of people. I did not really understand how scared the people were, though, until I looked over at one of the group's officers and saw that his hands were trembling – and that he could not stop them.'

It was into this atmosphere that Ashe walked, looking as calm as ever to anyone who didn't know him, but Arthur's limbs used to get a little stiff when he was really nervous and he was not walking freely now. No wonder. Some people were shouting, "Power, power!" But others were calling out, "Shame, shame!" As he moved towards the front Arthur heard someone mutter, "Uncle Tom!"

An early speaker laid it on the line. "You come here, our people play in a tournament once, and the situation remains unchanged. The black man still has his place – cleaning toilets. You stay away, all of you. All right, Arthur?"

I stood there and just admired this special man who had become my friend as he was put through this ordeal. You had to be there to know how intimidating it was. Arthur had no training to deal with situations like this. West Point had taught him how to handle himself – although certainly no better than his father and Dr Johnson – and it was their teachings he drew on now as he struggled to stay composed in the face of the onslaught.

"Cut off South Africa! Boycott it!" someone else called out. "Don't you see, we blacks wouldn't suffer any more than we already do. We are used to suffering. Only the whites would suffer more."

"Your presence delays our struggle. You go back to New York. Stay away, stay away!"

Speaking in his even, unfussed tone, Ashe replied, "Sanctions won't work. When there's a choice – money over morality – it's always money that wins out. There's ten African nations trading with this country today. If the blacks cannot keep up a boycott, what makes you think the whites will?"

He admitted that the United States was a not a proper analogy but he used the example of Rosa Parks refusing to sit in the back of the bus. "She said, 'No! I'm not moving!' and the whole thing started for us from there."

The hawks in the crowd always had an answer. "She would have been banned here and Martin Luther King would have been put on Robben Island," a man shouted back.

Ashe may not have been convincing many of them that his arguments were correct but he was gaining their respect. And they listened when he told them: "Maybe I'm naïve, but I think when you're mapping out a plan for progress, emotion cannot be allowed to play a large role, except for drumming up support. I had a very wise man who taught me to play tennis, to play against whites, and in places no black man had ever been before. His name was Dr Walter Johnson and he used to say, 'Those whom the gods wish to destroy, they first make mad'."

Even Dr Johnson probably never envisioned his pupil having to test the ability to keep his cool in circumstances quite like this. The good doctor, with whom Arthur lived in Lynchburg, Virginia during his early teenage years, had focused, naturally enough, on teaching Arthur how to deal with whites in a totally white dominated sport. Here he was having to deal with the wrath of blacks caught in a time warp of history over which he had no control.

There were those who spoke up for him. One man said that Ashe's presence acted as an inspiration, "not just to excel at something but not to be intimidated by the bully."

Another said that Ashe was not an inspiration to him, but a challenge. "I see you and other free blacks who come here and it is a challenge for me to be like you, free, and, if not me, my sons."

We escaped into the night air and found Don Mattera waiting patiently, just to say good bye. "Go well, brothers," he said, clasping Arthur's hand. "Go well."

We didn't see him again but we saw what he wrote in a poem about Arthur and it was both illuminating and brilliant. The Government wanted to silence this man but instead he was read by more people, not fewer – probably millions more because we used the poem in the Sunday Times and it has been re-printed in countless articles and stories about Arthur Ashe over the years.

I am happy to ensure Mattera's work lives on by doing so here:

'I listened deeply when you spoke
About the step-by-step evolution
Of a gradual harvest,
Tendered by the rains of tolerance
And patience

Your youthful face,
A mask,
Hiding a pining, anguished spirit, and
I loved you brother –
Not for your quiet philosophy
But for the rage in your soul
Trained to be rebuked or summoned.

As for me,
When I asked them for bread,
They gave me a wheat field,
And I thought they loved me.
When I asked for water,
They gave me the well,
And I thought they cared.

When I asked for freedom
They took back the wheat field

And the well,
Tightened the chains
And told me I asked too much.
Now I no longer wait for
The wheat and water, but fight
For freedom ...'

Mattera had seen in Arthur what many of us did not yet comprehend – the rage in his soul, trained to be rebuked or summoned. Don was a fine poet and a remarkable man. And the Boers could not silence him.

At Ellis Park, Ashe beat Bob Hewitt and his friend Cliff Drysdale, the South African No. 1 who, unfairly, was booed by a few people in the black section but, in the final, his hopes of finishing his visit with a flourish were dashed when Jimmy Connors beat him 6-3 in the third set in the final.

The final was played on a Monday as no formal sport was allowed on Sundays, so Ashe had grabbed the chance to head into the notorious township of Soweto and give a clinic which was conducted by the ever-ebullient Bud Collins. A few days earlier, Ashe had made use of the car and driver Owen had put at his disposal to take a quick look at this sprawling urban township situated seventeen miles from Johannesburg.

In 1973, Soweto was probably home to upwards of one million people but grew rapidly over the years. In those days, all the houses were owned by the government; there was one hospital, one fire brigade and no public transport within the township. There was one switchboard with just 500 phones. Oh, and while whites got their education free, blacks had to pay for tuition – if they could afford it.

Facts such as these go some way to answering the question of how approximately three million whites managed to control and subjugate over twenty million blacks. Apart from the hardship of daily life, it was lack of proper education that enabled apartheid to function. Most inhabitants of Soweto had to walk to work and, at all times, they had to have upon their person the hated Passbook which gave them permission to travel in white areas. Anyone forgetting it was fined, jailed and probably beaten.

Ashe was trailed by a BOSS car during his quick tour around Soweto but when he returned on the Sunday he had a very different look at the place as about 1,500 people turned out to see him, with a few kids taking the opportunity of a quick tennis lesson on one of the only twenty courts in the whole of Soweto.

I was struck by how pleasant everyone was to us. Personally, I was greeted by smiles and handshakes and I kept wondering, "Why are you being so nice to me? I'm a white man!"

The atmosphere of bonhomie was disrupted somewhat as we were about to leave, as a group of young men appeared and started berating Arthur with all the arguments we had heard at the journalists' meeting. It all got a bit tense as an even greater number of people shouted back, "God bless you, Arthur!" There was jostling as he edged his way to the car and it was lucky no one was hurt.

That was a relief in more ways than one because, although we were headed for the home of Dr Methlane for a reception being held in Ashe's honour, the doctor, one of very few in this vast township, was too busy to attend himself. God knows when he ever got any sleep.

With Mrs Methlane in charge of the hospitality, it was a pleasant affair and, as we were about to leave, everyone sang, "For He's a Jolly Good Fellow!" and someone put a lucky amulet around Arthur's neck. Everywhere we went, emotions were close to the surface.

The day after the singles final, Ashe teamed with the talented Dutchman, Tom Okker, to win the doubles title over South Africa's Rob Maud and Lew Hoad, the ageing former Wimbledon champion whom I considered the greatest player I had ever seen before Roger Federer came along. As we shall see, Lew became a special friend to me.

So, satisfied that he had at least gone into history as the first black man to win a tennis trophy in open competition in South Africa, Ashe led us off on the next stage of this somewhat unreal journey. We boarded a plane to head over to Durban where we would stay the night at the elegant Edward Hotel before continuing north for a planned meeting with the great Zulu chieftain, Gatsha Buthelezi, who was considered to be the most powerful black man in South Africa.

Marshall Lee of the Rand Daily Mail, a fearless writer for that liberal leaning journal, joined us for the trip and we were all a bit hot and sweaty by the time we arrived at the hotel. Unless Chief Buthelezi had been admitted for some official function, Arthur Ashe was almost certainly the first black man to walk up the front steps and through the front door of the Edward Hotel, which was Edwardian in every way. It was obvious little had changed since the days of General Smuts and the rules said that we had to wear jackets and ties for dinner. So Marshall and I went up to our rooms to shower and change, returning to the splendid dining room properly attired.

It was then that I let my mischievous sense of humour get the better of me. I was seated next to Arthur who was sitting there in his safari-type jacket, open necked shirt with the African beads that had just been given to him, around his neck. Obviously, the management, already nervous at having to entertain a black guest, had not dared suggest that he needed to change, too.

So when the poor maître d' came to take our orders, I couldn't help myself. "Excuse me," I said politely. "I don't quite understand why Mr Lee and myself have to wear a tie and Mr Ashe doesn't. Is this some kind of discrimination?"

I was being kind. I could have inserted the word 'racial' but I spared him that. In any case, it was enough. His expression was clear. He could have killed me. The twisted smile and spluttering reply which made little sense was enough to let us know I had scored a bullseye. Arthur, trying to suppress a grin, bit his lip and we proceeded with an excellent dinner.

A ten-seater aircraft had been hired for us the next morning as we headed up the coast to Chief Buthelezi's headquarters in the heart of Zululand. We had been flying for about 45 minutes through banks of nasty looking clouds when the pilot, receiving weather predictions in his ear, decided to call it off. We were heading for a small airstrip with no modern amenities to deal with poor visibility so we never got to see the great Zulu, although I believe Arthur had the chance to meet him on a subsequent visit.

Our next stop was Cape Town and, after a quick lunch, we headed out to Stellenbosch University, considered South Africa's finest educational establishment which is set amidst the splendour of the wine country. A meeting had been set up for Arthur with Christopf Hanekom, a professor of anthropology.

The professor had brought some of his students with him and we all exchanged niceties for a while. Ashe noticed, however, as the conversation developed, how quick his hosts were to pick out faults in the United States as a way of supporting their own injustices.

A tall handsome looking student picked up on the theme. "You see, Mr Ashe, it is so necessary to keep the balance in our country. This way, we don't have the riots that you suffer."

Ashe hit back quickly. "But perhaps riots are a small price to pay for freedom of expression. And besides, every day that goes by with apartheid increases the chances that the riot that does come will be even more violent, a huge conflagration."

Turning to Professor Hanekom, Ashe said, "Tell me professor, are you scared?"

After a pause, Hanekom replied, "No."

"Boy, I'd be if I were you," Arthur replied, laughing. He was trying to lighten up the conversation a bit but it soon got serious again. He pointed out the how the government were loath to admit the ease and frequency of racial murders, of the rapes and executions. Marshall Lee had provided him with statistics to back up the argument.

"But you must try to understand, Mr Ashe," the Professor interjected, "that we are still struggling with our colonial past. We are different cultures, different languages, trying to find our way together, and that is not an easy task."

The well-primed students butted in at every opportunity to support their professor's arguments and there came a moment when I found it hard to control my temper. I replied to one statement with a definite edge of anger in my voice but one look at Arthur told me he wanted us to keep it cool. Dr Johnson would have been proud of him.

Yet that did not mean Ashe was not going to stand his ground. When a student stated smugly that his people did not think that racial equality would benefit the whole society, a blinkered view if ever there was one, Arthur was on him in a flash.

"Oh? Can I ask you who you sampled in the whole society for that conclusion? Did you go up to Soweto for any soundings? How can you justify the whites making all the decisions?"

The answer, a student offered, was that one could not justify it except on the basis of evolution. But Ashe would not let them off the hook.

"Putting all the sophisticated evolutionary arguments aside, all the intellectual and political position papers forgotten – in your heart, do you think it's right?"

There was a lot of shuffling and looking at feet but before we received a coherent reply, Ashe forged on and pointed to someone we had brought along, Conrad Johnson, a well-dressed Coloured tennis official, an educated man who spoke well. "What about this man," Ashe demanded with a hint of aggression he had not shown before. "Why can you vote and this man can't? Why are you free and this man isn't?"

Professor Hanekom looked over at Conrad Johnson and then briefly at his black visitor and, lowering his eyes, replied in a despondent tone, "Mr Ashe, that is the ace up your sleeve. I cannot defend that."

Arthur Ashe had served many aces in his life. Few as satisfying as that one.

The visit, occasionally dramatic and never less than fascinating, still had a little drama left to offer, even as we reached the airport. Carole Dell was sitting on a bench as we waited to check in when an African man came and sat down next to her. Talking quietly, he said he had an envelope for her and would she mind going to the ladies room. When she came back, he said, the envelope would be waiting on the bench.

"I did what he asked and my heart was already beating fast even before I was taken away and strip searched a few minutes later!" Carole told me recently. "The police women just asked me to take off my outer garments without offering any explanation. I was trying not to look at the envelope which I had placed, as casually as I could, on the table. They never looked inside!"

Carole was allowed to proceed to check-in after a few minutes and did not dare to open the envelope until we were airborne. When she did so, she found a signed photograph of Winnie Mandela whose husband, of course, was incarcerated on Robben Island at the time. The envelope also contained Don Mattera's poem. We had not been able to meet Mrs Mandela but the photo and the clandestine method of delivery offered a farewell reminder of how apt Alan Paton's description of his country had been. South Africa was an odd country.

Chapter 17
GAYLE

Before taking you off to Africa, I mentioned a personal relationship. As an itinerant bachelor roaming the world over the years, there had been many relationships of varying intensity since my marriage to Glenys had ended but, ironically, it was my former wife who was responsible for setting up the next one of real significance.

In the intervening years, Glenys had married Doug Hayward, a bright, ambitious and charming young man from the wrong side of the tracks who had used his skill as a tailor to move into the upper strata of London society by opening a men's tailor shop in Mount Street, which joins Park Lane and Berkeley Square.

Because Doug was always as sharp in conversation as he was with a needle, he gathered about him a list of clients that included many of the movers and shakers to be found in the British entertainment industry in the sixties and seventies. The suits Michael Parkinson wore for his hugely popular talk show were all Doug Hayward creations and, if you dropped by his shop of a morning, you could well find coffee being dispensed to Michael Caine, Terence Stamp, Richard Harris or the photographer Terry O'Neill. Doug's place served as an information centre for the 'in crowd'. If you wanted to know what was happening in London, Doug was your man.

At any rate, Glenys met him on her return from America and they got married. Soon after, they bought a large flat right opposite the shop on Mount Street and Glenys produced Polly, who turned out to be as beautiful as her mother. But the marriage didn't last and, by 1975, Doug was no longer living across the street. Glenys, incidentally, still is – clever girl.

As December '75 rolled around, Glenys decided to have a Christmas Eve party and invite a few of her girl friends as a sort of celebration of freedom from ex-husbands. For some reason, being one husband removed, I suppose, I didn't fall into that category and anyway, apart from remaining on speaking terms with me, Glenys was still in the habit of popping round to see my mother at her flat in Dolphin Square for a gin and tonic, or two. They had always got on well and so we were both invited.

One of the girl friends was Gayle Hunnicutt who had her five-year-old son Nolan in tow. Nolan's father was David Hemmings, whom Gayle had met several years before at the beginning of her Hollywood career during a party at Peter Lawford's beach house in Malibu. Hemmings was a genius. An outstanding child singer before his voice broke, David went on to star in the iconic movie *Blow Up* and numerous others. He was charming, mercurial, hopelessly talented in a variety of fields and possessed a very nasty streak. Gayle had been swept off her feet when they met but he couldn't remain faithful for two minutes after they got married and, occasionally – in between all the charm and romance – treated her appallingly.

Gayle and I looked at each other at Glenys's party and something clicked. The majority of women in the world, unhappily, find me as sexually interesting as a piece of cod on a fishmonger's slab. But, more encouragingly, I have found a minority who react very differently. It was my good fortune that Gayle was one of them. A couple of days after the party, I asked her to have dinner with me at Alexander's, a basement restaurant on the corner of Markham Square and the King's Road, decked out with candles and check tablecloths, which had become a haunt of the tennis crowd (the owner, Jose, was a member of the Queen's Club). Before we had imbibed more than a couple of glasses of wine, Gayle looked me in the eye and said, "I think I want to make love to you."

I made some inane response about that being possible and so it started – a romance of some intensity that quickly saw me move into Gayle's duplex apartment in the Boltons.

For those unfamiliar with the name, Gayle Hunnicutt was one of the world's most beautiful actresses. Born in Fort Worth, Texas, she had gained a scholarship to UCLA where she studied under the great French director Jean Renoir (son of the Impressionist) and, on graduation, eventually got her first part in a biker movie called *Wild Angels* with Peter Fonda after working briefly as fashion model and a receptionist at the advertising agency Young & Rubicam. *Wild Angels* was not type casting. Gayle was not a biker sort of girl although she always possessed the ability to muck in and behave, to a degree, like one of the boys.

A George Peppard movie called *P.J.* followed and by the time she starred in *Marlowe* with James Garner, Gayle was becoming established as a young actress who could decorate any movie and, almost incidentally, act. It was not until she moved to London with David and landed the part of Charlotte Stant in the Henry James saga *The Golden Bowl* for BBC television that the extent of her acting ability became clear. Needless to say, she looked stunning in period costume but she was rightly acclaimed for her performance in an excellent production. The role of Tsarina Alexandra in *Fall of Eagles*, also for BBC television, enhanced her reputation still further and soon she was accepting parts on the West End stage as well as roles in Shakespeare productions like *The Tempest*, when she played Miranda at the Oxford Playhouse. I relished the chance of learning more about theatre while sitting in on numerous rehearsals.

Her career might have been in fine shape but her marriage was not. By the time we met she had filed for divorce from Hemmings who had run off with his secretary and Gayle, more recently, had been seeing Charles Douro, son of the Duke of Wellington. With an address of No. 1 London – it is the house that stands at Hyde Park Corner, near the beginning of Park Lane – Douro was able to entertain her in some style but she had not fallen in love with him, so it proved to be no obstacle to our romance.

I was still European Director of the ATP at the time and, with a tournament coming up in Cairo at the beginning of the year, I asked Gayle to join me. She flew out for the final weekend and, after introducing her to some of the players like Ismail El Shafei, Egypt's greatest player, John Feaver and Mike Estep, who seemed suitably impressed, we flew down to Luxor and went walking amidst the towering temples of Karnak. While in Cairo, the largest of the three pyramids had impressed me by being far bigger than I could have ever conceived and I felt much the same about the remaining obelisk that stands at the entrance to Karnak. Mut, the great goddess of Egypt in the 18th dynasty, had built two of these enormous pillars but only one survives. It is the tallest surviving ancient obelisk in the world.

Wanting to explore a little after dinner but feeling a bit tired after traipsing around Karnak, Gayle and I flagged down a horse and buggy cab outside the hotel and told the young driver to take us for a ride down the banks of the Nile. In limited English we began talking and soon the young man, probably no older than eighteen, started imploring us to visit his house. Despite an initial hesitation on my part, I agreed because Gayle was all for it. So, we trotted on for a bit down some ill-lit side streets until we came to a little, white painted, concrete structure that was basically one room, divided inside by some hung carpets.

Our driver ushered us in, lit some candles and quickly put a kettle on after lighting a primitive stove so he could offer us tea. I was searching for something to say when I noticed a large photograph of Bobby Charlton, in his Manchester United strip, hanging on the wall.

"So you like Bobby Charlton?" I said by way of starting up a conversation.

"Oh, so very much, sir," he replied. "Bobby Charlton is very good player."

After that the conversation flowed, as best it could, and Gayle, whose interest in games did not extend far beyond tennis, was given a fascinating example of how sport, and football in particular, can bring people together – even in a concrete hut in the back streets of Luxor.

Living with Gayle took me into a different world. Having people round to dinner meant sitting down with Robert Bolt, who wrote *A Man for All Seasons* and *Dr Zhivago*, and his wife, the actress Sarah Miles. We went to parties where one found oneself chatting to John Hurt, who delved so deeply into the intellectual connotations of some play he was in that I lost him half way through. Meanwhile one would find Patrick Litchfield, the royal photographer, snapping away happily, taking yet more pictures of Gayle.

We went on holiday to Gstaad where my friend Kobi Hermenjat, who ran the local sports store as well as the ATP tennis tournament, put us up in Peter Sellers' chalet. Kobi, who knew everyone, was in the renting business, too!

I was trying to become sort of a father to Nolan who was a lively six-year-old and, quite frequently, needed bringing into line. One day, when he was becoming more obstreperous than usual, I adopted the shock and awe tactics to discipline and, picking up a large handful of snow, shoved it straight into his little face. He tended to listen to what I had to say after that.

Back in London, Gayle was negotiating with the BBC for the title role in Tolstoy's *Anna Karenina*. After her success in *The Golden Bowl*, the director, James Cellan Jones, felt she would be perfect for the part and it seemed like a done deal. The BBC, however, was going through one of its finance-driven internal upheavals and, suddenly, the project was shelved. Gayle was devastated as it was a part she coveted more than most and she knew, having observed the way things work, that once a big production is put on hold, a different cast of backroom characters tend to get involved and that original choices can get changed overnight.

Unhappily, she was absolutely right although it took several months to sort itself out. When it did, Cellan Jones was no longer the director and the part of Anna Karenina had been given to Debra Paget.

In retrospect, the loss of that part and the example it offered of how hopelessly unreliable the acting profession can be only enhanced Gayle's need for security and a stable existence. The fact that I parted company with the ATP midway through our relationship in 1976 only emphasised the fact that security was not high on the list of attractions I could offer a woman and it was probably inevitable that someone more eligible in that respect would come along.

Gayle met Simon Jenkins at a film premier, I think it was, early the following year and that, basically, was that. Ironically, Simon was editor of the Evening Standard at the time and it would not be long before he became editor of The Times. He was the shining new star of British journalism, with Welsh parents whose down-home values were not far removed from her own in Texas so Simon was able to offer Gayle everything she craved.

So we broke up and, apart from the fact that Virginia Wade won Wimbledon, I don't remember 1977 very fondly. My mother's heart began to fail and she was not well enough to join Margot, Frank and their two young daughters, Fiona and Fleur, at Tregunter Road for the usual Christmas gathering.

I was in Jamaica a few weeks into the New Year when Margot called me to say Mummy had passed away. I couldn't have asked for a more devoted or loving Mum and now she was no longer there. I flew home for the funeral feeling bereft and sadder than I had ever been before.

Chapter 18
BOOKS

As we shall see, Gayle did not depart from my life forever but many years passed before I saw her again. In the meantime, she had played a vital part in a project that enabled me to start earning a reputation as a writer as well as a journalist. During the last months we were together, the opportunity of writing a book about Ilie Nastase had arisen. A private publisher called Aidan Ellis was interested and approached me.

I needed a bit of encouragement to take on the task and Gayle provided it. Complimenting me on my writing one evening in the upstairs study at Bolton Gardens, she told me to go for it. So I took the plunge. Having already had three books published, I had some idea of the amount of work required. Apart from *Whineray's All Blacks*, written fourteen years before, I had ghosted Marty Riessen's book *Match Point* in 1972 after Donald Dell suggested it might be a good way to give one of his clients, who tended to be overshadowed by the superstars in his stable like Arthur Ashe and Stan Smith, the kind of visibility he deserved.

Riessen was one of the game's most popular people and hardworking pros. He was always a threat on the WCT tour and, remarkably, ended his career with a winning 4-3 record over Rod Laver. I was travelling on the circuit virtually non-stop at the time so it was easy to chronicle Marty's thoughts in places like Stockholm, Bologna and Cologne.

I think *Match Point* offered a good insight into what it was like to be a touring pro in the early days of Open Tennis but, sadly, it was written before Marty met his second wife on an American Airlines flight. April, a lady of great gentility and beauty, bore him two lovely daughters and the couple were clever enough to use some of Marty's prize money to buy a big house with a tennis court in Santa Barbara which, even back then, was a sought-after place to live. Now? Well, let's just say that Oprah has built a place down the road.

About five years later I entered into a very different collaboration with Allen Fox, the only Davis Cup player with a doctorate in psychology, which was the theme of the book. We both felt like we needed a couch by the time we had finished. Actually it was fun working with Allen, because he is a very amusing and stimulating guy but, intellectually, it was stressful. When I went to live at his house on 14th Street in Santa Monica, we used to sit at the kitchen table writing sentence by sentence, arguing over every tenth word. Or so it seemed. Allen is a perfectly good writer but a deliberate one with an academic mind and, despite our splendidly robust arguments, I think he appreciated my ability to turn a phrase and move things along.

We called the book, *If I'm the Better Player, Why Can't I Win?* and Allen came up with some good answers. There has never been anything wrong with Allen's brain but his living habits? Well, it was a good thing he met the delightful Nancy soon after. With me, his idea of dinner was to cook up some pasta and eat it straight out of the saucepan without sitting down. I think Nancy had something to say about that – probably before they got married.

Nastase presented yet another challenge. I met up with 'Nasty' as he was called by friend and foe alike – he had more of the former than the latter although opinion was definitely divided – and we came to an agreement that he would give me sufficient access to write his life story.

Inevitably that meant spending a couple of weeks in Bucharest to get a proper feel of where this mercurially talented athlete had grown up. His parents' original home was located within the grounds of the Progesul Tennis Club – a house randomly chosen by the bank his father worked for. By happy chance, their second child turned out to be a genius with the tennis rackets that were available at the courts outside his bedroom window and so a Romanian superstar emerged to create headlines around the world.

Of course, it was not just his ability to play tennis that caused so much excitement once Ilie started to play on the international circuit, but the wildly volatile temperament that went with it. Often he was quite impossible and would have been more so had not Ion Tiriac, the senior member of the Romanian Davis Cup team, been around to give him a cuff around the ear – quite literally on occasion – when the antics got out of control.

Nastase was bright enough to learn from Tiriac but, in the early days, their relationship was almost as explosive as the earthquake which had hit Bucharest a few months before my visit. At one stage they fell out so badly that they spent an entire year playing Davis Cup doubles together without uttering a word to each other. By then, of course, they knew each other's game so intimately that words were hardly necessary. Tiriac, a loyal friend despite a gruff manner, went on to become one of the great figures in the game and a genius at making money. He is now one of the richest men in Romania.

The bad side of Nastase was pretty bad. He could say some disgusting things to umpires, officials and even opponents and he was always being fined and threatened with suspension. But, as was the case with John McEnroe a few years later, the amateur umpires in those days had no idea how to control such a tempestuous character and often made difficult situations worse. Once, during a tournament in California, when I was working with the ATP, Ilie started acting up while playing the straight-laced Ken Rosewall and Jack Kramer asked me to intervene.

"Try and calm him down, Richard," the ATP boss said. "I have no idea what to do with him!"

For a man who had dealt with Pancho Gonzalez at his worst, that was some admission and I did not really appreciate the assignment. Taking a deep breath, I walked up to the side of the court at a change over and tried the softly, softly approach. "Ilie, try and cool it," I pleaded. "You're going to get yourself defaulted if you go on like this."

I received a Romanian stare straight out of Dracula casting but we were good enough friends for Nastase to take heed and he calmed down sufficiently to finish the match. I think Rosewall won.

The Nastase family had moved to a big house in a tree-lined avenue in Bucharest and Ilie kindly invited me to stay while we worked on the book. Apart from having to eat too much – his mother became very upset if you did not partake generously of the massive offerings spread across the dining room table – it was a most enjoyable stay, frequently enlivened by being driven around Bucharest by Nasty in his mustard coloured Fiat sports car. He drove like he played and luckily for the pedestrians in the vicinity, his lightning fast reflexes enabled us to avoid disaster. Red lights were obeyed depending on his mood of the moment and when a young policeman had the temerity to pull us over, his courage deserted him when he saw who was driving. Ilie roared off, gesticulating at the very thought of being fined. Nastase's fame in his country was already well established.

One evening we were invited to a party being held by Horst Dassler, the man who founded Adidas (his brother did likewise with Puma) which was being held way out of town by a lake. Ilie knew the general direction but needed to ask for help when we got close. Two grinning local yokels pointed in opposite directions at precisely the same moment when we stopped to ask them so we drove on and soon turned down a side road. Suddenly the Fiat's headlights illuminated a vast yellow, and obviously ancient, wall.

"Ah, I think we go wrong," Ilie muttered. "That's Dracula's Castle."

No kidding. It was, indeed, the one-time home of Vlad The Impaler and I was quite pleased when Ilie did a quick U-turn and got us out of there. When we finally found Horst's alfresco barbecue, the castle looked a little less forbidding in the moonlight on the other side of the lake.

Ilie Nastase was as complex a character as you could find – at least until John McEnroe came along; and maybe it was not a coincidence that Johnny Mac became my second subject for a book. Like any journalist, I have had the privilege of peeking behind the mask of the famous; of seeing what the public doesn't see and of trying to knit together the various aspects of someone's character so that readers get to understand that a one-dimensional public image does not do justice to the whole person.

Instinctively, I reject the easy evaluation of public figures – especially young ones. However, persuading people, especially critics, that there is more to a person than immediately meets the eye through the strictly limited prism of a newspaper headline is difficult. My first book on McEnroe, *A Rage for Perfection*, which I wrote when he was about 22, was hammered in the New York Times because I dared to suggest that the 'foul mouthed brat' actually had a brain and rather a good none at that. Suggesting that John was loyal, considerate and incredibly sharp in the brain department didn't fit the narrative.

With Nastase, it was a little easier to get the message across because Ilie was funny. Unlike McEnroe, who has a very good sense of humour, Nastase had the natural timing of a real comic and was not afraid to use it during matches. He could have his audience in stitches within minutes of behaving really badly. McEnroe would have loved to have been able to do that but he was always too intense and too wound up with the business of winning and of trying to play the perfect tennis match. Often, Nastase was more occupied with the show than the result.

The extent to which Nastase was able to win people over was particularly evident in Britain. On numerous occasions at Wimbledon, I overhead terribly English ladies in their cardigans and pearl necklaces chatting away, saying how much they adored the enfant terrible, seemingly oblivious to the wicked diatribes he was capable of producing, using words that had never, ever, been uttered in their drawing rooms. Quite simply, they fancied him. Heaven knows how he must have filled their dreams.

To suggest he was contrary was an understatement. I once suggested to him that he might like to swear in Romanian instead of English (or French or Italian which he also spoke fluently) so as to avoid getting fined for the abuse of umpires.

"But I want to let the sons of bitches know what I think of them!" he retorted. "I WANT them to understand!"

If nothing else, that attitude revealed a certain honesty, an honesty that has always drawn me to athletes more than politicians and people in other more devious walks of life. Although there are exceptions, athletes are very open and honest. They really have no choice. Coming into a press conference and trying to fool a roomful of knowledgeable tennis writers that you really played quite well despite losing 6-1, 6-0 doesn't cut it. Mostly, excuses don't fly.

McEnroe offered a prime example of this. I remember a bad loss he suffered in the ATP Masters at Madison Square Garden one year. He had played very poorly by his standards and hadn't behaved very well either. Pencils were sharpened (we still used them in those days) and everyone was busy thinking up some tough questions when he entered the room.

But his opening statement left us with nowhere to go. "If I ever play that badly again, I will no longer have the right to call myself a professional athlete," McEnroe said. He was always his own worst critic and frequently used press conferences as if he was on the psychiatrist's couch.

Away from the arena, Nastase was the most generous of souls. During his title-winning years in Europe, hardly a night passed when he didn't take a dozen people out to dinner, always picking up the tab. On one famous occasion, a Romanian cyclist tried to break some record by cycling to Paris from Bucharest. But by the time he arrived, his bike was ruined. Ilie bought him a new one.

Both Nastase and McEnroe went on to write ghosted autobiographies much later on, but I was glad I had been able to get to know them so well and reveal more of the real people behind the crazy mask. John was as good as gold to work with and I was impressed when he was very firm with Tatum O'Neal, to whom he was married at the time, telling her after practice one evening at Madison Square Garden, "Richard needs to talk to you. Sit down with him and tell him what he needs to know."

The result was a fascinating 45 minutes with an actress who was obviously bright and in love with her husband but who was finding the business of being a wife on the non-stop tennis caravan a difficult experience. Wives on tour inevitably find themselves with time on their hands in each other's company and Tatum wasn't into that. She had grown up very young with a father who had her in high heels at eleven and took her to all the Hollywood parties. She was used to sophisticated male company rather than shopping expeditions with the girls.

It would be easy to say that she fell for John McEnroe because, like Ryan O'Neal, he was a combustible Irish-American super star. But Tatum laid out the differences between the two men very clearly when we talked.

"John is more direct and more sensitive," she said. "My father is much more temperamental. If someone told him to be quiet in a movie house, you never knew how he would react. Going out with him in the evening was what you might call an exciting experience because you never knew how the evening would end. He was quite capable of getting into a brawl which John would never do. I suppose you could call my father a bully. He likes to assert his authority and flaunt his fame. This is quite the opposite of John, who goes out of his way to make sure people do not feel uneasy in his company just because he is famous."

Tatum had picked up on one of the most fascinating aspects of McEnroe's character. Judging by the way he behaved on court, one would have expected him to be a great bar room brawler. But to the best of my knowledge this was never the case. I have seen drunks – notably one night at a hotel in Nice when he was very young – taunt him unmercifully. But after trying to ignore the man and his sniggering companions, he just got up and left.

By the time the McEnroe paperback had come out and been translated into French (selling twice as many copies in France as Simon & Schuster had managed to sell in the US) Nigel Newton had left Sidgwick & Jackson and had founded a British publishing house called Bloomsbury which managed to remain independent in an age of publishing takeovers off the back of one brilliant decision. Having received a manuscript for young readers from someone called J.K. Rowling, Nigel gave it to his eight-year-old daughter to read.

"Oh, yes, Daddy, this is wonderful," said the perceptive child. "You must publish it."

And so, with a deal that included a percentage of everything sold under the Harry Potter trade mark under its belt, Bloomsbury has becoming one of the great publishing success stories of all time.

Long before that happened, I had approached Nigel about a book I had been wanting to write. Having been a witness to most of what had transpired, I felt the need to get the story of the birth of Open Tennis down on paper. I was fearful that the complicated, and in many ways sensational, story would get twisted in the telling if someone who did not know all the facts started relating it.

Encouraged by the success of the McEnroe biography, Newton assigned me Kathy Rooney as my editor and we began a collaboration that eventually encompassed several books for Bloomsbury, including an updated version of the McEnroe story, this time entitled *Taming the Talent*, and a first-person account of David Lloyd's life as a British Davis Cup star and creator of the David Lloyd Leisure Clubs.

But it was my book *Open Tennis*, first published in 1988, that started it all and I think it achieved its goal – laying out in detail the story behind the tumultuous happenings as tennis went 'Open' in 1968 and the subsequent game-changing boycott of Wimbledon in 1973.

Bloomsbury was also involved in the publication of two coffee table style books which I edited, chronicling the first two years of the re-styled ATP Tour beginning in 1990. The books had (mostly!) well written stories on all 80-odd tournaments held worldwide during those initial years, with colour photos to illustrate the cities and sites at which they were played. Apart from anything else, they offered a pretty good geography lesson.

Bloomsbury asked Robert Sackville West's company Toucan to take on the project as they were specialists in that kind of book. The first year required an incredible race against time as we only decided to go for it after Wimbledon and books were eventually produced in late October. Not sure how we managed that, but Robert had some great young technicians putting it together while I assigned the articles and leaned on my photographer friends to produce the pictures. I wrote a few pieces myself and was aided throughout by Pidge Hutton (later Mrs Matthew Freud and then Lady Spencer after she married Princess Diana's brother Charles). Pidge was amazing, the sort of dream assistant who never needs to be asked to do something twice. Happily, Pidge became a great friend, as did Robert who fell in love with, and married, his wife Jane while all this was going on.

When I started asking about how to get a batch of ATP books down to our offices in Monaco, Robert told me, a little surreptitiously I thought, that he would take care of it. In fact he turned it into an excuse to take Jane off across France on a sort of pre-honeymoon and the happy couple turned up at my apartment in Fontvieille in a hired van with the books stashed in the back. Nothing like a publisher who delivers!

Both Pidge and Robert and Jane have been incredibly hospitable to me over the years (while producing seven children between them!) – Pidge at her splendid houses in Little Venice and, later Ladbroke Grove, and the Sackville Wests at the family estate in Sevenoaks.

Knole doesn't really fit the description of a country house because you will not find in England – nor, I should imagine, anywhere on earth – a house that encompasses 352 rooms, 52 stair cases, 7 courtyards and a roof that covers 7 acres. That's correct – 7 acres, all guarded by 27 stone leopards.

An Archbishop of Canterbury started building it in 1456 but his successor, Thomas Cranmer, was unfortunate enough to be ejected by King Henry VIII who wanted it so that he could hunt the deer. Their descendants still roam the 1,000 acres which surround the house today.

Knole came into the possession of Thomas Sackville, who was a cousin of Queen Elizabeth I, in 1603 and has remained in the family ever since. Much to Vita Sackville West's disgust, the property is only handed down to male members of the family, most of whom, according to the enraged Vita, "were nearly all stark staring mad." The description would not fit the charming, level-headed Robert who inherited his portion (most of it is owned by the National Trust) in 2008 and moved his family into a renovated section, having previously lived in the gardener's cottage.

With his uncle's death came the title, but Lord and Lady Sackville have no airs and graces. You are as likely to be lunched in the kitchen as the wood-panelled dining room with portraits of Congreve, Swift, Pope and Dryden staring down at you. The kids run free, out onto the vast lawn to throw cricket balls at each other or play tennis or swim. Robert, a keen cricketer like his son Arthur, stages matches on the patch of green by the side of the house.

There are paintings, tapestries and books everywhere, a few written by Robert himself, and you walk through the Colonnade room on the way to bed, past Knights in Armour (I always expect one to shift and clink) while walking on floors trod by Kings, Queens, Shakespeare and any Prime

Minister you want to name. Personally, I love being that close to history and luckily for the future of this amazing house, so do the Sackville Wests.

At about this time Glenys came back into my life as one of my publishers! She had started a small publishing company called LibriMundi and when I asked her if she would take on a project Vijay Amritraj and I had been talking about, she agreed.

As with Nastase, it meant travelling to the source which, for Vijay, was the family compound on Sterling Road in Madras before the city changed its name to Chennai. I use the term compound because the large, sprawling property encompassed a cardboard-making factory in the back where Maggie Amritraj employed numerous young women in their colourful saris who came pouring through the front gate every morning.

Maggie and Robert Amritraj, as their first names suggest, were both members of the minority Catholic community in India (by Indian standards some ten million is a minority) and both were delightful people. They had produced three sons and Maggie, a keen tennis player herself, had decreed that all three would win the Indian Junior title and play Wimbledon. They did – Anand first, then Vijay and then Ashok actually held the Indian Junior title between them for nine years! And one year, all three made the singles draw at Wimbledon.

Vijay had been sick as a child, suffering from a lung congestion problem that must have been dangerously close to the incurable Cystic Fibrosis (coincidentally the first charity that the ATP had adopted). Doctors suggested that goat's milk would alleviate the problem and so it was that a goat became part of the family, tethered to the kitchen door, dutifully producing milk for Vijay's breakfast.

He recovered sufficiently to partake in Maggie's exercise regime which entailed sending all three boys off a for a run in the neighbourhood in the early morning hours before the worst of the heat set in. When someone snitched on Vijay and told his mother that he was running round the corner and sitting on a wall, she put a stop to that practice by driving behind her sons in her little Austin Seven. The ritual became quite a sight on Sterling Road which, by chance, was also the address of another international star called Viswanathan Anand who grew up to be world chess champion and whose father, like Robert Amritraj, worked for Indian Railways.

I had a thoroughly enjoyable time staying with the Amritrajs despite being hotter than I have ever been in my life before or since – it is not called Madras curry for nothing – and even survived a game of tennis on the family court. Survival was really the name of the game because Robert was a sufficiently good player to serve you wide out in the deuce court so that you found yourself trying to scrape the ball off the wall of the graveyard that adjoined the property. And the chances of you ending up in the graveyard permanently were quite good, because the branches of a large tree hung over one baseline and if your opponent lobbed and sent the ball into the tree, snakes tended to fall on your head! I suppose they weren't poisonous, otherwise I wouldn't be writing this.

Ashok, the youngest, used his easy charm and sharp brain to turn himself into a highly successful Hollywood film producer while Vijay and Anand pursued their tennis careers. They won eight doubles titles together on the ATP tour and also reached the semi-final at Wimbledon in 1976. With other partners, Vijay collected an additional five titles and Anand four.

With a little bit of extra speed, the tall, graceful Vijay would have made a far greater impact on the game. As it was, his big serve and volley style took him to No. 16 in the world in 1980 and, during a long career, he won sixteen ATP singles titles, beating Jimmy Connors five times along the way.

I was with them in Stockholm in 1974 when they began to realise that their dream of playing in the Davis Cup final, which they had fought so hard to achieve, was going to be ruined by politics. By chance their opponents in the final were South Africa. Sports boycotts against the Afrikaaner government's apartheid regime were beginning to take hold and despite pleading with the Indian Prime Minister to let them play, on the basis that winning the Davis Cup for the first time for India, which they might well have done that year, would be most beneficial for national prestige, the answer was 'no'. The final was never played.

It is testament to the brothers' longevity and dedication to a sport they loved so much that they were able, with the help of the wonderfully talented Ramesh Krishnan, to lead India to another Davis Cup final thirteen years later. Sweden proved too strong in Gothenburg but the occasion provided a fitting finale for Vijay and Anand who had given so much to Indian sport.

Ramesh, incidentally, was one of the few sons of great players to equal, if not surpass, his father's achievements. He did not, like Ramanathan, reach two Wimbledon semi-finals but, like his father, won the junior title there before turning pro. He went on to win eight ATP singles titles and reached a ranking high of No. 23 in the world.

Ramesh, a man of great charm and intellect, invited me round to the family house where he had learned his tennis on the court situated right outside the living room. I was about to ask Ramanathan how he had managed to raise Ramesh to be a player of equal stature to himself when he informed me that it had been his own father, T.K. Ramanathan who had coached young Ramesh, thus diminishing the problem so many young male players have of trying to emulate the deeds of their famous fathers.

Allen Fox lays down a whole thesis about this in our book, basically stating that boys have a terrible time trying to be as good as highly successful fathers and the record in tennis, which as opposed to team games is a highly individual sport, appears to bear this out. Too many sons of Grand Slam champions have failed to follow in their father's footsteps for it to be a coincidence. In fact there is not a single instance of the son of a Grand Slam champion winning one of the four majors himself.

My next major book writing project was on behalf on the International Tennis Federation. I was asked to write the history of the first hundred years of the Davis Cup and it was a project I really enjoyed. A considerable amount of research was involved but a good deal of it was made easier when Gene Scott, founder of Tennis Week magazine, arranged access for me to the New York Racquet Club library on Park Avenue. Scott, of course, was a member, winning numerous US titles on the club's Real (or Court) tennis court and this was just one of many ways in which this charming, erudite, demanding and controversial figure smoothed my path in American tennis circles.

The Racquet Club library is extensive and I was able to dig out fascinating information about Dwight Davis' family and the man who, in 1899, designed the beautiful rose bowl which is displayed so proudly on top of its ever-growing plinth at Davis Cup ties all over the world. He was a red-bearded Englishman called Rowland Rhodes who had emigrated to America from Newcastle-under-Lyme before going to work for a company in Concord, New Hampshire called William B. Durgin. Mr Durgin wanted nothing to do with new-fangled ideas like silver plating. He dealt exclusively with the best – solid silver.

As a result Rhodes' beautiful creation still looks as lovely as ever, despite being carted around the world for more than a century. In many ways it reflects the purity of Dwight Davis' idea – an international tennis team competition between nations. The USA and Britain started it at the Longwood Cricket Club in Boston in 1990 and the stories that rolled forth in subsequent years were worth the telling. Still are – although I am one of those who believe the scheduling of the event, which even avid fans find very hard to follow, needs modernising.

More recently, I had fun helping my Boca Raton neighbour Bill Norris write his book about the 35 years he spent on the tour as the ATP physio. Appropriately, we called it "Pain, Set & Match." Bill and Sherie Norris and their daughter Lisa have become great friends since I moved to Florida although, of course, I had known Bill for years. Only a person as open and caring and kind as Bill could have survived 35 years in a sweaty, competitive locker room and emerged with no enemies. But he is a special person with a zest for life that remains undiminished.

In the meantime, there had been two regular assignments which had become staples of my writing life. Neither made me rich but both gave me a platform from which I could air my opinions about tennis and establish some sort of a reputation as an observer worth listening to – even if you didn't agree!

The first came about when Gene Scott founded Tennis Week in the mid seventies and asked me to contribute. Gene, who combined extraordinary athletic skills with a probing, intellectual curiosity about our game, began writing his Vantage Point column which quickly became a 'must read' for everyone in tennis. Soon, my reports morphed into a column I called The Roving Eye, filching the name from my old World Tennis contributions.

Maggie Sullivan, Carole Graebner, Bobby Faig and numerous other devotees made the whole thing work as Tennis Week moved offices around Manhattan over the years and I was able to help Linda Pentz land the job as editor, a task she performed with some skill for a demanding boss, for several years.

Linda, whose father, Mike Pentz was the leader of CND, the Campaign for Nuclear Disarmament in the UK, eventually moved on and, finally, found her soul mate in Paul Gunter, a leading anti-nuclear advocate, and settled just outside Washington DC after their marriage. Linda and Paul, battling through endless bureaucracy, did rather better than I had managed with Vietnamese children and adopted two daughters, Tuyet who has grown up to be a fine singer and Tra My, who is very sporty.

At about the same time as I forged my relationship with Gene, Jean Couvercelle invited to write a column we called 'Autour du Monde' for his monthly publication Tennis Magazine in Paris. It was a collaboration that endured through decades until he sold it in 2015 and one that I valued a great deal. With an amazing group of reporters and editors through the years, headed primarily by Guy Barbier, Bruno Cuaz and Yannick Cochennec, and aided by that ace photographer Serge Philippot, Jean managed to have Tennis Magazine selling on the kiosks of France on the Wednesday following a Grand Slam with 16 pages of reports and colour photographs. No other tennis magazine in the world came close to achieving such a feat. Happily, under the ownership of Benjamin Badinter, the tradition continues.

Chapter 19
RADIO

As a freelance journalist you have to get out of bed in the morning and do something. Call someone, go somewhere, even if it means dipping into reserves and buying an expensive air ticket. Unless you have managed to make yourself hugely in demand, no one is going to come knocking on your door – you have to be at a venue where you can make yourself useful.

Almost always I found that by just being at a tournament some extra work would materialise and, often by the seat of my pants, I managed to keep my bank balance in the black.

However at the beginning of the 1980s, I felt that I needed to add more strings to my bow. The Nastase book had been a success and Sidgwick & Jackson had agreed to publish my John McEnroe biography *A Rage for Perfection*. I was writing on and off for the Guardian and various other Fleet Street newspapers and still felt I could be doing more.

Listening one day to BBC Radio covering tennis with live commentary (5 Live was yet to be born) I thought, 'I can do that'. To be honest I was not particularly impressed with the efforts of the ex-player who was summarising alongside Gerald Williams, a hugely accomplished broadcaster, and, full of conceit, I extended that thought to 'not only can I do it, but I can do it better!'

So I phoned Slim Wilkinson. I had met the head of BBC Radio Sport on occasion so introductions weren't necessary and as Slim was an extremely outgoing and personable sort of fellow I had no qualms about suggesting that I might be able to help out. Maybe he had been looking for someone because the reaction was more welcoming than I had anticipated.

"Good, come and find us at Queen's next week and we'll see what we can do," was Wilkinson's swift reply.

So, returning to the club where my tennis career had started some twenty years before, I now took another step forward – or rather, upwards, wobbling up those rickety stairs to the makeshift commentary boxes that look down on the court with the old pavilion on your left.

"Right," said Wilkinson, by way of greeting, "Why don't you do the next match with Christine?"

Of course, why not? Just do it, go live on air on the BBC and see if you can avoid making a fool of yourself. A word of advice, perhaps? A little bit of coaching for what is widely regarded as one of the more demanding forms of sports radio commentating? No chance. The BBC seemed to be of the Reg Hayter school of thought – you've got yourself on the diving board, so jump.

"Coming to you live in 30!" a disembodied voice said in my headphones. Gulp.

"Good afternoon, everyone, welcome to the Queen's Club. I have Christine Truman alongside me and we will be bringing you this first round match between …"

You know, I have absolutely no idea what match it was. A state of suppressed panic probably fused the wavelengths to the memory bank in my head. Maybe it was John Lloyd playing Paul McNamee – I simply can't recall. At any rate, having Christine sitting next to me helped enormously.

Christine Truman Janes had been the darling of British sport for a couple of decades when she was winning Roland Garros in 1959 and, two years later, reaching the final of Wimbledon where she lost to Angela Mortimer in a memorable all-British duel.

Christine is unique. A tall lady with rosy cheeks and a cheeky smile, it would be impossible to find anyone more English. She had a terribly English brother called Humphrey who served on the Wimbledon committee for several years and then she married Gerry Janes, a suitably large but gentle man who had somehow managed to summon up enough ferocity on Saturday afternoons for play in the second row for Wasps Rugby Football Club. If Gerry happened to accidentally punch you at the bottom of the scrum, I am sure he was very apologetic later on in the bar.

Christine had this self-effacing way about her, too, always appearing to be not quite sure of herself while achieving more than most people dream about. She has been a mother and a wife, a top ranked tennis star and a long-serving and much loved commentator, all the while giving off an air of slight surprise. In reality, Christine always knew what she was doing.

We went on to spend many amusing days together in the Wimbledon commentary box and you could always rely on her to come up with something a bit daft after a serious period of play. Once, when some poor man had played precisely the wrong shot at the wrong moment, I paused for breath and Christine piped up, "Oh, that's rather like putting the ice cream in the oven and the roast in the fridge, isn't it?"

No wonder housewives across the country were glued to her commentary as they prepared dinner.

Apparently my efforts at Queen's passed muster and the next week I found myself on the roster of BBC Radio commentators for Wimbledon. We covered Centre, No. 1 and No. 2 Courts in those days but after a couple of matches outside I was given the honour of a seat in the Centre Court commentary box, which is situated just to the left of the Royal Box. There is no better seat in the house but you have to sing for your supper!

A word about radio commentary. It is, of course, a different art from talking on television. There are no pictures to relay information to the listener and the first thing you have to realise is that you are the eyes of the listener, not least for blind people who have no choice but to listen to their favourite sports on the radio. If the sky is blue, say so. If there's a guy with a funny hat sitting court side, describe it. It's all about description – and talking fast.

No one ever talked as fast as my revered predecessor Max Robertson who barely missed a shot in the most frenzied rally. Max was also an expert on the technical side of the game and knew the sport inside out, which brings me to the next important point about radio commentary – your knowledge has to be instinctive; right there on tap in your head. There is no time for checking on a fact. You can't know them all but you have to have enough at instant disposal to be able to say with certainty that, for instance, Mats Wilander won three Grand Slams in 1988 but only reached the quarter finals at Wimbledon that year. On TV, commentators have time to take a peek although the best ones don't need to. But on radio there is no option. Everything is happening too fast.

Max Robertson was one of the BBC commentators I had grown up listening to at school – Raymond Baxter on Motor Racing; Rex Alston on athletics, Raymond Glendenning on football and John Arlott, Brian Johnston and Jim Swanton on cricket. They were my heroes and now I was trying emulate Max, which was an impossible task.

Robertson was let go by the BBC far too early and he resented it, which was hardly surprising because he still had much to offer. But he was unfailingly nice and helpful to me which I appreciated. That first year I needed all the help I could get but the only person I remember offering a piece of technical advice was Barry Davies who, for decades, was the voice of British football commentating on television along with John Motson. Only last year at the Wimbledon media party, I had the chance to thank Barry as I joined him, David Mercer and John Inverdale at an impromptu table – three old sweats and Invers, a slightly younger one. We enjoyed swapping tales about our profession and how it has evolved over the years. I was lucky to have enjoyed twenty years at Wimbledon during which time BBC Radio 5 Live came into being and provided, I think it is fair to say, one of the best outside broadcasts of the summer.

But, to get back to the beginning ... there were moments, I must confess, when I got stuck for words. There was that split-second moment of panic when you think, "What the hell am I supposed to say next?" The way out is to just repeat the score and keep talking. It's like warming up in tennis – hit a few more balls and you get into a rhythm. Radio broadcasting in tennis is all about rhythm and to find it you need summarisers who are on your wavelength.

I had some excellent ones over the years, none better than my good friend Frew McMillan, the great doubles champion from South Africa who has lived in Bristol for most of his life. In his younger days, Frew was known for his acerbic wit and he was able to bring a bit of that to the microphone. But, mainly, it was his ability to come up with a pertinent observation in about seven seconds just when I needed it – sometimes, after a long rally, when I had literally run out of breath. It was a partnership which, I like to think, developed into a fine one over the years and Frew certainly made my job easier.

During the first half dozen years I had someone else sitting to my right in the far corner of the box. Fred Perry had been a member of the BBC Radio team for years before I arrived, using his vast knowledge and sharp mind to illuminate any match he worked on.

Perry, of course, was the great icon of British tennis who remained the last British player to win the men's singles at Wimbledon from 1936 right up to the moment Andy Murray seized the crown 77 years later. The son of a Labour Member of Parliament who invaded the snob-ridden world of tennis in the thirties with the wrong accent and a chip on his shoulder, Perry won Wimbledon three times and led Britain to Davis Cup triumph from 1933 to '36. He was a wise-cracking, cocky, arrogant champion who got up opponents' noses and thoroughly enjoyed cocking a snoot at the establishment.

Those All England Club members who could never quite come to terms with his success had their worst suspicions confirmed when he turned professional in 1936 and went to America where he played exhibition matches and eventually bought the Beverly Hills Tennis Club with Ellsworth Vines,who preceeded him as Wimbledon champion. They had some glamorous backers in Errol Flynn, Charlie Chaplin, Groucho Marx and a few other Hollywood stars who were serious tennis players.

But like Pancho Gonzalez, who was growing up a few miles away in a rough Latino neighbourhood of Los Angeles at the time, Perry mellowed in later life and, for me, he was an easy-going companionable colleague. The naughty twinkle in the eye remained and it was always fun to spend time with him on and off air. Obviously I learned a great deal from what he had to say as I threw questions at him and he always had interesting off-the-cuff answers, even when I interrupted his letter writing! During matches, he used to answer fan mail as I nattered on but I could never catch him out. Looking up in mid-sentence, pen in hand, he would say something like, "Oh, Lendl should stand further in to receive that McEnroe serve – try and cut off the angle." And then he'd continue with his letter. Been there, done it all, seen it all – Fred didn't need to watch every shot to know what he was talking about.

He lived long enough to see his statue erected on the grounds of the club that had been so reluctant to accept him when he became champion and he was overwhelmed by the honour. The chips had fallen from the shoulders as the years passed and it was clear, listening to him commentate, that he was in love with Wimbledon and its fabled Centre Court which held so many golden memories.

Perry died in Melbourne in February 1995.I last saw him at a dinner held at the Hilton in honour of Ken Rosewall and Lew Hoad, who had died a couple of years before. The previous evening Fred had slipped in the shower and bruised his ribs. He was all trussed up under his dinner jacket but was still looking as dapper as ever when he passed my table. "Hurts like hell," were the last words he said to me. Four days later he died in hospital. He was 85.

Just a few months ago I was driving through the Place d'Italie in Paris and caught sight of a young man carrying a sports bag with the name Fred Perry plastered across it. The company lives on, although I doubt whether the chap with the bag had much understanding of what the name meant to generations of tennis fans.

For a couple of years – 1982 and '83 as far as I can remember – I also had the privilege of commentating with Perry's great friend and companion in arms from Davis Cup days, Dan Maskell. The opportunity came about because, after a couple of years with the radio team, BBC television came calling. Obviously I was flattered and accepted the offer although I felt a pang of regret at leaving a bunch of people I had enjoyed working with.

I made the switch with eyes open, realising that I would be further down the pecking order with television. Dan Maskell was established as Britain's Voice of Tennis and John Barrett, a good friend of mine who had been Davis Cup captain soon after his playing days ended, was becoming established as Maskell's backup.

So I spent a lot of time doing doubles on Court 2 while waiting for a Centre Court match to come my way. It did one afternoon when I found myself sitting alongside Dan as his summariser for one of Slobodan Zivojinovic's matches. The previous year I had filled the same role at Roland Garros, commentating on the final that saw the 17-year-old Mats Wilander pick up Bjorn Borg's mantle by beating Guillermo Vilas in the final. The BBC only covered the men's and women's finals of the French Open in those days so they did not have a big team in Paris but, as I was there anyway, they asked me to sit in with Maskell – another instance of how being on the spot pays off.

Working with Dan was a joy. He was old school in the most charming way, a quiet-spoken man who revered the game and its traditions and did his level best to keep them alive. His autobiography, which John Barrett helped him write, was entitled *Oh! I Say!* – it being his most usual reaction to a particularly splendid shot.

Born in Fulham of modest means, Maskell had become a coach in the late twenties and quickly made a name for himself at the Queen's Club before being appointed head coach at the All England Club. The role of trainer to the Davis Cup team soon followed and Dan was a member of the triumphant squad that won three consecutive Cups.

The success of the team was enhanced by the bond forged by Maskell and Perry, which went some way to easing the snobby social restrictions of the day. When the British team travelled to Paris for the final against France in 1933, they were put up in some splendour at Le Crillon on the Place de la Concorde – everyone, that is, except Maskell. He was a professional, you see, servant class.

Perry was furious and insisted that Dan be rescued from his digs down a back street and installed with the rest of the team. They used to dine together after Dan had put Fred through his paces on court and given him a good massage. Once, when they found a restaurant near Roland Garros in the Bois de Boulogne, the band struck up 'God Save the King' as they were shown to their table. It said something about Perry's fame and the eagerly awaited Davis Cup final.

One of the pleasures of working with the television team was getting to know Bill Threlfall who spent many of his later years as Tennis Director at the Hurlingham Club next to Putney Bridge. Bill's earlier career had been a trifle more exciting. He had been a Royal Navy fighter pilot during the war, landing Hurricanes and Beaufighters on the shifting, rolling decks of aircraft carriers – a feat which tests a pilot's skill like no other.

Bill's sense of humour and dare-devil antics knew no bounds and he came up with the most unique and persuasive way of proposing. He took Ann up for a spin in a two seater Beaufighter, flipped the thing upside down and yelled, "I'm not turning it right side up until you say 'Yes'!". Shock treatment worked. They were married until the day Bill died.

Commentating with Bill could be a rough ride, too. One day, we were told to rush off to No. 1 Court – the old No. 1 Court which was situated where the players & members' facilities sit today – and record a women's doubles so it could be used as a filler in case of rain. The match happened to be between two Czech ladies and a couple of Russians. I had never set eyes on any of them before in my life. There had been no time to prepare and we looked at this quartet in horror as they warmed up. So Bill, the bloody man, opened up by saying, "Well, Richard, you travel the world, tell us what you know about these ladies."

It was the wicked grin on his face that did me in. I morphed. I tried to answer, not knowing what the hell I was about to say, and started giggling. So did he. For about 30 seconds we were speechless. Thank God we weren't live. Eventually we managed to get our acts together and produced a seriously ill-informed piece of commentary. I hope it never got on air.

This little incident, thankfully, had nothing to do with the fact that BBC television dropped me from the team the following year. There was no room for me once they decided to bring in Mark Cox, the erudite, Cambridge-educated former British No. 1. Mark was an obvious choice once his playing career finished and he went to enjoy a distinguished career in television.

To my delight, Slim Wilkinson immediately invited me back. Returning to radio felt like going home and, for two weeks every year, it was just that.

Mike Lewis, a young BBC producer, soon took over from Wilkinson and remained in that post for many years until Joanne Watson, a highly efficient and dedicated BBC-type person, replaced him. (Mike, understated and always helpful, still works at the Championships as liaison officer for the All England Club and the vast multi-nation television operation.)

I was glad to have joined the BBC Radio team as early as I did because, through the late eighties and nineties, we saw considerable expansion. BBC Radio Five Live was born in 1994 as a separate channel and our wall-to-wall Wimbledon coverage was made for it. We were on air from first ball to last, offering much more live commentary than the programme does today.

It proved to be the perfect launching pad for a whole host of future radio and television stars who came in to join the stalwarts like myself, Gerald Williams, David Mercer (before both moved over the TV), the wry and amusing Tony Adamson and the incomparable Peter Jones, one of the best broadcasters I have ever heard, who anchored the programme. Peter, whose son Stuart later became football correspondent of The Times for a while, died, tragically, from a heart attack while commentating on the Varsity Boat Race. He was a wonderful colleague, professional to the core but always ready for a chat and joke in the bar.

Soon the newcomers starting filtering in. Jon Champion, Peter Drury – both now established as top football commentators as part of NBCSN's increasingly popular Premier League coverage in the States – were welcome additions. So, too, were Miles Harrison, who has gone on to make a name for himself as Britain's foremost rugby commentator, Mark Pugatch, Jeff Stelling and Marcus Buckland. Jeff and Marcus, who liked to manipulate the English language with words like 'riduculous', have gone on to be stars at Sky Sports. Iain Carter was another top broadcaster who took over from the popular Tony Adamson as the official BBC tennis correspondent in 1990. He was excellent in the job but his heart was always on a golf course and, after a few years, he became the full-time golf correspondent. Annabel Croft was never going to deviate from the sport that had seen her rise to the exalted position of No 1 in Britain and has become a regular analyst for Sky Sports' tennis coverage. Proving just how good women are at multi-tasking, Annabel has raised children; coached at Roehampton and, with her husband Mel Coleman, has created tennis camps in places like Cyrprus and the Algarve.

Soon a young lady called Clare Balding joined us. At the time she was known primarily as the daughter of the famous race horse trainer Ian Balding, whom I had covered years before in his days as full back for Cambridge University. Clare was a little shy to start with but had something about her which, coupled with a natural ease behind the microphone, marked her out as one for the future. Like Sue Barker, Clare has established herself as one of Britain's foremost broadcasters, capable of handling a multitude of tasks with ease in front of the camera or behind the mike.

In the nineties, a younger generation started filtering in – Chris Bowers, who became a close friend and colleague as well as co-owner, along with David Mercer, Craig Gabriel and myself, of Tennis Radio Network. Barry Millns was another versatile broadcaster who started his Wimbledon career with the BBC Overseas Service and, after Mercer retired, he became a valued partner at TRN. David Law, a giant of a young man from the Midlands who turned into a fine broadcaster while doubling up as a PR man for the Aegon Championships at Queen's and Eleanor Preston, who also mixed a career in radio with public relations jobs for the LTA were amongst the younger generation who soon became familiar voices on the airwaves.

Obviously, the more time you spend behind a microphone, the better you get as a broadcaster, but there are people who just seem to be born with the gift. I remember the first time Eleanor joined us and was sent off to some distant court to do updates. I heard her through my headphones and within two minutes I knew she was a natural.

The same was true of Gigi Salmon who was hired by Radio Wimbledon while working for Chelsea Football Club. Gigi quickly became recognised as a top-class play-by-play commentator and does a lot of work for us at TRN.

My BBC Radio career hit the stop sign somewhat unexpectedly in 2003. Like Max, I felt I still had a bit to offer but the BBC works in curious ways and various factors probably contributed to my receiving the 'Your services will no longer be required …' letter from Gordon Turnbull, one of the bigwigs who have to make these decisions. He thanked me for some twenty years of service and the way in which I had always tried to help newcomers to the team. He even offered to hold a farewell dinner for me but, although I am sure it would have been a lovely occasion, the thought of having to be nice when I wouldn't have felt like it led me to refuse the invitation.

Without any real proof, I just presume the pervading mood of the moment, which was for the BBC to promote regional accents, played a part. Also the fact that I had developed a bad throat the previous year which left me literally without a voice during the Roger Federer-Mark Philippoussis final probably hadn't helped. Joanne Watson, who had always been a big supporter of mine, heaped on a bit of pressure the previous day by saying, "Oh for God's sake don't get ill. We need you for the final."

Well, they got me for about a quarter of the final before I opened my mouth to describe a Federer forehand and nothing happened. Silence. Bit of a problem for a radio commentator. Thank heaven Jonathan Overend, who was just starting a period as a much-respected BBC Radio tennis correspondent, was already in the adjacent chair waiting to rotate with me so I literally dug him in the ribs and mouthed 'Help'. That, as it turned out was my less than glorious sign off. Such is life.

There was probably something else that didn't help my cause, too. I am going to break a rule I try to maintain which is never to be too beastly to my colleagues because, however much I might disagree or dislike something they say or write on occasion, I take the view that we are all in this crazy job together and none of us are perfect.

But I'll make an exception for Patrick Collins. A brilliant columnist for the Mail on Sunday, Collins has been a jovial and very popular member of the British sports writing world for decades.. I enjoyed his writing with one exception. Every year, he arrived at Wimbledon and proceeded to trash the place. Collins is Irish and the sight of middle-class Britain in all its finery was obviously a sight he could not abide. Taking a dig or two at the all the usual targets – the Royal Box, Pimms, and strawberries and cream – is all very fine but his attacks, which went on for three or four consecutive years, became a little tedious.

Finally, it seemed, he ran out of the obvious things to complain about so, in 2002, he turned on me. He needed some way to get at Wimbledon so he chose a BBC commentator whose accent and style obviously got up his nose. I genuinely can't remember exactly how Collins described me but it wasn't nice and I am sure it was read at Broadcasting House.

Maybe it tipped the balance, maybe it didn't, but I was surprised because, without being great buddies, we had always got on fine in the press rooms of the world. I never spoke to him again which was probably a good thing. I'm not Irish but I do have a temper.

Happily, I had developed other strings to my broadcasting bow, including some years earlier, a period when Tom Gorman and I did play-by-play commentary from an open-air corner of Louis Armstrong Stadium at the US Open for Mutual Broadcasting. I don't know how many of their affiliates picked us up; probably not enough because the deal collapsed after three years. But Tom and I had a lot of fun offering American audiences something they did not hear very often. A delightful character with an Irish twinkle in his eye, 'Gor' won a lot of matches on the WCT and Grand Prix during his career, including seven titles, and then became one of America's longest serving Davis Cup captains.

More recently, as TRN has expanded, new opportunities have arisen. We jumped in with an offer to provide a team of commentators when Tennis Channel won the contract to cover the French Open in 2007. They wanted to offer viewers in the US the chance to choose their own court during the early rounds by selecting from five matches in progress. To provide this service, they needed more commentators than they had at their disposal – certainly in Europe – and, utilising Chris Bowers' knowledge of who could or couldn't do the job, we mustered a team of eight with additional help from freelancers like Neil Harman, Simon Cambers, Matt Brown, Nick Lester and Eleanor Preston.

The regulars who have been mostly permanent over the past decade include the former Australian and US Open doubles champion Allan Stone; Elise Burgin, for many years a top player on the WTA tour; our TRN partner Barry Millns, Doug Adler from California, and Peter Marcato, who like Stone flies in from Australia. Tennis Channel have also seconded to us Leif Shiras, a good player who has become an even better commentator, and Katrina Adams. Katrina has had to reduce her commitment since she became USTA President but still managed to fill in a few slots during her first year despite the demands on her time. As the first ex-professional player and the first African American to become USTA President, Katrina is, as we say, a trooper, ready and willing to do anything she can to help her sport.

I lead the team as well as broadcasting myself which lands me with the job of fixing the next day's roster every night, not always a straightforward task with freelancers unable to pin down their availability, but that's what we're there for, and I think Bob Whyley, David Egdes and Tennis Channel team, led by the ebullient and always positive CEO Ken Solomon, appreciate not having to worry about it.

We have also taken on the role of providing commentators and summarisers for Tennis Australia who, as from 2009, started a play-by-play radio service on their website. In this digital age, fans can hear us on all manner of mobile devices and the global reach is incredible. We get texts and emails fed through to us on Rod Laver Arena and it is fun to get messages such as

'Listening to you on a beach in Thailand!' or 'I'm at London Bridge station. Train's late as usual and it's freezing. But you are keeping me warm'.

Television was supposed to kill radio but it hasn't. It remains the easiest and most effective way of communicating if you broaden the concept to include the web. There were no satellites above when I used to get up at 4.00 am to turn on our radio and, huddled in my pyjamas and dressing gown at our flat in London, listen to the crackling reception as Alan McGilvray and Jim Swanton described an Ashes Test match from Sydney or Brisbane.

So far away. It seemed like magic. Today, it's even more magical and for me, being able to participate, an even greater thrill.

Chapter 20
THE THATCHERS

So much of life is about contacts, who you meet when and where and what it leads to. A brief assignment in Paris for Rod Tyler led to my introducing him to his future wife. A brief phone call from Rod some time later led to an introduction to Carol Thatcher and a somewhat surreal period of my life.

Rod was a hearty, robust individual, full of insatiable curiosity and fun. He carved out an amazing journalistic career for himself which blossomed when Margaret Thatcher called him at 6.00 am one morning to invite him round for a lengthy chat, so impressed had she been by a piece he had written.

The pair formed a bond which led to Tyler writing many of her speeches, including the one which had her say, "Me? The Iron Lady?" and subsequently a highly praised account of her 1987 election campaign, written on the hoof, called *Campaign*.

We had become friends over the years and I was one of the first people he called when he realised he would be spending a few days in Paris. I had met the lovely Maggie, of Guyanan origin, about a year earlier and, after our original fling had cooled, we had remained good friends. So when Rod and I planned a night on the town, I invited her along. Love at first sight.

They were married soon after, had a daughter called Rachel who eventually went into the hotel business, and in those early days became regular hosts to a North London set of journalists, like Nick Lloyd and his wife Eve Pollard (a power couple of some magnitude in the 1990s when Nick was editing the Daily Express while Eve edited the Sunday Express!) and PR people like Mrs Thatcher's adviser Tim Bell. The wine flowed and the conversation was perky, to say the least.

Maggie was as good a talker as any, which is high praise considering the company she kept, and she did tremendous work over the years for The Duke of Edinburgh's Award.

The call that affected me so much came one morning when I was living on the top floor of my sister's house at Tregunter Road in Fulham. "My dear boy!" Rod's boisterous tones were unmistakable. "Carol Thatcher wants to write a book about Chris and John Lloyd and I told her you were just the person to help her. Why don't you give her a call. Here's the number."

So I did and so began one of the most memorable relationships of my life. It would have been special, even without the family aspect, because Carole is a personage in her own right and one of the most engaging, amusing, brightest people you will ever meet. When the twins were born, whoever it is that decides these things, gave Carol 100% of the humour quotient and her brother Mark 0%.

Even in the most trying circumstances – and there were many with a mother like hers – Carol always managed to see the amusing or downright funny side of the situation and bounced back.

In response to Rod's call, I set up a meeting at Wimbledon a few weeks later and, as a sort of 'thank you', Carol suggested we have dinner. We found we had lots to talk about and we quickly became more than dinner partners. Her zest for life was infectious and it was stimulating just to be in her company. Would I have found it all so much fun if it had not included invitations to 10 Downing Street to meet the Prime Minister? Unequivocally, I can say, yes I would. But it would also to be absurd to suggest it was not an added attraction.

When Carol first suggested we drop by to say hello to the woman who was busy running the country – and, in her spare time, the world it seemed – I found myself being led into the lift and escorted up to the private flat at the top of No. 10 where British Prime Ministers live. It is not spacious. Carol ushered me into a reasonably sized but far from grand living room and Margaret Thatcher immediately bounced up off the sofa.

"How good to meet you! Can I get you a drink? Vodka and tonic? Splendid!"

There was no flunkie waiting to mix it. The Prime Minister mixed the drinks and she did not hold back on the vodka. I mumbled my thanks and tried to take stock of this woman whose fame and reputation made her, along with her cohort Ronald Reagan, the most talked about politician in the world at the time. Three years into her Premiership, she had already been dubbed 'The Iron Lady' but up close she seemed far from that.

The first thing that you noticed about Margaret Thatcher in close-up was her femininity. The personality was certainly powerful but the hair, the make-up and the clothes – a tailored blue suit if I recall correctly – made you very aware that this was a woman and one who wanted to be treated as such. It offered a huge clue to the way in which she governed and the hold she enjoyed over her colleagues in government.

She might bark orders at you and slice up her Ministers with cutting remarks in Cabinet meetings but she never, ever, let you forget that she was a woman. It may be changing somewhat now but back in the post war years, English public schoolboys had tenuous relationships with women. They were not brought up with them at school and, apart from a sister or two, the closest they had ever come to having a relationship with a woman was with Mother or Matron. And they were not to be argued with.

So Thatcher's Cabinet did not find themselves on an even playing field. Having to deal with mother, matron and Prime Minister all in one package while trying to suppress any faintly erotic feelings they had for this perfectly presented example of middle-aged femininity frequently left them at a loss. After a Prime Ministerial dressing-down they felt like naughty fourth formers.

Her Foreign Secretary Lord Carrington was the only member of her Cabinet who had the nerve to test her sense of humour and make use of it. Peter Carrington, who I had the chance to meet occasionally at some of Frank and Margot's cocktail parties at Tregunter Road, was always able to see the funny side of life and, crucially, he made Mrs Thatcher laugh. Excusing himself from the gathering, he would say to my sister, "Sorry, Margot, got to run. My mistress is calling!"

Lord Carrington was also a man of principle. When Argentina invaded the Falkland Islands, he resigned. "British territory had been invaded which was a terrible blow to our national pride and I was Foreign Secretary. I had to go."

His going did the Prime Minister no good at all. She had lost the one person who could cajole her and re-direct her when her harsher authoritarian instincts took hold. She knew she was going to miss him and she did.

My own relationship with Margaret Thatcher never developed to the extent I could talk to her about such things but, at a certain level, she was extremely pleasant and hospitable towards me. After a couple more visits I found myself in the extraordinary situation of being able to hail a cab in Knightsbridge and say, "10 Downing Street, please," and mean it. There were no iron gates guarding the street's entrance in those days and, on being deposited outside the most photographed door in the world, I would be saluted by the policeman on duty and ushered in by the concierge with the words, "Please go straight up, Mr Evans. The Prime Minister is expecting you."

It's called access – access to power and you need to tell yourself very firmly not to get carried away. On one particular night, Carol had called to say she would be a little late for our dinner appointment so when I stepped out of the lift and somewhat tentatively opened the door to the living room, I found the Prime Minister ensconced with her Personal Private Secretary, poring over Cabinet papers.

Inevitably, she jumped up, bustled over to the drinks cabinet, made me a vodka and tonic and said, "Carol will be here any minute. Do make yourself at home. We'll go and finish off this stuff in the kitchen."

It was no use protesting about not wanting to interrupt in the affairs of government. The decision had been made. You didn't argue.

I had an absurd travelling schedule at the time – as an example the following year, 1983, I visited Guadaloupe, New York, Rio de Janeiro, Guaruja, Philadelphia, London, Kuwait, Paris, London, Paris, Brussels, London, Milan and Monte Carlo from the end of January to the end of March, approximately ten weeks. That year I took 61 flights on 21 different airlines. There were years when I topped 80 flights. Apart from anything else, I don't know how I paid for the air tickets because only occasionally did an assignment include expenses.

So Carol and I saw each other mostly during London stop overs, although she did manage to get a writing job that allowed her to accompany me to Fiji after the 1982 US Open. We were guests of John Newcombe who owned a tennis ranch at the Regent Hotel in Nandi at the time. The party included Dennis McElrath, a business partner of Newk's and the ever-amusing Ubaldo Scanagatta, one of Europe's leading tennis writers and a great friend of mine over the years.

Carol was the life and soul of every gathering – some achievement with such extrovert personalities as Newk and Ubaldo in the party – and was made guest of honour by a local village which went through all their elaborate rituals of welcoming an important guest. She had to squat in the middle of large circle and drink the local concoction out of a large wooden saucer. It was light brown in colour and gritty to the taste – an acquired taste, indeed!

Rather more to our liking were the rum punches and, as midnight approached after a sumptuous feast at the Regent's open air restaurant, Newk tended to finish off the evening with flaming sambucas, occasionally singeing his moustache in the process. We enjoyed the beach, sailed on catamarans and played a lot of tennis. For us, Fiji was living up to its reputation as paradise.

Autumn was fading into winter by the time we got back to London but the hectic lifestyle never stopped. Soon the question arose as to what the Prime Minister wanted as a birthday present. "I want to see *Cats*," she stated firmly. So to *Cats* it was. Denis, Carol and I took the Birthday Lady to the New London Theatre where the Lloyd Webber musical had opened in May 1981 and did not end its record-breaking run until October 2006. We found Sir John Mills, one of Britain's best loved actors, and his wife sitting behind us. The show was magical and the slinky cast, all dressed up as cats with whiskers, made sure they weaved around in close proximity to the Prime Minister as they did every evening with any member of the audience. Mrs Thatcher loved it. Appropriately, Andrew Lloyd Webber was amongst the guests who joined us at No. 10 for supper afterwards. Charles Douglas Home, editor of the Times who died tragically young of cancer a few years later, was there as was Richard Ryder, one of the PM's top aides who later became Lord Ryder of Wensum. More importantly for me, we became good friends many years later when I discovered Richard, a director of Ipswich Town, was a complete sports nut who seemed to know as much about football, cricket, tennis and rugby as I did.

Looking back amongst brief diary notes, it seems Carol and I spent more time popping in and out of No. 10 than I remember. I even dropped in one afternoon to get some photocopying done for an article I had written! Using the place as an office was a bit cheeky, I suppose.

Christmas 1982 produced a whirl of social activities that, in retrospect, seem a little unreal. On Thursday 23rd December, Carol who was living in her parents' house at 19 Flood Street just off the Kings Road, threw a cocktail party that included a wide selection of our friends. Margot came, as did Marshall and Kate Lee, Gabrielle Crawford and her footballer boyfriend Tommy Baldwin, Foulard Hadid, a popular and omnipresent member of the Queen's Club, Charles Benson, the famous racing correspondent of the Daily Express, John Ellison, who had been the Express bureau chief in Paris during my days as a correspondent there and, to my delight, Albina du Boisrouvray who had become good friends with Carol after I introduced them.

The evening ended at Annabel's in Berkeley Square and, somehow the nightingales had stopped singing by the time Carol and I found enough energy to get ourselves out to David Lloyd's new club near Heathrow for a game of tennis. From there we drove out to Chequers, situated not far from Great Missenden in the Cotswolds. Chequers was bequeathed to the Prime Minister of the day in perpetuity as a country residence after the First World War and, of course, the house has become part of British history. The Thatchers were holding a Christmas Eve cocktail party, with Peter Carrington and various Cabinet Ministers in attendance. Afterwards Carol and I sat down to dinner with her parents and brother Mark who, I seem to recall, was quite tolerable that evening.

Christmas Eve morning found us at the Tylers' in North London where Maggie was producing a delicious Guyanese breakfast. Later we were invited to tea at Albina's rented flat on Charles Street in Mayfair with Ted Tinling. Ted and I usually managed to see each other at Christmas wherever we happened to be in the world and I was pleased he could join us.

My family tradition was always to have a Christmas dinner with Margot, Frank and their two daughters Fiona and Fleur at Tregunter Road. So we had a great time there but left soon after 10.30 so that Carol could do her radio show on LBC. It was soon after midnight when we left the studio and had just started to cross Parliament Square when Carol's car conked out. I don't recall what the problem was but I vividly remember pushing the thing alongside the kerb not far from Churchill's statue while Carol tried to explain the problem to the young bobby on the beat.

"Look, I'm Carol Thatcher and I just been doing my radio show and my mother lives round the corner and …" The policeman started giving her the old soldier look but became a bit more attentive when Carol produced her driving licence. Somehow, help was called and, after about an hour, the problem solved.

Ironically we were heading for Chequers rather than the nearby Downing Street and it was just after 2.00 am by the time we drove through the gates. "I bet your mother's still up," I said to Carol.

"Oh, I don't doubt it," Carol laughed. "She's supposed to be on holiday but that doesn't mean she gets any more sleep."

Sure enough, we found the P.M. in the little studio which is situated just to the left of the imposing drawing room. She was watching re-runs of *Yes, Minister*, the hilarious BBC series starring Nigel Hawthorne and Paul Eddington. People who thought Margaret Thatcher didn't have a sense of humour should have seen her. She was laughing out loud as she told us how accurate so many of the scenes were.

It was just after 3.00 am when we all retired to our separate (!) bedrooms. I was wondering, as I drifted off to sleep, who else had occupied my bedroom. A wide variety of Cabinet Ministers and foreign Prime Ministers, I presumed.

I knew there was going to be no chance of a lie in on Christmas morning and, like Carol, I was downstairs for breakfast by 8.00 am. Having learned of her sleeping habits, I was not surprised to find the Prime Minister greeting us but I was a little taken aback when she told me the cricket score from Australia. "England batting – I caught it on the 6.30 news," she said briskly.

As usual, on holiday or not, Mrs Thatcher was existing on about three hours' sleep. The fact that she had noted the cricket score revealed another aspect of her character. First of all, she followed anything that involved 'England' or 'Britain'. I think she genuinely felt some sort of responsibility for anyone who was out there representing the nation. One time, Carol was speaking to her on the phone and said she was off to interview Lucinda Prior-Palmer, Britain's leading equestrian at the time. With a wink at me, Carol immediately held the phone away from her ear. She knew what was coming. A minute's Prime Ministerial bio of Ms Prior-Palmer. It was like punching a keypad. As far as anything British was concerned she was a one woman, non-digital Google.

The conversation that Christmas morning at Chequers was memorable for a whole host of reasons and, unhappily, became more so in retrospect. For a start, I never imagined that I would find myself sitting down to breakfast with a Prime Minister at Chequers. But, even more than that, it was the tone and substance of the conversation which unfolded that struck me as so unexpected.

Quite apart from the Iron Lady factor, Margaret Thatcher's policies were quite blatantly right wing, offering little evidence of concern for the plight of the poor or disenfranchised in British society. She had gone to war with the trade unions, especially Arthur Scargill's miners' union, and, basically, had earned herself the reputation as being as tough as old boots.

However, I am going to ask you to believe that the conversation at breakfast on 25th December 1982 was almost entirely made up of the Prime Minister talking about the need to care for others and the wonderful work done by so many of Britain's charities. Even Mark shut up and listened. If Denis didn't actually say, "Hear hear!" he certainly looked as if he wanted to.

So does one explain this virtual monologue about the need for concern for the poor by suggesting the lady was simply infused with the Christmas spirit and would have recovered her steely ways by New Year's Eve?

That would be difficult, because a frequent guest at her New Year's Eve parties was Jimmy Savile, the eccentric British comedian, TV presenter and philanthropist who, ironic as it will sound now, had been held up as the most wonderful example of a sweet, caring man during breakfast that morning.

This apparently genuine outpouring of affection for a man who, it seemed, spent his life doing good deeds, was a little hard to explain at the time and, later when the reality of Savile's 'deeds' were exposed, it surpassed irony. Within a year of his death at 85 ten years later, Savile was revealed as a serial child molester in an ITV documentary. Soon fourteen police forces across the UK were investigating his crimes which included numerous counts of rape and over 300 cases of sexual attacks on children as young as eight.

It goes without saying that, had Mrs Thatcher known of any of this, she would have been utterly appalled and embarrassed beyond belief. She had instigated Savile's knighthood during her last year in office and had always promoted him as one of the nation's most caring people. But Savile, in reality, was as nasty a piece of work as you could find.

When the extent of Savile's crimes came to light, my thoughts fled back to that breakfast conversation – more a Prime Ministerial monologue, really – and I reminded myself once again of how often people are not what they seem.

Was Margaret Thatcher the person people perceived her to be? Maybe the portrait I have drawn here of the private person, as opposed to the public figure, might give people a different perspective. Her politics were not my politics. I do believe she gave Britain a kick up the backside when she came into office in 1979 and the country needed it. It is difficult for the younger generation to understand just how depressed, listless and pessimistic Britain was by the time the last Labour Government under Jim Callaghan lost the support of the populace. Drastic action was required and, inevitably, the instigator of that action would need to take some ruthless and unpopular decisions.

Even so, many of the Thatcherite policies seemed brutal and from a distance it was easy to paint her as a woman of no soul and no sympathy. But, all I can say is that was not the woman I met. And, mainly in deference to Carol, of whom I was truly fond, I treated her with uncritical respect.

As I have intimated, Mrs Thatcher and I never got into a real political discussion. While I was simply Carol's boyfriend, I did not feel it was my place to start suggesting what I felt she should or should not do. She would not have listened to me anyway and who could blame her.

All that might have changed had I become her son-in-law. Those who know me recognise, I think, that I am a person who is not afraid to speak his mind (often at considerable cost to myself) and, had I become a figure of influence in the Thatcher family, I have no doubt at all that, sooner or later, I would have voiced my opinion. What kind of eruption that would have caused, I shudder to think. But it never came to that.

I was having to do some long, hard thinking about my relationship with her daughter. I knew myself well enough by that stage of my life to be able to judge my own feelings honestly. I loved Carol but I was not in love with her. We never talked about marriage in detail but both of us were increasingly aware that it was a subject that would have to be dealt with if we continued as we had been for the previous ten months.

I don't need to spell out the temptations from my standpoint. Had I proposed, and had Carol accepted, I would have found myself in a very special position in Britain. Access and influence would have been there for the taking and, quite possibly, I could have undertaken projects that might have helped some of the people who were not being helped by Thatcherite policies. I would have met anyone I wanted to meet and had doors flung open everywhere. And I would have had a lively, funny, charming woman for a wife.

But I knew myself too well. In the long run I knew that I would not remain faithful to Carol if we were married. There would be love from my side in our marriage but there would also be the ingredient of convenience and, in my mind, I couldn't get the balance right. The last thing in the world I wanted to do was hurt this woman who had been appallingly treated by Jonathan Aitken who, to all intents and purposes, had ended their relationship within days of Mrs Thatcher deciding not to give him a Cabinet post. Even by Westminster standards, it was seen as an exceptionally cruel piece of expedient uncoupling.

So I started to try and take our relationship down a gear. Inevitably it caused stress and tears but Carol, being the amazing woman she is, seemed to accept the idea of 'Can't we be friends?' and we continued to see each other on a regular basis for some months. I was always welcome at the dinner parties she gave at Flood Street and, one afternoon, we drove out to Chequers to take a look at the possibility of having a tennis court installed. We had been talking to John Barrett about it and, with his Slazenger connections, he was prepared to take on the task.

It was a lovely spring day, as I recall, and while Carol went off for a dip in the covered swimming pool, one of the RAF staff got me a drink and I sat out on the wooden bench in front of the flower beds and gazed out across the lawn to the unspoiled fields of the Buckinghamshire countryside.

Inevitably I thought of Winston Churchill and, indeed, other beleaguered Prime Ministers, sitting there, as they must have done, grappling with the horrendous decisions they had needed to make in times of war and hardship. For me, it was simply an unforgettable moment and I felt immensely privileged to be able to enjoy it.

Less enjoyable, as my thoughts turned to Carol and our relationship, was the question of how long she would put up with me as a friend. I had been receiving a few signs that the writing was on the wall. She must have said something to her parents because, a little later, when the Prime Minister threw a cocktail party at No. 10, Carol invited Albina and my great friend Ingrid Lofdahl-Bentzer, the former Swedish No. 1 with whom she had also become close, but omitted to invite me. Fair enough. I knew there wasn't going to be much more of having one's cake and eating it.

Eventually Carol moved out of Flood Street and bought her own place in Fulham. I went to the house warming party but she offered little warmth to me. My only regret was that I was about to lose a friend – a really good and special friend. But even now I think I made the right decision. I have not seen Carol since.

Chapter 21
WITNESS TO THE END OF APARTHEID

I had a hunch and this one worked. Unhappily, many didn't but, this time, I could hardly have imagined how an idea I had for a book would dovetail with such precision into a moment of history.

Firstly, I had always wanted to write a book about a cricket tour. For me, cricket is the prince of games, involving a greater variety of skills and intricate tactical thinking than any other sport I know. Despite being a particularly English invention, it has become, without too much exaggeration, the greatest legacy Britain has left behind in the Commonwealth countries it used to rule.

Literally billions of people follow it and millions play it – across the Indian sub-continent, to Australasia, Southern Africa and the West Indies. Mostly it has brought peoples together in fierce but friendly sporting combat but, inevitably, by virtue of its sheer popularity, it has, on occasion, been used a political tool.

This has never been more true than when many nations decided to use sport as a way to fight the apartheid regime that existed in South Africa. A virtual boycott of South African sport gave birth to 'rebel' tours, undertaken by a few top-class cricketers in defiance of their national governing bodies. Participants in one of the first tours found themselves banned from playing any form on top class cricket in their countries for three years.

They had been lured, of course, by money and it was not hard to understand why. County cricketers in England during the eighties and nineties were being paid a pittance and, even if you became a regular member of the England team, you would be lucky to make £50,000 a year. The offer to tour South Africa illegally was precisely that sum for just six weeks with the captain getting double.

These tours were organised by Dr Ali Bacher who was a former captain of South Africa. He was not an apologist for the Afrikaaner government and was, in fact, fairly liberal in his thinking. But his motivation was simple.

He was desperate to keep cricket alive in his country and he knew full well if there were no international matches and no heroes for kids to idolise, the game would die.

So he found some financial support and began organising these tours, one of which, in 1982, had been captained by Graham Gooch, one of England's finest batsmen. Like his team, he was banned from playing for England for three years but, eventually, was re-instated. Gooch returned to the fold at about the time Mike Gatting, a successful but controversial England captain, was running into trouble with the men in suits for having shouted at an umpire in Pakistan and poked him in the chest. Not the done thing, old boy. Poor form. Not cricket.

Gatting, who was a broad as he was tall and could eat for England as well as score centuries for them, was a man of action rather than words and would have laid down his life for the England cause. He became Mr Middlesex at Lords, leading his county to Championship titles and then captaining England on one of the most successful tours to Australia ever undertaken against the arch-enemy. In 1986/87 Gatt's team regained the Ashes – the best of five Test Series – while also winning the One Day Series and a special multi-national Benson & Hedges Cup held in Perth.

But then came Pakistan and, ridiculously, a Sun expose about a fling with a barmaid. To the horror of his team, their captain was sacked. There followed an absurd summer when England captains came and went, most of them unfit for the role and none of them remotely successful. So, ignoring his past indiscretions, the selectors turned to the former rebel, Graham Gooch. His ability was never in doubt but it was still a strange choice and one which Gatting found ironic.

There was a tour to the West Indies coming up and Gatting let Micky Stewart, the England manager, know that he would make himself available for selection even if he was no longer captain. He never heard back.

However, he did hear from the organisers of the next rebel tour which was due to get under way in early weeks of 1990. Fearing the response from such a loyal member of the England team, Dr Bacher's people only plucked up courage to approach him at the eleventh hour. It came as a surprise even though he had heard rumours of the party being assembled which included his Middlesex colleague John Emburey and numerous soon-to-be ex-England players such as Chris Broad, Richard Ellison and Bruce French.

Gatting's acceptance, born out of frustration and hurt, came as a surprise to the organisers, too, but Bacher was delighted to have signed up such a high-profile name. As it turned out, publicity became the least of his worries.

So English cricket found itself in a very strange situation and it triggered my first thoughts about writing a book. Mike Gatting, previously a loyal and successful England captain, was burning his bridges by heading off to captain a rebel tour in South Africa while Graham Gooch, who had been there and done that and been re-instated, was going to take the official England team to the West Indies.

Hang on, I thought to myself, shouldn't it be the other way around? The tours were being led by the wrong captains! That, in itself, was some sort of story but there was something else. Through my South African contacts I had been hearing of a shift in mood in that country. P.W. Botha, the archetypical Afrikaaner hard-liner, had stepped down and had been replaced by F.W. de Klerk.

Even when Botha was still in power there had been long, painful discussions amongst Botha's cabinet about how to handle the Mandela problem. Someone who was on friendly terms with many cabinet ministers in the National Party, although he did not share their views, related a remarkable story to me one night over dinner.

Apparently, in 1987, there had been a serious move to have Nelson Mandela released from Robben Island. My friend painted an amazing picture of how the Boers go about their business. One night on the veldt, virtually the entire Cabinet were sitting round a camp fire with braais burning. They had just enjoyed a day's hunting and were scoffing happily on the meat they had shot for themselves.

Suddenly, a senior Cabinet minister rode up, brandishing a piece of paper.

"We've got it," he exclaimed. "All the judges have now signed. It's legal. We can let him go."

Apparently, there had been a consensus among Botha's colleagues that the time had come to get rid of their longest serving prisoner whose continued incarceration was creating more and more anti-South African publicity worldwide. But they had needed the agreement of High Court judiciary to make the move legal.

"Great!" some exclaimed out of the darkness. "Now we can push the little kaffir out on to Robben Island station at the crack of dawn with his suitcase and send him on his way before anyone realises what's happening!"

Gutteral guffaws erupted around the fire. "Right," said President Botha. "It will be nine o'clock Monday morning, then."

But it never happened because the Army moved faster. They sent a deputation to Botha as dawn broke that Monday morning to let the President know that, if the government went through with its plan, they would resist with force. In other words, there would be a military coup. So Mandela stayed in jail for another three years.

These kinds of stories only fed my hunch that this was not going to be an ordinary cricket tour and that something really interesting was going to happen in South Africa. It might, I thought, be a very good moment to be there.

Never, in my wildest dreams, did I imagine that I would arrive in one sort of country and, three weeks later, leave from one that had been totally transformed. But it happened and Gatting's tour found itself the focal point of much that was about to unfold.

F.W. de Klerk had been turning a blind eye to what was known as petty apartheid – people of colour meeting with whites in public places – soon after he had become Prime Minister and he made an overt move towards a relaxation of laws when he decided to allow peaceful demonstrations. Prior to that moment, anyone producing so much as a placard with a critical message would find themselves beaten and dragged off to jail.

But suddenly demonstrations would become legal and guess who were the very first people to be demonstrated against? Mike Gatting and his rebel cricketers.

Having worked out the dates, I determined that I could cover Gatting's tour and then fly straight to Kingston, Jamaica, arriving in time for the second day of the First Test between Gooch's England team and the West Indies. I would do a diary, comparing the moods, ethics and differences of the two tours. They were stark.

So, on 31st January 1990, I found myself in Bloemfontein, capital of the deeply conservative Orange Free State. Remembering the oddities, if one can use such a mild word, of my trip seventeen years earlier with Arthur Ashe, I knew we were in for a strange ride and, as I noted in my diary of the book that became entitled *The Ultimate Test*, the point was quickly made.

'The abnormality begins at breakfast at the otherwise splendid Landrost Hotel. If you want the black waiter to bring you a pot of tea, it is necessary to convince him that you are not a member of the English cricket team. The team are in an alcove around the corner, near the self-service buffet, cordoned off from the main, multi-racial dining room. The irony is not easy to miss. Apartheid at breakfast.'

Later, with the chants of the first group of legalised demonstrators audible from outside the gates of the recently built Springbok Park, I had a chance to sit down with Ali Bacher who quickly made it apparent where his political sympathies lay even if his sporting initiatives had put him on the 'wrong' side of the political divide.

Explaining, in very brief terms, the problem between the Afrikaaner Government and the ANC (African National Congress) which had spawned Nelson Mandela and other brave men, Bacher said, "The National Party wouldn't talk to the ANC in the old days so they decided to start fighting people, which was reasonable enough. Then Gorbachev arrived on the scene and told the government that he had got a problem in Afghanistan and couldn't help them anymore. And the whole picture changed. The Nats knew the country's economy was bleeding and the ANC found their funds drying up. Everybody had to start talking. There was no alternative."

Although I didn't realise it at the time, Bacher was laying out an explanation for what was about to happen. His crystal ball was clear but not, I believe, clear enough to see what would transpire in a matter of days.

In the meantime, the focus of the tour was on Mike Gatting. There was a large press corps, both South African and English, following the tour and they knew that virtually every word the captain uttered would produce some sort of copy. Gatting was on a tight rope and it didn't take him to long to fall off.

On February 1st, with the match under way, we received word in the press box that the leaders of the demonstration we had been hearing outside the gates wanted to enter the ground to hand Gatting a petition. Gatt had said from the start that he would be prepared to meet 'anyone representing factions opposed to the tour' and it was arranged for the tea interval.

So the foreign press corps which included Malcolm Folley from the Daily Mail; Paul Weaver, then writing for Today; John Etheridge of the Sun; and John Jackson of the Daily Mirror joined the South African journalists inside the police cordon on the field to watch proceedings.

It was a picture set up. One of the three men allowed through to present the petition, John Sognoneco, who looked years younger than his actual age of 25, suddenly ripped off his shirt and presented his back to Gatting and the tour manager David Graveney. It was peppered with buckshot wounds as a result of some police action that had occurred in the townships a couple of nights before.

Gatting did not have the right response. "Did that happen at the ground?" he asked. When told that it hadn't, he replied, "Then it's nothing to do with us. We can't be held responsible for anything that happens away from the ground."

Gatt would learn a little about diplomacy as the tour went on but this was very early in the proceedings and it was a response that was too blunt and too defensive. On being told that the media would make meal of it, the captain immediately agreed to hold a press conference back at the hotel to try and clarify his comment but, even in that cumbersome age of communication, the stories had been wired and the headlines were being set back in London as well as Johannesburg.

Gatting talked to the media twice before we packed our bags for the long road trip to Pietermaritzburg and I was chatting to Chris Broad and John Emburey in the lobby when the chastened captain joined us.

"How was I?" he asked.

"Better," I replied. "You almost kept a straight bat this time." Gatting gave a little smile and waddled off to supervise the team's departure.

The journey took six hours across the vast, brown landscape of Natal. Great flat-top mountains erupted at intervals of every twenty to thirty miles. It is Gulliver country, and our little bus, smaller and more rickety than we had expected, scurried along like a beetle, dwarfed by everything around it.

There had been apologies for the lack of air conditioning but with the windows open, we were less concerned about that than the bloody radio. That didn't work either. On the principle that timing is everything, this proved not to be the moment to be out of communication with the world. The extent to which that was true was revealed when, having skirted Lesotho and come within striking distance of Ladysmith, we decided to stop for a bite to eat at a Wimpy bar in Harrismith. It was there that Graham Morris, one of cricket's ace photographers who had been following us in a hire car with a radio that worked, told us the news.

"De Klerk's unbanned the Communist Party as well as the ANC; suspended all executions and promised that Mandela's release is imminent."

Cheeseburgers got stuck half way to our mouths. Jaws really do drop. Ours certainly did. F.W. de Klerk, who, for years, had been a staunch and unquestioning member of the National Party's cabinet had, in a stroke, virtually dismantled apartheid. In the sweeping changes he had just announced F.W. had gone further than anyone had expected. It seemed as if he was trying to turn himself into a Southern Hemisphere Gorbachev who, during the preceding years, had been manipulating the changes that would lead to the demise of the Soviet Union.

I had been told by some of my liberal friends that de Klerk had been showing signs of having 'seen the light' and now it seemed that it had been a very bright one. And it appeared to be true. I had heard from what reporters in Westminster would have probably described an 'unimpeachable source' that the President had insisted that he literally 'saw the light' on his knees in church. Evidently, he had seen a vision of a new South Africa which released him from the agonies of indecision with which he had been wrestling and allowed him to set out on a straightforward path that would lead, ultimately and inevitably, to black rule – "even if that means I am no longer President."

My source, who had known de Klerk for years, was staggered by this revelation because F.W. is a Dopper, a term used to describe those who belong to the most conservative branch of the Dutch Reform Church. A conversion to liberalism, I was told, would be virtually unheard of and an incomprehensible occurrence for anyone with his background.

But it had happened and South Africa would never be the same country. The changes he had instituted in the face of God knows how much opposition from members of his party were beyond dramatic. They would create a new society, a new way of living. And they would release upon an unsuspecting public a man who would turn out to be his nation's saviour, and take his place as one of the most remarkable and revered figures of the twentieth century.

Within days we would get our first look at Nelson Mandela and no one would forget it.

However, on 3rd February, there was still a cricket tour going on and there were still people who objected to it. Five thousand of them, actually. We were in Pietermaritzburg and the crowd, which had assembled in Churchill Square (yes, he had passed that way) and which proceeded to march towards the cricket ground seven abreast, was made up predominantly of Zulus with a sprinkling of Indians and Coloureds, most of who were acting as marshals. This was something much larger and better organised than we had seen before.

They set up camp outside the main gate and sent a note in to Ali Bacher during the afternoon's play. They had a petition – no surprise there – and wanted to hand it personally to Mike Gatting. Bacher agreed and, at the tea interval, led the England captain towards the waist-high brick wall which formed the perimeter of the ground. That was as far as Bacher wanted anyone to go. But the leaders of the demonstration were not satisfied.

"No, no, we want you to receive the petition on that podium over there," one of them said to Gatting. "Safe in, safe out. We guarantee it!"

He might have meant it but he could guarantee no such thing. The podium they had set up was about 150 yards away. Not far? Ringed by 5,000 chanting Zulus it looked like another world. And there were no Red Coats in sight. Not that Michael Caine or Stanley Baker could have done much about it. This was real life and it didn't need an imaginative movie script to suggest that one spark, one thrown Coke bottle, one over-excited demonstrator, could have set off a riot that would have engulfed Gatting and our entourage.

The captain was escorted by two policemen as we left the ground but that was it. The rest of us – Bacher, Emburey, Graveney and a few members of the press corps – were on our own. Even now, I can say that I haven't been in many more nerve-racking situations in my life. The possibility of disaster was balancing on the tip of a spear.

You would never have known it watching Mike Gatting. Out he strode like the original British bulldog; up he climbed onto the podium and received the petition after speeches were made. I can't remember if he said anything himself. It was not a moment to hang around. So we started the journey back and I stopped to ask one of the Indian marshals, who were doing a great job, what he thought.

"He's a very brave man," the marshal replied. "But I still think the tour should be stopped."

That decision would be taken later but, for the moment, Gatting had a cricket team to lead and, marching back through the gate as if he had just been out to stretch his legs, he walked into the dressing room and said, "Come on, lads! Time to go!" And then he bowled the second over after tea.

For an old-fashioned example of British stiff upper lip, it wasn't bad. Bacher, who was a bag of nerves by the time it was all over, was quick to unburden his thoughts.

"I am very emotional right now," he told me. "That was one of the most courageous acts I have ever seen by a sportsman off the field of play. You guys have vilified Mike for making a couple of silly remarks about the situation here after being in the country a few days. White South Africans say stupid things every week after living here all their lives."

That was true. Much cleverer people than Mike Gatting had put their foot in it over the topic of apartheid and he had learned that deeds are often better than words in situations like the one we had just faced, and he had emerged with honour.

It was interesting to get a copy of the actual petition and learn that it was basically making a complaint about the lack of sporting facilities for non-whites in the Pietermaritzburg area. Even the numbers that made up the local population made fascinating reading, offering as it did a microcosm of South Africa itself. There were 53,000 Whites; 63,000 Indians and Coloureds and 260,000 Africans. But, of course, the minority ruled.

Sports facilities just offered an example of how that played out. Whites had 11 hockey fields; 8 rugby pitches; 18 squash courts; 3 swimming pools and 44 tennis courts. Africans? 0.

Of all the facilities available, Africans had 8 soccer fields and 6 tennis courts. The Indians and Coloureds fared hardly any better although they did have 11 soccer fields.

The cricket statistics were even worse. White schools had 11,567 pupils and 32 cricket fields, 22 of which had turf wickets. Indian & Coloured schools with 13,608 students had ONE cricket field with an inferior matting wicket. Welcome to apartheid.

While no one is suggesting for a moment that the England cricketers were in South Africa for altruistic reasons, another fact is unassailable. Those figures would never have been published anywhere had not the demonstrators been a given a target to aim at. At least their voices had been heard and Gatting was not the only member of the touring party who was happy about that.

In the nation as a whole, it was a moment for everyone to recover their breath and start assessing just what President de Klerk's uprooting of so much of what his Afrikaaner party stood for would bring. Change would be swift in some ways and not so much in others. Paul Weaver, who went on to enjoy a long and distinguished career on the Guardian, had written a particularly damning piece for Today about the riots that had erupted at the airport upon our arrival three weeks before.

He was reminded of it somewhat suddenly on 6th February when two large policemen knocked on his door at the Sandton Hotel in Johannesburg at 10.00 am. They handed him a piece of paper which told him to get out of South Africa by midnight. It reminded me of Don Mattera being banned during Arthur Ashe's visit. They couldn't ban a non-South African so expulsion was their way of dealing with criticism. It would change, of course, but those orders move slowly down the pipeline and Paul had no alternative but to be on that plane.

Apparently, Malcolm Folley, John Jackson, the BBC's Frank Partridge and the rest of us were still just about persona grata as we made our way down to Johannesburg for a so-called 'Test' between what was billed an a South African XI vs and England XI at the Wanderers.

Gordon and Frances Forbes had invited me to stay and it was wonderful to be lodged in a welcoming home rather than a hotel for a change. It was also incredibly convenient because Gordon showed me a short-cut down a little path and through a hole in a wire fence leading to the Wanderers ground, which was which was less ten minutes away. The cricket would be even more of a side-show now but that did not stop another group of demonstrators showing up to wave banners and chant outside the gates.

I went to have a look and, by chance, found myself being given a close up view of the racial hatred that was so deeply embedded in South Africa at that time.

A group of some twenty white males had gathered inside the gates and were hurling abuse at the demonstrators. "You're just a bunch of gorillas, man," yelled an overweight, swarthy individual who was blissfully unaware that he closely resembled an ape. "You want to come in? Hey, let them in so we can show them who's boss around here!"

It's very easy to play the big man when you are secure behind bolted iron bars and a row of armed police. It was an unedifying sight but I was particularly interested in the behaviour of the police. All their careers they had been taught to bash demonstrators over the head and now, here they were, with orders to protect them. They looked confused.

However, there was no doubting where their sympathies lay. Once the demonstrators' time was up and they had been led away, one tall young policeman, who had been standing directly in front of the ringleader of the anti-demo mob, turned and patted him on the back. "Well done, that was great, man!"

President de Klerk was going to have to watch his police. It's tough to get leopards to change their spots. There was, in fact, probably only one man in Africa who could even attempt it and, on 11th February 1990, he walked out of his prison cell to face the world as a free man for the first time in 27 years.

We watched Nelson Mandela emerge from Victor Verster prison on the outskirts of Cape Town, from where he had been brought from Robben Island, on television. It was a moment of history that is, of course, etched in the memory. Apart from his actual appearance – tall, calm, elegant – it was what he proceeded to do that left everyone stunned.

If you have been locked in a prison cell for a long time, speaking to only one or two people at once, psychologists will tell that the vast majority of people need a period of re-adjustment before they can face big crowds. Big? There were over 50,000 people packed onto Cape Town's Grand Parade when Mandela walked up to the microphone and his voice rang out, strong and clear.

"First, let me say, I do not come to you as a prophet."

With such a clear understanding of how he was being viewed; of the expectation that had built up around him and the daunting task that lay ahead, Mandela knew it needed to be said. But the media, worldwide, still treated it like a second coming and he knew he would be expected to perform miracles at every turn. For us, just seeing him there, a free man, unbowed and seemingly in control of a media circus, the like of which he had never known, appeared to be a miracle all on its own.

The following day Mandela found himself facing questions from some of the most famous TV faces in the world – Tom Brokaw, Dan Rather, Ted Koppel and David Dimbleby – but he barely stumbled and answered each question on its merits instead of fudging questions like so many politicians in Britain or America. Watching him, I remember thinking, this man is remarkable. He is almost living up to advance publicity.

Winnie Mandela had a home waiting for her husband in Soweto and he flew up there almost immediately to begin a new life. For me the 14th February was a day I shall never forget. Unhappily, it had nothing to do with finding a beautiful Valentine but there were serious compensations. I got to see a man who would shape South Africa's future and meet a woman who had battled with incredible bravery and determination to preserve something good from the past.

I had not really expected to see Mandela when Ronnie Van't Hof, a financial consultant and former tennis player, offered to drive me into Soweto. He had set up a trust fund to develop grass roots tennis in the townships. I wanted to have a look at what he had achieved while also verifying what I had heard about courts that Arthur Ashe and Owen Williams had worked so hard to get built.

Sadly, what I had heard was true. The Ashe courts had fallen into disrepair, largely because of riots in Soweto in 1976 which had thrown so much into chaos. Also, pressured by so many of his black colleagues in America, Ashe had ended the numerous visits he had been making. Van't Hof and I surveyed the desolate scene. The eight courts that had been built lay baking under the hot Soweto sun, grass flopping over the edges of the concrete while pylons, which were to have carried floodlights, stood like rusting sentinels over some half-forgotten dream.

Although it wouldn't take that much money or effort to get the place up and running again, Van't Hof pointed out that the community had other priorities. "We can't do anything until we are asked. We cannot impose ourselves on these people. We have to wait until things change."

But they were changing and when Ronnie casually mentioned that the one shining beacon of hope for the future lived just a few roads away, I leapt at the chance to see what was happening at the Mandela home.

The house stood on an unpaved road and there were two oil cans blocking immediate access. So we got out of the car and walked up to a group of some 40 reporters and cameramen who were milling around. Van't Hof knew some of the photographers and one told me, "He's in the garden right now. Here, stand on this, and you will be able to peek over the fence."

He was pointing to his steel camera case, which would take my weight, so I clambered up and peered through the single strand of loosely coiled barbed wire that sat on top of the fence. From that uncertain vantage point, I stared down at the face of a man no one had seen for 27 years until three days before.

Nelson Mandela was sitting in a chair, no more than twenty yards away, being interviewed by ABC's Ted Koppel whose Nightline programme was considered one of the best of its kind in the world. I raised my little automatic camera, which was about the size of some of the Samsung mobile phones we use today, and fired off a few shots. It struck me right then that I could be shooting off shots of a different kind. There had been next to no security. There were some police visible further down the road but they paid scant attention to me. Someone on a different mission could have changed the course of history.

In retrospect, it is remarkable that no one did. Especially during those early months of freedom, Mandela was a huge target for the seething anger that was emanating from the most traditional elements of the Afrikaaner community over what their President had done. They did not need to be told what lay ahead. Free elections would have only one result. Mandela would replace de Klerk as President. You didn't need a calculator to check the figures.

So the stage was set for bloodshed and, indeed, there was a little here and there. But the conflagration never happened. Mandela performed his miracle aided, it must be said, by the transformed de Klerk. He achieved it by revealing himself to be a statesman of incredible magnitude. He did it by showing that he would demand no retribution on any major scale. He did it by insisting all races in South Africa could live in peace if they tried. Mandela did it by refusing to rub Afrikaaner noses in their own beloved soil.

There is a scene in the excellent film *Invictus* when Mandela, played superbly by Morgan Freeman, stands firm in the face of angry opposition from his own advisers over the issue of whether to allow the South African rugby team to retain the name 'Springbok'. One must credit Clint Eastwood, an American director, for understanding so clearly what part rugby played in the everyday lives of the Afrikaaner nation. Yes, English-speaking South Africans played rugby, too, but the national team was always dominated by names like du Toit and van der Merwe. Their rugby team was their pride and joy; it was the vessel that carried their power and their worth to the world. And they were called Springboks.

It was for precisely these reasons that so many blacks wanted to eradicate the name Springbok from South African life. It had become a symbol of everything they hated. Mandela understood that fully and it was exactly why he refused to let his supporters destroy it.

"If we are going to have peace in our country, we have to learn to live with these people," he insisted in front of a restless, unforgiving crowd. "And we cannot gain their trust and their co-operation if we take away what is dearest to them."

That was how Nelson Mandela worked his miracles – through reasoned argument; through a refusal to get carried away on a wave of euphoria or revenge; to understand the enemy and to appeal to his own people's finer instincts. Given the history of what had gone before, there was probably not another person on earth; or in the entire history of South Africa, who could have managed it.

Memorably, of course, Mandela went on to show how far he was prepared to go to embrace those who had imprisoned him for 27 years when he wore a Springbok rugby jersey on the day South Africa played their arch rugby rivals New Zealand in the 1995 World Rugby Cup Final. He had become friends with the South African captain, Francois Pienaar, who led his team to a nail-biting 15-12 victory against the mighty All Blacks that day.

Mandela had put on Pienaar's spare jersey with No 6 on the back and buttoned it up to the neck. Maybe the fit wasn't perfect but the symbolism of the gesture could not have been more so. When the man who had become his nation's President – this black man, this 'convict' – handed the trophy to the tall, blond Afrikaaner captain and 65,000 mostly white spectators cheered themselves hoarse, South Africa came together as one country. Oh, yes, the union has not been perfect but it would never have got off the ground without Mandela's understanding of what was required and of how to use the tools at his disposal. And sport, to a huge degree, was one of the most important.

"Sport has the power to change the world," Mandela had said. "It has the power to inspire; it has the power to unite people."

On an insignificant, personal level, it was good to hear him say that. It made me feel that a life's work of promoting sport through my writing had been, in some small degree, worthwhile.

But to return to that memorable 14th of February 1990. The woman Gordon Forbes took me to visit after I had returned from Soweto had led a life unique in the history of politics and she must, on occasion, have wondered whether it was all worthwhile.

But Dame Helen Suzman never even contemplated giving up. Not even when the representation of her Progressive Party in Parliament had shrunk to one. Herself. Just her, this small female surrounded by a House of hulking Boers who were irritated beyond belief that she would challenge them, argue with them and denounce them for their inhumanity day after day after day. And she did it for over 30 years. Stamina, determination, deep-seated belief in what was right and what was wrong – oh, we need to redefine those words and phrases when talking about Helen Suzman.

It is so hard to be able to put oneself in somebody else's shoes and imagine what it is really like to be them. So many of us don't even try. And I certainly struggle to comprehend what it must have been like for a woman to wake up every morning knowing full well that her day was going to be one of struggle against absurd odds; of abuse; of contradiction and, of course, of ultimate failure. For 30 years.

Sixteen of those years she was totally alone and you better believe her fellow parliamentarians did not let her forget it. She was harassed and threatened outside parliament as well as in the chamber but her quick mind and ready wit beat them back. When one National Party member asked her why she kept asking questions that embarrassed South Africa, she shot back, "It is not my questions that embarrass South Africa, it is your answers."

It was futile, too, to try to reach her at home with abusive phone calls. She replied by blowing a very loud whistle down the mouthpiece.

So I knew I was going to be privileged to meet this special person, especially when it transpired that Dame Helen had only just returned from a holiday on the coast to deal with endless requests for interviews and was due to be up at 5.00 am to talk to Ted Koppel for his Nightline programme that would be transmitted live to New York.

The lady herself opened the front door of her lovely house in Sandton when Gordon and I arrived. Presumably there were servants around somewhere but they were not in evidence. Apologising for sounding sleepy when Gordon had called, she fetched us some drinks and settled down on the settee of her spacious, book-lined living room, giving way to a large lawn. The house has an English feel about it, as does the lady herself, although she had Jewish-Lithuanian origins.

She must have been 71 at the time and she was wearing her years well. Petite and fine-boned, she gave off a distinguished air of unpretentious charm. However, it was not simply her charm that had enabled to survive such a lengthy political ordeal.

When the conversation turned to Mandela, whom she had visited frequently on Robben Island during his 27-year incarceration, she related how her visits had eventually been curtailed when she said something that had annoyed the then Prime Minister P.W. Botha even more than usual.

"One of the problems with P.W. was that he was a bully," she said. "All this finger-wagging stuff. So unattractive. And, frankly, he was third rate. Not in de Klerk's league intellectually."

We did not need to mention how that had been made evident by de Klerk's startling changes of the previous few days, and I turned the conversation to sport. I was anxious to hear her views on how sport should be handled as far as boycotts were concerned.

"Sporting bodies that have moved away from apartheid and have made a real effort in that direction need encouragement," she said. "Sport is an area where great progress can be made and the people running sports like cricket, tennis, athletics and soccer here should be helped to achieve it."

It turned out that Dame Helen was not quite in accord with the ANC over the questions of sanctions in general and was not afraid to take a little dig at the hero of the hour.

"Did you see in the papers that Labour leaders in London were saying to the Prime Minister, 'How dare you think you know more than Mandela!' Well, I'm sorry but, much as I love Nelson, the fact is that she does know more about a lot of things concerning sanctions than he does. Margaret Thatcher has been running a country while he has been in prison for 27 years. Nelson is a fine man but there are a lot of things that he can't possibly comprehend just yet."

Gordon Forbes, who had known Dame Helen, whose niece, incidentally is the great actress Dame Janet Suzman, for most of his life, then posed a question he had been wanting to put to her for years. Not needing to remind her that white liberals, as well as black activists, had been assassinated by the secret police, he asked her if she ever been really afraid.

"Oh, there was never time to be afraid, really," she replied with a little smile. "Too much to do. You just put it out of your mind."

Some mind. One began to see how she had survived in the apartheid den; morally incorruptible, fearless, outspoken, always prepared to stand up for what was humane and decent while her army of opponents tried to defend the indefensible. What an uncomfortable little pin she must have been, pricking away at the remnants of their conscience.

Before we left, she showed us a book by Natan Sharansky, the Soviet Jew who had spent nine years in a KGB prison camp. She had taken it to Mandela on her last visit and he had sent it back to her soon after she retired from formal political life with an inscription of which she was obviously, and justifiably, proud.

It read: 'The countless tributes that you have received on retirement from Parliament show that you have acquitted yourself beyond words.' It was signed 'Nelson. 6.7.89.'

Now the man who had been a prisoner that day in July the previous year was receiving tributes of his own. What a pair they would have made had Helen Suzman and Nelson Mandela been allowed to serve in Pretoria's Parliament together.

And so it was back to the cricket tour – or what was left of it. A press conference had been called at the Wanderers to announce that the itinerary had changed. There would be no 'Test' in Cape Town and only four one day matches instead of seven – none of them in Cape Town, East London or Port Elizabeth where the protests were expected to be strongest.

The reason? It was not immediately clear but Ali Bacher, in evasive tones, stated that a 'third party' had called from overseas, imploring that a solution be found to end, or at least reduce, the increasingly hostile demonstrations that continued to make headlines and mar the sudden new hope for a better future in South Africa.

Later, it transpired that the call had come from an English country estate called Mells Park House in Somerset which was being used by a group of South African businessmen who, with foresight, were wanting to start a civilised dialogue with the ANC. There had been a gathering over the same weekend that the Johannesburg 'Test' had started and the Gatting tour had been at the centre of the conversation.

No less a figure than Thabu Mbeki, who would become South Africa's second black President when Mandela stepped down in 1999, was present as was Mof Terre'Blanche, a close friend of de Klerk's as well as other Afrikaaner businessmen. They put it to Mbeki and his ANC colleagues that it would best for the country if the demonstrations were called off. Initially, Mbeki would not hear of it but, when he was given a hint of the radical changes that were about to be announced, including the imminent release of Mandela, he realised that something needed to be done.

So the phone call was made and suddenly Bacher found himself working out a compromise that would drastically cut back the rest of the tour's itinerary. The deal was thrashed out with Krish Naidoo, the lawyer who headed the National Sports Congress, and the result of their efforts were now being presented to us.

It was made clear that the South African government was not exerting any pressure in the matter and was leaving it up to the parties involved to work together in 'depoliticising sport'.

Mike Gatting, in comparison to his earlier efforts, was positively eloquent. "It is very heartening that the NSC and the South African Cricket Union will be able to get together, to sit down and talk, which they haven't done for a long time and get around to normalising sport here in South Africa. Hopefully this new spirit of compromise will take both parties a long way down the road towards complete understanding."

Bacher still looked like a worried man and with reason. He had been at the epi-centre of the maelstrom that had surrounded the tour from the beginning. Here was the Liberal who had compromised his own political beliefs by working with a government he basically despised to ensure that there was some hope of keeping South African cricket alive. He had been shot at from all sides and we were all grateful that the shots had been nothing more than verbal.

As is clear from Rodney Hartman's excellent biography *Ali*, the former South African captain had been shaken to the core by the virulence of the demonstrations and had feared for his life, as well as those of Gatting and the rest of us, during that nerve-racking walk amongst the Zulus in Pietermaritzburg.

Speaking a long time later, Hartman quotes Bacher as saying, "People must have been insane to believe the second leg of the tour was possible (as scheduled). It was sheer madness even to consider it. The anger and fury around that tour was something I had never experienced before and I was truly afraid someone would die if it went on the way it had begun."

By removing matches from the hot spots, the tour did continue but the ironies were glaring. The next match, which was the first officially sanctioned by the ANC after the compromise had been reached, was played in a town named after the father of apartheid in front of a packed stadium of 15,000 without a black spectator in sight.

The recently built, high-tech Centurion Park is situated in Verwoerdburg, a little Silicon Valley type adjunct to the nation's capital, Pretoria. With the threat of demonstrations removed, cricket lovers flocked to the ground and saw a reasonably competitive match which South Africa won.

So the tour dribbled on, the media back in the UK lost interest and, with surprising speed, the cricket establishment at Lord's chose to forgive and forget. Although Gatting never played for England again, he was eventually given a senior role by the English Cricket Board (ECB) and later was elected President of the MCC for the customary two-year term. The tour's manager, David Graveney, who had played such a leading part in proceedings, also soon found himself embraced by the powers on high and was Chairman of Selectors for the England team from 1997 to 2008. Chris Broad was appointed a Test match referee by the ICC and Bruce French has been an England wicketkeeping coach. Any lingering resentment towards the rebels faded fast.

But the last word should go to the man at the centre of everyone's thoughts during the amazing few weeks I have tried to describe. Half way through the day's play, Christopher Morris of Sky News arrived at Centurion hot-foot from Soweto, where he had finally managed to get an interview with Nelson Mandela.

I was chatting with Johnny Woodcock of the Times when Morris offered a fascinating little insight into how closely Mandela was following events in the country he would soon have to lead.

"You know the first thing Mandela asked me as the crew were setting up?" Chris asked. "Did I know Mike Gatting! I said that I had met him professionally, hoping that I would not get thrown out of the garden, but he just went on to comment that, in his view, the team shouldn't have come and that it was bad for South Africa and bad for South African sport."

More memorable for me was the answer Mandela gave when asked, on the eve of his first trip to New York two years later, he was asked who he would like to meet. "Arthur Ashe," he replied. Arthur did not have long to live but as Jeannie Moutoussamy Ashe has told me, her husband relished, like no other, his meetings with the man he had been unable to see on his visits to South Africa.

WEST INDIES

It was a rush to get to Kingston for the first Test between West Indies and England but I made it and enjoyed a completely different experience covering a tour with no racial overtones.

Coming straight from South Africa there was an element of irony in the fact that two of England's leading batsmen, Allan Lamb and Robin Smith, whose partnership of 172 at Sabina Park helped England open the tour with an unlikely victory, were both South African born and bred. They would never have switched allegiance but for apartheid.

The other main factor in England's win was Devon Malcolm, a hold-your-breath-and-hope selection for the tour who was known for speed and wicket-taking ability but not for accuracy. And where did Malcolm hail from? The West Indies. But that did not stop him taking four wickets in each innings. With sheer speed, he dismissed Viv Richards, the imperious West Indies captain twice. In ths second innings, Richards was on 37 when he swung through an arc that normally resulted in a six over long on. But Malcolm's yorker hit the base of the leg stump. As he turned to inspect the damage, the expression on Viv's face suggested that this outcome had not featured in his list of poissibilities when he selected the shot.

England might have gone two up in the seriues had not a black cloud, which appeared out of nowhere, dumped an unreasonable amount of water on the Queen's Park Oval in Trinidad when England only needed a mere 150 to win. In the end, they fell just 30 short of their target as darkness fell.

Reality set in after that and, with Graham Gooch out of action with a broken thumb, West Indies won the final two Tests in Barbados and Antigua by wide margins.

The tour had been a joy to cover and problems of race were never a factor, although one silly incident did manage to rear its head as I tried to hear what the West Indies manager, Clive Lloyd, had to say after his team's win in Antigua. Like all media affairs on cricket tours at the time, the press conference was poorly organised and a scrum formed round Lloyd, populated mostly but not entirely by accredited reporters.

Trying to hear what Lloyd, who spoke softly, was saying, I tried to get as close as possible when a young Antiguan, who had no badge, elbowed his way past me.

"Excuse me," I said in as mild a tone as I could muster. "This is supposed to be a press conference and if you do that I won't be able to take any notes."

The reply I got was laced with irony. "This isn't South Africa!" he shot back. "You can't tell me what to do here. This isn't South Africa!"

Oh, Lord have mercy! Where to start? I didn't try until the conference was over and then I attempted to explain that South Africa really didn't have a lot to do with whether I should be allowed to write down the utterances of a West Indies hero on an island that was no longer a colony. I'm not sure he was convinced but we parted with a handshake.

That evening I was on a British Airways 747, heading home for a frantic couple of days' work at Partridge Press putting the book to bed with the help of my editor Debbie Beckerman. When both Christopher Martin-Jenkins in The Cricketer and David Frith, a tough critic who edited Wisden Cricket Monthly, gave it excellent reviews, it made the whole mad endeavour seem worthwhile.

As a fitting postscript, I was back in the Tavern at Lord's a week later, having a drink with Mike Gatting, John Emburey and Desmond Haynes, the West Indies vice-captain. They were all wearing their Middlesex blazers; black and white playing for the same team.

Chapter 22
ENTERTAINMENT TONIGHT

Over a period of eighteen months from the end of 1983 to early 1985 I took on a completely different role thanks to an old friend being in the right job at the right time.

I had first met Bridget Byrne when she turned up at the Pacific South West Championships at the Los Angeles Tennis Club in 1968. She had been sent to cover the tournament because her sports editor, who didn't have a clue about tennis, said, "Oh, you're English so you must have been to Wimbledon, you go and cover it!"

Bridget, provocatively bright and very attractive with flowing blonde hair, had just started writing theatre reviews for the Los Angeles Herald Examiner which was a step up after starting her career on the paper as someone's secretary.

But this daughter of a family doctor from the very English town of Midhurst in Sussex was never going to remain unnoticed. Trinity College, Dublin had taken care of her higher education and, as soon as the editors at the Herald Examiner realised how well she wrote, she became a star on the second biggest paper in L.A. which, of course, meant Hollywood.

So, moving on from theatre reviews and women's features, Miss Byrne was appointed one of the paper's two movie critics, which made her a hugely influential figure in the capital of the film world. There are beautiful girls by the limousine load in Tinsel Town but not all of them have looks, intellect and a pen that refuses to be influenced by PR people spinning a line.

There are rules you are supposed to follow if you buy into the Hollywood game but Bridget wasn't interested. If she thought a movie stank, she said it stank – even if she was having an affair with the head of the studio. When she got the inevitable enraged call from the CEO the day her review came out, her reply left him flabbergasted.

"I thought it was a terrible movie," she said. "What do you expect me to say? That I liked it just because I am sleeping with you?"

Oh, dear, that was not the way the game was supposed to be played but Bridget wasn't interested in those sorts of games. She had plenty of her own which included going out with the likes of Clint Eastwood and skinny dipping in Jim Brown's pool. The gridiron star had a chequered reputation with his girlfriends but, naked or not, he always treated Bridget with total respect. Hollywood soon came to realise that you took Bridget on her own terms or not at all.

Inevitably that eventuality resulted in a parting of the ways with the Herald Examiner (which was to meet its own demise in 1989) but she quickly found a place writing features at Women's Wear Daily. After a few years, Jim Bellows, the editor at the Herald who had fired her, took an editorial position on a new TV programme called Entertainment Tonight. Realising that getting rid of Bridget had not been one of his cleverest moves, he immediately lured her away to become one of the programme's assignment editors.

Recently, I read Barbara Walter's fascinating autobiography in which she makes it abundantly clear that the success of a programme like 20/20 or The View is all about the quality of guests you can attract. That requires contacts and Bridget had them.

Given Bellows' background as a top news editor, there was a serious attempt in the early years to provide hard news concerning the movie industry. "Jim tried to make it journalistic," Bridget told me. "But not everyone had an understanding of what made a story. I was at the Directors' Guild Awards one year and got Warren Beatty to stop and talk to me which was a bit of a miracle because he never, ever gave interviews. But my producer at the time didn't run it because he said the sound wasn't great. He completely missed the point that simply having Warren talk to camera with an ET microphone in front of his face was a news story in itself."

But Bridget and her colleagues snared enough stars and produced enough gossip from their headquarters at Paramount Studios to ensure that that Entertainment Tonight became one of the most watched shows on American television. By 1985 Mary Hart had begun her incredible 29-year run as co-host and, as I write, ET remains the longest running entertainment news programme on television.

Back in 1983, when I was passing through L.A., Bridget had an idea. "You travel all over the place going to tennis tournaments, would you ever have time to pick up a crew and do some interviews for us?"

The answer was 'Yes!' It had begun with a dinner Bridget and I enjoyed at

Morton's on 18th October 1983. At that time, Morton's (not the steakhouse chain) was the sort of place where you would find yourself dining next to a galaxy of Hollywood stars and it was certainly true on this occasion as David Hemmings arrived to join Michael Caine, Joan Collins and George Hamilton, who were all celebrating the 25th wedding anniversary of Leslie and Evie Bricusse.

I had met David Hemmings on a couple of occasions when I was living with Gayle in London – dropping Nolan off at David's house in Onslow Gardens. Now, he gave me a vague, "Hello, mate," as he passed our table, probably wondering where the hell he had seen me before. Leslie Bricusse was responsible for writing those great songs Anthony Newley sung so well, including 'What Kind of Fool Am I', and, like everyone else there that night had been close friends with Gayle in earlier years. Now Gayle was married to Simon Jenkins and time had moved on.

However, Bridget's suggestion that I should do some work for Entertainment Tonight meant that I would be moving back into that world and we cemented an agreement a few days later when she invited me round to the studios to meet her colleagues.

Bridget did not waste any time finding me an assignment. Back in London on 29th October I found myself being sent out to Canning Town down by the London Docks where an NBC TV series movie called *First Olympics* was being filmed. It starred Angela Lansbury, Jason Connery – Sean's son – and, could you believe it, Gayle Hunnicutt!

We both laughed when I told her what I was doing and that I would make her my first ET interview. I'm not sure whether I mentioned our past relationship to Deirdre Reilly, the ET producer who had flown over from London to help with the series of assignments Bridget had laid on, but the interview was conducted with great professionalism!

I found Jason Connery to be a bright and engaging young man who seemed to be handling the difficult task of making his own way in the business, while saddled with the Connery name, in his stride. His mother was Diane Cilento, the fine Australian actress who I had the pleasure of meeting later on.

It had been freezing down by the docks so a warming noggin was required by the time I met Carol at No. 10, where Peter Osnos of the Washington Post was also a guest that evening. After a late supper at Flood Street, I was off to Paris in the morning for my second ET assignment.

The movie was *American Dreamer* with Tom Conti and JoBeth Williams and the interiors were being shot, like virtually every other French movie you've ever seen, at the studios in Boulogne-Billancourt, less than a mile from Roland Garros. So, for me, it was easy to find, which was not quite the case the next day when Deirdre, our VisNews crew and I set out to find a village near Melun called Vaux le Visconte where location scenes were being shot at a splendid chateau.

Even back in those days, I realised that any interview I did was not going to get air time of more than a minute or two at best (now they would better be described as sound bites) so I was not about to subject my interviewees with too many deep and probing questions. My approach was to get them to relax so that they might come up with a few amusing anecdotes.

Tom Conti, the Scottish actor who had been nominated for an Academy Award for his role in *Reuben, Reuben* and JoBeth Williams both got the message and were charming. We got their interviews in the can and then stuck around until after lunch so that I could talk to the director Rick Rosenthal. And that meant more than an hour's hiatus at best. This was France and the crew were French. So you stopped for lunch. No grabbing a sandwich, either.

The food truck pulled up alongside the cloisters of the Chateaux and tables were unloaded, soon to be covered with red and white check table cloths. Then the first course of a meal prepared by a serious French chef was served; then the second and then the third. All washed down by bottles of red wine. If an American director had dared suggest that none of this should happen, there would have been a strike. The French have their priorities!

As the year drew to a close, I was having to juggle my priorities. For the first time in my life I started to think it might be nice to have a secretary! Apart from the wonderful Dominique during my time with the Evening News in Paris, I had never had anyone helping to manage my affairs but now with tournaments to cover in Stockholm, London and Melbourne; publishing *Tales from the Tennis Court*, an anthology of tennis writings I had put together at Sidgwick, and answering Bridget's requests for ET I needed to keep a close eye on my schedule of appointments. But I never got a secretary!

The week of 7th November 1983 starts to give the flavour of my life at the time. Having watched Mats Wilander beat Tomas Smid to win the Stockholm Open, I flew back to Gatwick, picked up a brand new Alfa Romeo rental, apparently paying no more than £105 for the week according to my diary, and drove straight to the Old Vic in the Waterloo Road to interview Tim

Rice on the occasion of the old theatre's re-opening. I did a couple of 'stand-ups' on the stage and then rushed over to a studio in Chelsea for editing. Got to bed at 2.00 am.

The Benson & Hedges tournament had started at Wembley's Empire pool by then so I spent time there as well as picking up books at Sidgwick's. The week included a Memorial Service at St Bride's in Fleet Street for David Gray, a dear friend who had died during the US Open that year. The former Guardian writer had finished his career as Secretary General of the ITF but, at heart, he was a journo, and it was fitting that, as members of the Lawn Tennis Writers Association, we all chipped in to pay for the lovely service. Lance Tingay of the Daily Telegraph read a fine tribute to one of the most skilled writers ever to have covered the game.

Somehow, in between commuting between Tregunter Road in Fulham and Wembley I managed to have dinners with Gabrielle Crawford and Heather MacLauchlan – one of many Heather and I used to enjoy around the world while she was working for IMG and then Ion Tiriac – and was back out at Wembley to see John McEnroe win the title for the 5th time in 6 years by beating Jimmy Connors in the final.

Monday the 14th saw a stark change of venue as I went in search of Marvin Hamlisch at the National Theatre on the banks of the Thames for ET. I found the great composer seated at a piano in the lobby, tinkling away at tunes like 'The Way We Were' and, of course, I encouraged him to continue so we could get it on film. The poor man seemed cold, having just flown in from California and he commented enviously on the big fake fur coat that I used to wear at the time. "I didn't come properly equipped for your English winters," he said.

The next day Bridget cancelled a proposed interview with Sir Peter Hall, Britain's leading theatre director who was in charge of the National at the time and that, at least, gave me more time to catch the Gulf Air flight to Bahrain where I would be joining Bjorn Borg and Vitas Gerulaitis on an exhibition tour of the Gulf States.

Once again, being where the action was, paid off when we reached Dubai. The promoter, Christopher Davies, son of the former head of Rank Films, greeted me with far greater warmth once someone told him I was a commentator. It transpired he was desperately looking for someone to handle the local broadcast and could I help him out? The match was due to be played in about six hours. Nothing like forward planning!

So I found myself sitting courtside, leading the broadcast with a lovely Iranian newsreader called Shahraz Petravan with the time at changeovers being filled by an Egyptian tennis coach sitting behind me and analysing proceedings in Arabic! I was never sure when he would stop talking but we managed to get through it somehow.

So Kipling might have described the previous ten days as how to fill '60 seconds worth of distance run' and I was quite pleased to be able to take a few days off in Spain before heading off Down Under by the end of the month.

The big movie in Australia in 1983 was *Phar Lap*, the inspiring story of the Aussie's greatest race horse and, continuing my ET assignments, I interviewed the young human, as opposed to equestrian, star of the movie, Tom Burlinson. *Phar Lap* was a hit – another Australian production called *Coolangatta Gold* less so, but we did not know that at the time so I headed up to Queensland to do some location filming on the Gold Coast.

The visuals, on beaches and sugar cane plantations, were gorgeous but that did not save the movie, despite the efforts of its lively and lovely PR person, Prue Ryan. We laugh now when we look back and remember conversations we had on the set about Prue knowing virtually nothing about tennis. It is funny because, after a spell at the historic Windsor Hotel in Melbourne, Prue took a job with Tennis Australia and has been a stalwart member of the team at Melbourne Park over the past decade. She is now a fund of information about Australian tennis and all the young players they hope will carry on the great tradition of Hoad and Rosewall, Newcome and Roche and Rafter and Hewitt amongst so many others.

Back in Europe, the ET requests kept coming and within a week at the start of February I had interviewed Hayley Mills, the drag artist Danny La Rue, Fanny Ardant in Paris, and Boy George. I also had dinner with Roman Polanski at a Parisian nightclub off the Champs Elysees. But no interview. He had fled the United States after being charged with under-age sex and did not want to talk to an American media outlet. The dinner was delicious, the company charming but the answer was no. He was one of the few people who ever turned me down.

By March I was in India, covering a Davis Cup tie between India and France in New Delhi which Yannick Noah and Henri Leconte nailed down for the French, their task made easier by the fact that Vijay Amritraj was not fit to play.

Bridget was delighted to hear that I was in India because, with perfect timing, David Lean had just started filming *A Passage to India* in Bangalore. So, to set myself on the way, I flew down to Madras, as it was called until changing its name to Chennai, and waited for a VizNews crew to join me a couple of days later. It was fun being shown around this hot, teeming city by Vijay who took me to Higginbotham's bookshop amongst other places.

Higginbotham's is irresistible to any book lover, steeped in history; musty and slightly chaotic with salesmen clambering up ladders to find old volumes high above your head. Kipling shopped there. Now you could buy his work and feel his ghost.

Later, I took a walk by myself down TTK Road, which stretches for miles through the heart of the city. Humanity and animal life was everywhere; mothers cooking, children playing; old men pushing their ox carts; cows wandering. People lived, ate, made love and died cheek by jowl and they were all far too busy to take any notice of me. No one begged. It was not a tourist area. And I felt far safer than I had walking down the side streets of Manhattan a few weeks before.

The poverty was shocking, of course and, like any first-time visitor to this extraordinary country (this was before I returned to write the book with Vijay) I was appalled by the conditions in which so many millions lived. And the contrasts were incongruous. All along TTK Road, the endless rows of shacks were frequently interspersed with modern structures selling cooking utensils or even televisions. There was business going on but the profits did not go far.

When the crew arrived – Japsid Kapoor and his assistant Singh – Vijay took us onto the set of a Bollywood movie that was being shot. It was a scrum because, apart from being well known as a tennis star, Vijay had achieved even greater fame the previous year when he had played a prominent part in the James Bond movie *Octopussy* with Roger Moore. Once he had signed a sufficient number of autographs, we were allowed inside a caravan to interview Hema Malin, a beautiful actress who was charming in a regal sort of way.

Making space outside the somewhat scruffy looking entrance to the studios, I began my stand-up piece with: "Although the similarity may escape you, this is India's answer to Hollywood."

There was, indeed, little resemblance to Paramount or MGM but, Madras, to be fair, was not the real heart of the Indian movie industry. The 'B' for Bollywood stood for the fact that most of the action was based in Bombay, now called Mumbai. It was there that Indian producers churned out the glamorous, wildly imaginative offerings that entranced Indian audiences. And they did so at a rate, and at a cost, that was making Hollywood producers drool with envy.

I don't have figures for 1983 but twenty years later, when the ratios would not have changed much despite soaring costs, a Bollywood production cost an average of $1.5 million as against $47.7 million for a film made in Hollywood. And there were 1000 produced a year in India – twice as many as in Los Angeles.

But the man I was heading up to the elevated and lovely city of Bangalore to interview had nothing to with Bollywood. Despite a career that had lain dormant for fourteen years, David Lean was established as one of the greatest directors the British film industry, or indeed Hollywood, had ever known. From black and white beginnings during World War Two with *In Which We Serve* and then *Brief Encounter* and the movie that scared me so much as a child, *Great Expectations*, Lean burst into widescreen colour with his Oscar winning epics *Bridge on the River Kwai* and *Lawrence of Arabia*. *Dr Zhivago* followed, and that trio alone elevated Lean into the pantheon of those great directors who could tell deeply personal stories against the backdrop of breathtaking panoramas as he put advanced cinematographic technology to its greatest use. Many critics, in fact, would put Lean top of the list.

The making of *A Passage to India* had not, of course, been straightforward. Film rights to E.M. Forster's classic novel, set in India in the early part of the 20th century, had been much sought after before Lord Brabourne, whose father had been Governor of Bengal, bought them and asked Santha Rama Rau to write it. Lean, who had been so dejected by the critical reaction to his last film, *Ryan's Daughter*, that he had virtually retired, was persuaded to take on the task of directing a story that had so much cinematic potential.

But Lean did not like Rau's stifling script, which read more like a play for the theatre and, after spending some months in New Delhi to get a taste of the country, he settled in Zurich to re-write large parts of it, typing out the screenplay himself.

"The very mention of India conjures up high expectations," said Lean at the time. "It has sweep and size and is very romantic."

The quote encapsulates David Lean's whole approached to film making – sweep, size and romance. High expectations, indeed, or, in the eye of the movie going public, great expectations. And, of course he delivered. *A Passage to India* won Lean still more acclaim, including the New York Film Critics Award for Best Director.

Much of the filming in Bangalore was taking place at the slightly decayed Bangalore Palace, built as a model of Windsor Castle. However the Maharaja did not, apparently, have the financial resources of The Queen and whole place needed a lick of paint. Lean was not going to provide that. He wanted atmosphere.

The extent to which he would go to get it became apparent when we eventually got to see him at the West End Hotel, where other important scenes were shot by a pond in the lush tropical gardens. Despite receiving a very warm welcome from one of the producers, Richard Goodwin, who was a good friend of Bridget Byrne's, the PR people appeared somewhat nervous about the whole thing.

"He's very busy, you know," I was told somewhat needlessly. "And he's not a young man any more!"

Lean had put his age to good use when successfully persuading the great British actress Peggy Ashcroft to take on the important role of Mrs Moore. She had been reluctant.

"Oh, David, it's a very big part and I am 75, you know," she said plaintively.

"So am I," Lean shot back. End of that argument.

By chance, Miss Ashcroft was the very first person I saw on entering the lobby of the West End Hotel. For those of us, which meant half of Britain, who had been watching the TV series *Jewel in the Crown* which was also set in India, one's reaction was, "Well, of course she's here. Where else would she be?"

So we were put on hold but I didn't sit about kicking my heels. I interviewed Victor Banerjee, the Indian star of the movie, who appeared quite nervous about the whole thing, and had a quick word with James Fox. Judy Davis, the Australian actress who was the female lead, flatly refused. Nothing personal, I was told. She just hated the media and refused all interviews. She may have had good reason to hate the media but if you work in a profession that depends on the public buying tickets to watch you, there are certain professional requirements that go with the job. She really should have listened to her director who was about to give us a master class in the subject.

The next day, word came through that David Lean would see us. Everyone still seemed to be holding their breath but the great man greeted me warmly when we got down to the little summer house by the pond. Running my eyes quickly over the scene, it appeared that the door leading to the pond was being taken off its hinges so that it could open the opposite way. James Fox had said it was too awkward to say his lines when he first tried it. So the carpenters were called in.

Earlier, the painters had been there, draining the pond so they could paint the bottom black before refilling it. Lean had wanted the mysteriously curled branches of the ancient tree standing next to the pond to reflect more sharply off black water. I was beginning to understand what was meant by his craving for detail.

We chatted very briefly while his assistant cameraman took a shot of Alec Guinness, who was playing the Indian, Professor Godbole, walking down the side of the pond. No dialogue was required. It was just a filler shot.

Suddenly, Lean interjected. "Er, just a minute Alec. I wonder if you would be kind enough to do that once more?" Guinness, who had made five films with Lean, gave him that look of mild surprise that we have come to know so well on the screen and, with a small shrug, turned and walked back to his mark.

In the meantime Lean had dismissed his cameraman and, after positioning my crew behind him, had gone behind the camera himself. So as the great actor walked down the side of the pond, we had Alec Guinness being filmed by David Lean. Just for us.

"Will that be OK for you?" he asked, knowing full well that Entertainment Tonight couldn't have asked for anything better.

"Perfect," I replied. "Thank you so much."

As we made our way back through the hibiscus and frangipani, I muttered to Japsid and Singh, "Isn't it wonderful to deal with a professional?"

And I meant it. No fuss. No bother. Lean knew what we wanted and, wasting the minimum amount of time, delivered it. I do love pros.

Back in England, I found ET still taking up a good deal of my time. I drove down to Salisbury Plain where a version of *The Wizard of Oz* was being filmed and did interviews with Piper Laurie and Jean Marsh. Both were charming but also a little nervous. "Oh, thank you for not asking nasty questions," Miss Marsh said afterwards. "My stomach just churns in knots when they do that."

Her reaction gave me an insight into how people view being interviewed with a certain dread. But I was not trying to be Jeremy Paxman. The more one could put people at ease, the more likely you were to get an amusing soundbite and that's all ET were after.

On 20th March 1984, I broke my record by getting four interviews in the can in one day. With my faithful cameraman Pat Lett in tow, we drove out to Pinewood Studios in the morning to talk to Bruce Beresford who was directing *King David* and then dashed back to the Royal Albert Hall to interview to Red Skelton who was full of jokes as one would expect.

I had arranged to meet Christopher Reeve at the Theatre Royal in the Haymarket at 6.00 pm where he was appearing in *The Aspern Papers* by Henry James. We met in the manager's office, which was a virtual museum of all the great plays that had been performed there during the previous 264 years of the theatre's existence.

To my surprise, Reeve walked in accompanied by Vanessa Redgrave. 'Superman', in the days before his tragic accident which left him paralysed, cut an imposing figure and, in a kind but very firm way, he seemed to be in charge of Vanessa. I have no idea what their relationship was but I got the impression he had persuaded her to do the interview, which I had not asked for, and virtually directed her through the proceedings. I wish I had a transcript of our talk but one would have to delve into the Paramount vault to find it now.

Vanessa, like so many actresses I interviewed, came across as shy, nervous and vulnerable, so unlike the commanding presence she offers on screen or stage. Reeve, articulate and extremely bright, had some interesting things to say about the differences between acting in the theatre as opposed to film and I just wished ET had given more of it airtime.

The next day, I was at the Apollo Theatre in Victoria where Andrew Lloyd Webber was preparing *Starlight Express* and he too was charming in a vague sort of way. My great friend Keith Turner was his lawyer around that time and we had met before. But Andrew showed no sign of remembering. His focus was on the upcoming production which required ripping out sections of the Circle to install the runway for the train that was all part of the extravaganza. His contribution to the musical genre over the past several decades has been astonishing.

By 26th March, I was back in Paris to interview Anthony Hopkins, who was making *Arch of Triumph* about the Nazi Occupation with Donald Pleasance who, inevitably given his talent for portraying sinister characters, was playing the Nazi. Waris Hussein was directing and gave me an interview that was far too intellectually stimulating for ET. The female lead was being played by the lovely Lesley Ann Down and I joined them all on a freezing

Parisian night for some supper in the warmth of the crew mess tent, set up on the banks of the Seine.

In June I broke with tradition and left London during the Queen's Club tournament. The reason, I felt, justified it. I was going to interview Sophia Loren. Thanks to her being such a gracious lady, it all went off well although she had every reason to be annoyed because I was late. I was half an hour late. To say I was mortified was putting it mildly. I am never late. In fact, I sometimes annoy myself by being so hopelessly punctual. It stems, I think, from working on the Evening Standard at such a young age. With nine editions during the day, you always had your eye on the clock. It was no good providing copy at 10.59 because the edition had closed at 10.55. Missing an edition was a sin.

The sin I committed with Sophia Loren was, unhappily, far from romantic. I was late because we had driven out into the hills in the morning to interview Jane Birkin's brother, Andrew Birkin, who was the writer on the aforementioned *King David*. Richard Gere was the star but for reasons I forget, we could not get him. We hung around too long in the hope of grabbing other members of the cast and misjudged the time it would take to get back into the centre of Rome in the afternoon rush hour.

Miss Loren was filming on a street in Parioli and the interview was to be conducted in her caravan. I found her inside, perched on a corner couch, looking absolutely ravishing in a beige mohair cardigan. Being the consummate actress she is, there was no hint of annoyance in the dazzling smile I was offered as I spluttered out some inane apology. As I had noted all those years before at the gala in New York, she is, as the Americans might say, one classy lady.

The movie was an Italian production called *Aurora* and her 11-year-old son, Carlo Ponti Jnr, was in it, acting with her. She talked about how much fun that was for both of them. Although insisting that the relationship was completely professional on the set, she admitted to being overcome, on occasion, by waves of motherly pride. When we had finished, she gave me another of those Loren smiles that never quite fade from the memory.

So it was back to London to watch John McEnroe sweep all before him at Wimbledon and then off to Paris again, this time to interview Ian Charleson who was filming a segment of the mini-series, *Oxbridge Blues*, at Versailles. I had talked to Hugh Hudson, the director of *Chariots of Fire* in London a few weeks earlier and, of course, it was in the role of the religious Scottish runner

Eric Liddell that Charleson had produced his best remembered performance.

It was a tragedy that Charleson died just six years later of AIDS, working up to the end in no less demanding a role than Hamlet. He was one of Britain's finest actors and a delightful man.

By the skin of my teeth I managed not to be late for the next interview which was just as well. It was Richard Burton. He was filming the mini-series *Ellis Island* at the country estate Luton Hoo, which is just over an hour's drive north of London. As the appointment was for early afternoon, I thought I had time for a haircut at Michaeljohn in Mayfair. The haircut was fine but a problem presented itself when I left the salon. My car had been clamped.

In a controlled state of panic, I grabbed a cab and told him to drive the short distance to that vast parking lot which sits in a murky dungeon under Hyde Park and tried to get through the expensive formalities as soon as possible. Trying to hurry them along with protestations about being late for Richard Burton would not have helped. The coppers down there have heard more fanciful tales than that.

So, on Wednesday 18th July, I just about made it up to Luton Hoo and received a pleasant welcome from the famous Welshman whom I had only seen once before off stage (his performance in *Equus* remains one of the greatest I have seen in the theatre). That had occurred in the incongruous setting, one dark and rainy night, at Abertillery Rugby Club several years before. Burton had been brought up in nearby Port Talbot and members of the family still lived there. He had also been a fine rugby player before he was told to stop risking his looks when Hollywood beckoned.

So he had wanted to see his old club play and, of course, he brought his wife along. Why not? Except that the boyos in the bar were not used to having Elizabeth Taylor down a pint or two at their elbow after the match – which she did with relish.

Now, on a contrastingly warm summer's day outside Luton, I had to decide where to place him for the interview. There was an empty field right next to the main house so I nabbed one of those canvas director's chairs that were lying around near the TV trucks and, walking out into the middle of the field, sat him down in it.

I made sure he was comfortable because I knew he had been ill, although he looked fine and showed no sign of what lay ahead. He told me that he had only taken the part because Kate Burton, the daughter he had with his first wife, Sybil, was in it and had always wanted to act with him. In that baritone voice that, I hope, is being used as an example of perfect diction in every acting class at RADA, he started telling me tales. (How appropriate that Burton's first ever leading role in a school play was that of Professor Higgins in *Pygmalion*.)

One story concerned him returning from watching Wales lose to England at Cardiff Arms Park and how he had drowned his sorrows on the train all the way back to London.

"So, I get off at Paddington, you see, and this English bloke starts having a go at me over Wales losing the match as we walk down the platform. So I gave him one. Went down like a log."

I tried to give him an out by suggesting the man must have been to blame for riling him. "No, no," he replied with a little smile. "It was all my fault. I started it. I was pissed."

I never saw Richard Burton and Richard Harris drinking together but, my goodness, they must have been quite a pair after a few in the pub.

I was pleased with the interview, for the content as well as the way he looked, sitting in the field, and we parted with him giving me re-assurances concerning his health. "I'm feeling fine, old boy!"

I was back at Luton Hoo the next day because Terry O'Neill, the celebrity photographer who had been part of Doug Hayward's set, had arranged for me to cut through the red tape and arrange an interview with Faye Dunaway who was also in the film. He could get it done because, at the time, he was her husband.

"She's scared to death of doing interviews but I said you will be gentle with her," Terry told me. I assured him I would because, as you have seen, Faye was not the first nervous interviewee I had had to deal with.

She talked about the part and what it was like working with Richard and, afterwards, thanked me, saying, "Oh, that really wasn't so bad at all."

Do most interviewers behave as if they are conducting the Nuremberg Trials? Or am I just a pussycat? All that mattered, as far as I was concerned, was that Bridget and her colleagues in LA liked what they were getting.

I flew down to Malaga a few days later and was having a drink with Lew Hoad at the bar of his club near Mijas when he said, "Have you heard? Richard Burton died yesterday."

It was just nineteen days since I had said goodbye to him at Luton. He had returned to his home in Switzerland and had suffered a brain haemorrhage. So I have the unwanted distinction of being the last person to interview one of the giants of screen and stage who had chased the glamour and glitter of Hollywood while never forgetting his roots in south Wales.

As it turned out, I did little for ET after that. There were changes amongst the hierarchy at Paramount and the programme was losing any pretence at being a news outlet. There was a limit to how much mindless gossip and PR puffs Bridget could tolerate and, inevitably, given her outspoken nature, there came a parting of the ways.

For me, it had been quite a ride. I had met some fascinating, creative and charming people while making a bit of money on the side. It was, in fact, about the only time in my life when I had been able to accumulate a little surplus cash so I went down to Andalucia and bought some property. Unexpectedly, Spain became a focal part of my life for several years.

Chapter 23
LEW HOAD IN SPAIN

Before Roger Federer came along to grace the world's courts, I always felt Lew Hoad was the best tennis player I had ever seen. He was certainly one of the strongest and so blessed with power and skill that, occasionally, it became a handicap.

One night, after a beer or two at the bar of his club near Mijas, he admitted, "Yeah, mate, I did get confused sometimes, not knowing which shot to hit, because I had a few too many options!"

The plight of the super talented! Such was the strength in his wrist and forearm that he used to cut an inch off the end of his racket handle so he could wield his Dunlop more like a table tennis bat. Lew won Wimbledon twice, in 1955-56. In 1955, he won the first three Slams, and was two sets away from completing the Grand Slam when he won the first set off his old mucker Ken Rosewall in the final at Forest Hills before losing in four. Had he concentrated a bit harder, he could have joined Don Budge in an exclusive club of two – before Rod Laver came along.

I first met Lew when everyone was gathering at Marble Arch for a cricket match between the players and the press in the early sixties. Hoad was banned from playing Wimbledon because he had turned pro with Jack Kramer and was just hanging around London seeing some mates and having some fun. But, with his blond good looks and superb physique, he was still one of the most recognised sporting stars in the world. But he was never one to make much of that.

"Hello, my name's Lew Hoad," he said, grasping my hand. It was one of those moments when you want to reply with something silly like, "You don't say!" but the way he said it precluded that. He just honestly believed you might not know who he was.

Hoadie, as his Aussie mates called him, was a straightforward, no bullshit Sydneysider from humble origins who, like so many of his countrymen, took you at face value and expected you to play the game straight, be the game tennis, cricket or life. As I came to realise later, he was a great bloke to have as a friend.

Hoad was plagued with back problems for the latter part of his career and by 1966, he was looking for something else to do. However, there was still a stigma concerning the word 'professional' in Australia and the tennis authorities seemed scandalously uninterested in making use of this great champion's talent. So eventually Lew looked elsewhere.

His wife Jenny, whom he had married at St Mary's Church on the hill above Wimbledon in 1956, was enjoying a holiday at Torremolinos on the still unspoiled Costa del Sol that year while her husband played a series of tournaments with the Kramer tour in South Africa.

A friend mentioned that there was a piece of land a few miles up the coast that might be for sale. When Jenny found it, she immediately cabled Lew to say 'Come and have a look!'

You had to turn down a donkey track off the winding road up to Mijas to get to the property which consisted of a whitewashed farmhouse perched on sloping ground, surrounded by a few acres of olive trees and terraced plantings of potatoes and onions which the owners sold in the local market.

It required a special vision to see how one could turn the place into a tennis club but the Hoads did precisely that. With Lew often driving the earth-mover himself, they created a little paradise with six courts, one of which was carved out as an amphitheatre. There were ponds with water lilies and frogs and a huge variety of plants, many of which had never been seen in Europe before.

That was because an old friend, Alan Watt, who had decided to change his life by giving up a desk job in Sydney to join in this audacious project, had smuggled in plants from Australia and China in the back of the car he had bought on arriving in Rome. Within a year, palm trees had been planted and the orchids and jacaranda were blooming. The beauty of the Campo de Tenis Lew Hoad, as it became known, was, in no small measure, due to the gardening talents of Alan Watt.

News of all this had seeped onto the tennis circuit and whenever I ran into the Hoads at tournaments they were telling me to 'come on down'. For various reasons, it took me a long time to do so but, finally, in 1981, I took a plane to Malaga and it changed my life. The place was as lovely as people had been telling me and when I noticed that an apartment complex was being built at the bottom of the hill leading up to the clubhouse, I thought, "Why not?" and bought one that was still not finished.

And that was not the end of it. After a few days, Lew said, "We're going up to Castellar – want to come?" El Castillo de Castellar de la Frontera is a 13th century Moorish fortress situated high above Sotogrande near Gibraltar. Lew Hoad had told me about it in Paris a few months earlier.

"Bloody spectacular! Couldn't resist it, mate." When we got there, you could see why. The castle was reached by turning off the main road at the Hotel Sotogrande, driving past the famous Valderrama Golf Course and then, through the cork trees, up into the mountains for twenty minutes. Once there, you could stand on the battlements and look out over Andalucia, across the great Rock of Gibraltar and, on a clear day, all the way to the Riff Mountains in Morocco. The thought of the commercialised and increasingly garish Costa del Sol being only half an hour away was ridiculous. This was a completely different world. In the early eighties, there was no phone connection, no restaurant and no Guardia. We were a self-policed community which did not stop petty thieving but, otherwise, seemed to work despite the dubious characters – partially re-habilitated hippies from the old Moroccan drug trade – living in self-built dwellings outside the walls.

The entrance to Castellar, through the King's Gate, was too narrow for motor cars so there was no fear of being run over as you meandered through the four little cobble-stoned streets. The interior consisted of about 70 small two-storey houses, most of which were deserted at that time because only a few years earlier, the population, which was growing too big for the place, was moved down the mountain to a sterile new village.

A few bold foreigners like the Hoads had seen the amazing possibilities on offer and bought some houses. Lew and Jenny had taken three and moulded them to fit round a little courtyard. With Jenny's artistic flair to the fore, the place looked fantastic.

Immediately next to the Hoads, there were two houses which, I discovered, were for sale. For £20,000. Done. Suddenly, I seemed to be a property owner in southern Spain! Of course, both houses needed a huge amount of work (the smallest one had been home to colony of bats) and I could never have got it done without the incredibly generous help of an English couple, Terry and Kate Leahy, who lived round the corner.

Kate led me through all stupefying Spanish bureaucracy required for an ex-pat to buy property from a Spaniard while Terry not only found me a wonderful four-man team of builders but joined in the work himself. Cutting a very long story short, I was installed in my apartment at the Campo de Tenis by 1984 and the houses at Castellar were habitable the following year.

So Spain became my 'go-to' bolt hole in between charging around the world covering tournaments for various clients like the Times, the Melbourne Age and BBC Radio. I seemed to have managed about four trips a year, staying as long as three weeks at a time on occasion. Castellar, especially in winter sitting in front of my roaring fire, proved to be a wonderful place to write on my electric Canon typewriter – a major technological advance from my old manual Lettera 22! – or just to catch up on some reading.

I waded through Andre Gide's autobiography, switching occasionally to an Andre Brink novel; Kundera's *The Incredible Lightness of Being* or *The Art of Captaincy* by Mike Brearley, one of England most astute cricket captains.

It provided a great change of pace and a lot of the time I was on my own. Lonely? Up to a point, but I also spent some memorable weeks when friends visited. I enjoyed showing the castle to my old prep school pal Nick Evans; Charlie Wilson who was editor of the Times during that period; Balasz Taroczy, the Hungarian Wimbledon doubles champion and Gordon and Frances Forbes from South Africa. Kate Lee also came as did, a little later, her novelist son Jeffrey Lee and his friend Hassan Amini with whom he was making a film.

And then there were my friends from Jamaica. Alison Lopez came for an extended stay in the summer of 1984 and the following year Castellar was introduced to reggae and much laughter when those beautiful sisters, Nancy and Virginia Burke, and our friend Andrea Hutchinson all came at once. Sleeping arrangements were cramped but we managed! For some reason, Maxine Walters, who was the big mover and shaker of the Jamaican set, never made it, probably because she was too busy finding locations for TV commercials and documentaries all over Jamaica. Somehow, Maxine had found time to have a daughter, Chloe, and I was honoured to become her Godfather. It has been one of the joys of my life that we have all remained lifelong friends.

Stan Reilly, with his partner Nikki Stolee, were also visitors – and with good reason. Stan wanted to buy Sotogrande, lock, stock and barrel. Stan, a small robust Irish-American with an impish smile, was one of those people whose expansive imagination and ambition struggled to keep up with reality. The Sotogrande project never worked but Reilly came agonisingly close to pulling off a building coup that might have brought the Olympic Games to London sooner than 2012.

In the mid-eighties, Reilly pulled together a consortium consisting of Laing Construction; a Dutch company, and Doug Fox, chairman of The Tulsa Tribune in Oklahoma, with a view to building a 23,000 seat, state-of-the-art indoor stadium in the London docks. I joined them as a consultant to work on the project and it was fascinating.

With offices in Dover Street in Mayfair, we beavered away for over two years, working with Reg Ward at the London Docklands Development Corporation to try and add to what the LDDC was already helping to create – Canary Wharf, Surrey Quays shopping centre and London City Airport among other vast projects.

Driven by Stan's gung-ho optimism, the London Dome project, which was to be situated on Victoria Dock, came within £10 million pounds of succeeding. Reilly's consortium had secured £90 million of the £100 million required and pleaded with the Government to meet the gap. It refused. The LDDC itself was wound up in 1998 but, by then, it had transformed east London, creating some 120,000 jobs in the process. There could have been more. Stan Reilly was a special guy who deserved better.

Back in Spain, I played a lot of tennis at the Hotel Sotogrande down the hill and also at the Hotel Puente Romana in Marbella, where the tennis club was being run by Manolo Santana. Thanks to Manolo's ever welcoming hospitality I was able to use the club as a staging post between Castellar and the Camp de Tennis which, in those days before the highway was built, took a little over two hours. Having an occasional hit with the great Wimbledon champion himself was an extra bonus.

Life at the Campo de Tenis moved at a different pace to Castellar. Although the club always struggled to make money, Lew's reputation had ensured that he had some income from coaching as well as proceeds from the excellent restaurant, not to mention the bar.

In the early days during the seventies when the Marbella Club was attracting the smart set, numerous people from the acting world dropped by to hit a few balls or just drink on the shaded terrace. Sean Connery was living on the coast in those days and the Hoads were also friends with Peter Ustinov, a tennis fanatic, Richard Burton, Deborah Kerr, Stewart Granger and Ava Gardner.

The great saxophone player Stan Getz became a good friend, too, and after staying a few days with his Swedish wife and nine-year-old son Nicky, he asked if he might leave Nicky behind for a couple of weeks while he went off to play some gigs in Scandanavia. There were three young Hoads running around at the time and they all got along famously; so Lew said, of course.

All of nine months later, Stan Getz turned up out of the blue and, without explanation, whipped Nicky off the airport. You never know with musicians.

Financially, the Hoads survived largely by selling off parcels of land around the club on which people built villas. But Lew also landed a couple of jobs, one as coach at the nearby Los Monteros Hotel and, more importantly, as coach to the Spanish Davis Cup team. Apart from Santana, the talented left-hander Manolo Orantes became an admiring pupil of Lew's and both credit the Australian with having a major influence on the development of Spanish tennis. Rafael Nadal would have loved him.

The early days had been tough and during the opening months of the club's existence, Lew's only pupil was an English teenager called Ashley Compton Dando. He had talent but also a handicap. Hard of hearing, he could not hear the sound of the ball on the strings. Lew decided the best way to coach him was to stuff his own ears with cotton wool so that he could understand the game the way Ashley needed to. The gesture took empathy in coaching to a new level.

I could fill pages with the fun times and the people I met in Spain but it was in Perth, during the Hopman Cup in 1994 that I knew there was a very dark cloud on the horizon. Lew had been invited by Paul McNamee and Charlie Fancutt, the originators of the Hopman Cup, to visit the tournament and, after we had finished playing in a Pro-Am, I took a picture of Lew. When I had it developed, I found myself looking at a dying man. It was as if he had no blood in his veins. The photo was shockingly accurate and revealing. Ten days later at the Australian Open, Charlie's mother, Daphne Fancutt, told me Lew had undergone tests at a hospital in Adelaide and that the results weren't good.

We all hoped for the best but, agonisingly, Manolo Benavides, who was married to the Hoad's youngest daughter Sally, knew that hope did not exist. Benavides was a doctor specialising in leukaemia. As soon as he saw the medical report, he knew that it would be only a matter of months. Lew was suffering from a strain of the disease for which there was no cure. Poor Manolo had to drip feed this knowledge gently to the family over the following months, trying to prepare them as best as possible for the worst.

By the time Wimbledon came round six months later, Lew was starting to have bad nosebleeds and was no longer able to walk up the hill from their house to the club. Paul McNamee suggested the idea of a celebrity tournament at the club to help raise some money for medical care and the response, unsurprisingly, was enthusiastic. The tournament took place but Lew wasn't there.

On the 3rd July 1994, Lew watched the women's final at Wimbledon on television and correctly predicted Conchita Martinez's shock victory over the great Martina Navratilova. "Conchita has the ability to chop and change her shots and vary the pace," he told Jenny. "She won't let Martina find her rhythm."

The next morning, as Pete Sampras was preparing to play Goran Ivanisevic in the final, Lew, ashen-faced, was barely able to get out of bed. Frantic messages were sent to Manolo and Sally who were on the beach and, with much difficulty, the family managed to get Lew into the car and drive him to the hospital. He died within a few hours.

The tournament became a Memorial event for Lew Hoad just a few days later. Full of laughter and tears, I think it did justice to the man who had meant so much to all of us, and Lew would have loved the standard of tennis served up by Paul McNamee and Peter McNamara, Fred Stolle, Manolo Santana, Manolo Orantes, Roger Taylor, Buster Mottram, Bob Carmichael as well as Ken Rosewall, Lew's 'twin' who sadly, was making his first ever visit to the club. Tony Trabert, Lew's great Davis Cup rival and life-long friend, flew in from London, Butch Buchholz arrived from Miami and then Rod Laver appeared.

Laver only got the news when he stepped off the plane at Los Angeles from London. Buying a new ticket, he flew straight back to Spain. The gesture told you all you needed to know about what Lew meant to Rod.

I was asked to be the Master of Ceremonies and introduce the matches on the crowded terraced court. "We are here to honour a great friend but we have arrived a little late," I remember saying. "I think Lew will forgive us."

Jenny and the kids, Jane, Peter and Sally, held up very well and, somehow, we managed to have a good time. Just the way Hoadie would have wanted it.

Chapter 24
LYNN & ASHLEY

It was the way she wore her blue beret that made me take a second look. It was more than that, of course – the dark hair, strikingly attractive features, the posture, the way she walked and bore herself. But the angle of the beret added a certain something and the second glance led to the love of my life.

We were in Moscow in 1993, milling around in the cavernous indoor Olympic Stadium where my friend and Tennis Week publisher Gene Scott had agreed to take on the daunting task of running the Kremlin Cup – a new tournament on the ATP Tour.

The story of how I met and eventually married this New Jersey girl called Lynn Zanconato takes a circuitous path of irony and fate and has much to do with a man, Pierre Darmon, who had twice been instrumental in my leaving the ATP. So allow me to backtrack.

Towards the end of the 1980s another revolution was brewing in men's professional tennis. The player reps on the Pro Council were becoming totally frustrated with having to deal with the ITF and, led by Ray Moore and Harold Solomon, set in motion the eventual breakaway move that led to a new entity, The ATP Tour, which consisted of just players and tournament directors.

All that needs a book in itself and I am not going to write it here, other than to weave in critical factors that impacted so hugely on my own life. It began with Moore and Solomon making an audacious stab at getting a very high profile figure to become the new organisation's first CEO.

The man they went for, and somewhat surprisingly, secured, was Hamilton Jordan, President Jimmy Carter's former White House Chief of Staff. The world soon got to know about it because Jordan did not take long to make the most of his political savvy by making the USTA look a little foolish.

During the 1989 US Open, Hamilton wanted to hold a press conference to announce the formation of the new ATP Tour and asked if he could hold it on site in the Media Centre. Miffed at being associated with the ITF, the group which had just been cut out of the new order, someone who wasn't as smart as Jordan said no.

The old pro's eyes lit up. "Then we'll hold it in the parking lot!" he said mischievously. So, having acquired a lectern which was strategically placed right in front of the main gates at the subsequently named Billie Jean King Tennis Center, Hamilton Jordan and a group of leading players called in the media and made the historic announcement with every piece of symbolism clear for all to see. The players were in charge.

I had been getting a little tired of the hand-to-mouth existence of travelling the world and picking up work as I went along, and I let it be known that I would be interested in re-joining the ATP. That led to a strange meeting held at the Waldorf Astoria in New York between myself, Jordan, Moore and the other candidate for the job of European director, Colin Dowdeswell, the former British No. 1 who had been busy assembling staff in readiness for the opening of the new ATP Tour European headquarters in Monaco.

I call the meeting strange because, for about ten minutes, I was given reason to believe I was going to run Europe again, as I had done back in the 1970s. Jordan was obviously not sure of which call to make – he had met Dowdeswell but barely knew me – and suggested that we both take the job as joint CEOs.

Dowdeswell, a charming, soft-spoken and very bright man who had worked for Merrill Lynch following his retirement from the tour, suddenly became very decisive and refused point blank. "Joint leadership is always a disaster," he said.

I tended to agree with him but, as I liked Colin personally and felt that our very similar backgrounds would automatically remove some potential conflicts, I said I was happy to go along with whatever Jordan decided.

At that point Franco Bartoni burst into the room, demanding to know what the decision was because, down the hall, he had a roomful of European Tournament Directors and wanted to give them a definitive answer. Bartoni, an Italian who had been a Supervisor on the tour before being elected to represent the European tournaments, put the question to Jordan, heard the story and then said, "Right, Richard – he has agreed whatever the conditions; Colin, he has not, so Richard is European Director!"

Bartoni, no particular friend of mine, just wanted a solution. Jordan held his ground and was non-committal and remained so until the end of an indecisive meeting. Bartoni was frustrated and I was left uncertain of what the final decision would be.

A couple of days later Moore told me Jordan had decided on Dowdeswell. But not all was lost. Fast forward several months and Jordan had quit – arguing with tennis players rather than Heads of State had finally got him down – and Mark Miles, a promoter from Indianapolis who had run the Pan American Games, had been appointed in his place.

Miles took me to dinner at a little place in the Trastevere in Rome during the Italian Open and offered me the job of Communications for Europe. But there was catch. He had fired Dowdeswell and appointed Pierre Darmon to run Europe from Monaco.

I immediately told Mark that Pierre and I 'had previous' to use a Cockney term, and that it had not ended well. I was assured Darmon had no problem with the idea of working with me again so, against my better judgement, I accepted.

The salary wasn't great but gaining Monaco residency as a result of being employed in the Principality offered a huge bonus. I paid no taxes. People who are put off by a collection of millionaires living cheek by jowl in a tax-free paradise on the shores of the Mediterranean understandably have an ambivalent view towards Monte Carlo, but I discovered it was easy to live a normal life away from the glitzier part of town. I found a flat with an enormous roof terrace in Fontvieille, an area which had been re-claimed from the sea barely a decade before, and settled into a new existence which, of course, continued to include virtually non-stop travel.

The fact that Prince Albert was a tennis fan made all our lives easier at the ATP and, in his low-key, charming way, he invited me to lunch at the Yacht Club by way of a welcome to the Principality he would run after his father, Prince Rainier, died several years later

I inherited a young and energetic team of Communication Managers – Anna Legnani, Meg Donovan, George Rubenstein, Lauren Goldenberg and Pidge Hutton. Later, we hired a charming young French lady called Patricia Jolly and at least one of this group were to be found handling press conferences and all media matters at all the ATP tournaments Europe.

Although Pierre Darmon continued to view me with suspicion, we might have made it work had it not been for Mark Miles appointing a former New Times correspondent called Peter Alfano to replace Jay Beck, a very pleasant and experienced PR man, as Communications Director for North America which, in effect, meant he was my boss. Not only was Alfano a disastrous choice but Miles had not uttered a word to me before making the appointment.

I heard, from many colleagues, that Alfano had admitted to not liking tennis even as he wrote about it for the New York Times (poor Alison Danzig, one of his illustrious predecessors, must have turned in his grave). Yet he was going to have to espouse the glories of the sport to many former colleagues who knew the depth of his ambivalence, if not hypocrisy.

I knew there would be a problem when he called me from the ATP offices in Ponte Vedra, Florida to establish communication between us. Instead of asking a few questions and having an exchange of ideas, he proceeded to spend precisely one half hour unloading everything he knew about tennis in a non-stop monologue. It was extraordinary. Was he trying to impress me? How? By telling everything he knew I knew?

Needless to say, our relationship was strained from the start and when Byron Quann, an affable executive from IBM, arrived to head up the entire department, he and Alfano, finding no resistance from Darmon, basically ganged up on me. The details of the arguments that blew up between Darmon and myself were trivial in retrospect but I think I made both of them nervous and Quann was persuaded to fire me.

Mark Miles, who had stayed out of it, took me to lunch the next day and said he was sorry but what was he to do? Fire three of his top men so he could keep me? I could see his point.

It had been fun while it had lasted and I especially enjoyed helping to run the new ATP World Tour Finals – previously called the Masters during its lengthy stay at Madison Square Garden – in its new setting at the lovely Festhalle in Frankfurt.

Apart from my own hardworking staff, there were some good people in the Monte Carlo office as well and I particularly enjoyed the company of Russell Barlow, a multi-lingual Australian and former tour player, who had a very sharp brain and was as frustrated as I was at too many decisions concerning Europe being taken with very little consultation from across the Atlantic. Russell was very amusing company but Miles did not always see the funny side of Barlow and he left of his own accord soon after me and returned to Australia. He was a loss to the European game.

Happily, I did not have to move out of Monaco and so reverted to my previous life – picking up old contacts and becoming a freelancer again. As I have noted, helping to form Tennis Radio Network a few years later was an important step and I found myself drawn ever further into the fabric of this wonderful sport when I was invited to join the nominating committee for the International Hall of Fame.

The group of some twenty people who meet at Wimbledon every year to decide which names should be put forward for induction into the Hall which is based at its historic headquarters at Newport, Rhode Island comprises as good a brain's trust for tennis that exists anywhere. For years Tony Trabert was our chairman and now Stan Smith has taken over with Todd Martin arriving as CEO.

The fact that the discussions turn lively and argumentative is hardly surprising when you start to list some of the names around the table: Pam Shriver, Fred Stolle, Frew McMillan, John Barrett, Gordon Forbes, Mary Carillo, Jan Kodes, Ingrid Lofdahl Bentzer, Joel Drucker, Steve Flink, Mark Woodforde, Brad Parks, Bjorn Hellberg, Nancy Jeffett.....the list is incomplete but the depth of knowledge knows no bounds.

Choosing candidates for nomination demands examination of so much criteria that hard and fast conclusions become elusive. All I can say is that every angle of a candidate's record is poured over in minute detail and, in the end, it is left to over 100 people in the tennis media to produce a 75% affirmative vote to put someone into the Hall.

Nothing much would have changed in my personal life had Gene Scott not invited me to cover the Kremlin Cup in Moscow. If I had remained with the ATP Tour I would not have been able to accept because Russia, for some reason, fell under the jurisdiction on the ATP's Sydney office. (Somebody hadn't looked at a map.)

But, now there was nothing to stop me going. So, it was on a cold November day in 1993, that I spotted the girl with the blue beret. We chatted occasionally during the week and, on the Saturday evening escaped from a bun-fight of a party at the Kremlin and ended up, along with Harry Cocowitch from the Meadow Club in Southampton, Long Island and Lynn's friend, Cynthia Porter, at the Manhattan disco.

I must have been smitten then because, the next morning I got up at an ungodly hour to play in the media tournament – just to impress Miss Zanconato! Nothing much happened immediately, although I realised the attraction must be mutual when I started getting phone calls from New Jersey after I returned home. So we met on my next trip to the States and, before she could start having second thoughts, I quickly whisked her off to the Caribbean.

We went to St Maarten, lunched at the lovely La Samanna resort which was still owned at the time by the family of Ivan Lendl's wife, Samantha

Frankel, and then on to Anguilla, that little British island which had become famous in 1969 for the most fatuous reason. A local dispute over certain aspects of British sovereignty had broken out and when a new Commissioner, William Whitlock, arrived to try and sort things out, he was escorted off the island at gun point.

Harold Wilson, the British Prime Minister at the time, took offense at that and, enacting a last gasp of the British Empire, sent in the 2nd battalion of the Parachute Regiment and 40 London bobbies.

Bemused Anguillans stood around on the beaches watching the troops charge ashore, all ready to deal with some sinister enemy. But they couldn't find a gun anywhere. I remember flying down a few weeks later to find out what was happening and, after being thrown about the skies in an RAF Hercules – you get to appreciate commercial flying after being a guest of the RAF – I discovered nothing other than those 40 policemen, well-tanned and well-rested, managing to keep the very peaceful 6,000 residents out of trouble. As a Whitehall farce it topped the bill.

Nothing much had occurred since and, like thousands of other tourists, Lynn and I enjoyed the luxury of a room leading onto a golden beach and some lovely local restaurants. From then on we became a couple and, when she came to stay with me in Monaco, we took a walk down the path that leads along the coastline of Cap d'Ail one day and, as the waves crashed against the rocks, decided to get married.

There was a considerable age difference but her parents, Tony and MaryAnn, took it well and laid on a lovely wedding in the little town of Randolph, New Jersey on 10th December 1995. A thick layer of snow made it a white wedding for Lynn in every sense and we were thrilled that so many people showed up, including George and Heather Mitchell who had been married in New York on precisely the same day one year before. Andrew Malim was my best man and Herb FitzGibbon, representing the tennis world, was the usher. There was no complaint about that from the lady guests, many of whom enjoyed being ushered by someone so tall, dark and handsome!

By the time we settled down to married life in Monaco, I had found a different flat in Fontvieille, right on the water with a little terrace that we used for alfresco dinners on balmy Mediterranean nights. I set about finding Lynn some freelance jobs with television companies like ESPN and USA so that she could travel with me and earn a bit of money.

If you enjoyed watching the famous Davis Cup tie in which Pete Sampras overcame cramps to help the USA beat Russia in Moscow in 1995, you have Lynn to thank. Three days before the tie, the ESPN producer Bob Feller was nearing state of panic. A certain lack of foresight and understanding of how things worked in a country whose bureaucracy was still held in a Soviet straightjacket had led ESPN to send all their cameras and equipment to Moscow with only ten days to spare.

Needless to say, Russian Customs did not operate to that kind of times-cale and there appeared to be a real danger that the cameras would not be released in time. So Feller asked Lynn to go out to the airport with a Russian Federation official and plead their case. I may not have mentioned that Lynn, apart from a year at Sorbonne, had also spent nine months at Moscow University around the time Boris Yeltsin was climbing onto his tank, and, with her flair for Slavic languages, spoke fluent Russian.

And she knew how to use it. Several times during our Moscow visits, I was taken aback at how aggressive my sweet wife became when speaking Russian, but probably not as surprised as the Custom Officer at Moscow Airport when confronted by this very determined American woman yelling at him in his own language. Lynn was either going to get arrested or get the cameras. She got the cameras.

Other assignments were more peaceful and, at places like Prague, Indian Wells and the US Open, her job often entailed feeding Cliff Drysdale or Patrick McEnroe well researched pieces of information while they were on the air. She enjoyed it – up to a point. Basically, the whole world of television did not enthral her and she let it drop after a while.

Lynn did, however, play a leading role in the Vitas Gerulaitis Grassroots Challenge, an event that had lain dormant for several years after Andrew Malim, a business partner, and I had created it several years before. I had wanted to achieve what the LTA never seemed capable of – namely discovering some tennis talent amongst inner-city kids. I knew something must be going on around the Brixton area of London so we cooked up a plan. Andrew and I would stage a tennis match on Clapham Common. Richard Russell was in town with a couple of young Jamaicans so I corralled John Feaver, Richard Lewis and John Paish into forming a Britain team to play Jamaica.

In the dead of night, Andrew, who was always up for a good caper, and I drove round Brixton, plastering posters on any available space – we were lucky not to get arrested – and hoped some people would show up. Not many did but, after a few minutes, I spotted a Jamaican fellow who looked suspiciously like a tennis coach. His name was Orville Brown and he ran a tennis school in nearby Brockwell Park. Bingo! Just the man I was looking for.

Shortly after I persuaded Arthur Ashe, Harry Hopman, the great Australian Davis Cup captain, and Vitas Gerulaitis to come and take a look at Orville's kids and we hatched another idea. After enlisting the help of Mike Silverman, who was in charge of tennis for New York Public Parks, we staged a New York v London match for boys of fourteen or under. It worked for a couple of years but finding funds and airline tickets proved impossible and there was a hiatus until I joined the ATP Tour and asked Rolf Hoehn, the Lufthansa PR Director, if he would back us with airline tickets if we expanded the concept to include eight teams. As Lufthansa had signed up as one of the new ATP Tour's first sponsors, Rolf was more than willing to help.

So, in the nineties, we gave scores of kids from underprivileged backgrounds the chance of a lifetime. Almost all of them had never been on a plane before and the exercise was more cultural than sporting. We drew on inner city programmes from New York, Boston, Washington DC, Palo Alto, California as well as Soweto, Madras and Melbourne where Paul McNamee ran a big programme.

Ingrid Lofdahl Bentzer offered enthusiastic support and virtually ran the tournament when it was held in Battersea Park one year and then, in 1995, we moved it to Spitalfields Market in the City of London where mini-indoor soccer pitches offered enough space to set up two tennis courts.

That was where Lynn came into her own, using her organisational skills in dealing with shops, restaurants and suppliers, trying to decipher broad Cockney accents as she negotiated good deals with local traders. Surprisingly, there was less of a communication problem between the boys themselves. It was fascinating to see them size each other up on arrival, this disparate bunch of black, white, Christian, and Hindu kids from various corners of the globe. Showing how quickly sport can unify, they all seemed to be best friends by the time the weekend was over.

We took them to an ATP party at a club near Piccadilly Circus and I was delighted that Orville Brown was given the Arthur Ashe Humanitarian Award for his involvement in the project. Being staged just before Wimbledon, it never got much publicity, despite John Roberts and Steve Tongue of the Independent showing up to do a couple of pieces, and I got zero assistance from the LTA. So, once Lufthansa ended its sponsorship and Ashley arrived to take up Lynn's time, I had little option but to close it down.

But we continued to travel together and I had never been happier. The happiness level was raised considerably when we discovered Lynn was pregnant on arriving in Paris for the 1997 French Open. We were ecstatic and, secretly, I was a little apprehensive. I was going to be quite an old father and that can raise the risk of complications.

But all was well. On the 30th of January 1998 at 1.53 pm on a lovely afternoon in Monaco, Lynn gave birth to Ashley Anthony Evans at the Princess Grace Hospital. As all parents know, there is nothing to compare with the joy of a child being born. The last few minutes of the birth had not been fun for Lynn but she was soon cuddling him in her arms and when he opened his eyes, his first sight must have been a perfect view of the sparkling Mediterranean. Not a bad start to life.

And it only got better for the young man. After about eighteen more months in Fontvieille, we found an amazing apartment down the coast towards Nice in a large white villa on the pathway that links Beaulieu to Cap Ferrat. The Villa Sicard was still family owned, as it had been since being built in 1886. It is situated a few steps from the beach and a three minute walk from the little village of St Jean. At night you heard nothing but the lapping of the bay on the rocks. Miraculously, the rent was very reasonable. We could barely believe our luck. Paradise at an affordable price!

We tried to make the most of it, inviting special friends to stay like Tommy and Betty Tucker from Palm Springs and Paul and Linda Gunter from Washington DC as well as Lynn's parents. We had some magical times.

By the time we made the move, Ashley was already a seasoned traveller. The poor child had no option. We had whisked him off to New Jersey to stay with his grandparents, then out to LA for a few nights with Pamela and Nik Wheeler in their beautiful house just off Mullholland Drive and then to Indian Wells for the tournament. And he was not yet one before he found himself in the nose of a British Airways 747 heading for Australia.

My travel agent was still producing cut-price Business Class tickets so we were on the upper deck sharing the compartment with just one other passenger, a very large young man with a rich, deep voice. Somewhere over the Indian Ocean, he volunteered to play with Ashley and, while Lynn sank into a much-needed sleep, he got down on all fours and spent at least an hour engaging Ashley in all sorts of games that eleven-month-olds enjoy.

When she woke up, Lynn offered profuse thanks and remarked on his voice, asking if, by any chance he was a singer. "Actually, I sing opera," the young man replied. "I am going to try to sing Falstaff at the Sydney Opera House which is a very difficult role so I thought I had better go a long way away to do it!"

So we asked his name. "Bryn Terfel," he replied. Thank you, Bryn.

We had a room by the pool at the Hilton-on-the-Park opposite the Melbourne Cricket Ground (it's a Pullman hotel now), and it was there that we gave Ashley his first birthday party, just before Martina Hingis defeated Amelie Mauresmo to win her third consecutive Australian Open title. Several of my colleagues – John Parsons, Barry Flatman, Chris Bowers, Barry Millns and Iain Carter – came round to help blow out the single candle on the cake. Ashley had a big grin on his face. It was a nice way to celebrate No. 1.

To say I was enjoying being a father was a considerable understatement. For the first few years, we were able to take Ashley all over the world and, along with his outgoing Mum who seemed to make friends with everyone, he radiated a great deal of infectious happiness. People seemed to love him and I was very proud.

However, by 2003, things were starting to get difficult between Lynn and myself. Apart from missing her parents, she could not find a job, a task made virtually impossible because of the need to look after Ashley and, when he turned five, having to drive him to the International School in Nice which was a daily nightmare in the rush hour.

It might have worked had I been able to hang on to my two main sources of income. I have already related how I was laid off by BBC Radio and then, just a matter of months later, Alex Butler, the sports editor of the Sunday Times, decided he wanted someone less independently minded as his tennis correspondent. I had been under contract for ten years but was not on the staff. So when, for instance, I said I was going to attend the 2002 ATP Tour World finals in Shanghai and he said he didn't want any coverage, I said 'OK but I'm going anyway'.

Understandably, Butler was somewhat embarrassed. The man who covered two pages of his broadsheet publication at every Grand Slam and had acquired a certain following as a tennis writer was going to be at the world's fifth most important tournament and he was not going to use him. Odd … and unnecessary. Neither of us would back down – I couldn't afford to because of my commitments – and so the Sunday Times took agency copy.

A few months later, Barry Flatman left the Daily Express, where he had come to know Butler when Alex had been an editor there. So a ready-made alternative to yours truly became available and Butler took it. In a matter of a year, I had lost well over 60% of my income.

Annoyingly, my departure from the Sunday Times & its huge platform for tennis co-incided with the precise moment Judy Murray was launching her two sons onto the tour. Jamie was the first to win a Wimbledon title, winning the Mixed with Jelena Jankovic in 2007 but it was Andy who rose to heights British tennis never dreamt it could attain by becoming the first British man since Fred Perry to win the Wimbledon singles title. What an emotional moment that was! By then he had already won Olympic Gold at Wimbledon and the US Open and when he won Wimbledon again in 2016 & defended his Olympic title in Rio, there was no way he could be denied a knighthood. Andy is Britain's finest athlete and when he rose to No 1 in the world it was a triumph beyond measure.

My departure from the Sunday Times did nothing to make Lynn feel any more secure and when she suggested moving to the States, I didn't have much ammunition to fight back. Economically, it made sense because there would be a huge difference in the cost of living if we moved to Richmond, Virginia where Lynn's brother, Michael, had been at school. Her parents were, in fact, already searching for a house there.

So, in early 2004, we left our little corner of paradise and bought a house in a new suburban development in a town called Midlothian in Chesterfield County. The choice was not random. We had researched the local schools and Chesterfield County was listed amongst the best in America. I was full of trepidation at first but, looking back, I can have no complaints about the way my son was educated.

However, the fact that he did so well – finally earning a Dean's Scholarship to Lynn University in Boca Raton, Florida – was in no small part due to the support and extra tuition he received from his mother who finally managed to instil in him the work ethic he enjoys today. The name of his future college was a funny coincidence but entirely appropriate. As Lynn said, "No change. He's been at Lynn University all his life!" And she was right.

Thankfully, we quickly found a continuing theme in his young life for Ashley in soccer which, when we arrived, was beginning the huge growth in popularity it has enjoyed in the States over the past two decades. Ashley was already an Arsenal fan (yes, mea culpa!) and I had the chance to take him to Highbury for one of the last matches ever played at that iconic stadium before we attended the first ever match at The Emirates. I even managed to get him a couple of days training at Arsenals' Junior training ground at Hale End thanks to David Court's hospitality. Unfortunately, the Under 9-year-olds were not training on the days we were there so he was flung in with the incredibly fast and skilled Under 11s. Alex Iwobi may well have been amongst them. Ashley was a bit out of his depth but when he was presented with an open goal he didn't miss. So he has scored at Hale End!

I owe my Arsenal connections to Sue Mott, my predecessor at the Sunday Times who introduced me to David Dein, the man who brought Arsene Wenger to the club. David has been a wonderful friend over the years, getting me tickets for numerous matches including some away games in Genoa and Rome when I was living in Monaco. I knew David, then Arsenal's Vice-Chairman, in his heyday as one of the busiest men in world football. Incredibly, this never stopped him calling back within an hour of me calling him no matter where he was. As I had little to offer other than support I found this remarkable. How many people do you know who have good reason to get back to you and never do?

When David was ousted in a boardroom coup it was a sad day for Arsenal and Wenger. They worked brilliantly as a team with Dein using all his contacts in Europe to bring in the players Arsene wanted. It was a huge waste of talent when David left.

Ashley had honed his footballing skills during the lunch hour at the International School in Nice by joining in kickabouts with boys much older than himself. So he had a better grounding in the game than a lot of the kids he found himself playing with in the States under an excellent Scottish coach called John Addison, who ran the Richmond Kickers programme.

Soccer soon became a major part of Ashley's life and remained so, all the way through to the first team at Cosby High School, who were ranked in the top ten in the country. The training was tough and our little boy grew into a strapping and very fit athlete who now stands 6' 5"! I could not help feel a little bit proud about that, remembering all those hours we spent kicking a ball in the driveway at the Villa Sicard when he was three and four, using the big iron gates as the goal.

He had played a bit of tennis, too, but never enough to become really proficient despite occasional coaching sessions with Richard Russell in Jamaica, Manolo Santana at his club in Marbella and my good friend Bob Brett at the Monte Carlo Country Club. He was a lucky boy just to get on the same court as those guys but tennis requires relentless practice and, back home in Virginia, soccer took up too much of his time.

The saddest thing was that my relationship with Lynn was deteriorating to the point where ceaseless arguments were beginning to impinge on Ashley's happiness. There is no good way to solve a problem like that. Our decision, for better or worse, was to get a divorce while resolving to stay friends. Telling Ashley was the worst day of my life. I can't write about it coherently so I will say no more.

By February 2008, I needed to find somewhere else to live and, by chance, the next tournament on the ATP calendar happened to be Delray Beach. I had only been there once before when Butch Buchholz used the Laver Tennis Center (owned at the time by a cousin of Rod Laver's) as the site for his first ATP event which, as a result of his vision and boundless enthusiasm, he turned into one of the world's great tournaments on Key Biscayne near Miami.

But, since then, a terrific new Tennis Center had been built, right downtown on Atlantic Avenue and the city itself had improved beyond all recognition. Immediately I realised Delray Beach would be a place I could live and, strangely, the decision to move there hinged on an airline schedule. Jet Blue had a non-stop flight between Fort Lauderdale and Richmond. If there hadn't been such a flight, it would have been a deal breaker because easy access to Ashley was the prime reason for my staying in America and we were not going to put him on a flight that required a change. So thank you, Jet Blue – airlines may not always realise how they can affect people's lives!

So I settled in Delray and continued my life much as before, until I suddenly got a call from Glenys to say she had given Gayle my phone number. I had read that Gayle had broken up with Simon Jenkins so, on a whim, I invited her to stay. She came and didn't leave. After a gap of 32 years we virtually picked up where we had left off!

Gayle hardly knew Florida but soon decided to buy a house just off Atlantic Avenue and everything was fine for about three years until she started to slip into deep depression. Mental health is unfathomable and only now are people starting to treat it with the seriousness and respect it requires.

It was soon after she had sold her beautiful house on Regent's Park Road, and bought another one just outside Great Missenden in Buckinghamshire, that the illness started to take hold and led to almost two years of hospitalisation and time in clinics.

She had a year of remission before needing more treatment and no one seems to know what the future holds. She never wanted to return to Florida, so our relationship came to an end.

The whole episode made me incredibly sad but, for me on a personal level, life improved when Ashley got his scholarship to Lynn University, which is fifteen minutes from where I live. Believe it or not, Lynn soon followed him and bought a little apartment downtown. That's fifteen minutes in the other direction. So it almost feels like family. It's good to have both of them so close.

That's about it. I've written too much and still left out incidents and people I wanted to mention. I have just returned from covering the 2017 Australian Open, which I have figured, must have been my 196th Grand Slam and one of the best. Roger Federer's recovery from 1-3 down in the fifth set to beat Rafa Nadal and so win his first major title since Wimbledon 2012 produced a final that somehow exceeded the pre-match hype and I was lucky to be commentating on the fifth set for AO Radio with Steve Pearce and Kate Kearns as the drama reached its climax.

The omens for this Aussie Open were good from the moment I ran into Chris Evert and Martina Navratilova in the Qantas lounge at LAX. It says so much about the spirit of our game that these two totally amazing and completely different personalities, who competed fiercely against each other for fourteen years, remain the best of buddies. Martina and I – with Chrissie chiming in occasionally – have struck up a different kind of relationship in recent years on Twitter. Politically, we seem to be on the same page and find it a good way to vent our frustrations.

The link to the past through long forged friendships came into focus again in Melbourne and it was fun chatting and doing interviews with those great Australian champions who I have been lucky enough to know for decades. John Newcombe and I had enjoyed our bi-annual chat during the tournament and, at the Legends lunch, held this year for Ashley Cooper, there had been more stories and laughter with Roy and Joy Emerson, Neale Fraser, Fred and Pat Stolle, Ken and Wilma Rosewall, Marty Mulligan, John Alexander and that man I noticed in the white tuxedo on the front page of the Sunday Express all of 65 years before, Frank Sedgman. They really are a special bunch of people.

I still get a kick out of it. It has been a hell of a journey, and thanks for coming along for the ride. I'll stay in the saddle for as long as I can!

ACKNOWLEDGMENTS

There are so many people who have helped me along the way who do not get proper credit here. Many of them work in the public relations area of professional tennis. Some who come most immediately to mind are Rod Humphries during his time at WCT in Dallas; David Newman who left the USTA for the Mets too soon for our liking, Mark Beal and his successor at Indian Wells Matt Van Tuinen; Nick Imison who marshalls the players for us at the Grand Slams; and Nicola Arzani who took over from me at the ATP in Monaco and has made the difficult business of being the buffer between players and press his life's work. I know how hard it can be.

And so, some thanks --to my niece, Clare Sholz and her husband Andy for handling our family affairs; to Barbara Daniel for offering support when I had to speak at Ted Tinling's Memorial Service; to Richard Jones for his endless ideas and enthusiasm at the Tennis Gallery bookshop; to John and Alison Feaver for providing the lawn where Ashley kicked his first goal; to Jane Jones, the most devoted Arsenal fan I know; to Cino Marchese whose expansive hospitality used to make the Foro Italico a place of welcome; to Vittorio Selmi, the opera-buff who keeps generations of ATP players connected; to Henrik & Pascale Sundstrom for being such good neighbours in Fontvieille; to Jennifer Shand and Mike Hurst for all the hospitality in Sidney; to Kevin Hand for making me feel welcome in the Middlesex commentary box; to Larry Keating for working with me on the Anthony Wilding project (we'll get it done one day, Larry!) to John Beddington for decades of friendship; to John Lampl for all his help at British Airways; to Rahul Jacob, an astute tennis fan who helped me with assignments at the Financial Times; to Stefano Papaleo for offering Ashley such a warm welcome at Lynn University; to Chris Kermode for giving the ATP the kind of leadership it needs; to Mary Carillo who never ceases to brighten our lives and to all those other colleagues who have kept me sane on the road for so many years – Andrew Longmore, Neil Harman, Christopher Clarey, Leo Schlink, Steve

Bierley, Alix Ramsay, Chris Jones, Sandra Harwitt, Kevin Mitchell, Mike Dickson and so, so many more stretching back to the eccentric Laurie Pignon and three who have been around as long as I have, Reg Brace, Ron Atkin and Nigel Clarke. And not forgetting Joel Drucker who remembers more about what I wrote than I do myself.

More? Of course but I must get this book published and for that I have to thank Gareth Howard and Hayley Radford at Authoright in London for agreeing to take this project on.

Thank you all for being part of my life.

BIBLIOGRAPHY

"Point of Departure" by James Cameron – McGraw-Hill

"The Best & the Brightest" by David Halberstam – Fawcett-Crest

"Robert Kennedy – A Memoir" by Jack Newfield – Dutton

"A Thousand Days" – by Arthur M. Schlesinger Jnr – Houghton Miflin Co.

"The Heir Apparent" by William. V Shannon – Macmillan

"Robert Kennedy in his Own Words" edited by Edwin O. Guthman & Jeffrey Shulman - Bantam

"River of Time" by Jon Swain – Heinemann

"A Portrait in Motion" by Arthur Ashe with Frank Deford – Houghton Miflin Co

"A Handful of Summers" by Gordon Forbes – Heinemann

"Sixty Years in Tennis" by Ted Tinling – Sidgwick & Jackson

"The Life of Fred Perry" by Jon Henderson – Yellow Jersey Press

"My Life with Lew" by Jenny Hoad & Jack Pollard – Harper Collins

"Ahead of the Game" by Owen Williams – SMSI Press

Reference Book Annuals: John Barrett's World of Tennis and The ATP/ WTA Media Guide.

CPSIA information can be obtained
at www.ICGtesting.com
Printed in the USA
BVOW11s0740310717
490699BV00011B/92/P